ANTHROPOLOGIES OF
ORTHODOX CHRISTIANITY

ORTHODOX CHRISTIANITY AND CONTEMPORARY THOUGHT

SERIES EDITORS
Aristotle Papanikolaou and Ashley M. Purpura

ANTHROPOLOGIES OF ORTHODOX CHRISTIANITY

Theology, Politics, Ethics

CANDACE LUKASIK AND
SARAH RICCARDI-SWARTZ
EDITORS

FORDHAM UNIVERSITY PRESS
New York • 2026

For EU safety / GPSR concerns: Mare Nostrum Group B.V., Mauritskade 21D, 1091 GC Amsterdam, The Netherlands, gpsr@mare-nostrum.co.uk

Library of Congress Cataloging-in-Publication Data available online at https://catalog.loc .gov.

Printed in the United States of America

28 27 26   5 4 3 2 1

First edition

CONTENTS

FOREWORD

Sonja Thomas

This edited volume offers groundbreaking perspectives on the anthropology of Christianity and Orthodoxy. Recent scholarship has witnessed the discussion of the divides between theology and the anthropology of Christianity and attempts to transcend those divides. The chapters in this volume do not merely add Orthodoxy to this existing scholarship. Rather, the authors' interdisciplinary perspectives and their attention to a global Orthodoxy give readers a greater understanding of how the bridging of theology and the anthropology of Christianity can and should be done, what such a bridging offers us, and how these bridges can create new avenues for future ethnographic and theological research on Christianity.

Theology is often seen as the realm of authority in a religious community because it works to explain an entire community's relationship to God. This carving out of communities and definitions of practice provides the substance, backdrop, even a manual (if you will) for lived practice—even as lived practice is not necessarily the focus of the field.

Anthropology, on the other hand, traffics in the lived experience of religion. Through the method of ethnography, the creation and maintenance of religious identity is explored within the larger sociopolitical landscape of a religious community. This research is (supposedly) conducted objectively and often with a secular, cultural relativist frame. As Sarah Bakker Kellogg describes in this volume, theology "is an uncomfortable space for secularist social scientists with a political attraction to alterity."[1]

However, both the anthropology of Christianity and theology are interested in questions of morality and being in the world. Both fields have continually drawn from each other in their respective analyses. Further, both fields have undergone changes over the last few decades that have sent each discipline into a deep self-reflexive mode that has questioned field formations and simultaneously opened up new possibilities for what can be considered an "object" of study.

As Joel Robbins discussed in the introduction to his *Theology and the Anthropology of Christian Life*, the anthropology of Christianity is a very new subfield of anthropology.[2] Starting in the 1990s and continuing today, anthropologists are grappling with the "postmodern" or "postcolonial" turn, questioning the imperialist foundations of anthropology, where Western privileged scholars participated in fieldwork in the non-West, interviewing "informants" to become experts on the "exotic other." In this framing, the "exotic religious other" was a non-Christian "other," while the West was implicitly Christian and the definers of a static and unchanging Christianity. Indeed, as Rowena Robinson describes on scholarship of Indian Christianity, Hinduism received the most attention, while Christianity was seen as "something that was in no need of definition. . . . Many practices, thus, were not even seen as worthy of attention—because they were viewed as being the same everywhere universally and therefore, not exotic enough to be considered worthy of anthropological interest."[3] Academic anthropology distanced itself from missionary anthropological works in large part because Christian missions were viewed as entities that would destroy the native "exotic" culture that proper anthropologists were striving to record.[4] As a result, "Christian mission was written out of anthropology, and mission scholars studying it, traditionally in a rather confessional and uncritical manner, were not potential academic partners."[5] All this made studying Christianity, and specifically Christianity in the non-West, an afterthought in anthropology.

That started to change in the 1990s, when anthropology began both to question the position of the researcher and to take on "new" objects of study, such as Christianity in the Global South. However, much of this literature is focused on Pentecostal and Charismatic Christianity. As Joel Robbins explains, the rise in the anthropology of Christianity coincided with the enormous growth of Pentecostal and Charismatic worship and churches.[6] This often means that the scholarly research attempting to bridge theology and the Anthropology of Christianity tends to view Pentecostal and Charismatic Christianity as its particular Christian object, thus neglecting Orthodoxy.

Theology, too, has been questioning the Western self. The intellectual history of theology has had a heavy focus on (Western) Protestant Christianity. This view of Christianity implicitly centered the Western Christian subject as the invisible referent, creating a corpus of literature myopic in its scope. However, there has been a new interest from privileged scholars to read and platform the theology of the marginalized and to center works by scholars who are located in the Global South. Dalit theology, for example, is increasingly being read, cited, assigned in graduate coursework, and shared in South Asian academic circles (academic circles that are predominantly dominant caste, engendering problematic tokenism and virtue signaling even as it simultaneously reveals the immense amount of work that must be done by theologians and ethnographers with privilege who are saturated in Western/Orientalist knowledge production in the academy).

One may ask, then, where is Orthodoxy in this self-reflexive and critical scholarship? As the authors in this volume reveal, Orthodoxy provides a unique lens to the bridging of theology and the anthropology of Christianity. While theology understands a religious community as discrete, *Anthropologies of Orthodox Christianity* shows us how these believed boundaries are, in actuality, blurred and crossed constantly. I am a scholar of Indian Christianity, and in my own research I have argued that Indian Orthodox Christians and Syro-Malabar and Syro-Malankara Catholics need to be understood in conversation with each other as they have the same apostolic origin story, the same dominant caste status in India, and have worked politically to protect not just the boundaries of their community but to maintain their caste and class status. Chapters in this volume likewise examine Orthodox Christian life in larger religious lifeworlds. As Christopher Sheklian's chapter reveals, this can be seen in the ways that diasporic Armenian Orthodox Christians participate in unofficial modes of veneration and write themselves into the city of Maastricht, the Netherlands. Or, as Clayton Goodgame writes, Palestinian Orthodox Christians connect horizontally with Evangelical and other denominations through marriage and holidays while also connecting themselves vertically "as a community persisting through time." Or, as Sarah Bakker Kellogg writes, there is a diasporic Syriac world which unites Syriac Christians, Orthodox and non-Orthodox alike, through a shared language politic and sociopolitical kinship with one another in the diaspora.

What these chapters show us is that the object of the anthropology of Christianity cannot be assumed (as Pentecostal/Charismatic). Nor can theology, in its awareness of discrete denominational differences, be approached unidirectionally. If the bridging of anthropology and theology has previously focused on Pentecostal/Charismatic Christianity, Orthodoxy gives us a more holistic and accurate view of the anthropology of Christianity. Orthodox Christians are often minority religions in particular nation-states. They may face persecution or marginalization as they fight to maintain their practices and traditions in the face of a dominant majority. Diasporic Orthodox Christians may be ethnic or racial minorities in the diaspora, while becoming part of a majority Christian religion in the United States or European countries.

Within contexts such as national/religious belonging, Christian life under authoritarian governments, settler colonialism, the forces behind migration, and church schisms, chapters in this edited collection provide us with a keen eye to the social and political realities that produce power and domination, marginalization and subordination, and resistance and persistence in a given society.

Orthodoxy is a constant reminder that divides between the Occident and Orient, or the Global North and Global South—divides that anthropology still grapples with—are not static or always definable. Rather, they are blurred and shifting. Orthodoxy allows us to ask questions of what is "new" research or "new" perspectives in the anthropology of Christianity and in theology. If the anthropology of Christianity was a newer field of scholarship because Christianity is assumed to be the Western researcher's religion, studies on Orthodoxy in Russia, Ukraine, Syria, Palestine, Egypt, Ethiopia, or India always already have done this "new" work. *Anthropologies of Orthodox Christianity* shows us how the East/West divide is continually played out, played upon for political purposes, or approached critically by scholars attempting to do the difficult bridging of theological and anthropological perspectives. For example, as Jacob Lassin shows us in his chapter, charges of "Eastern Papizm" problematically gain political traction among Russian Orthodox because the Russian Orthodox Church positions itself as the defender of the East/Orthodox against Western influences. Examining the invention of rhetorical devices at play in this positioning becomes a key site of analysis and pushes scholars of religion to think through our normative assumptions concerning the West and the rest.

As Sarah Riccardi-Swartz and Candace Lukasik tell us in their Introduction, this volume emerged from an interdisciplinary ethos. This is more than just being multidisciplinary. Mia Liianson and Ulla Holm define multidisciplinarity as a "collaboration between disciplinary approaches, without exceeding the disciplinary borders, their theoretical or methodological frames . . . multidisciplinarity reinforces the distinction between disciplines and leaves traditional disciplines unchallenged."[7] While multidisciplinarity is useful, important, and often practiced by both the theologian and the ethnographer, this isn't the same as transformation. As Joel Robbins explains, while dialogue between anthropology and theology may produce good work, they do not have "discipline-altering effects" that are truly "transformative."[8]

Interdisciplinarity, on the other hand, involves a bridging of the gaps between disciplines, a transformation of existing methods, or the creation of new methods.[9] One must be willing to think through different objects of analysis and question rather than wholeheartedly accept existing methods or paradigms. It is hard work because it requires immense disciplinary breadth without sacrificing methodological depth. In academic circles more familiar with disciplinary or multidisciplinary research, it is difficult to explain who the audience is for an interdisciplinary study or what the new methods are, as they may not be recognized by the traditional ethnographer or theologian. Quite frankly, it is difficult to publish in our discipline's normative journals. As Cindi Katz has argued, "It is far easier to consume interdisciplinarity than produce, maintain, or make a living from it."[10] What this volume does is this difficult work of bridging.

In an interdisciplinary ethos, conventional sites of ethnographic research and archives of Christianity need to be explored and rethought. It is no surprise, then, that digital ethnography features prominently in this volume, such as Robert Saler's exploration of UFO conspiracy theologoumenon in diasporic US Russian Orthodox online forums. Rather than just assume that lived experiences of religion resides in the practices of believers, we can think through and question where "lived Christianity" resides, as Aaron Michka writes about through his examination of church authority and the lived interaction between laity and Orthodox priests. "Shared connections," "sonic maps," and "worldliness" are phrases that pop up to describe this interdisciplinary bridging that the authors in this volume attend to. Because it gets interdisciplinarity right, *Anthropologies of Orthodox Christianity* speaks to disciplines beyond anthropology and theology, including religious studies, migration and diaspora studies, media and communications, gender and women's studies, race and ethnic studies, and particular area studies.

The volume is timely in its focus and is an important step forward in self-reflexive and interdisciplinary research. It goes beyond just adding Orthodox Christians and stirring. It helps us question conventional modes of analysis and branch out by compelling readers to think through what it means to be ethnographers of Christianity.

Notes

1. Sarah Bakker Kellogg, "Imperial Ecclesiologies and Ethnographic Imaginaries: Situating Syriac Christianity in the Anthropology of Global Orthodoxy," *Anthropologies of Orthodox Christianity: Theology, Politics, Ethics* (New York: Fordham University Press, 2025), 72.

2. Joel Robbins, *Theology and the Anthropology of Christian Life* (Oxford University Press, 2020), 8–13.

3. Rowena Robinson, *Christians of India* (Sage, 2003), 22–23.

4. Mika Vähäkangas and Karen Lauterbach, "Faith in African Lived Christianity—Bridging Anthropological and Theological Perspectives: Introduction," in *Faith in African Live Christianity: Bridging Anthropological and Theological Perspectives*, ed. Karen Lauterbach and Mika Vähäkangas (Brill, 2019), 2.

5. Vähäkangas and Lauterbach, "Faith in African Lived Christianity," 2.

6. Joel Robbins, "World Christianity and the Reorganization of Disciplines: On the Emerging Dialogue Between Anthropology and Theology," in *Faith in African Live Christianity: Bridging Anthropological and Theological Perspectives*, ed. Karen Lauterbach and Mika Vähäkangas (Brill, 2019), 20.

7. Mia Liianson and Ulla Holm, "PhDs, Women's/Gender Studies and Interdisciplinarity," *Nordic Journal of Women's Studies* 14, no. 2 (December 2006): 118.

8. Robbins, *Theology and the Anthropology of Christian Life*, 5.

9. Liianson and Holm, "PhDs, Women's/Gender Studies and Interdisciplinarity," 118.

10. Cindi Katz, "Disciplining Interdisciplinarity," *Feminist Studies* 27, no. 2 (Summer 2001): 524.

ANTHROPOLOGIES OF
ORTHODOX CHRISTIANITY

Introduction

Thinking About Orthodox Christianity in an Anthropological Perspective

Candace Lukasik and Sarah Riccardi-Swartz

Orthodox Christianity, currently the third-largest branch of Christianity globally, has long been the focus of both theologians and ethnologists (subsequently anthropologists), often with neither group taking the other seriously.[1] This historic disciplinary divide is ultimately to the detriment of both fields since Orthodox Christianity is not a static form of spirituality unmoored from social structures, cultural constructions, and political paradigms. Among Orthodox theologians, anthropology is typically understood as *theological* anthropology, or what it means to be human as lived out in relationship to and with God.[2] The Orthodox Christian human is theologically understood as ontologically different— as first and foremost oriented toward God. By contrast, anthropological renderings of Christianity in recent years have sought to translate ethnographic engagements through a relational orientation to God. At the same time, they remain in tension with the secular demands of the discipline, approaching the edge of God's sovereignty without fully endorsing it and expressing implicit concern over the (im)possibility of maintaining an objective view of religious community. The divide between anthropology and theology, then, rests both on the ability of the social scientist to accept God's omnipresent agency among their Orthodox interlocutors and the ability of the theologian to understand theology as an interpretation of the divine *in* the world. Moreover, recent conversations between anthropology and theology have often eschewed discussions of how political conditions shape theology and religious practice. Specifically, the anthropological study of Orthodox Christianity (as well as Christianity more broadly) has typically decentered the impact of power dynamics—from histories of colonialism to the emergence of authoritarian national formations and contemporary imperial formations—in theology, practice, and institutional change.

This volume is arguably the first project of its kind to think about the intersections of anthropology and theology alongside the entanglement of theology and politics among contemporary Orthodox Christians. Much of the anthropological literature on Christianity tends to be focused on Protestant (and marginally Catholic) Christian communities of the Global South for historical reasons of missionization as connected to Western colonial projects of domination, as well as out of a sense of theological kinship to the secularized renderings of Western political and social life. In some contrast, Orthodox Christianity has largely been rendered marginal in mainstream anthropological engagement because of its theological and social alterity from Western anthropological traditions of knowledge production—offering a unique perspective into how Orientalism works in knowledge production on Orthodoxy in the West. In this way, Orthodox Christian lifeworlds in and beyond the academy are created, contested, and transformed in relation to various "others," whether they be religious, political, secular, or historical, with an eye toward the opposition between modernity and Orthodoxy. In this opposition, Orthodox Christian communities are varyingly framed in their distance from modernity—as clinging to "material attachments, political structures, and external practice."[3]

Yet, geopolitical interest in Orthodox lifeworlds has increased dramatically over the past decade, most especially as it pertains to Russia and the Middle East, which has spurred anthropological inquiry along with it.[4] With its authoritarian crackdown on any forms of religiosity that could threaten its regime, the end of Soviet power brought with it a turn to public religion and the return of Orthodox publicity in many postsocialist Eastern European countries and, especially, in Russia.[5] These national and local contexts in the former Soviet Union became active field sites for anthropological inquiry into their political conditions, social transformation, and, finally, religious belief and practice.[6] In addition to postsocialist Europe, the increased violence against and migration of Orthodox Christians, especially from the Global South (and particularly the Middle East) to the West, has increased their anthropological and social relevancy to the academy and broader public policy world. Both social phenomena—

between authoritarian aftermath and minority violence—have presented anthropologists and other social scientists with new social, political, and religious challenges, connecting broader interests in diaspora and minority politics, nationalism and transnationalism, and religious pluralism and interfaith relations to Orthodox lifeworlds.

Along with these shifting intellectual traditions and geopolitical fields in and beyond anthropological inquiry, more Orthodox Christians have also sought degrees in higher education to think through ministerial practices and theological difference in diaspora. In scholastic pursuit, however, the ethnographic texture and diversity of everyday Orthodox life is often displaced from the emic interpretation of the divine *in* the world. This volume contends that the theological is imbricated with the political, with far-reaching impacts for a new this-worldly orientation to politics but also for a reoriented understanding of how religious practice and theological affects feed into social action.[7] The chapters in this volume texture a new trajectory in the study of Orthodox Christianity, one that takes seriously the theopolitical aspects of Orthodox life—between institutional and lay orientations—through anthropological inquiry. And this differentiation between lay/institutional theologies is a long-standing one in anthropology and the study of religion more broadly, channeled through an inquiry into what counts as authoritative. This older debate has been superseded by an acceptance that such divisions are arbitrary and are negotiations of power to determine what constitutes "correctness." This volume aims to engage and move beyond the tension between populist and institutional framings of religion and most especially regarding Orthodoxy—from the seminary to the academy. The dynamic experiences in and of Orthodoxy, both institutional and vernacular, can only be understood through interdisciplinary, holistic engagement. The volume, then, is an intervention that addresses the ontological gap in both fields as Orthodox Christianity continues to expand in social, cultural, and geopolitical interest.

Geopolitical Power, Global Orthodoxy, and Theopolitical Difference

Thinking anthropologically about the relationship between religion and politics in Orthodox lifeworlds goes beyond subordinating religion to secular forms of comprehension—political, social, economic, racial, or otherwise. Rather, geopolitical crises in Orthodox contexts are enmeshed in other historical (as theological) ruptures and imaginaries that have broad impacts for thinking about contemporary social theory and transformation.[8] History is theologically laden. Thus, the following chapters show how theology and power cannot be disentangled. Such is the case with the ongoing Russian war in Ukraine, a catastrophic political enterprise theologically authorized by Patriarch Kirill of the Russian Orthodox Church. In early 2022, at the beginning of the war, Kirill and Russian president Vladimir Putin both evoked the theological dimensions of the conversion of ancient Rus' to Orthodox Christianity, arguing for a state policy of intervention that centers on Russian theopolitical claims to the space and inhabitants of Ukraine. Both men repeatedly suggested that Ukraine and Russia have a shared religious history in the Kievan baptismal font and that Russia should have control over the territory. Religious history, even theological mythos, for Putin and Kirill, becomes a means through which they curated the narrative of state violence into a story of nationalistic Christian unification and cultural belonging. To understand theopolitical phenomena such as the authoritarianism emerging in contemporary Russia, anthropologists must wrestle with the theological (or the perforation between human and divine) and not simply the religious language, beliefs, and imaginaries of the Russian Orthodox Church (as opposed to modern, secular arrangements). Geopolitics, population displacement, human rights violations, and questions about nuclear disarmament are not unmoored from theological values and ideas; put another way, such seemingly geopolitical predicaments are structured by deeper questions of God's theopolitical revelation in the world.

Looking to another Orthodox geography beyond Eastern Europe, the Middle East has been a geopoliticized place of great importance to the United States and other Western locales for centuries, and more recently, since the onset of the global War on Terror. The emergence of ISIS in 2014 reignited counterterrorism efforts, prompting new military targets, policy initiatives in Washington, and increased attention from think tanks focused on defeating the group. The fall of Mosul in June 2014 saw the systematic removal of and violent attack against Christians and other minorities in northern Iraq and Syria. In February 2015, on the shores of Libya, twenty Coptic Orthodox Christians and a Ghanaian man were beheaded by ISIS affiliates; only three months later, thirty Ethiopian Orthodox men met a similar fate. Present conditions and the collective memory of violence and persecution among Orthodox in these geographies have been translated through Western religious interest in preserving global Christian identity in the face of Muslim extremism. At the same time, little concern has been given to the theological dimensions of Western religious (often evangelical and increasingly Catholic) interest in shaping the politics of global Christianity; conversely, theological agency is often denied to Middle Eastern Christians by Western actors who essentialize the persecution of these communities for theopolitical means.[9]

Western interest in the persecuted bodies of (Orthodox) Christians in the Middle East, for example, has been transposed onto transnational religious contexts and taken up by various actors for the purposes of ecumenical unity, symbolic capital, and political expediency. (Orthodox) Christians between here and there are caught between their empathy for suffering kin in their homelands and Western imperial interest in "saving" Eastern Christians, shaping how they articulate their entangled histories between East and West. These theo/geopolitical circuits are not cordoned off by modern, national borders but gesture to transhistorical/theological phenomena. In bringing anthropology and theology together, this volume moves beyond the interpretation of theological concepts as social instrumentalization—as simply a system of symbols in the Geertzian lineage. Rather, (Orthodox) Christian theology is (Orthodox) Christian history that weaves bodies, affects, and materialities together in translation from a divine perforation. The enfleshing force of Christianity—in its global asymmetries—is irreducible to either difference or sameness with secular ontologies. Therefore, we argue for a broader attunement to the theological difference that the anthropology of global Orthodoxy makes in unfolding the contradictions in moves of Christian homogenization, as it offers new ways to think about tradition, authority, belonging, and empire beyond the historical problematic binaries of divine/profane, global/local, East/West, and secular/religious. Global Orthodoxy responds to the equating of Christian theology and secularity[10] and to the broader scholarly and public proclivity to separate the theological from political-material force in the world (extending beyond a regulated and administered category of "religion").

As we make the argument for a theologically conversant anthropology of global Orthodoxy, we also note the critiques of difference between Eastern and Oriental Orthodox lifeworlds. The volume articulates certain formations that are shared between these two families without ignoring the theological and imperial differences between them. The schism between these two Orthodox branches emerged in AD 451 after the Council of

Chalcedon, focused on the question of the relationship between the divinity and humanity of Jesus Christ, and thereafter saw the development of an imperial Byzantine church, dominating and regulating Christian traditions in the East. What are today understood as Oriental Orthodox churches (including the Coptic, Armenian, Eritrean, Ethiopian, Syriac, and Indo-Malankaran church hierarchies) remained in defense and response to both Western and dominant Eastern Christian worlds. The nineteenth and early twentieth centuries saw both the nationalization of Orthodox churches as territorially bound and tied to political authority as well as the onslaught of colonial rule throughout the Middle East, Africa, and South Asia. These modern histories of authority and subjugation transformed the Orthodox tradition rooted in specific localities. (Eastern) Orthodoxy's historical relationship with empire affects how Eastern Orthodox communities today understand their Byzantine pasts and troubled ecclesiastical presents. For Oriental Orthodox communities, many of whom were/are subjugated by the Byzantine Empire, subsequent Islamic empires, European colonial regimes, and American imperialism, it is important to situate scholarly claims "about the past within the very traditions of imperial Christian heresiology, ethnography, and historiography."[11]

In the contemporary moment of Oriental Orthodox migrations to the West caused by economic, political, and social upheavals (many events stemming from postcolonial aftermath and neocolonial forms of governance), there has been an ecumenical push between the two Orthodox branches out of conditional need but also because of new forms of imperial encounter.[12] The entangled histories of past and present migrations and the aesthetic formation of liturgical life articulate a tradition that is shared among all Orthodox communities (without ignoring important theological and imperial differences).[13] In this context, this volume asks: How does the tension between specificity (of Orthodox churches) versus commonality (of the Orthodox tradition) play out in global Orthodoxy—between church and state, homeland and diaspora, and in contexts of the Global South, in minority-majority relations? What is foregrounded in the different anthropologies (or forms of life) of Orthodox lifeworlds, and what is backgrounded?[14] And, more importantly, how does theology matter, anthropologically, and anthropology matter, theologically?

These questions come into stark relief as we consider how Ukrainian Orthodox Christians, in the wake of the 2022 Russian invasion, practice their faith. Ukrainian Orthodox Christians have found themselves positioned between the Ukrainian and Russian governments' lack of understanding regarding the lived theological dimensions of Orthodoxy on the ground.[15] The nationalistic divisions between competing Orthodox churches in Ukraine have been either critiqued or dismissed at the governmental level, which has created fraught theological and canon law issues for believers living in the war-torn nation. In 2024, the Ukrainian government issued a bill that would prohibit Russian Orthodox churches from functioning within the borders of Ukraine, creating ontological anxieties in Ukrainian Orthodox Christians and concerns over religious freedom. At the same time, the Russian Orthodox Church has been theologically complicit and supportive of Putin's war in Ukraine. Faced with these challenges, questions abound. Where do they attend church? Who is their patriarch? What liturgical calendar should they follow? For a theologian, these issues would be theological, perhaps raising larger questions about the ethics of war, church-and-state relationships, ecclesiastical polity, and canonicity. For an anthropologist, these conflicts are assessed through social, cultural, and political framings, paying attention to questions of rights, borders, migration, and ritual sociality. However, these issues contain within them theological concerns that transform and are transformed by social realities and political subjectivities. Orthodox religious traditions are not simply symbolic cultural systems in need of interpretation by the anthropologist. Orthodox traditions—from scripture and saintly writings to the material life of icons—are a means by which practitioners reach the divine on earth, make spiritual meaning for themselves, and often shape their ontological framings of everything from social politics to eschatological perceptions themselves in relationship to the cosmos.

Taking seriously the fraught lifeworlds of Orthodox Christians around the globe, then, means thinking about the theological with the social, cultural, and political as enmeshed with one another. Arguably, theology itself is beholden to social understandings of divinity. Steeped in historical contexts, contoured by time, theology is a gendered, raced, classed product that often tells us as much about the writer(s) and their audiences as it does about human comprehensions of the divine. Thus, theology is a product of the social, with all its attendant structures of power, and as such should be fully drawn into social science-based assessments of Orthodox worlds. At the same time, theology must reckon with its social construction, rather than assuming a place of privilege as unchanging guardian of a universal truth. These assumptions of inerrant and unchangeable truth are part of what early anthropologists were trying to distance themselves from as they moved away from engagement with theological ideas about humanity and the missionizing actors who used them to assess communities around the world.[16] As a field rooted deeply in Enlightenment principles and formations of the secular, anthropology privileges data-driven experiences that take seriously the ontological lifeworlds of interlocutors, without deferring to a universal idea of what counts as real or true. Yet how can we understand and take seriously Orthodox practitioners if we fail to see how essential theology is for their ontological lifeworlds and the political-material conditions that shape how they comprehend supernatural figures and ideas?

The intent, then, of engaging with theology is not to reify claims of truth, impose universalizing ideas about Orthodox practitioners, or even smuggle in missionary claims. Rather, we aim to expand the anthropological, analytical lens to include how theology and politics play out in life and social action. Orthodoxy can be understood through vernacular and institutional debates over correct practice and belief while also being experienced through institutional, aesthetic, material, ethical, and political orientations and kinships (even as they are contested among practitioners).[17] In this way, we need to take seriously the ontological difference expressed in Orthodoxy. If we critically assess and take seriously the theological imaginaries of Orthodox Christians in the way that, for example, Eduardo Kohn did with the indigenous Runa communities in the Amazon of Ecuador, we begin to move away from a sole focus on materiality and praxis and forward into better understanding the interiority and moral networks formed by the Orthodox faithful around the globe.[18] In doing so, we can better understand how theology and its political-material force are enmeshed in sensory practices and bodily disciplines that continually create and sustain Orthodox lifeworlds. Theological knowledge is also a formation of power—in that theological conversations, councils, and synods are predicated by political problems. Thus, it is neither devoid of the effects of messy human interaction nor completely static. Orthodox Christianity takes seriously the notion that theology is living. To be clear, though, Orthodoxy's orientation to a living theology is not argued through the fundamental transformation of Christian doctrine or that somehow new interpretations of Scripture and tradition will render new interpretations of God's revelation. Rather, theology is living in Orthodox perspectives through its conditioning and contextualizing in this world. Thus, theology's political-material force should be understood in its unfolding in the sociocultural aspects of a person's lifeworld.

Too often, however, the approach to studying theology in Orthodox lived theological experiences is to assess them through the lens of Western (Christian) histories, practices, and beliefs. The American religious historian Sydney Ahlstrom once noted that these churches had been—or still are—a "closed book": "A Greek was a restaurateur, not a bearer of a rich and ancient Christian tradition. A Russian is variously suspected as White or Red. The historic testimony and ways of about one hundred thousand Unitarians or four hundred thousand Christian Scientists or a handful of Shakers are better known, even in many seminaries, than the faith and practice of America's nearly three million Orthodox."[19] Alstrom's indictment of his own field in the 1970s mirrors that of social scientists working on Orthodoxy in the early 2000s and 2010s. In 2007, Peter McMylor and Maria Vorozhishcheva noted that Orthodoxy was affected by the "manifold" way in which "cultures, especially alien ones," are examined. Even when scholars attempt to think through the relationship between theology and culture, McMylor and Vorozhishcheva argue that there is a "profoundly misplaced historicism at work, which profoundly distorts our understanding of Churches per se and leads frequently to a kind of theological reductionism in which the supposed aspects of church theology are seen to lead to certain social outcomes."[20] Tom Boylston, also concerned about framings, noted the lack of research on Orthodox Christianity in 2013, suggesting then that "entwined histories of Christianity and colonialism" have ensured that Protestantism is not just a bias in the anthropology of Christianity but part of the hegemony of secular modernity.[21] In other words, Protestantism and its attendant forms—on a global scale—shape not only academic inquires but reality itself. Boylston argues that Orthodoxy provides a helpful intervention through its theopolitical histories and living communities. He writes: "What do politics and territory have to do with truth, light, and beauty? Orthodox Christianities are not alone in dealing with these questions—just the opposite—but their approaches and solutions are interesting, important, and understudied. Which is good reason to get to work."[22]

As Boylston noted, the theological traditions and lived practices of Orthodox Christians have often been marginalized in scholarship, ecumenical partnerships, social discourse, and broader geopolitical considerations because of their alterity to Western intellectual and social conceptualizations of Christianity. Yet Western (Christian) social actors also reconceptualize and/or utilize the suffering of Eastern/Orthodox Christians around the globe as part of a political project aimed at the deconstruction of secularism or their own eschatological imagination of geographically displaced death for salvation.[23] The enmeshment of geopolitics and theology among Eastern Orthodox and Oriental Orthodox communities globally exhibit how religious practice and ethical commitments are transformed and made possible through their unfolding *in* the world. To fully understand how Orthodox traditions are conditioned by their lived contexts, an anthropological attunement must already include their theopolitical and ontological difference. Put another way, anthropological engagement with Orthodox communities requires accounting both for their difference from other Christian traditions (in our case Protestant and Catholic forms) as well as for how their theology and geopolitical positioning affects the ways they understand themselves and how they are understood, administered, and governed in transnational contexts of power and subjugation.

Foregrounding and Backgrounding in the Anthropology of (Orthodox) Christianity

How does Christianity become foregrounded and backgrounded in anthropological inquiry? Is Christianity a comprehensive tradition (like the anthropological study of Islam has been), or does Orthodox difference reshape what looks "recognizably" Christian?[24] Within the history of anthropology as a discipline, the subfield focused on Christianity remains relatively new, even as there have been calls to move past it by its founders.[25] While it is true that the anthropology of Christianity has come into its own as a distinct subfield, its historical emergence shows how contested the study of Christianity was in the social sciences. In 2003, Joel Robbins argued:

> Christians are too similar by virtue of drawing on the same broad cultural tradition as anthropologists, and too meaningfully different by virtue of drawing on part of that tradition that in many respects has arisen in critical dialogue with the modernist ideas on which anthropology is founded. Both the similarities and the pointed nature of the differences make Christianity more difficult than other religions for anthropologists to study.[26]

Underlying this claim is a normative understanding of the discipline—as conditioned and scaffolded by Western networks of power and frameworks of legibility. But there is also a normative understanding of the ontological positioning of anthropologists themselves—as wading in Western Christian water and enmeshed within those imperial networks of power.[27] Beyond this, however, anthropologists also carry the legacy of Western transformations in the social positioning and study of a distinct category of "religion," a category differentiated from other aspects of life. In the 1990s, Marshall Sahlins recognized this when he noted that Judeo-Christian cosmologies (what could be construed as theologies for our purposes) were vital to the creation of Western social science, arguing that over time these cosmologies became "bourgeoisified" as free will transformed into rational choice.[28] Bourgeois sociality and politics were thought to have liberated humans from the burden of Christianized morality, and thus, Christianity was no longer needed to understand culture or in the study of religion.[29] Much like the rest of the social sciences (and humanities), however, anthropology has a long genealogy before the Enlightenment that includes theological and philosophical ideas directly related to transformations in Western Christian thought.[30]

Seeking to separate themselves as scientists, early anthropologists including Malinowski, Radcliffe-Brown, and Spencer (and many others) created paradigms and theories about social practices that revealed the structure and function of social worlds without explicitly naming and engaging Christian cosmologies.[31] While recent turns to a "theologically engaged anthropology" have opened up the discipline to forms of analysis that challenge these long-standing ontological orientations in the field,[32] there remains an uneasiness within anthropology about engaging with theology. Furthermore, when anthropological engagements at the intersection of theology and anthropology do occur, they remain oriented toward a Western (mainly Protestant) frame of legibility that contours not only what counts as their main analytical use in the anthropology of Christianity but also within anthropological inquiry on religion writ large.[33]

Bridging from the seminal critiques of Talal Asad, the anthropology of religion and subsequently the subfield of the anthropology of Christianity have long had to respond to this idea of Protestant bias in anthropological inquiry—from the emphasis on meaning to the focus on interiority.[34] Over a decade ago, the anthropologist Chris Hann critiqued the subfield and anthropology writ large for the absence of inquiry into Orthodox lifeworlds.

In the Introduction to the volume *Eastern Christians from an Anthropological Perspective* (2010), Hann and his coeditor Hermann Goltz emphasize that the future of research on Eastern Christianity would involve comparative studies, thinking about similarities and differences between Eastern and Western Christians past and present. Hann and Goltz seem to suggest that Eastern Christianity can only be understood through the lens of Western Christianity. Comparing Orthodoxy against Western forms of Christianity, though, implies that Protestantism and Catholicism are the standard by which faith traditions are to be assessed. This presumption further complicates the position of Orthodoxy, presenting it, in some ways, as a minor object of study in anthropology. Hann and Goltz frame the place of Orthodox Christianity in scholarship as resting upon a history of political power struggles and crumbling economic infrastructures that cannot compete with the machine of Western modernity that is tied to the Protestant work ethic and its ideologies. They note: "Our broader aim with the research agenda initiated in this volume is simultaneously to free the category 'East' from the political distortions of the Cold War era and to transcend the legacy of centuries of scholarly 'Orientalism.'"[35] In the gaze of Western Christianity and its enmeshment in past colonial and missionary endeavors to remake the "East," Hann and Goltz both identify the material-political power dynamics at play in keeping Orthodoxy in intellectual alterity without wholly addressing the foundational conditions of this division. The exceptional centering of Orthodox Christianity in anthropological studies of religion (as well as secularism) often creates a myopic focus on the West, implicitly perpetuating an Orientalist East/West dichotomy and reinforcing long-held colonialist notions of Eastern Christian and Orthodox alterity; the tradition's inclusion is rendered as exception, an addition to the study of Christianity's "diversity." These scholarly conditions are still pressing despite how Orthodox diasporas have grown throughout the West (including North America, Europe, and Australia) over the past two decades of revolutionary political upheaval and neocolonial economic restructuring.

Foundational to thinking about Orthodoxy's (non)place in the anthropology of Christianity, Susan Friend Harding's work on American fundamentalists and more specifically on the televangelist Jerry Falwell made a pathway to take Christianity seriously as a field of anthropological inquiry and also zoomed in on the frames of scholarly exclusion in the discipline.[36] Harding's work attempted to open a space for anthropologists to research and write about Christianity in ways that paid attention to the "repugnancy" of certain Christian forms. Instead of dismissing those forms, which were publicly understood as being in opposition to progressive politics, Harding shed light on the secular, liberal underbelly of anthropology. Harding's work became, it seems, a model for how to approach Christianity anthropologically—with a serious accounting of practitioners' lifeworlds that does not reinforce secular tones of dismissal. Thus, she neither marginalizes nor praises groups on the fringe of Christian studies, calling instead for scholars to pay attention to all forms of religion, even if they are in complete opposition to the implicit secularity of anthropological inquiry.[37] The anthropological study of Orthodoxy has faced similar challenges in taking seriously its theological orientations and political praxis on its own terms. Seeing Orthodox contexts anthropologically has often meant focusing on other socially acceptable forms of alterity, such as race, class, and/or gender, and eschewing direct and contentious engagement with the theological lifeworlds that construct an Orthodox political-material ethos.[38]

In this way, engaging the seminal question of the subfield—"What difference does Christianity make?"—translates quite distinctly for anthropologies of Orthodoxy because of the historical-theological context it arises from.[39] While the late 1990s saw anthropological interest in Christian religious life in colonial and postcolonial contexts dramatically increase (where missionaries' converts were making Christianity their own), scholarship sidelined (or briefly mentioned) the continuing conditions of subjugation and imperial frames of legibility that made that Christianity a source of Western intellectual interest in the first place. Since the conversion of the Global South originated from the Western Christian traditions and historical-imperial contexts of the Global North, their study was made commensurable with anthropological interest. Thus, the anthropology of Christianity's focus has predominantly been on the flow of Christian life starting "historically in the West and expand[ing] to cover the globe."[40] In some contrast, we are interested in a project that decenters Christianity from its Western normativity or captivity, asking what might be possible if we start at the margins, with arguably the oldest forms of Christianity in existence.

In 2003, Joel Robbins noted that early anthropological study of Christianity struggled with and at times was "dependent upon missionary infrastructure."[41] One of the central claims of the anthropology of Christianity was the discipline's unease with studying Christians *as* Christians or even with Christian anthropologists studying communities of their own religious tradition. (Arguably, anthropologists who are also practicing Christians have become the suspect Other within the field, and this has produced a dynamic debate at the intersection of ontology, theology, and politics.)[42] Since Robbins's early writings, anthropologists of Christianity have consistently contended over what the "object" of the anthropology of Christianity should be—what is a Christian? What is Christianity? Whose Christianity? In quite a presentist way, this line of inquiry has sidestepped how being a Christian in a postcolonial or post-Soviet locale is quite different from being one in places of both privilege and anxiety, like the United States. Yet the focus on making Christianity at home in a variety of spaces of difference—a plea to a kind of liberal politics of diversity—has certainly missed out on the interconnections between Western missionization and legacies of conquest, colonization, and enslavement.[43] At the same time, it also fails to fully interrogate the dynamics of conversion, belonging, enculturation, and appropriation that often accompany Orthodoxy in the Western context. When we pay attention to all these dynamics, we begin to recognize that "not all Christians have been able to make Christianity at home in equal ways."[44]

The anthropology of Christianity has tended to privilege a study of ethics and cultural rupture over confrontations with the historicity and political economy of (Western) Christianity because the latter would require us to rethink the idea of Christianity as a religious tradition among others. Along with his aforementioned coedited volume on Eastern Christianity, Chris Hann has critically assessed the subfield's intense focus on the microlevel variation of religious practice. He argues that these shifts are not products of local cultural difference but rather a result of macrolevel political economic processes, in terms of the comparative wealth and resultant power of Western Christians to influence Christians across the Global South.[45] Granted, Joel Robbins and others suggest that the focus on culture and radical rupture encompasses political, social, and economic factors.[46] Yet in focusing Christianity through the prism of culture (as a cultural fact), it has reframed Christianity as a totality, with a shared cosmology and worldview. This culture move decenters institutions (Christian or otherwise) that shape the contours of a given tradition, provide structures of communal belonging, and enable forms of politicization. As the anthropology of Christianity coalesced around notions of "rupture" and "sincerity" as tools of analysis, communities and denominations who have focused on tradition, established rituals, and cultural continuity (at least in a discursive, institutional manner) found themselves outside the narrow gauge of the field[47]—a gauge that typically fails to fully understand and critique the ontological distinctions of Orthodoxy. Orthodox theology is not largely focused on rupture but instead on continuity and repair. To repeat, the tools of analysis, then, are, in many respects, products of the long history of latent Protestant bias largely within the humanities and social sciences, and they fail to encompass other concepts that fully interrogate the problems and possibilities of Orthodoxy—such as sensorium, emplacement, or even (neo)patristics.

Most scholars within the subfield, whether critics or caretakers, work within the given confines of the broader field of anthropology, taking small steps toward an anthropology of Christianity that can overcome both its innate Western biases and its maligned status as a product of Western dominance and colonial authority. In the reframing of an anthropology of Christianity to be inclusive of Orthodoxy, a geopolitical accounting to the asymmetries of Christian difference must be taken up—foregrounding political-material-historical difference and backgrounding perceived cultural cohesion and connection. Studying Orthodox Christianity—whether in its Oriental or Eastern forms—anthropologically and theologically is conditioned by whom and by how it is being studied and by what knowledge is produced from such encounters. To understand the "East/West" divide in the anthropology of Christianity, engaging theologically with Orthodox Christianity—and its diverse communities and traditions—provides a new perspective on the theological underpinnings of contemporary political-material orientations and forms of social action.

What Difference Does Orthodox Theology Make?

The chapters in this volume illuminate the ethnographic possibilities of another way of approaching more-than-human forces in this world. Drawing together anthropology and theology, then, is an opportunity for social science scholarship to consider the limits of its implicit secularity, a historical intervention that pushes back against the earliest notions of anthropological objectivity before the reflexive turn of the late twentieth century. As the anthropology of Christianity has developed over the first two decades of the twenty-first century, so too has its engagement with religious texts, theologies, and doctrines as other corners of the anthropology of religion have as well.[48] In his ethnography of Evangelical Bible study groups, James Bielo highlights how important religious documents are in the study of Christianity: "Sacred texts—like Christian scriptures—are not only sources of spiritual revelation; they are also powerful incitements to action."[49] In thinking about Orthodox Christianity, engagement with the writings of the Church Fathers and Mothers, lives of the saints (for example, the Coptic Synaxarium), canons, *Akathists* (hymns), the Lenten Triodion, the Festal Menaion, and various jurisdictional iterations of traditional prayer books are crucial to understanding the written revelation of Orthodox theologies. Yet the institutional authorization of these textual, liturgical, and material parts of the tradition are always in conversation with community practice and local vernacular theologies. The determination of "correctness," then, can be described as a negotiation of power between structures of legitimacy. Institutional decisions, doctrines, and decrees become authoritative through their vernacular deployment, acceptance, and/or contestation. These vernacular theologies are the embodiment of the church's institutional authority at the local level. Put another way, the anthropological as well as theological tension between "populist" and "institutional" framings of religious tradition eschews how theology is lived, expressed, and brought to life through its embodiment and praxis.

In this volume, the differentiation between lay and institutional theologies is conditioned by the histories and the politics of knowledge production in the field. Yet even anthropologists of Orthodox Christianity have often struggled with how to take seriously the political-material force of a theology that extends beyond the traditionally understood category of "religion"—in belief, prayer, and the text (institutionally authorized forms of the tradition). This tension was once personified in the late Sonja Luehrmann's reaction to an article on religious materiality as connective forms of media. Luehrmann's scholarly inroads into Orthodox Christian spirituality zoomed in on Orthodoxy through prayer and conceptualized it as tradition, skill, and aesthetic formation. However, in describing the broader structures of authorized tradition through the institutional church, Luehrmann also left out the political-material forces undergirding the theological thrusts of her argument, disentangling theology and power. As we argued earlier in this Introduction, theological controversy throughout Christian history has been predicated by a political problem, and such history is theologically laden.

Luehrmann's edited volume *Praying with the Senses: Contemporary Orthodox Spirituality in Practice* was published in 2018. As part of an earlier iteration of the project, the Reverberations: New Directions in the Study of Prayer forum commissioned, through the Social Science Research Council (SSRC), essays at the intersection of prayer, religious materiality, and Orthodoxy. Based on extensive fieldwork in the United States, Aaron Sokoll and Sarah Riccardi-Swartz argued that icons and other forms of the material holy serve as haptic and visual agentive interfaces that allow for transrealm communication and prayer, highlighting the icons themselves as interlocutors in a conversation between practitioners and members of the celestial realm.[50] These findings were based entirely on interviews with interlocutors about the theological role of icons in their lives. However, in response to the essay, Luehrmann wrote, "I think that part of the point of a social-scientific analysis of religious practices is always to produce a picture that's a little different from that which a normative account of the religion would produce. The saints and theologians can say much better than we can how prayer is supposed to work from the inside of its practice. What we can add as social scientists is a framework that's slightly shifted to include aspects that the devotee herself does not consider relevant."[51] While acknowledging how the social embeddedness of interactions with holy things intersects theological elaborations of social hierarchy and everyday ways of thinking about kinship, gender, and reproduction, she also seemingly argues that the anthropologist must see beyond what the interlocutor produces, that anthropologists are not simply stenographers. Luehrmann was a rigorous anthropologist whose legacy continues to shape how we think about Orthodox Christianity as well as secularism, yet her response to the assessment of vernacular theological belief about iconography more broadly highlights the ongoing tensions between anthropology and theology, as well as internally within the two disciplines. Luehrmann's statement is problematic for several reasons; it suggests that we as anthropologists, and our interlocutors, should be demure to the ideas and theological authority of clerics and hierarchs in our assessment of what is happening within a given field site. It also speaks to a negation of agency on the part of one's interlocutors, suggesting that they themselves cannot speak about their beliefs as they are practiced. Finally, it reinforces the historical fissure between theology and anthropology, resuscitating the arguments of E. E. Evans-Pritchard and others had about the secular/scientific nature of anthropology as oppositional to theology.[52]

Luehrmann's comments might stem from a larger disciplinary conception of religion, which already assumes it is an effect rather than a cause. Or, to frame it another way, "religion" is understood as one particular form of life divorced from larger structures of power, and theology is relevant only in the context of its textual tradition rather than its lived and negotiated character. Thus prayer, as a theological practice, is not seen as being part of the purview of anthropological inquiry beyond notions of praxis and power. In many respects, this view is a byproduct of the fact that Orthodoxy seems to be viewed outside of the normative anthropological understanding of what Christianity was and is within pre- and postcolonial (neocolonial) worlds and how it functions in relationship to other social-material-political forms of life. This seems to be what Timothy Jenkins is alluding to when he suggests that anthropology is interested in Christianity as "something encountered in the field."[53] In other words, Christianity is studied as a phenomenon that is a facet of a particular cultural and social habitus within the given field rather than being the field itself. To take this even further, anthropologists view religion (particularly Christianity) as a visible effect of underlying sociopolitical and ethnocultural ideas, tensions, and negotiation, whereas scholars of religious studies often approach topical issues through a cordoned-off category of "religion"—it becomes a way of understanding the actions, practices, and beliefs of people that are often removed from theology, presence, and divine agency. As Angie Heo has argued in response to Saba Mahmood's *Religious Difference in a Secular Age: A Minority Report*, "Christological discourse travels, its weight and force in late antiquity differing from its work in the contemporary present of majority-minority inequality and clerical authoritarianism."[54] Again, history is theologically laden, and theology is predicated by political controversy. In response to the emergence of the anthropology of Christianity subfield, the editors of *The Anthropology of Catholicism* reader argue that Catholicism's "invisibility" (as opposed to the "visibility" of Pentecostalism and other Protestant forms) in anthropological inquiry can be interpreted as the ability of Catholicism (and Orthodoxy) to "structure communities at all levels." They speculate that Catholicism's "presence-as-non-presence" is part of its "politico-historical legacy and subsequent naturalization in the institutional sense."[55] The present volume addresses the theological (and particularly secular) underpinnings of this conceptualization of Catholicism's and Orthodoxy's alterity.

Orthodoxy's ontological difference is manifested in the practices and beliefs of adherents as they live out the theological teachings of the church in the "presence-as-non-presence" of their everyday lives. In a theological world of damnation, purgation, and hellfire, Eastern Orthodoxy's philosophy, for example, with its emphasis on a lifetime of theosis (deification), communal salvation, and hell as an ontological separation from God's love rather than a literal, physical place of torment, is outside of the normative Western Christian stance on salvation.[56] Many scholars of anthropology do not take this ontological difference into consideration. Cannell, for example, writes that the general view in anthropology is that "Christianity is the religion of a god who is at best intermittently present in a world of immanence . . . that is, many of its practices are understood as attempts to compensate for the appalling distance which is felt to be placed between man and the Christian God."[57] This concept of Christianity both privileges Protestant ontologies and flattens the rich diversity of theologies that abound, such as the Orthodox belief that God is "everywhere present and filling all things" or that spiritual beings are present when the divine services occur.[58]

In contrast to the dualistic notions (even Gnostic) of the body and spirit that pervade much of Western Christianity, Orthodoxy sees a mingling of corporeality and spirituality.[59] In Eastern Orthodoxy, this is evidenced particularly in the concept of theosis; Eastern Orthodox Christians, through participation with the rituals of the church, holy materiality, and bodily contouring through kinetic prayer, fasting, and feasting, transform over time, conforming to the image of God. This lived theology aspires to the words of Saint Athanasius from the fourth century: "God became man so that man might become God."[60] While theosis is still a contested theological concept among Oriental Orthodox Christians for reasons of historical, imperial contexts, among others, they also understand this lived theology through the incarnational truth of Christ's divine and human enmeshment—allowing for a both/and approach.[61] As Sarah Bakker Kellogg argues in her chapter in this volume: "The Chalcedonian Definition affirms that a human is defined by more than what happens to her in her life because Jesus is defined by more than what happened to him living on Earth. In Cyrillian Christology, first the word *physis* and then the word *hypostasis* convey this integration of different parts into a cosmic, spiritually significant wholeness." While belief and faith are important aspects of

Orthodox spirituality, practice is at the heart of salvation, for it is through communal participation in the life of the church that one is saved.

Drawing from the New Testament, the Russian Orthodox theologian Sergei Bulgakov commented that "faith without works is dead."[62] The actions of Orthodox practitioners—both Eastern and Oriental—are not symbolic; rather, each ritual is a material aid for spiritual transformation. This not only differs from Protestant notions of salvation, but it also stands in tension with the subfield of the anthropology of Christianity, which is haunted not only by the ghost of Max Weber but also the specter of Clifford Geertz and his theoretical model of belief and the symbolic. Max Weber's *The Protestant Ethic and the Spirit of Capitalism*, while devoid of ethnographic material, is foundational reading for the anthropological study of religion. Seminal English-speaking anthropologists such as Talcott Parsons and Clifford Geertz used Weber's theories about Protestantism to launch methods of cultural analysis that focused on the symbolic aspects of culture.[63] In contrast, the influence of Talal Asad's work on discursive tradition, religion, and power has been less of a focus in the subfield of the anthropology of Christianity, despite the subfield's inspiration from Asad's own interventions in thinking about the idea of an anthropology of Islam. Asad's focus on power and historical-political-material conditions (which also shape the possibilities of action and practice) has been eschewed for more agential perspectives of sincerity and rupture (paradoxically themselves shaped by colonial and geopolitical/theological circulations).

Bridging from the anthropology of Christianity, as noted earlier, recent conversations in the newer field of theologically engaged anthropology has broadly facilitated a dialogue between anthropologists and theologians, albeit focused on Protestant and Catholic perspectives. Joel Robbins has emphasized that the relationship between these two disciplines should be one of "transformation." In his book *Theology and the Anthropology of Christian Life*, Robbins argues that this transformation should not be of "theology borrowing anthropology's method and anthropology treating theological arguments as ethnographic data bearing on the nature of Christian thought, but as one that takes place between two theoretically ambitious disciplines with their own varied versions of systematic thinking about how the cosmos, and the human beings who inhabit it, come to be the way that they are . . ."[64] This volume argues that there is no universalizing theory of how to anthropologically understand Orthodox Christianity theologically. Rather, Orthodoxy is context dependent, integrating the enmeshment of theological and political-material forces into its accounting. This volume collectively considers the possibilities of reframing the anthropology of Christianity in a way that centers Orthodox Christian thought and practice rather than marginalizing it, while acknowledging the intersectional aspects of religiosity and spirituality with other social phenomena, cultural constructions, and material (co)presences.

Outline of the Volume

While much of this Introduction has focused on the more institutional and scholarly conversations and debates in anthropology and recent inroads into the conversation between theology and anthropology, the following chapters provide ethnographic texture to how theology is engaged in contexts from Palestine to Ethiopia to the United States and beyond. From tracking the imperial traces and continuing sociopolitical importance of the Council of Chalcedon to the ethics of clerical-anthropological engagement in the field, the volume contributes to an expansion of conceptual resources for theologically thinking about the difference that Orthodoxy makes to the anthropological study of religion, politics, and ethics.

Part I of the volume, "Living Theology and Anthropological Theories," considers how Orthodox Christian life is theologically transformed in various geopolitically important contemporary and historical contexts, showcasing how kinship and ethnicity should be reconsidered theologically. Clayton Goodgame's chapter, "Orthodoxy from the Outside: Palestinian Christian Kinship and the Evangelical Theology of Love," explores how traditions are oriented and remade in relationship to one another by examining a case of theological transmission from Palestinian Orthodox Christianity to Palestinian Evangelicalism. In it Goodgame argues that while Orthodox and Evangelicals in Palestine approach the transmission of divine experience in profoundly different ways, their real difference lies in "the way the latter conceptually separate the category of kinship from that of faith." Through the tension between the Orthodox discourse of "sacred descent" and Evangelical forms of "love talk," Goodgame shows how traditions are remade and the boundaries of what counts as "religion" are redefined in pluralist societies. This move has profound effects for thinking about the difference Orthodox Christianity makes in political orientation and theological reason in Palestine and beyond it, with attention to how imperialism and settler colonialism have transformed theological transmission.

Bridging from Goodgame's consideration of the anthropology of Orthodoxy and kinship, Sarah Bakker Kellogg takes up imperial a/effects on Oriental Orthodox divisions between religion/ethnicity in diaspora, looping through an analysis of the theologically laden histories that condition such imperial presents. In her chapter, "Imperial Ecclesiologies and Ethnographic Imaginaries: Situating Syriac Christianity in the Anthropology of Global Orthodoxy," Bakker Kellogg reflects on extensive fieldwork among Syriac Orthodox Christians in the Netherlands to explore "what an Orthodox framing enables, as well as forecloses, in producing ethnographic descriptions and analyses of Syriac lifeworlds, lived theologies, and ethicopolitical commitments." Specifically, she draws together the shadow of Chalcedonian Christianity's historical relationship with empire and how the Syriac world has been "constituted in the shadow of multiple empires." Through careful attention to theological reason and historical context, Bakker Kellogg brings the volume into the specific Syriac context to show how power dynamics formed the Syriac world—at times in response to imperial Christianity and at other times vastly removed from its conversations and concerns.

Thinking through a methodological discussion of anthropology and theology's social enmeshment and the ethical subjectivities of anthropologists, clergy members, and Orthodox believers in the field, Aaron Michka foregrounds social transformation through an ecclesiastical pondering on "The Lives of Priests in the Coptic Imagination." Through the Coptic tradition, Michka connects the idea of continuity and apostolic succession to the everyday life of the priest beyond church doors. Engaging the role of the priest, Michka explores how anthropology and theology can better contend with each other, specifically asking: "How might the figure of the priest, caught between the stability of the church and the flux of society, help us rethink the relationship between these two disciplines?"

Part II of the volume, entitled "Social Transformation and Orthodox Theologies," zooms in on ethics in different forms—from ethical subjectivities to the ethical dimensions of everyday Orthodox practice under sociopolitical constraints—bringing together a set of chapters that focus on everyday forms of social life and how conflict, ecumenism, and relationality redefine Orthodox Christianity in new ways. Christopher Sheklian's chapter, "Hagiographic Emplacement: St. Servatius, the Armenian

Community of Maastricht, and Oriental Orthodox Christians in Europe," focuses on how kinship is materialized through theological placemaking in diaspora and how the "concerted use of theological arguments and liturgical practices regarding saints" forges connections to place in migration. Through the idea of "hagiographic emplacement," Sheklian argues for "careful attention to the liturgical and theological encounter of different traditions in the minority migrant experience," specifically in Western Europe. While Sheklian thinks about Orthodox migrations' impact on theological thinking, John Dulin's "Dynamic Honor: How Ethiopian Orthodox *Keber* Mediates the Secular, the Islamic, and the Religiously Plural" examines how the Ethiopian Orthodox practice of respect, or *keber*, through means such as prostration, or *sigdet*, mediates Christian social and particularly interreligious imaginaries in Gondar, Ethiopia. Interreligious *keber*, then, enables mutuality to define Muslim-Orthodox relations in Ethiopia, even in tension with geopolitical influence on the local specificity of such kin forms.

Combining the engagement of Dulin with theological form and social practice and Sheklian's methodological discussion of anthropology and theology's social enmeshment in migrant societies, Amber Lee Silva intimately outlines the complex convergences between soteriology and sociality among Old Rite Russian Orthodox Christians (or Old Believers). In her chapter, "The State of Grace: Old Believers' Determinations of Coreligiosity and Moral Life in the Days Between the Mysteries," Silva argues that grace is a "third element" of coreligiosity that warrants greater consideration in anthropological studies of Old Believers' inter- and intrareligious delineations of association. In this way, grace is thought to be "a divine social boundary between the saved and the doomed" that has influence over Old Believers' everyday moral decision making and ecclesiological determinations of "what we believe and who belongs."

The third and final part of this volume, "Theological Anxieties and Cultural Constructions," takes us to the digital worlds of religious nationalism and nation building among Russian Orthodox Christians and to American Orthodox theological considerations of the believability of UFOs, with an attunement for overlapping considerations of geopolitical conspiracy and controversy. In his chapter, "The Heresy of Eastern *Papizm* in Russian Orthodox Online Discourse," Jacob Lassin unpacks how the rhetorical strategies of the Russian Orthodox Church and its allies frame Ukrainian autocephaly as a tangible example of the threats that the West poses in the Russian nation. Focusing on how theology is intimately tied with soft power and neoimperial statecraft, Lassin shows how ecclesial conflicts are intertwined with the conflicts of various modern states and how Orthodox Christian church structure—online and off—creates the theological boundaries and social separations between Orthodox and heterodox heresy. Shifting to one of the key twentieth-century theological figures from the Russian Orthodox Church Outside of Russia (ROCOR), Fr. Seraphim Rose, Robert C. Saler considers the Americanness of Eastern Orthodoxy, conversion, and conspiracy within the broader sweep of Orthodox presence in the United States and online. In "UFOs, Conspiracy, and American Eastern Orthodoxy: Narrative Performance of the 'Patristic Mind,'" Saler concludes the volume with discussion of the idea of the "patristic mind" and how figures like Fr. Seraphim Rose have been imagined as an Orthodox authority on what appear to be conspiratorial matters beyond the realm of "modern" legibility. Several contemporary Eastern Orthodox influencers have argued that UFOs are not extraterrestrials but rather demons; in addition, they have tied these assertions directly to conspiracy theories about the government's role in fostering the New World Order. Saler argues that Rose's authority is connected to his "credibility in enacting a sort of patristic reinscription, a performative recasting of anxieties relating to extraterrestrials, the paranormal, and conspiracy that, crucially, lend themselves to being updated and recapitulated in ways that make their deployment all the more fraught in our time." In this exercise, Saler posits that interrogating what morally constitutes "real" Orthodoxy is not helpful if we understand Orthodox Christian practice as dependent upon sociopolitical context *and* contested theological engagement in a digital age.

Building on the frameworks articulated in this Introduction, Angie Heo bookends the volume's chapters with an afterword drawing together contemporary geopolitical contexts from Ethiopia to Russia to show how Orthodox identity and transformation is a living and contentious endeavor negotiated between the everyday and the structures of institutional power that condition theological reason and religious practice. Instead of recapitulating the tired binary separation between East-West in Christian forms, Heo reiterates one of the volume's aims—to show that Eastern and Oriental Orthodox Christians are not simply assimilable into the category of "Eastern Christians." Rather, such Orthodox Christians are interpellated into an East-West divide differently in distinct ethnographic contexts, lending itself to the questioning of such a binary that demarcates a global Orthodoxy in the first place. Heo reminds us that the volume unravels typical renderings of Orthodox Christianity as sutured to the nation-state and instead challenges this methodological nationalism in the social sciences at large—with consequences for both theological imagination and anthropological inquiry.

Notes

Editorial note: To reflect the interdisciplinary spirit of this volume, we encouraged our authors to use citational practices they are most familiar with in their disciplines.

1. Pew Research Center, "Orthodox Christianity in the 21st Century," November 8, 2017, https://www.pew-esearch.org/religion/2017/11/08/orthodox -christianity-in-the-21st-century/.

2. John Behr, *Becoming Human: Theological Anthropology in Word and Image* (St. Vladimir's Seminary Press, 2013); Matta El-Meskeen, *Orthodox Prayer Life: The Interior Way*, trans. Monastery of St. Macarius the Great (St. Vladimir's Seminary Press, 2003); Nonna Vera Harrison, *God's Many Splendored Image: Theological Anthropology for Christian Formation* (Baker Academic, 2010); Alexis Torrance, *Human Perfection in Byzantine Theology: Attaining the Fullness of Christ* (Oxford University Press, 2020).

3. Ayala Fader and Vlad Naumescu, "Religious Orthodoxies: Provocations from the Jewish and Christian Margins," *Annual Review of Anthropology* 51 (October 2022): 326.

4. Michael Jackson, *Lifeworlds: Essays in Existential Anthropology* (University of Chicago Press, 2012).

5. Much of the social science work on religion in the post-Soviet context comes from outside of anthropology, with theologians conducting interviews and sociologists, political scientists, and ethnologists doing qualitative research. While not intended to be exhaustive, see the Introduction's notes for sources.

6. Jeffers Engelhardt, *Singing the Right Way: Orthodox Christians and Secular Enchantment in Estonia* (Oxford University Press, 2014); Sonja Luehrmann, ed., *Praying with the Senses: Contemporary Orthodox Christian Spirituality in Practice* (Indiana University Press, 2018); Sonja Luehrmann, "Objects, Anti-Objects, and Efficacious Interpretations of Prayer," Reverberations: New Directions in the Study of Prayer, 2013, http://forums.ssrc.org/ndsp/2013/11/06/objects-anti -objects-and-efficacious-interpretations-of-prayer/.

7. Jeanne Kormina and Vlad Naumescu, "A New 'Great Schism'? Theopolitics of Communion and Canonical Territory in the Orthodox Church," *Anthropology Today* 36, no. 1 (2020); Carlota McAllister and Valentina Napolitano, "Political Theology/Theopolitics: The Thresholds and Vulnerabilities of Sovereignty," *Annual Review of Anthropology* 50 (2021):

109–24; Sarah Riccardi-Swartz, *Between Heaven and Russia: Religious Conversion and Political Apostasy in Appalachia* (Fordham University Press, 2022); Robert Cady Saler, *"Death to the World" and Apocalyptic Theological Aesthetics* (Bloomsbury, 2024).

8. Kormina and Naumescu, "A New 'Great Schism'?"

9. Mitri Raheb, *The Politics of Persecution: Middle Eastern Christians in An Age of Empire* (Baylor University Press, 2021); Mitri Raheb, *Decolonizing Palestine: The Land, the People, the Bible* (Orbis, 2023).

10. Gil Anidjar, *Blood: A Critique of Christianity* (Columbia University Press, 2014).

11. Sarah Bakker Kellogg, "Perforating Kinship: Syriac Christianity, Ethnicity, and Secular Legibility," *Current Anthropology* 60, no. 4 (2019): 475–98; Fader and Naumescu, "Religious Orthodoxies."

12. Lieba Faier and Lisa Rofel, "Ethnographies of Encounter," *Annual Review of Anthropology* 43, no. 1 (2014): 363–77.

13. Birgit Meyer, *Aesthetic Formations: Media, Religion, and the Senses* (Springer, 2009).

14. Simon Coleman, "Anthropology on Shifting Grounds," *Ethnos* 77, no. 4 (December 2012): 556–63.

15. Regina Elsner, "Living 'Holy Rus' or 'Kyivan Tradition'—the Socio-Ethical Perspective on Common Roots and Diverging Identities," in *Churches in Contact and Collision*, ed. Heta Hurskainen and Teuvo Laitila (Brill/Schöningh, 2023); Catherine Wanner, *Everyday Religiosity and the Politics of Belonging in Ukraine* (Cornell University Press, 2022).

16. Timothy Jenkins, "The Anthropology of Christianity: Situation and Critique," *Ethnos* 77, no. 4 (December 2012): 459–76.

17. Fader and Naumescu, "Religious Orthodoxies," 326.

18. Eduardo Kohn, *How Forests Think: Toward an Anthropology Beyond the Human* (University of California Press, 2013).

19. Sydney E. Ahlstrom, *A Religious History of the American People* (Yale University Press, 1972), 985–86.

20. Peter McMylor and Maria Vorozhishcheva, "Sociology and Eastern Orthodoxy," in *The Blackwell Companion to Eastern Christianity*, ed. Ken Parry (Blackwell, 2007), 463.

21. Tom Boylston, "Orienting the East: Notes on Anthropology and Orthodox Christianities," 2013, http://www.blogs.hss.ed.ac.uk/anthrocybib/2013/05/26/orienting-the-east/.

22. Boylston, "Orienting the East."

23. Candace Lukasik, *Martyrs and Migrants: Coptic Christians and the Persecution Politics of US Empire* (New York University Press, 2025).

24. Coleman, "Anthropology on Shifting Grounds."

25. Joel Robbins, "The Anthropology of Christianity: Unity, Diversity, New Directions," *Current Anthropology* 55, S10 (December 2014): S157–71.

26. Joel Robbins, "What Is a Christian? Notes Toward an Anthropology of Christianity," *Religion* 33, no. 3 (2003): 192.

27. Candace Lukasik and Jason Bruner, "Power Circuits: Asymmetries of Global Christianity," *Journal of the American Academy of Religion* 91, no. 3 (September 2023): 519–41.

28. Marshall Sahlins, "The Sadness of Sweetness: The Native Anthropology of Western Cosmology," *Current Anthropology* 37, no. 3 (June 1996): 397.

29. Sahlins, "The Sadness of Sweetness," 397–98.

30. Sahlins, "The Sadness of Sweetness," 398.

31. Sahlins, "The Sadness of Sweetness," 399.

32. Derrick Lemons, ed., *Theologically Engaged Anthropology* (Oxford University Press, 2018); Joel Robbins, *Theology and the Anthropology of Christian Life* (Oxford University Press, 2020).

33. Notable exceptions to this framework have included collective anthropological work on Orthodoxy including and especially Luehrmann, ed., *Praying with the Senses.*

34. Talal Asad, "The Idea of an Anthropology of Islam," Occasional Paper Series, Center for Contemporary Arab Studies, Georgetown University, Washington, DC, 1986.

35. Chris Hann and Hermann Goltz, *Eastern Christians in Anthropological Perspective* (University of California Press, 2011), 22.

36. Susan Friend Harding, "Representing Fundamentalism: The Problem of the Repugnant Cultural Other," *Social Research* 58, no. 2 (1991): 373–93; Susan Friend Harding, *The Book of Jerry Falwell: Fundamentalist Language and Politics* (Princeton University Press, 2000).

37. Harding, "Representing Fundamentalism," 391–93.

38. Since the 2010s, there has been a burgeoning conversation on Orthodox Christianity in anthropology, with much of this literature focused in postsocialist Europe, the Middle East, Ethiopia, and India. See, e.g., Andreas Bandak, *Exemplary Life: Modelling Sainthood in Christian Syria* (University of Toronto Press, 2022); Tom Boylston, *The Stranger at the Feast: Prohibition and Mediation in an Ethiopian Orthodox Christian Community* (University of California Press, 2018); Angie Heo, *The Political Lives of Saints: Christian-Muslim Mediation in Egypt* (University of California Press, 2018); Vlad Naumescu, "Pedagogies of Prayer: Teaching Orthodoxy in South India," *Comparative Studies in Society and History* 61, no. 2 (2019): 389–418; among several others. To be clear, this volume seeks to channel these conversations into a cohesive whole, bridging the gap between the difference that Orthodoxy makes in each of those ethnographic contexts and a broader, burgeoning

conversation between anthropology and theology (Lemons, ed., *Theologically Engaged Anthropology*; Robbins, *Theology and the Anthropology of Christian Life*).

39. Fenella Cannell, ed., *The Anthropology of Christianity* (Duke University Press, 2006). Cannell's edited volume was one of the groundbreaking works in the subfield, and while it focused on notions of orthodoxy, it pointedly failed to include Orthodox Christianity as an object of study, which suggests how the subfield understood the parameters of study in its formative years. In our view, including Orthodoxy would have shown even more clearly the answer to Cannell's question about the difference that Christianity might make.

40. Joel Robbins, *Becoming Sinners: Christianity and Moral Torment in a Papua New Guinea Society* (University of California Press, 2004), 118.

41. Robbins, "What Is a Christian?," 192.

42. Anthropologist of Orthodox Christianity Timothy Carroll has recently elaborated on these contentions through his own positionality and work at the intersection of theology and anthropology. See Timothy Carroll (Revd Dr. Boniface), "Meditations on the Incarnation: Humanity, Society, and the Church," Institute for Orthodox Christian Studies, Cambridge, 2023, https://www.youtube.com/watch?v=lWVSST4O9lo; Timothy Carroll, *Orthodox Christian Material Culture: Of People and Things in the Making of Heaven* (Routledge, 2018). For a broader consideration of positionality in the anthropological study of Christianity, see the recent conversation between Jon Bialecki and Eloise Meneses, "A School of Thought in Christian Anthropology: A Discussion on Ontology, Religion, and the Limits of Secularity," *Religion and Society: Advances in Research* 14 (2023): 60–73. This conversation, though, is not new but harkens back to earlier debates in the subfield. See Brian M. Howell, "The Repugnant Cultural Other Speaks Back: Christian Identity as Ethnographic 'Standpoint,'" *Anthropological Theory* 7, no. 4 (2007): 371–91.

43. Lukasik and Bruner, "Power Circuits," 7–8.

44. Elayne Oliphant, *The Privilege of Being Banal: Art, Secularism, and Catholicism in Paris* (University of Chicago Press, 2021), 590.

45. Chris Hann, "Reconciling Anthropologies," *Anthropology Today* 23 (2007): 17–19.

46. Robbins, "The Anthropology of Christianity," S162.

47. Lukasik and Bruner, "Power Circuits," 8.

48. Basit Kareem Iqbal, "Reprising Islamic Political Theology: Genre and the Time of Tribulation," *Political Theology* 23, no. 6 (2022): 525–42.

49. James Bielo, *Words Upon the Word: An Ethnography of Evangelical Group Bible Study* (New York University Press, 2009), 159.

50. Sarah Riccardi and Aaron Sokoll, "Connective Implications of the Material Holy," Reverberations: New Directions in the Study of Prayer, 2013, http://forums.ssrc.org/ndsp/2013/10/09/connective-implications-of-the-material-holy/.

51. Luehrmann, "Objects, Anti-Objects, and Efficacious Interpretations of Prayer."

52. E. E. Evans-Pritchard, *Witchcraft, Oracles and Magic Among the Azande* (Oxford University Press, 1976).

53. Jenkins, "The Anthropology of Christianity," 459.

54. Angie Heo, "Secularity and Thinking About the Hermeneutics of Theological Controversy," *Syndicate*, July 2016, https://syndicate.network /symposia/theology/religious-difference-in-a-secular-age/.

55. Kristin Norget, Valentina Napolitano, and Maya Mayblin, eds., *The Anthropology of Catholicism: A Reader* (University of California Press, 2017), 4.

56. Sergei Bulgakov, *The Orthodox Church*, trans. Lydia Kesich (St. Vladimir's Seminary Press, 1988); Daniel Clendenin, *Eastern Orthodox Theology: A Contemporary Reader* (Baker, 1995); Stephen Freeman, *Everywhere Present: Christianity in a One-Storey Universe* (Ancient Faith, 2011); Vladimir Lossky, *The Mystical Theology of the Eastern Church* (St. Vladimir Seminary Press, 1976); John Anthony McGuckin, *The Orthodox Church: An Introduction to Its History, Doctrine, and Spiritual Culture* (Blackwell, 2008); John Meyendorff, *Living Tradition: Orthodox Witness in the Contemporary World* (St. Vladimir's Seminary Press, 1997); Kallistos Ware (Bishop of Diokleia), *The Orthodox Church* (Penguin, 1993).

57. Fenella Cannell, "The Christianity of Anthropology," *Journal of the Royal Anthropological Institute* 11 (2005): 339.

58. Holy Trinity Monastery, *Prayer Book* (Holy Trinity Monastery, 1988).

59. Michael Pomazansky, *Orthodox Dogmatic Theology*, 3rd ed. (St. Herman of Alaska Brotherhood, 2009).

60. Athanasius 54:3, PG 25:192B.

61. One example of this Orthodox division over theosis comes from the Coptic Orthodox bishop Raphael. See "The Theosis Heresy—Bishop Raphael," YouTube video, https://www.youtube.com/watch?v=zbWm5dMI15A.

62. Bulgakov, *The Orthodox Church*, 107.

63. Charles F. Keyes, "Weber and Anthropology," *Annual Review of Anthropology* 31 (2002): 239.

64. Robbins, *Theology and the Anthropology of Christian Life*, 5–6.

PART I

LIVING THEOLOGY AND ANTHROPOLOGICAL THEORIES

ORTHODOXY FROM THE OUTSIDE

PALESTINIAN CHRISTIAN KINSHIP AND THE
EVANGELICAL THEOLOGY OF LOVE

Clayton Goodgame

In recent years, anthropologists have worked to better engage with theology in their studies of Christianity, be it written scholarship or theological discourse among Christians in different social contexts. As the discussion of theology in the anthropology of Christianity has been mostly concerned with Protestantism, this volume will hopefully take a step toward broadening its analytical scope.[1] Here, however, I address another potential problem for anthropological engagement with theology, which is a common methodological tendency among scholars to associate theological knowledge with discrete religious communities. Orthodox theology, in other words, produced by Orthodox Christians, and Catholic theology by Catholics. In my own fieldwork this is often not the case, and I think the same is probably true for any society in which multiple religious traditions coexist—which is to say, most of them.

As a result, this chapter seeks to advance the anthropological discussion of theology by examining a case of theological transmission from one denomination to another—in this case Palestinian Orthodox Christianity to Palestinian evangelicalism. In doing so, I hope to substantiate two arguments about theological knowledge, at least in the Christian tradition. First, while others have pointed to theology-in-practice as fertile ground for understanding religious experience, I argue that areas of crossover between religious traditions are particularly helpful in revealing how religious traditions change the societies in which they emerge. Second, I argue that to fully appreciate how theology matters in the lives of Christians, scholars must pay attention to the occlusions that inevitably emerge in the translation of theology from one tradition to another. For along with the content of theology, for example, questions of Christ's humanity or divinity, which differs according to tradition, the boundaries of theological knowledge—what classifies as theology at all, as opposed to biology or astronomy—are also variable. As these latter distinctions are often implicit, comparison between traditions helps throw them into sharper relief.

In the Palestinian example, the theological theme I discuss is an Orthodox view that divinity is embodied in each generation of the church: that the transmission of generational kinship is also a form of divine transmission—a sort of apostolic succession for everyone. As the chapter is focused on the transition from Orthodoxy to evangelicalism, I will only briefly outline the Orthodox perspective, which I describe in more detail elsewhere.[2] I will then go on to describe the rising public profile of evangelicalism in Jerusalem during the 2000s, highlighting the difference between evangelicals and Orthodox through the former's emphasis on personal conversion and love. Finally, I single out a particular thread of evangelical "love talk" and a theology of Jewish origins that often accompanies it. Engaging with written sources in Arabic and English and fieldwork discussions with theologians and lay Christians, I argue that while Orthodox and evangelicals approach the transmission of divine experience in profoundly different ways, their real difference lies in the way the latter conceptually separate the category of kinship from that of faith. Crucially, they do so using an idiom of genealogical relatedness adopted from the Orthodox.

The Palestinian Orthodox Tradition

At least in part, Orthodoxy is a tradition of carrying divine presence forward in time. As I have argued elsewhere, this tradition materializes in the Palestinian context in part through the veneration of saints and the way their shrines are ritually and historically linked to Palestinian land. The Eastern Orthodox Patriarchate of Jerusalem is composed of a Palestinian laity and a Greek monastic hierarchy, and while the division of authority between these groups has been a major source of conflict between them, both parties regularly describe their relationship to the church in the same terms: as a lineage.

This is not a lineage reckoned through kinship and filiation alone but through a relationship that includes ancestors, saints, and sacred landscapes and that is mediated through the substances, objects, and sensations they all share.[3] This extended sense of descent is not formally expressed by professional theologians, but one can find its presence all over the Orthodox tradition, both in writing and in everyday expressions of faith. It is visible first in the doctrine of apostolic succession, which is a key part of the Jerusalem Patriarchate's identity: the idea that each patriarch of the church is a spiritual descendant of James, the first bishop of Jerusalem and the brother of Christ. This form of spiritual descent is transmitted in several ways, including ritually, when the patriarch is installed, then at each anniversary thereafter, and finally when he is interred with great pageantry alongside his predecessors. Genealogical relatedness is also transmitted among those monks who are not patriarchs but share in their leader's personhood—through ritual contact but also idioms of human kinship (including sharing meals, a common birthplace, etc).[4]

One can find explicit links between this institution and more general Orthodox theology in the concept of *theosis*, or "deification," made famous by St. Gregory Palamas in the fourteenth century but originating with St. Athanasius and his fourth-century battle against Arianism. In 2020, Patriarch Theophilos III of Jerusalem reiterated Athanasius's famous dictum in his annual Christmas message:

> Today, the Church . . . proclaims to the world and the whole universe, the bond and the union of heaven with earth, and the meeting of God with man. Today, God's word "I will dwell in them, and walk in them" is fulfilled. . . . As the hymnographer says, "God becomes man, in order to make man a God". As the established Father of the Church, Saint Athanasios says: "the Word of God became incarnate, so that we may be deified. . . ." This heavenly and God-originated mystery is being witnessed by its descent and manifestation in the course of the human history. . . . The Church is not only the testimony of Christ's beneficial incarnate presence on earth, but also the continuator of His mission.[5]

In other contexts, Theophilos and other patriarchs describe the church's continuity with Christ and its divine quality in explicitly genealogical terms as a *genos* or *phyle* (lineage, race, kind), but here it is also an expression of divine personhood, an idea emphasized by scholars associated with the ontological turn in Orthodox theology. Christos Yannaras, for example, argues that the aim of all Orthodox life is not to efface human individuality for the sake of union with God but to draw out the aspects of the human person that reflect the divine personhood.[6] In the process, one shares in the being (and the divinity) of Christ. Theologians like Yannaras and his intellectual predecessor, Vladimir Lossky, decry what they call the obsession of Orthodox Christians with "passing down" traditions from the past.[7] They emphasize instead the essence of tradition, which is this process of eliciting the divine in human beings through the institutions of the church. For them it is less important whether a certain hymn or ritual is historically authentic than if it produces the right kind of relationship between human beings and God. Understandable though this attitude is, I would suggest that it is somewhat disconnected from the actual experience of Orthodoxy among lay Christians. During my fieldwork, it was indeed through rituals that are historically repeated and passed down that my interlocutors were able to experience divine presence, and disputes over authenticity—or politics in general—were an inevitable part of the process.[8]

The second expression of genealogical faith is the liturgical theology of life-cycle rituals and marriage in particular. In the Orthodox tradition, the wedding ceremony allows the church to recognize its members in a new way. At baptism or a convert's christening, individuals are embraced by the church and adopted by godparents. At marriage, however, the couple becomes linked to what theologians like John Meyendorff call the "chain of generations." The priest invokes the great couples of Jewish history, starting with Abraham and Sarah, and positions the new couple as their spiritual successors.

> The genealogy of Christ, going back to Abraham . . . or Adam . . . witnesses to the fact that the chain of generations was leading to a goal: the coming of Christ, the Messiah. . . . In Biblical history, marriage was . . . leading to a point when God "from the root of Jesse according to the flesh, didst bud forth from the ever-virgin one. . . ." The [wedding prayer] asks God to place the bridegroom and the bride in the company of . . . holy couples, the ancestors of Christ, to bestow upon them the same blessing.[9]

Meyendorff stresses that generation is not an end in itself, as he claims it was in Judaism, but rather serves an eschatological purpose.[10] But whereas many evangelicals—like Pentecostals who wish to "make a complete break with the past"[11]—describe Christ as the breaker of lineages, the Orthodox theologian merely emphasizes the fact that the lineage looks both backward and forward. Thus the chain of generations leads the Orthodox faithful forward toward the second coming of Christ, just as it originates in the holy couples of the past.

At Palestinian Orthodox weddings, this emphasis on continuity is marked, for example, by the queue of relatives representing the bride and the groom. These men and women stand in the courtyard or hall of the church and greet all who attend the service after it ends. Later that evening, when guests arrive at the reception hall, the same relatives queue again at the entrance. The guests enter, shake each person's hand, and present their wedding gift. This custom is also performed at funerals, only then the queues are usually separated by gender, with men and women sitting in adjacent halls. Both occasions, however, serve to establish generational continuity: in one case by bringing a bride into the family and in the other by recognizing the succession of a father by a son (or brother, cousin, etc.). The climax of the Orthodox wedding is the crowning ceremony, sometimes called the "dance of Isaiah," during which crowns of metal or garland are placed on the heads of the bride and groom. They then circle the altar three times, "a symbol of eternity [that] emphasizes marriage as a permanent commitment."[12] The tradition appears to have both Jewish and ancient Greek roots, but as a sacrament, the crown represents the divine personhood within the bride and groom, which they share with their ancestors and which their descendants will carry to the end of history.

The Orthodox Christian tradition is, of course, far more complex than I have presented it here. My aim in outlining its genealogical dimension is simply to express that it is one significant stream of the tradition and to describe enough of its form so that the evangelical community's own genealogical claims can be clearly differentiated. We now turn to this latter community, beginning with what I take to be its central emphasis on love, which I then link to its unique view of descent.

An Ethnography of Evangelical Love

During my fieldwork I often visited with an Orthodox woman in her sixties called Yvette, whose nephew, Ra'id, had converted to an evangelical church. Sometimes he would pass by when I was visiting and chat about religion. Other times we could hear him passing in the street, whistling and singing church hymns on his way home.

Ra'id's relationship with his aunt was cordial but awkward. He would often attempt to evangelize her, raising thorny theological questions and criticizing the Orthodox. "You should visit my church," he would suggest. But she would only roll her eyes: "I live next to the tomb of Christ and I'm going to pray in some house?"

To Yvette, theological differences were less important than her nephew's behavior, which she felt changed after his conversion. When I asked how, she couldn't put her finger on it, but their encounters provided some indication. One day, for example, Ra'id brought her groceries from the market. He knocked on the screen door:

"Yvette!! Open the door!"

"Who is it?"

"Open the door!"

"Oh," she said, observing him through the screen. "What do you have with you?"

"Carrots."

She unlatched the door, and he brushed past her into the kitchen. She watched as he set the bag down. They exchanged greetings in Arabic: "How are you? Praise God. You? Thank the Lord."[13] And with that, he started out; he had to get back to work. "Do you need anything?" "Just your peace." As she closed the door he turned around, already halfway down the steps. He called out to her, in English this time:

"Yvette! I love you!"

"What?" she asked in Arabic. She returned to the screen.

"I . . . *love* . . . you!" He said again in English.

"Okay," she replied in Arabic, turning back inside. He left.

This was an ordinary encounter, but Ra'id's impromptu "I love you" appeared out of place. They do not speak this way to each other, and the fact that he said it in English only highlighted the miss. Yvette said that this "love talk" was something he picked up "over there," at his church in the Quarter. And indeed, as I came to discover, this phrase is central to the wider ethos of the evangelical movement, which emphasizes the transformative and transgressive power of religious love. Among evangelicals, love is not just a feeling. It is a powerful vehicle for religious and social change.

One of the first evangelical leaders I met was Yohanna Katanacho, a prominent Palestinian evangelical pastor and theologian. I had been conducting interviews in Bethlehem and ended up staying too late to catch a bus back to Jerusalem. I had to spend the night in town and found a small hostel run by a middle-aged couple, essentially a family home with rooms for rent. When I arrived, I noticed a Bible in the room, which was unusual even for Christian families. Then the next morning, when I was getting ready to leave, my host asked me where I was heading.

"Bethlehem Bible College," I told her. "Do you know it?"

"Yes! We are born again! Who are you meeting there?"

"Yohanna Katanacho."

"Yohanna! I've known him since he was five years old. He is a good man."

As it turned out, she volunteers every week for an evangelical church and holds worship meetings in her basement. Eager to help me, she called her son and asked him to take me

When I interviewed Katanacho, he was working as the academic dean for the Bible College. We met at the college, a large complex with an office building, hostel, gift shop, and a new academic building. I had seen him at ecumenical events in the past and found his criticisms of the traditional churches interesting but confounding. He openly condemned the occupation, which some evangelicals avoid doing, but he also vehemently criticized his Palestinian colleagues for privileging politics over the Bible.[14] Once in his office, I asked what was different about his perspective. "I will answer your question with a story," he replied.

> I was invited to go to a conference in Sweden with several Israeli Jewish colleagues. During the conference one speaker after the other went up and talked about the terrible Palestinians, how awful and unwilling to compromise they are. I waited for a long time and then finally I raised my hand and stood up and said, "I am a Palestinian and a Christian and I love you." And I sat down. And they were shocked.

He went on to say that evangelicals subscribe to an ethics of love that the Orthodox and other traditional churches do not. Evangelicals confront every problem with the love that appears in the Bible. "Love for Jesus is my spiritual bank account," he said, the measure by which everything in this world must be weighed.

The Rise of Palestinian Evangelicalism

Evangelical churches have been a part of Palestinian society for a very long time, but their presence has always been small. For two centuries, Protestant missionaries struggled in vain to win converts from Islam, Judaism, and the Orthodox Church. Today, Palestinian Christians continue to resist formal conversion, but in recent decades, evangelical influence has grown through the establishment of NGOs. Even more than ecumenical organizations, which are a major part of the Christian landscape, evangelicals have benefited from Israel's dramatic turn to neoliberalism in the 1980s and the increasing links with Western Christian institutions that came with it. With the advent of the Christian NGO, it became possible for evangelicals to reach Palestinians uninterested in conversion by offering educational and political programs to Christians of any background. In the 1990s, Palestinian evangelicals began to develop a new approach to Palestinian Christianity, founding or expanding a host of organizations including Musalaha and the Bethlehem Bible College. And in Jerusalem, a new cadre of evangelical leaders emerged among Palestinians who had grown up in Orthodox and Catholic families, converted, and become pastors and youth activists after the First Intifada (1987–1993). Their churches remain small, but they are active and closely associated with NGOs that reach Christians from evangelical and nonevangelical backgrounds alike.

When Yvette spoke to me about her nephew's desire for her conversion, her comment that she did not want to pray "in some house" was telling. She was referring to several evangelical churches in Jerusalem located in former houses. For her, though, it was not the feel or look of the building to which she objected but the lack of tradition. The Orthodox Church matters to her, at least in part, because its history is tied up with that of her own family and Palestinian past. For evangelicals, on the other hand, a house is precisely the kind of place to encounter God. What matters to them is the preparedness of one's own heart, which in practice often means staying away from Orthodox churches, symbols of imperial Byzantium. One person who embodies this attitude is Salim, an Old City resident from an Orthodox family.

Salim had a relatively typical conversion experience for the area: He was walking out of the Holy Sepulcher Church—for him, a symbol of corruption where Orthodox and Catholic monks fight over space—when he felt drawn to the sounds of hymns nearby. Wandering over, he heard a

Protestant pastor speaking about a personal relationship to God, which made him curious.

> I started wanting to know more. I went to a Bible study group and I discovered that the Bible tells us a lot of things we don't know. . . . [Previously] I thought, faith in Christ I take it from my father and mother. If my father is Christian, *khalas*, I'm a Christian [too]. I discovered that [this isn't true] . . . every person has the responsibility to request Christ to be in his life. I requested Christ, began my life in personal faith . . . and I started speaking to others on the importance of a personal relationship with the lord, because we cannot inherit it.

Evangelicals around the world speak as Salim does about the need to testify, about maintaining a personal relationship to God; here, however, Salim situates true faith in Old City society specifically in opposition to descent, against thinking of Christianity as something one "inherits."

And in his case, the challenges of conversion were clearly framed in these terms. When he first converted, he caused a major split in his family. His uncles and cousins threatened to take his children to the Orthodox Church and baptize them while he was at work. For them, conversion was not about him as an individual but the family as a whole. This is because evangelical or not, his children will follow his own church affiliation rather than that of his agnates. As such, it was not him they threatened to force back to Orthodoxy but his children.

Leaving the Orthodox Church is thus complicated by the fact that it is not only a "religious" institution. It is also legally, historically, and socially tied to the organization and life of the family. Baptism is not just a symbol of belonging, of an implicit affinity between members of the same faith. Rather, it determines things like which school or scout group a child will join, who her friends will be, and whom she will marry. Because of its conservative politics and apparently "Western" style of worship, evangelicalism is stigmatized. Thus when Salim's relatives sought to baptize his children, they were likely less concerned about his desire to study the Bible than the social implications of converting for his children and the family as a whole.

Salim was fortunate in that he eventually reconciled with his cousins and uncles. His story, however, illustrates the social weight of evangelical conversion and provides some indication of how rare the result was. He was able to formally convert and to keep his children out of the Orthodox Church without being cut off from his extended family. The process is not usually so smooth; in general, conversion requires concessions to kinship.

Tamer, for example, was perhaps the most outspoken critic of the traditional churches that I met. A small business owner in the Old City and evangelical, Tamer writes articles on theology and shares videos of biblical commentary on social media. "I don't buy anything from any church," he once told me. "I examine everything, and I choose what to believe and what to reject." Nevertheless, though he married an evangelical, he did so in the Orthodox Church to please his Orthodox father. Many evangelicals tell similar stories: They maintain a strong interior faith consonant with the evangelical tradition but agree to get married and buried in their natal church.

The experiences of Salim and Tamer raise an important issue in the anthropology of Christian conversion. Birgit Meyer's famous quotation about Pentecostal conversion, that "you have to make a complete break with the past," is often repeated in the literature, but perhaps less well remembered is that for Meyer's interlocutors, this "often boils down to a break with one's family."[15] I would suggest that this point, the association of kinship with the past, is much more significant than anthropologists of Christianity have generally acknowledged and is crucial for the understanding of evangelical difference.

Faith in the Present, Family in the Past:
Orthodox and Evangelical Conversion

Apart from evangelical churches, conversion in Palestinian Christian society generally takes the form of a wedding. When a man and woman from different churches wish to marry, the woman generally converts. This does not mean such women do not continue to feel Catholic or Lutheran at heart or even that they stop attending the liturgy in the church of their birth. But it does signify entering a new family and a new communal structure. In the case of an Orthodox wedding, the couple's children will be baptized in the Orthodox Church, disputes will be arbitrated in the Orthodox ecclesiastical court, and records will be held by the Orthodox lay council of *wukala'* (trustees).

Marriages involving conversion from one church to another are common. In most cases the procedure has been streamlined and the significance of spiritual change diminished. The bride's original baptism is accepted by the new church (though this sometimes contradicts canon law); before the wedding day, she is merely blessed with holy oil to signal her new allegiance. Though a significant change of affiliation occurs in this process, from one church to another, the emphasis is on continuity in another domain of social life. Usually, theologians call this the family, as the emphasis in the marriage union is partly on childbearing, so the "chain of generations" is being reproduced through the groom's family lineage, which the bride has just converted into. In other words, conversion here serves the purpose of perpetuating the Orthodox family, just as marriage among two born Orthodox does. The institutions of conversion and marriage thus merge, each being ritually assimilated into the other.

As in the examples of Orthodox sacred kinship from the previous section, here as well the marriage traditions do not always accord with classic theological accounts. This is not to say that such traditions are merely customary, however. As Kallistos Ware put it, "Tradition is not static but dynamic . . . inwardly changeless (for God does not change), [Tradition] is constantly assuming new forms."[16] In the Middle East, where the colonial legacy of sectarianism looms large, Orthodox theologians and lay people argue for a view of catholicity among the sects. "Nous sommes d'empire," the prominent Lebanese Orthodox Bishop Georges Khodr often puts it.

> "[W]e blend with the existing "empire" . . . we have been through [*sic*] with the Roman Empire, then that of the Arabs, the Mamaleek [pl. of Mamluk], the Ottoman and the nation of the Mandate (France) . . . the Sunnis were right in saying openly that they do not accept the classification of our society according to sects. . . . We, like them, did not speak of confessionalism because we believe that we are the catholic universal Church or that we are from Her.[17]

For Khodr in the Lebanese context and for many of my Palestinian Orthodox and Catholic interlocutors, denominational differences are subordinate to a sense that all Arab Christians are a community that has changed form over centuries according to the empire of the day but that remained in a deeper sense a catholic unity.[18]

For Palestinians, this element of communal rather than simply familial continuity is compounded by their status as a very small minority, even by Middle Eastern standards. For them, the distinctions between the churches (again, not including the evangelicals) are purposefully muted when it comes to intermarriage for the sake of continuing "the church," understood in the broadest possible sense of a Christian community. Among many Palestinian Christians, including Catholics, Syriacs, Anglicans, and Lutherans, the Orthodox Church still holds a special place in their own religious identity as the largest and oldest church in the country. In a sense, it still represents them—even if their family history or personal faith led them to prefer a different denomination in their daily lives. On the one hand, the Orthodox Church represents their past, the heritage of the Christian community as a whole (as most non-Orthodox Christians have Orthodox ancestors). But as I have written elsewhere, this heritage is not only temporal. Orthodoxy is literally part of the Christian landscape now. Its shrines are the focal points of diversified Christian towns and villages, the events of its history marked on the streets and the shops and on Palestinian homes (many of which, even for non-Orthodox, are owned by the Orthodox Church).[19]

Where Meyendorff writes of a chain of generations in an abstract sense, Orthodox Palestinians speak about interchurch marriage in terms of communal solidarity and survival. The sense of continuity is present in both, but for Palestinians it is much more practical and immediately important. Virtually every family I know includes relatives from different church traditions. Even the proudest or most activist Orthodox are married to Catholics or mainline Protestants and have non-Orthodox among their parents, grandparents, aunts, and uncles. They do not see this as a problem. When I asked women in these families who converted for marriage, or their children, who grew up with parents from different churches, they spoke above all of unity.

A Jerusalemite woman called Rima, for example, grew up in the Latin Catholic Church but married an Orthodox man. Following tradition, they married in the Orthodox Church, and Rima accepts her new status; nevertheless, she does not love the Orthodox Church. She finds the Greek-speaking priests aloof and unkind and the services long, arduous, and difficult to follow. When I visited her and her husband, she would complain about their parish: "It's like the *suq* [market]!" she said. "At the Catholic church, there is a queue for the Eucharist, it's organized, not a crowd." Hearing this, her husband smiled: "The Orthodox are simply eager to receive the true body of Christ," he quipped. "Catholics stand patiently because secretly they know: only the Orthodox receive the true body, so they are in no hurry to eat wafers." Rima and her husband joke about these differences, but I heard serious criticisms along the same lines all the time. "The Orthodox arrive late to the Divine Liturgy [mass]," their critics say. They talk during the service and walk in and out of the church as they please. After the liturgy, they rush the altar to shake the priest's hand and decamp to the courtyard for coffee.

Rima sometimes slips and tells strangers she's Catholic. She still occasionally attends the Catholic Church with her parents, and even though she baptized her daughter Orthodox, she also makes sure to bring her to Catholic feasts and parades. She says that in the future, if her daughter grows up and marries either an Orthodox or a Catholic, she will be happy. But keeping her mother church close clearly means a lot to her.

Individuals like Rima accept that conversion for marriage marks a transition into a new family. They accept entering a new church community because there is a certain sense that the traditional churches are fundamentally similar and that the Palestinian Christian population is so small that the various parishes—which are linked socially, religiously, and historically—comprise a single community. One example of this is the religious calendar. The Orthodox Patriarchate uses the older Julian calendar, so its feast days occur on different days than the Catholic and Protestant ones. As a solution, Palestinian and Jordanian Christians celebrate Easter on the Orthodox date and Christmas on the Catholic one. The higher clergy of the respective churches do not follow this custom, but lay Orthodox families generally celebrate Christmas on December 25, and Catholics take part in the Holy Fire ceremony, a primarily Orthodox ceremony.

This arrangement reflects broader sentiments about relations among the established churches. Palestinian Orthodox often maintain relations with nuns or monks of a particular convent and attend the feasts there even if they do not care for the liturgy or understand Greek or Russian. This is also true of lay Christians visiting other church communities. For a particular feast, they will attend the service of others without taking communion and then join their friends for the food, cognac, and coffee afterward. Some of my neighbors and friends during fieldwork even attended services at other churches for "religious" reasons, for example because they found the hymns at the Lutheran Church or the Lenten traditions at a Greek Catholic church especially powerful.

Beneath all these cases is a sense that the churches are connected horizontally—that is, through wedding conversions and shared holidays—because they are also connected vertically, as a community persisting through time. For Christians of the traditional churches, conversion is a form of alliance with a new family and a new church more than it is a break with one's past affiliations. Without doubt, there is a clear change involved, but one's relationship to the past and to unconverted relatives is not usually broken in the process. For Palestinian evangelicals, conversion is a process diametrically opposed to this one, representing a break not only from individual relatives but also from the traditional concept of the family as both human and divine.

Love as Conversion

Bruno Latour once made a comparison between religion and what he called "love talk." Religion, he argued, does not seek to provide information but transformation. "[The question] 'Do you love me?' is not assessed by the originality of the sentence—none are more banal, trivial, boring, rehashed—but by the transformation it generates in the listener, as well as in the speaker."[20] Latour is writing about religion in general (though from a Catholic perspective), and for him, love talk is an analogy for religious talk. It has many parallels in linguistic anthropology and speech act theory, in which words and utterances matter less for their semantic value than for the social force they impose on the listener. For Palestinian evangelicals, however, love talk is quite literally the medium of religious transformation.

In the previous section, I suggested that conversion in the Palestinian Christian community is often tied to marriage and that both rituals are linked to a sense of past and future generations, both of the church and the family. The conversions of Salim and Tamer reveal the difference of evangelicalism—its emphasis on an individual and immediate relationship to God—and the resistance that evangelicals face when they try to extend their conversion to their children. The problem is once again one of continuity.

Some evangelicals are attempting to make this process easier by gaining the right for their churches to grant marriage licenses and by buying cemeteries to bury their members. Such efforts are complicated, however, by the fact that evangelical churches have few official members and therefore few people to marry or bury. But evangelical leaders have also changed their priorities. Instead of encouraging people to convert formally, many now say they prefer for converts to remain inside their denominations and change them from within.[21] Jack Sara, president of the Bethlehem Bible

College, made this clear to me: "This is an evangelical institution but at the same time . . . we want to work with all the churches. And we never encourage someone to leave their church; we want to have him or her experience the faith, and the spirit, and the word of God. To change their minds, fill their minds with the word of God, change their heart, and then your actions, your ministry could [fill] any church."

For Sara, conversion doesn't require a formal change of affiliation, only a change of heart. There are important historical and political conditions affecting this position, as we will see, in addition to the widely recognized evangelical emphasis on interiority. For Sara, Orthodox and Catholic clergy "are not helping people discover God": "They're helping them discover the church. . . . The priest wants to encourage their faith [but] he doesn't tell them 'come closer to God.' [He says] 'come closer to the church.' So the church is the end, not God." This is why, for Sara, it is possible to remain Orthodox or Catholic while also becoming a born-again believer. I met him through his work with young men of the Christian Quarter when he was a local pastor there and for which he is still respected. He grew up in the Old City in a Catholic but not particularly pious family. His transformation occurred after years of activism during the First Intifada landed him in jail. He became disillusioned with the Communist Party, in which he had been active, and when he returned home, he started searching for a new path. After encountering an evangelical youth minister, he had a powerful conversion experience. He attempted to remain Catholic at first, attending youth meetings and Bible study sessions with his fellow Catholics. Eventually, however, he felt rejected by his fellows for his evangelical ideas and ended up moving to the Alliance Church.[22]

Now, Sara says, institutions like the Bible College have fostered an environment in which remaining Catholic or Orthodox is possible while still maintaining a strong evangelical faith. Other organizations, such as the Palestinian Bible Society, have followed the same model, partnering with traditional churches for specific projects, for example, Arabic translations of the Bible or youth training programs, while distinguishing their members—whom they call "nominal" Christians—from true believers (*mu'minin*).

It is in this context that I suggest evangelical love talk gains special significance. It indexes a form of religious conversion that produces a radical change in one's faith but nevertheless does not require leaving one's natal church or extended family network. Such a discourse allows someone in

Salim's position to convert at heart without breaking from his family and the risks such a break entails. But it also opens up a new field of potential converts—albeit of a different kind.

I once asked Katanacho why evangelicals are so reluctant to engage with political issues. The Orthodox Church has been historically connected to Arab nationalism, Palestinian resistance, and socialist political parties. The ecumenical organizations constantly write about the occupation and engage in civil disobedience. What are the evangelicals doing? Again he spoke of love. He told me about a youth project he organized in Upper Nazareth, a Jewish enclave built in the 1950s on the hilltops around the historic Palestinian town to slow the latter's expansion.[23] They put on T-shirts with the phrase "I love you" printed on the front and went around the Jewish neighborhoods cleaning the streets. The idea was to show Israelis that Palestinians are not dangerous or threatening but willing to be good neighbors. Compared with nonevangelical organizations, for which youth activity often means civil disobedience, this type of behavior may seem ludicrous. But for Katanacho, it is radical.[24]

This is in part because the message of love and reconciliation is also a message of conversion. Just as Orthodox Christians who have become "believers" are encouraged not to leave their churches, Muslims and Jews are encouraged to "love" without necessarily leaving their traditions. Here, however, the scale of evangelical discourse changes to fit the national categories of Israel/Palestine and its three religions. The language of love is still paramount, but it is joined by marriage and reconciliation.

Since the 1990s, a significant Messianic Jewish population has emerged in Israel.[25] Messianic Jews identify as Jews but also believe that Jesus is their messiah. From an evangelical point of view, this appears to be a Jewish version of Sara's philosophy—Jews who are (Christian) believers at heart—and as such Palestinian evangelicals spend considerable energy attempting to link their own community with the Messianic one. Salim Munayer, a Palestinian evangelical, founded an organization with a Messianic Jew called Musalaha, or "reconciliation." In an interview Munayer explained the impetus for founding it: "I realized that our identity in Jesus is a bridge not only to God but between our [Israeli and Palestinian] communities. The identity issue is one of the biggest issues [we face] . . . as long as the Palestinians and Jews are not going to embrace their neighbors in their identity we're not going to see a solution."[26] Musalaha thus attempts to "build bridges among Muslims, Christians, and Jews," but it does so primarily by building a link between Palestinian Christians and Messianic Jews, framing them not as distinct or opposed religious groups but as a single, united faith with different "identities."

Some people attend programs at Musalaha as they would a secular organization like Seeds of Peace, a well-known American initiative that gathers Palestinians and Israeli students for a summer camp in the United States where they bond over sports and leisure activities and discuss some political issues. But the "reconciliation stories" Musalaha disseminates as evidence of its success make clear that for them, "real" reconciliation—like "real" belief—requires conversion. In one such story, a Palestinian participant wrote: "When I first met with an Israeli, I didn't know what I was doing, but slowly Jesus opened my heart and I saw that this woman was human."[27] Another Palestinian wrote in similar terms: "I have learned so much about God in meeting [Israelis]. When I first went away with Musalaha, I had so much hate inside me. I didn't go to church. I was so angry . . . [but w]hen we were rowing on a lake . . . I heard from God. I cannot describe it. I felt so much love. I had this big hate inside me, and it all vanished."[28]

In these stories, mutual understanding between two national groups is expressed as a relationship with divinity: God-love leads to love of neighbor. But Musalaha's "theology of reconciliation" describes this process of human and divine love in an interesting way: as a marriage. The organization's theological primer for participants reads, "Jesus is able to take us and create 'one new humanity'":

> This does not mean that our unique identities should fade away, or blend into one colorless, bland uniformity. We retain our distinctiveness, even as we become one body. We can think of it like marriage between a man and a woman. Through sacred bonds of marriage, they are joined together and become one, but they still retain their distinctive qualities as male and female.[29]

The text identifies "marriage" as joining Palestinian Christians and Messianic Jews while also retaining certain differences. "As Israeli Messianic Jews and Palestinian Christians," it goes on, "we both have a rich heritage to draw on . . . We must retain our identities, but remember that our primary identity is in God."[30]

The key term is "identity." Just as Sara spoke of love connecting Christians while maintaining their denominational differences, Musalaha speaks of love uniting people from different "heritages" that "must" remain distinct. Katanacho spoke in a similar vein about Jewish residents of Upper Nazareth, to whom Palestinian evangelicals expressed their love. An employee of the Bible Society, another evangelical organization, put it even more clearly: "I read the other day . . . that one in every three Jews in the United States believes that believing in Jesus is an extension to the Jewish identity. There is a shift happening . . . we are loving people and we are telling them . . . you need to consider Jesus Christ.[31]

Clearly, loving and evangelizing are conflated here, but the language of identity is also being paired with the language of believing. As we will now see, this is not accidental. It speaks to a well-developed theology in the evangelical community that distinguishes between faith and identity and between religion and kinship to turn the three Abrahamic religions into separate ethnic groups with one faith. This is accomplished by translating sacred descent into affinity.

The Seed of Abraham

Thus far I have described how the increasing visibility of Palestinian evangelism occurred alongside a more general growth of ecumenical organizations led by traditional churches. The evangelicals, however, became increasingly critical of the social justice paradigm of their compatriots. Their own answer to the problem of injustice was the paradigm of love. I thus explored the two contexts in which love talk appears most prominently: first from evangelicals to other Christians, who are encouraged to convert at heart without leaving their families or churches, and second from evangelicals to Jews and Muslims. Peace between religions is envisioned as a marriage of peoples who are separate in heritage but united in Christ.

This is all rooted in an evangelical theology of the Abrahamic covenant that goes back to Saint Paul. Just as Orthodox Christians do, many evangelicals speak and write about the place of Arab Christians in the Bible and in the history of the church. But unlike the Orthodox, the argument they make often focuses on the relatedness of Arabs to the ancestors and descendants of Abraham. Katanacho, for example, describes how the Abrahamic lineage is reckoned in various contradictory ways in different parts of the Bible text and how these variations often end up including Arabs and other non-Jewish, non-Hebrew, non-Israelite peoples within the lineage:

Although the descendants of Jacob preferred tribal intermarriages, they were not a closed group . . . Judah married a Canaanite wife . . . Joseph married an Egyptian (Gen. 41:45) . . . we have children who belong to a certain pedigree but are partially foreign to that lineage. . . . We see it not only in the story of Abraham and his son Ishmael (Gen. 16), but also in the story of Judah. . . . In short, borrowing [the prophet] Ezra's language, we can see that the "holy seed" has mingled with many nations.[32]

For Katanacho, the existence of Arabs and other "nations" within the lineage of Abraham does not serve as evidence of the Jewish roots of Palestinians but rather of their persistence through time as the Jewish other: related, but distinct.[33] With the appearance of Christ, this relationship changes. Following Paul's letter to the Galatians, Katanacho claims that Jesus broke the barrier between Jewish and Gentile lineages:

In Paul's words, "If you belong to Christ, then you are Abraham's seed, and heirs according to the promise" (Gal. 3:29). Paul is here refuting the Judaizers' claim that becoming part of the physical seed of Abraham through circumcision secures becoming part of the Abrahamic promises. Christ alone is the legitimate seed of Abraham in whom the promises will be fulfilled (Gal. 3:16). To be associated with Him is the only legitimate means for belonging to the seed of Abraham.[34]

With Christ, in other words, the Abrahamic lineage is no longer measured in terms of descent but faith, or ' belonging to Christ."

This argument comes very close to one of the dominant narratives of Western modernity: the idea that with Christ, the Jewish religion ceased being a "closed" religious system and transformed into a "universal" one built on faith alone, rather than law or descent. That idea has been closely examined by historians, theologians, and social scientists. In anthropology, it influenced Dumont's thesis on Christian individualism, Leach's theory on the egalitarianism of the early church, and Goody's work on the development of the European family.[35] Though very different in content, all three arguments developed in part out of an analytic division between Christianity, which banned close-kin marriage and defined faith in purely spiritual terms, and Judaism and Islam, which continued to endorse religious law, endogamy, and agnatic descent.[36] Christian difference is thus defined, at least to some extent, in opposition to kinship and descent.

In an important critique of this division, Jonathan Boyarin and Daniel Boyarin trace its origins to the Pauline tradition, "the fountainhead of Christendom."[37] They begin their essay with the assertion that "group identity has been constructed . . . on the one hand as the product of a common genealogical origin and, on the other, as produced by a common geographical origin."[38] The first of these forms, they argue, has been maligned in modern scholarship as racist, while the latter has become normative, for example as discourses of indigeneity linked to land have been enshrined in human rights law. Historically, they argue, claims to both land and lineage have led to violence and oppression, but criticism has fallen disproportionately on the latter. For them, the Western distaste for descent originates in Paul's letter to the Galatians, quoted by Katanacho above. For them, Paul represents an ideological shift. When he wrote "there is neither Jew nor Greek," the ritual of baptism "substitute[ed] an allegorical genealogy for a literal one":[39]

> In Christ, that is, in baptism, all the differences that mark off one body from another as Jew or Greek (circumcision is considered a "natural" mark of the Jew [Rom. 2:27]), male or female, slave or free are effaced, for in the Spirit such marks do not exist. Accordingly, if one belongs to Christ, then one participates in the allegorical meaning of the promise of the "seed of Abraham," an allegorical meaning of genealogy. . . . The individual body itself is replaced by its allegorical referent, the body of Christ.[40]

In response to this view, the authors attempt to resuscitate the notion of a genealogical identity in the Jewish diaspora, showing that it is only with the joining of genealogy and land in Israel that the Jewish lineage discourse becomes exclusionary.

What interests me about this argument is the claim that the "Christian" view of genealogy is the Pauline one. That view is incorrect, however, because it does not represent a large proportion of Christians, including contemporary Christians and many of those in early modern Europe, Byzantium, and late antiquity. By contrast, at least among the Orthodox, the link between religious faith and social descent is central and broadly similar to Jewish contexts. Among Palestinians, it is not Christianity but evangelicalism that produces a change in the way genealogy is viewed, and even there the concept does not disappear so much as it is transposed into a new register.

The evangelical way of reckoning with the Pauline legacy speaks directly to the problem that Jonathan Boyarin and Daniel Boyarin raise. Mirroring their characterization of Paul almost verbatim, Katanacho writes, "Christ alone is the legitimate seed of Abraham in whom the promises [of the covenant] will be fulfilled."[41] As much Western scholarship has done, he claims a universality for Christianity that overcomes the allegedly narrow scope of Judaism. However, the genealogical vision of Palestinian evangelicals also diverges from this tradition in a crucial way. As we will now see, evangelicals do not actually discard genealogical ties for universalist, spiritual ones. On the contrary, they often insist on their significance. The difference is that they define them as ethnic and biological ties, not religious ones.

Being and Believing: DNA, Descent, and Race

Some of the most instructive experiences I had with evangelicals were those that involved encounters with Christians from other denominations. One example involved a meal I shared with my landlady, Abla, and her friend. During my fieldwork, Abla and I often went out to eat with other Orthodox for religious feasts. On one such Sunday, however, Abla knocked on my door and asked me to come out with her and a friend called Rana from Nazareth, whom she introduced as being from a well-known Orthodox family. Sitting at lunch, Rana asked us to pray over the food before we ate. "As you like," Abla said, "but that isn't Orthodox." Rana responded bashfully that she didn't know what was correct, but personally, she liked to do it. We waited while she prayed aloud, head bowed, thanking God for the meal and the presence of friends.

During the meal, Rana spoke about moving to Be'er Sheva (Bir Seba'a in Arabic), a city in southern Israel. She left Nazareth for work, she said, but enjoys living there in part for the spiritual life. She was born Orthodox but in Be'er Sheva came to prefer what she called "praying by the spirit, not by conventions." "I'm someone who doesn't like regulations and structure. Some people need structure, but I don't." She still attends life-cycle rituals at the Orthodox church in Nazareth, is fascinated by the tradition, and enjoys reading about the early saints. She continues to *be* Orthodox, she said, but her faith is now guided by evangelical principles: the spirit, not

conventions. What matters most, she stressed, is one's personal relationship with God and other believers.

In practice, this means that Rana does not attend one church but a wide
variety of evangelical parishes. But she singled out one tradition in particular: Messianic Judaism. Be'er Sheva is home to a small Messianic population, a significant proportion of which appears to be Russian Israelis who
immigrated in the 1990s. Out of concern for space I cannot describe this
population here except to note that while many of the 1.6 million Russian
Israelis who emigrated from the former Soviet Union fully identify as Jews,
the population is also known for retaining elements of Christianity in their
forms of self-identification and worship. They also rarely keep *kashrut* dietary laws, particularly with regard to pork.[42] In a few cases, Russian Israelis have even taken over old Orthodox churches and begun celebrating
the liturgy.

Others have joined Messianic congregations with a much more evangelical style of worship but that also allow them to retain Christian and
Jewish elements of their identity. Rana feels at home in these congregations, despite being a Palestinian with no Jewish background, because she
too identifies as *being* one thing and *believing* something else. As someone
who grew up inside the 1948 borders of Israel, she speaks both Arabic and
Hebrew fluently. Her Orthodoxy is a part of her identity as an Arab Palestinian, and she associates life-cycle rituals and seasonal feasts with the maintenance of that identity. However, when framed in terms of "religion," Rana
saw conventions as tying Orthodoxy to the past, whereas praying by the
spirit freed her of such structures. I would suggest that this separation
from the past is what encouraged her to join a Messianic community.

Separating one's ethnic identity from one's faith resonates powerfully
with recent scholarship on Messianic Judaism and the relationship between
evangelicals and Israel more broadly. Hillary Kaell's research on Christian
pilgrims to the Holy Land was an important landmark for the latter because
it demonstrates, in contrast to so many studies of Christian Zionism, how
this relationship forms through the religious experience of the evangelicals
themselves. Particularly important for this discussion is her finding that
many of those who might be called Christian Zionists do not speak of their
support for Israel in primarily political or eschatological terms, as previous
scholars had suggested, but in terms of a discovery of Jewish "roots."[43]

Similarly, in an article on Messianic Jews and Jewish-affinity Christians
in the United States, Kaell and Sarah Imhoff argue that the rediscovery of

Jewish roots often emerges through "gene talk," the ascription of lineage links to Jewish ancestors through websites that trace DNA linked to the Cohanim, or Jewish priestly class.[44] What makes these Messianic Jews unique, the authors argue, is the extent to which they highlight the racial or ethnic character of Jesus:

> For Messianics contemporary "ethnic" Jews will play a unique role in the coming apocalypse and, just as important, are also understood to be genetically related to Jesus. The latter idea is especially crucial for the heirs of pietistic Christianity—such as North American charismatics and many evangelicals—who prize an intimate relationship with Jesus. To feel this closeness . . . takes on a radically new meaning if one thinks of [Jesus] as raced, that is as an ethnic Jew. . . . [Messianics] strongly embrace this view. For them, it means that having Jewish "blood," or at least being in close contact with Jews . . . is a tangible way to propel the coming End Times and to nurture closeness with the incarnated Son of God.[45]

For Messianics, the ethnically Jewish character of Jesus is significant because it allows them to draw closer to him not only through faith but also through his physical substance. Ethnic Jews talk about genes as "a way to talk about the distinctiveness or peoplehood, even the specialness of Jews and Jewish history, without the hubris of biblical chosenness."[46] Messianics, on the other hand, insist on the chosenness of the Jewish people because it gives them the feeling of uncovering their hidden Jewish roots without having to change their Christian faith.

Imhoff and Kaell emphasize the extent to which studies of gene talk ignore its religious dimensions, which, in the Messianic case, are central. They also emphasize the centrality of gene talk's racial element, which helps produce a hierarchy that privileges the European-associated Ashkenazi over North African or Iberian/Middle Eastern–associated Sephardics.[47] This combination of factors affords a valuable point of comparison. As we have seen, Palestinian evangelicals do not trace their lineages through family genealogy or DNA technologies but through the Bible: through Eber, Joktan, Shem, and Ezra. Nevertheless, like those technologies, the Old Testament is treated as a kind of group or tribal genealogy, but only until the time of Jesus. After that, only love for the messiah can make one a member of the elect. But why? If Jesus unites all, what difference does it make which pre-Christian lineage one represents?

Palestinian evangelicals seek to establish difference from Jews on theological grounds—that is, Paul's "universal" genealogy—rather than racial ones. Nevertheless, they continue to uphold genealogical differences because doing so allows them to claim Jewishness as a culture, not a faith. A Messianic Jew, according to this logic, is utterly Christian at heart but continues to "be" Jewish—including practicing Jewish customs and rituals—in her ethnic identity, which is associated with descent. Palestinian evangelicals, by comparison, do not want to claim Jewishness but do support an ethnic view of Judaism (or Orthodox Christianity or Islam) that opens the door for a "Jewish" faith in Christ.

As a result, following Imhoff and Kaell, I argue that race and ethnicity provide evangelical discourse with something that "religion," in the modern sense of the word, cannot. One is either a believer or not in the evangelical worldview. Palestinian evangelicals thus appear to be replacing the descent rhetoric of Orthodox Christians (and "ethnic" Jews), which conflates religious tradition and communal continuity, with a rhetoric of *ethnic* descent and *religious* affinity: Jewish roots and Christian faith. If a person carries her ancestors in her veins, there is no need for a theology of mediation so central to the Catholic and Orthodox traditions.[48] Instead, lineage continuity is inscribed in the blood.

Recognizing Religion in Descent

This chapter began with a description of the way Palestinian and Greek Orthodox Christians describe their church in genealogical terms—both in explicit theological statements and through the experience and practice of everyday ritual life. It then attempted to draw a line from that tradition to the Palestinian evangelical community, the members of which often hail from Orthodox families. I showed on the one hand how evangelicals establish their difference from the Orthodox through idioms of love, which encourage potential converts to experience Jesus in the present moment. I then showed how, at the same time, evangelicals move to redefine Orthodox life-cycle rituals as part of the domain of kinship while actively reclaiming that domain as their past. My discussion of Katanacho described that past as a form of Christian descent stripped of the divine qualities it carries in Orthodoxy. The Christian-ness of the lineage remains only through the kinship institution of patrilineal endogamy. This ensures the perpetuation of Christian families through intermarriage among Christian denominations (facilitated by relaxed conversion regulations) and life-cycle rituals that associate Christians with Christian social institutions: schools, social clubs, and church housing. Faith now exists only as a personal relationship to God. Though it remains, the church becomes an appendage of the family.

This process of religious change informs the discussion of Orthodox theology in important ways. The theologian Sarah Coakley has pointed out that many anthropological definitions of theology wrongly assume that theological scholarship is normative in a way that anthropology is not.[49] Though definitional problems are hardly unique to theology, Coakley's response that the normative and categorical features of theological knowledge are variable and should always be investigated alongside the content of any religious tradition is highly instructive. The parameters we establish for what counts as theology change the content of that theology, both in social life and its analysis.[50] In this chapter, I have attempted to show how those parameters change as theological knowledge is translated across denominational boundaries. Ethnographically, I showed how evangelical theology is produced in conversation with Orthodox ideas and how those ideas change in the process. By isolating one of those ideas, sacred descent, I demonstrated how Palestinian evangelicals refashioned the Orthodox tradition into a new, naturalized form. From a theoretical perspective, the intersection of Orthodoxy and evangelicalism exposes theology's influence on social life in a much more general way.

The intervention is twofold: On the one hand, changing theological perspectives transform the content of a religious tradition—here through the language of love and personal contact with Christ. On the other hand, they reconfigure the conceptual scaffolding that defines for a society how that tradition is related to the other domains of social life. The first part of this process is often highlighted by anthropologists of Christianity, who show how explicit assertions about the tradition become a part of everyday religious life, but the latter is not. Much more often, it is addressed by political anthropologists who highlight how religious change is bound up within a larger conceptual matrix, for example, of modernity, secularism, or capitalism. Whereas such work sometimes appears "outside" everyday religious life, here the latter aspect is as intrinsic to the Christian experience as the former. The kinship outside to evangelical faith is a product of the theology, which informs when religion appears as such and when it appears as kinship instead. This double effect is not recognized enough, but it is one of the central means through which change is introduced to the Palestinian Christian tradition.

Notes

I would like to thank Candace Lukasik and Sarah Riccardi-Swartz for inviting me to join this project and for their invaluable feedback at multiple stages of the publication process. I would also like to thank Andraous Jahshan for his careful and incisive reading of an early draft and the reviewers for their very helpful comments.

1. E.g., J. Derrick Lemons, ed., *Theologically Engaged Anthropology* (Oxford: Oxford University Press, 2018).

2. Clayton Goodgame, "A Lineage in Land: The Transmission of Palestinian Christianity," *Journal of the Royal Anthropological Institute* 29, no. 3 (2023): 670–91. See also Sarah Bakker Kellogg's chapter in this volume on "liturgical kinship" among Syriac Christians, which is also imagined in historical and genealogical terms.

3. See Tom Boylston, "'And Unto Dust Thou Shall Return': Death and the Semiotics of Remembrance in an Ethiopian Village," *Material Religion* 21, no. 3 (2015): 281–302, on the materiality of Orthodox graves; and Timothy Carroll, "The Ethics of Orthodoxy as the Aesthetics of the Local Church," *World Art* 7, no. 2 (2017): 353–71, on the ritual affordances of palm branches, basil, and bay leaves.

4. Cf. Claudia Rapp, *Brother-Making in Late Antiquity* (Oxford University Press, 2016).

5. "Message of His Beatitude the Patriarch Theophilos III," *Jerusalem Patriarchate Newsgate*, 2020, https://en.jerusalem-patriarchate.info/blog/2020 /12/22/christmas-2020-message-of-his-holy-beatitude-the-patriarch-of -jerusalem-theophilos-iii/.

6. Christos Yannaras, *The Freedom of Morality*, trans. Elizabeth Briere (1984; St. Vladimir's Seminary Press, 1996); Christos Yannaras, *Elements of Faith: An Introduction to Orthodox Theology*, trans. Keith Schram (T&T Clark, 1991).

7. V. Lossky, "Tradition and Traditions," in *In the Image and Likeness of God* (St. Vladimir's Seminary Press, 1974), 141–68. As an example, Lossky points to those "traditionalists" who refuse changes to sacred texts, "sometimes attributing a mystical meaning to stupid mistakes of copyists" (156).

8. This is not an anthropological critique of theology but, as Coakley puts it, a critique from one end of the theological spectrum, the local, of the other: "the middle distance" or "the vast." Sarah Coakley and Joel Robbins,

"Anthropological and Theological Responses to Theologically Engaged Anthropology," in *Theologically Engaged Anthropology*, ed. Derrick Lemons (Oxford University Press, 2018), 373.

9. John Meyendorff, *Marriage: An Orthodox Perspective* (St. Vladimir's Seminary Press, 2000), 36.

10. Meyendorff, *Marriage*, 36.

11. Birgit Meyer, "'Make a Complete Break with the Past': Memory and Post-Colonial Modernity in Ghanaian Pentecostal Discourse," *Journal of Religion in Africa* 28, no. 3 (1998): 316–49.

12. Meyendorff, *Marriage*, 42.

13. Orthodox Christians, like Muslims, generally use the former (*hamd'illa*), while evangelicals often use the latter (*nushkur al-rab*) to distinguish "believers" from "nominal" Christians.

14. Writing of contemporary Greece, Stewart echoes this idea: "In marrying, one participates in the same ritual, the same mystery as one's parents; it expresses the intention to engender children who in their turn will repeat this ritual (perhaps after one's death)." Charles Stewart, "Honour and Sanctity: Two Levels of Ideology in Greece," *Social Anthropology* 2, no. 3 (1994): 222.

15. Meyer, "Make a Complete Break," 329. A similar evangelical shift in the relationship between religion and kinship has been described in contexts where Orthodox Christianity was one of the traditional religions, for example in Ukraine (Catherine Wanner, "Advocating New Moralities: Conversion to Evangelicalism in Ukraine," *Religion, State & Society* 31, no. 3 [2003]: 273–87) and Kyrgyzstan (Mathijs Pelkmans, "Frontier Dynamics: Reflections on Evangelical and Tablighi Missions in Central Asia," *Comparative Studies in Society and History* 63, no. 1 [2021]: 212–41; cf. Mathijs Pelkmans, "Baptized Georgian: Religious Conversion to Christianity in Autonomous Ajaria," Working Paper, 71, Max Planck Gesellschaft, Halle).

16. Timothy Ware, *The Orthodox Church: An Introduction to Eastern Christianity* (1963; Penguin, 2015), 192.

17. Georges Khodr, "The Orthodox," trans. Riad Mufarrij, *Al-Nahar*, 2014, http://georgeskhodr.org/en/the-orthodox-14-04-2012/.

18. Cf. Georges Massouh, "Ana sar 'umri 72 [I am 72 years old]," *Al-Nahar*, 2014, https://www.lebanonfiles.com/news/683765/; Glenn Bowman, "Nationalizing the Sacred: Shrines and Shifting Identities in the Israeli-Occupied Territories," *Man: The Journal of the Royal Anthropological Institute* 28, no. 3 (1993): 431–60.

19. Goodgame, "A Lineage in Land"; Clayton Goodgame, "Custodians of Descent: The House, the Church, and the Family Waqf in the Orthodox Patriarchate of Jerusalem," *Jerusalem Quarterly* 89 (2022): 32–55.

20. Bruno Latour, "Thou Shall Not Freeze-Frame. Or How Not to Misunderstand the Religion and Science Debate," in *On the Modern Cult of the Factish Gods* (Duke University Press, 2010), 102.

21. In addition to the Bible College and Musalaha, another powerful institution that takes this view of evangelism is the Bible Society, a global organization but one that in Jerusalem focuses on increasing Bible-based faith among all denominations.

22. A global church loosely affiliated with Pentecostalism, with two parishes in Jerusalem.

23. Dan Rabinowitz, *Overlooking Nazareth: The Ethnography of Exclusion in a Mixed Town in Galilee* (Cambridge: Cambridge University Press, 1997).

24. There is an important political element to this attitude toward national politics, but here I wish to focus on the politics involved in separating the religious and social character of evangelical identity. For a broader political view of Palestinian evangelicalism, see Lena Rose, "Palestinian Evangelicals—a Theologically Engaged Anthropological Approach," *Ethnos* 86, no. 3 (2019): 444–59.

25. Twenty thousand, which is large in terms of Christians, not the general population. See Todd Johnson and Gina Zurlo, eds., *World Christian Database* (Brill, n.d.); Sarah Posner, "Kosher Jesus: Messianic Jews in the Holy Land," *The Atlantic*, November 19, 2012, https://www.theatlantic.com/international /archive/2012/11/kosher-jesus-messianic-jews-in-the-holy-land/265670/.

26. Julia Fisher, "What You Believe and Where You Come From," *Olive Tree Reconciliation Fund*, 2014, http://www.olivetreefund.org/ot221-identity-what-you -believe-and-where-you-come-from-dr-salim-munayer-with-julia-fisher-1-of-2.

27. "Amira's Story," Musalaha, n.d., http://www.musalaha.org/amiras-story.

28. "Leila's Story," Musalaha, n.d., http://www.musalaha.org/leilas-story.

29. "A Theology of Reconciliation," in *A Curriculum of Reconciliation*, Musalaha, 2017, https://musalaha.org/musalaha-test/.

30. "A Theology of Reconciliation."

31. Julia Fisher, "Syrian Refugees in Northern Jordan," *Olive Tree Reconciliation Fund*, 2014, https://www.olivetreefund.org/ot180-syrian-refugees -in-northern-jordan-labib-madanat-with-julia-fisher-1-of-2/.

32. Yohanna Katanacho, "Christ Is the Owner of *Ha'aretz*," *Christian Scholar's Review* 34 (2005): 432.

33. Specifically, they are agnates: "The first [biblical] scene of emergence of the Arabs was one linking them to Yaqtan [Joktan] and 'Aaber (Eber), from whom Abraham descended. Thus Abraham and the Arabs were born from the same ancestor, i.e. 'Aaber, from the seed [*nasal*] of Sam [Shem]." Yohanna Katanacho, *"Bidayat al-'arab fi al-kitab al-muqaddas* [The beginning of the

Arabs in the Bible]," *Come and See*, 2017, http://www.comeandsee.com/ar/post /2835508; translation mine.

34. Katanacho, "Christ Is the Owner of *Ha'aretz*," 440.

35. Louis Dumont, "A Modified View of Our Origins: The Christian Beginnings of Modern Individualism," *Contributions to Indian Sociology* 17, no. 1 (1983): 1–26; E. Leach, "Melchisedech and the Emperor: Icons of Subversion and Orthodoxy," *Proceedings of the Royal Anthropological Institute of Great Britain and Ireland*, 1972, 5–14; Jack Goody, *The Development of the Family and Marriage in Europe* (Cambridge University Press, 1983).

36. Cf. Don Seeman, "Kinship as Ethical Relation: A Critique of the Spiritual Kinship Paradigm," in *New Directions in Spiritual Kinship: Sacred Ties Across the Abrahamic Religions*, ed. T. Thomas, A. Malik, and R. Wellman (Palgrave, 2017), 85–109.

37. Daniel Boyarin and Jonathan Boyarin, "Diaspora: Generation and the Ground of Jewish Identity," *Critical Inquiry* 19, no. 4 (1993): 694. Cf. Nadia Abu El-Haj, *The Genealogical Science: The Search for Jewish Origins and the Politics of Epistemology* (University of Chicago Press, 2012), 175–76.

38. Boyarin and Boyarin, "Diaspora," 693.

39. Boyarin and Boyarin, "Diaspora," 695.

40. Boyarin and Boyarin, "Diaspora," 695.

41. Katanacho, "Christ Is the Owner of *Ha'aretz*."

42. Larissa Remennick and Anna Prashizky, "Russian Israelis and Religion: What Has Changed After Twenty Years in Israel?," *Israel Studies Review* 27, no. 1 (2012): 55–77.

43. Hillary Kaell, *Walking Where Jesus Walked: American Christians and Holy Land Pilgrimage* (New York University Press, 2014), 144–46; cf. Aaron Engberg, *Walking on the Pages of the Word of God: Self, Land, and Text Among Evangelical Volunteers in Jerusalem* (Brill, 2019), 117. On American Mormons who are given lineage ascriptions to the lost tribes of Israel, see Fenella Cannell, "The Blood of Abraham: Mormon Redemptive Physicality and American Idioms of Kinship," *Journal of the Royal Anthropological Institute* 19, no. 1 (2013): 77–94. Mormon converts are similarly "grafted" into the Abrahamic line, their blood transformed into Abraham's. Fenella Cannell, "'Forever Families': Christian Individualism, Mormonism, and Collective Salvation," in *New Directions in Spiritual Kinship: Sacred Ties Across the Abrahamic Religions*, ed. T. Thomas, A. Malik, and R. Wellman (Palgrave, 2017), 159–66.

44. Sarah Imhoff and Hillary Kaell, "Lineage Matters: DNA, Race, and Gene Talk in Judaism and Messianic Judaism," *Religion and American Culture: A Journal of Interpretation* 27, no. 1 (2017): 100; El-Haj, *The Genealogical Science*, 2.

45. Imhoff and Kaell, "Lineage Matters," 105.

46. Imhoff and Kaell, "Lineage Matters," 108.

47. Elsewhere I show how Palestinian genealogical idioms are influenced by the Israeli state's use of DNA technology. See Goodgame, "A Lineage in Land"; cf. El-Haj, *The Genealogical Science.*

48. Imhoff and Kaell, "Lineage Matters," 112.

49. Coakley and Robbins, "Anthropological and Theological Responses to Theologically Engaged Anthropology," 368–73.

50. Even Coakley's etymological definition, "talking about God" (Coakley and Robbins, "Anthropological and Theological Responses to Theologically Engaged Anthropology," 368), is rather different from Orthodox ones. Evagrius of Pontus famously described a theologian as "one who knows how to pray." Ware, *The Orthodox Church*, 200.

Imperial Ecclesiologies and Ethnographic Imaginaries

Situating Syriac Christianity in the Anthropology of Global Orthodoxy

Sarah Bakker Kellogg

The West Syrian fathers have not given a definition of liturgy. Perhaps it is felt unnecessary to define something self-evident, and so intimate to one's experience.
> —Father Baby Varghese, *West Syrian Liturgical Theology*

That fact that people of every country pray differently and have something which singles them out from the rest, goes to their credit, first because it indicates the wealth of their devotions and spiritual vigor, and secondly because it is a sign of the incomprehensibility of God, who wishes to be glorified in different ways in different countries and towns
> —Bishop Dionysius Bar Salibi (d. 1171), *Against the Melchites*

Awash in the sound of ringing bells and rustling vestments, the scent of incense and the taste of bread, rocked by the haptic connection to one's neighbors sharing the kiss of peace and the kinetic rhythms of standing, sitting, and bowing together, entering the space-time of Orthodox Christian liturgy synchronizes body, mind, and heart. During one of my earliest fieldwork experiences in a diasporic Syriac Orthodox Church, I witnessed a young boy—maybe seven or eight years old—in a white robe and crimson sash standing before the altar surrounded by elder deacons. He closed his eyes and lifted his head, and his clear voice, light but strong, rose in a crescendo of melodic prayer. In some other traditions, the microtonal complexity of his performance might be considered virtuosic in a child this young, but here in the Syriac Orthodox Church, his mastery over both the melodies and phonetics of classical Syriac, while certainly an accomplishment his family was proud of, was also not that unusual, as children this young can be found performing the liturgy with their elders in the diaconate every week in the global diaspora, from New Jersey to Sweden to Brazil.

In my fieldwork, as I rehearsed with several parish liturgical choirs in the Netherlands, I came to grasp how difficult the child cantor's performance actually was: On any given day, performing the liturgy means struggling to find the right note; slipping up the proper pronunciation and wincing at a moment of discord or a person singing a little too loudly; hurriedly flipping pages; sharing texts written in untransliterated Serto, the classical West Syriac script; keeping an eye out for mouthed instructions from the senior deacon, whose head peeks out occasionally from behind the altar curtain; and laughing affectionately at the sight of a toddler running up to the altar to say hello to the priest in the middle of prayers. This is worship and learning and learning-as-worship: a cyclical and intersensorial enculturation into being and becoming Syriac, Orthodox, and Christian.[1]

A few weeks after I first noticed the young cantor, I sat down with him and his parents at a focus group discussion I organized with the chair of their parish's governance board. As the conversation flowed, I asked the young boy: "Why do you sing in the liturgy?" He responded without hesitation: "I do it because it gives me a good feeling inside. I do it because it makes me feel at home."

In this chapter, I inquire into the methodological, epistemological, and political implications of situating this ethnographic scene in the world of Syriac Christianity—a family of liturgical traditions who trace their ecclesial origins to the Syriac-speaking congregations of the second-century Roman provinces of Mesopotamia, Osrhoene, Euphratensis, Syria I, and Syria II[2]—as well as in the emerging anthropology of global Orthodoxy. Reflecting on over ten years of fieldwork with Syriac Orthodox Christians, or Suryoye, as they refer to themselves in neo-Aramaic, in the Netherlands, as well as digital ethnography among the Assyrian/Syriac global diaspora, I revisit the temporal, spatial, cultural, linguistic, and theological horizons of my research to explore what an Orthodox framing enables, as well as forecloses, in producing ethnographic descriptions and analyses of Syriac lifeworlds, lived theologies, and ethicopolitical commitments encapsulated in the words "the liturgy makes me feel at home."

The ethnographic fieldwork that inspired these reflections formed the basis of my first book, *Sonic Icons: Relation, Recognition, and Revival in a Syriac World*,[3] which examines how Syriac Orthodox Christians fashion kinship—understood in an ethnic, cultural, *and* religious sense—through liturgical chant, and so this chapter serves as a methodological companion piece to that work. This chapter also shares a theoretical interest in "what classifies as theological knowledge at all" with Clayton Goodgame's chapter in this volume on Palestinian Christian kinship. In the early stages of defining my fieldsite, I experienced a pattern of disorientation as I navigated crucial relationships among my research participants that drew me beyond the boundaries of Orthodox ecclesiology as conventionally understood among pro-Chalcedonian Christians.[4] And yet these interlocutors also clarified for me the insight embodied by the young cantor: the centrality of a multisensory, affective, and ethical relationship with liturgy to Syriac Orthodox conceptions of identity and belonging.

The sights, sounds, smells, and haptic rhythms of the liturgy are woven together by the sound of the chant to shape a distinctly Syriac sensorium, which is reproduced across diverse political, linguistic, and cultural contexts to form a complex set of sensory cultures.[5] In *Sonic Icons*, I argued that the practice of sacred chant is itself an embodied mode of doing theology and as such grounds Syriac Orthodox understandings of sociopolitical identity in liturgical history, even for the most secularist articulations of ethnonational identity among Assyrian and Aramaean political movements, the two dominant sociopolitical identifications linked to Syriac heritage.[6] These connections produce the Syriac world.[7]

In this chapter, I take up one strand of this earlier argument to explore an unexamined tension between two distinct yet interwoven ways of thinking about and relating to "history." The first is a social scientific construct that understands history as neutral "context" to ethnographic description, while the second is an emotional, embodied investment in history as a personal story of family trauma saturated with theological significance. My discussion grapples with Christianity's relationship with empire—whether

Byzantine, Persian, Abbasid, or Ottoman—since the Council of Chalcedon in 451 CE and that legacy's influence on the divergent histories of pro-Chalcedonian and non-Chalcedonian churches. Given these histories, I examine how non-Chalcedonian Christianities are rendered ethnographically in the anthropology of global Orthodoxy to illuminate how certain narratives *of* the past, originating *in* these imperial pasts, endure within present-day scholarly constructions of ostensibly neutral, historical context.

This chapter proceeds in four parts: First, I recount moments of fieldwork disorientation when I became uncertain about how and where to draw the boundaries around Syriac Christianity as an ethnographic entity. Second, I offer an overview of the major barriers currently inhibiting the formation of a coherent anthropology of the Syriac world, working with methodological insights drawn from Mark Calder's notion of ecclesiological anthropology to map how these barriers index the Syriac world's intersections with global Orthodoxy.[8] Next, I examine the affordances of the anthropology of global Orthodoxy for an anthropology of the Syriac world—especially those approaches that foreground the world-building intersensoriality of Orthodox prayer. These approaches illuminate how liturgy can generate social formations, political orientations, and ethnic identifications. In the fourth and final part, I explore the limits of the "Orthodox" frame for characterizing the commitments of Syriac Orthodox Christians who identify as ethnically Assyrian, because this ethnic formation entails a strong sense of sociopolitical kinship with the Chaldean Catholic Church, the Syriac Catholic Church, and the Assyrian and Ancient Churches of the East, none of whom can be characterized as "Orthodox" in the sense generally meant by the anthropology of global Orthodoxy.

At stake here is how differently situated each ecclesial community is in relation to the history of state power, both imperial and national, and how these different histories come to be either recast or erased in ethnographic renderings of historical "context." Yet this abstracted rendering of history as context also intervenes *within* the ethnographic space of liturgical life as it coexists with a theological orientation toward history as Incarnation. This orientation, expressed in the epigraph by the twelfth-century Syriac Orthodox bishop Dionysius Bar Ṣalibi, materializes in the diverse stylistic traditions of Syriac chant. Ultimately, I argue for a both/and approach that neither assimilates these diverse communities into a Chalcedonian ecclesiological frame nor forfeits the anthropology of global Orthodoxy's ability to describe and explain liturgy's sociopolitical power.[9]

Ethnographic Disorientations

In my first summer of fieldwork at the Mor Ephrem Syriac Orthodox Monastery in the Netherlands, I met a Dutch Assyrian woman named Semela.[10] An elected representative in the provincial parliament for the eastern region of Overijssel, she had risen to international prominence among the global Assyrian/Syriac diaspora as an activist for Christians in the Middle East and as an advocate for a politically autonomous homeland for Assyrians on the Nineveh Plains in northern Iraq. In one of our early meetings at Semela's office in Enschede, she told me directly: "If I could, I would really rather just be a regular Dutch woman living a regular Dutch life. This work [in politics] is a constant source of headache," she said, with an exasperated shake of her head. "But," she continued, "my community has a history. I have an obligation to that history, or Syriac Christianity will disappear from the world." She paused for a moment, remembering: "It is when I hear the hymns especially. I sang in the choir when I was a young girl. When I hear the singing now I feel . . . emotional. I cannot let all that beauty disappear."

Early in her career, Semela relied on the ecclesiastical hierarchy to help her accomplish her political aims, despite her private doubts about the existence of God, or at least, she says, the kind of God described in her childhood church. This was the reason for our meeting at the monastery that first summer in 2007, where the recently installed bishop had introduced us. Semela told me that she relied on the church's cooperation and support not only because it was the primary source of authority and means of communication among Syriac Orthodox communities across northern Europe but also because it was the bishop's office that facilitated connections with local Dutch Protestant, Catholic, and secular human rights organizations. Representatives from these agencies saw the bishop as the community's de facto leader and spokesperson, which, she said, she found problematic. With a pained expression, she tried to choose her words carefully: "So . . . yes . . . it is tricky . . . the church is the 'location' of our culture, in a sense, and in the past, the church has always protected our culture's identity . . . but now . . . it seems to me that the church is keeping people ignorant . . . we are so focused on the religious side of things that not many of us are politically aware . . . and ironically that might be what causes us to disappear."

Semela returned to this theme frequently in our subsequent conversations, pointing out that a strong sense of religious identity was not enough to keep Syriac Christianity from disappearing from the world because in secular modernity, in her view, you cannot stake a public claim to political autonomy on religious identity alone; for that, you need an ethnicity, with all the ties to land and blood the secularist concept of "ethnicity" is presumed to entail. For Semela, it was important to make clear to outsiders that she was Assyrian because her family's history was both "Syriac" in terms of the language of the liturgy performed at their church and "Christian" in terms of a social and cultural belonging organized by and through that church. Ethnic ties to ancient Mesopotamia and to the Assyrian Empire, whose ruins dot the landscape of northern Iraq, were, in her analysis, reproduced over the centuries by and through the church. The church was therefore essential, but also not enough. To compound matters, she disliked attending Mass now as an adult, despite her love for the hymns. This she told me with a defiant air that only made sense to me once I discovered that many of her constituents were increasingly incensed by what they perceived as her public impiety (such as admitting in an interview with a local newspaper her discomfort with how the church characterized God), a grave breach in Syriac Orthodox social norms.

Such reactions could provoke frustration, as could the visiting anthropologist's naive questioning. But Semela was well-versed in social scientific theory and equipped to answer in terms I could wrap my brain around. Stuck on the fact that ancient Assyria had ended in the 600s BCE, I asked her to explain how exactly she linked her Christian upbringing to an empire that had been destroyed six hundred years *before* the birth of Christ. She threw up her hands and switched to English to bellow at me: "Everyone else gets to invent their tradition—why can't we? Our identity is no more or less constructed than every single other ethnic group in the world! That doesn't make us any less *a people!* Why should we be singled out as an exception?!"

In subsequent visits, I met several parish governance boards, many of whom looked at me with suspicion and asked the same question before agreeing to speak with me further: "You know who we are, right? You know that we are Aramaean?" Disoriented by what felt like a surreal shift in my research interlocutors' default terminology from my first summer with Semela, I learned quickly that getting this answer wrong could bar my access to the inner workings of many parishes. Unnerved by the intensity of the feelings my questions seemed to provoke, I worked up the courage to ask a woman I'd befriended whose young son was participating in the monastery's Syriac language and liturgical school that summer: "Can you help me understand? Why do some people here say that Syriac Orthodox people are Assyrian while others say you are Aramaean?"

She replied, emphatically but not unkindly: "Some people are very confused and have the wrong information. Assyrians are heretics. The patriarch said so! They belong to a different church. They don't believe the same things. But really, what you need to understand, Sarah, is that as far as our identity is concerned, we are just Christians. That's it!" This third layer—"just Christian!"—confounded me further: I had never considered the possibility that a person could be ethnicity-less, so naturalized was the English-language category of "ethnic" identity within my own secularist social scientific worldview. What, then, in my mind and in the minds of my interlocutors, was "ethnicity" and what was "religion," and what was the gap between our definitions? And why did the theological difference between the Syriac Orthodox Church and the Church of the East matter to some Suryoye and not to others?[11]

With the passage of time and participation in Syriac Orthodox liturgical life as both a singer in two parish women's choirs and in a "secular" Assyrian choir, I discerned the connective tissue linking these contentious and seemingly contradictory claims. As I have argued in my earlier work, this connective tissue is a shared sociopolitical commitment across disparate ethnoreligious and ethnonationalist ancestral narratives, enacted through ritual practice, to the historical and linguistic identity of the West Syriac liturgical tradition. This tradition was known throughout late antiquity and the medieval world as "Jacobite," for Jacob Baradaeus, the sixth-century bishop of Edessa. In the chants, melodies, texts, sights, sounds, smells, and rhythms of the daily and weekly offices of the church, and especially the Holy Qurbono, or Eucharistic Mass, this tradition reproduces liturgical memory through prayer. In retrospect, my early fieldwork disorientation was a function of my methodological and epistemological incapacity to grasp how these ritual forms, bound together in the Liturgy of St. James, constituted a practice of relating and, as such, Syriac Orthodox sociality, which in turn authorized political life. Liturgy, in this analysis, is a category, a practice, and a set of relationships infused with the power to shape sociopolitical imaginaries, binding far-flung communities into a connected, coherent, global formation—the Syriac world.

Syriac Orthodox self-ascriptions are shaped by complex spatiotemporalities of historical memory. Those who think about the public, political dimensions of their identity represent themselves through one of two distinct ancestral narratives: either as modern Assyrians, descendants of the ancient Assyrian Empire, or as modern Aramaeans, descendants of the ancient city-states of Aram referenced in the Bible. There was also a third possibility: For some of my interlocutors, the secularist concept of "ethnicity" was meaningless—as was the case for my summer-school friend at the monastery. For these Suryoye, the ground of identity was to be found in their parishes, ancestral villages, and monasteries. Yet these disparate configurations share a common thread. That which connects present sociopolitical identity to these ancient pasts is a practical theology of kinship enacted through liturgy. Ancient Assyria and Aram are linked to the present day *through* liturgical memories transmitted in parishes, ancestral villages, and monasteries. Thus while these three positions caused a great deal of controversy, everyone agreed that despite the name debate, they were all the same *people.*

The complexity and cosmopolitanism of their peoplehood was reflected in the complexity and cosmopolitanism of their liturgical sounds. The melodies of a given prayer sounded ever so slightly different as young cantors faithfully reproduced the sounds taught to them by their parish priests, liturgical teachers, and monastic uncles as a matter of village and regional identity. This theology of kinship imbued the repetitive, sensuous process of generating affective and ethical bonds through collective prayer with an irreducible, sacral relationality. This relationality exceeds and renders largely irrelevant questions of individual belief. Such was the case of skeptical Semela, who nonetheless understood the connection between modern Assyrian nationalism and the ancient Assyrian past to be the linguistic and liturgical forms of Syriac Christian history. As such, Assyrian, Aramaean, and Syriac historical narratives connect prayer—the corpus of sacred chants known as the Beth Gazo, or "Treasury of Chant," used throughout the liturgical cycle—to kinship. This liturgical subjectivity holds the Syriac world together even as it intersects with other sensory cultures, whether local secular nationalisms, Turkish urban culture, Arab music scenes, Kurdish village life, transnational ecumenical activism, or, indeed, global Orthodoxy.

My experiences of fieldwork disorientation raise two interrelated questions for ethnographers approaching non-Chalcedonian traditions through an analytical frame shared—and arguably dominated by—Eastern Orthodox churches of the Chalcedonian line. First, to what extent does the emerging Anglophone anthropology of global Orthodoxy rely upon an

implicitly Chalcedonian ecclesiology? If so, how much does this ecclesiological imagination emerge from culturally and politically specific experiences within Greek and Latin Christianity? To what extent do such Latin
and Greek Christian experiences shape Anglophone anthropology's assumptions about what makes Christian social life Christian? Finally, can
such an anthropology engage Semela the Assyrian (and the many thousands
of Assyrian Syriac Orthodox like her around the world) without erasing her
primary understanding of herself as Assyrian or the non-Chalcedonian dimensions of Syriac liturgical history on which her conception of being Assyrian is staked? It is to these questions that I now turn.

Toward an Anthropology of the Syriac World

Syriac Christianity has been a border-crossing political, cultural, linguistic, literary, ethnic, and social formation since the second century. That
this formation has thus far been largely ignored by Anglophone anthropology is a consequence of several disciplinary and methodological problems indicative of broader currents and conditions in contemporary social
science. The first problem is a siloed area studies approach to ethnographic
research. A coherent anthropology of the Syriac world would require scholars with wide-ranging linguistic training (e.g., neo-Aramaic/Assyrian vernaculars, Arabic, Turkish, Kurdish, and classical Syriac, in addition to
various diasporic languages) and transnational, multiregional expertise
(e.g., the ability to trace linkages among European, Middle Eastern/West
Asian, South and East Asian, North American, South American, and Aus-
tralian migration routes, kinship networks, and reading publics) to read
and speak to one another as part of a common conversation. In my own
fieldsite in the Netherlands, the majority of local Syriac Orthodox Christians hail from families who spoke primarily Ṭuroyo ("the mountain language"), a nonstandardized dialect of central neo-Aramaic that developed
in the highlands of Tur Abdin in southeastern Turkey, considered by many
to be the heartland of Syriac Orthodoxy.[12] Tur Abdin, meaning "the Moun-
tains of the Servants of God," is a rural and impoverished area densely
populated with Syriac Orthodox monasteries and Ṭuroyo-speaking villages
and was home to the patriarchate at the monastery of Deyr al-Zafaran until
1933.

In the global diaspora, Syriac Orthodox are predominantly either from
Ṭuroyo-speaking families if they are from Tur Abdin; from Arabic-speaking

families if they are from Syria, Lebanon, or the Arabic-speaking cities of southeastern Turkey, like Mardin; or are Turkish speakers, if they are from major urban areas in Turkey, like Istanbul; or Kurdish speakers, if they are from any of the smaller towns or villages where Kurdish clans dominated local politics.[13] Proficiency in classical Syriac, or *Suryoyo kthobonoyo* (the "book language"), meanwhile, is rare outside the highest reaches of the ecclesiastical hierarchy. Language politics is a key site for detecting the worldliness of the Syriac world. This politics manifests in debates over whether to maintain classical Syriac in Sunday services or to translate portions into local vernaculars to promote theological understanding; whether to revive classical Syriac as a spoken language through satellite television or to standardize and teach Ṭuroyo online through nonprofit initiatives; and whether speaking Arabic, Turkish, or Kurdish as one's first language undermines one's ethnic claim to being properly Syriac, Aramaean, or Assyrian. The answer to any of these questions can look radically different depending on where and when in the Syriac world one is located.

A second significant problem inhibiting anthropological study of the Syriac world is Anglophone anthropology's conceptual and ideological difficulty in grappling with theology as a political-material force that extends beyond the category of "religion." It is here where the anthropology of global Orthodoxy has been especially useful for ethnographies of Syriac Christianity. Theology, as the discursive terrain in which Christians and ex-Christians imagine, formulate, debate, and enact their understanding of what the universe is and how it works, is an uncomfortable space for secularist social scientists with a political attraction to alterity. Close attention to Christian theology can make explicit what many might prefer to remain implicit in the social scientific imagination: at best, ethnocentric (or perhaps theocentric?) concepts that have been decontextualized, universalized, and misapplied as secular analytical categories and at worst, essentialist and racializing intellectual habits rooted in the worst legacies of European Christianity.[14] The anthropology of global Orthodoxy, on the other hand, grapples explicitly with the ontological pluralism within Christianity itself. This pluralism unsettles modern social science's founding presumption that Christianity is interior to whiteness and Westernness—the unmarked *us* that makes it epistemologically possible to discern others as *different* enough to become objects of anthropological inquiry in the first place. It offers an expansive and clarifying perspective on the diversity of Christian theologies and their material-political force in its attentiveness to how sensory practices and bodily disciplines work together to create worlds. With an emphasis on the corporeal dimensions of corporate worship, the anthropology of global Orthodoxy enables us to ask important questions of personhood, tradition, authority, publicity, intimacy, belonging, and the human sensorium.

In *Praying with the Senses: Contemporary Orthodox Spirituality in Practice* (2018), a foundational text in the emerging Anglophone anthropology of global Orthodoxy edited by Sonja Luehrmann, a cohort of ethnographers working on both Chalcedonian and non-Chalcedonian traditions paint a compelling portrait of Orthodox Christianity as *a world*, as common stylistic features, ethical questions, and theological preoccupations reappear again and again, from Russia to Ethiopia to India and beyond.[15] When understood as a globalized aesthetic formation, following Birgit Meyer's apt phrase,[16] Orthodox Christianity makes Christian persons through diverse relationships among practitioners spanning multiple scales and modes of mediation. These relationships, in turn, are fashioned through ongoing processes of sensory exchange and the ethically attuned cultivation of individual capacities that enable such exchanges. This approach enables a crucial set of insights about the Syriac world in how it makes the sociopolitical potentialities of liturgical practice legible.

In sensory practices like icon veneration, sacramental listening, intercessory prayer, repetitive recitation, pilgrimage, and learning to read ancient sacral languages, Orthodoxy's aesthetics and ethics articulate with what the contributors to *Praying with the Senses* understand to be an authoritative discursive tradition in the sense that Talal Asad means it, in that it aspires to coherence as an ethico-theological corpus rooted in a genealogy of ecclesiastical authority.[17] For Syriac Orthodoxy, this is evident in the weekly recitation of the litany of saints, from St. Ephrem of Nisibis to St. Severus of Antioch to St. Jacob of Serug to Philoxenos of Mabbug, who are not only moral exemplars for Orthodox becoming[18] but also beloved ancestors, who as members of the family remain intimately and immanently involved in everyday life. In its sensitivity to the world-making possibilities of the sensory and the material in religious life, then, the anthropology of global Orthodoxy helps us grasp, ontologically, liturgy's generative, binding, capacious, and flexible power. Liturgy is, in a practical sense, what Christianity *is*.

History as Incarnation

Another way to discern liturgical power is through an explicitly "ecclesio-logical" anthropology, a methodology developed by anthropologist Mark Calder that "enables a rigorous engagement with local Christians' lives in their specificity while making space for the universal-oriented repertoire they articulate in their lives."[19] The *ecclesia*, a term drawn from the classical Athenian sense of a "called assembly," carries within it another shade of political meaning, one that evokes the civic duties toward the broader polity of those called. This civic sense repeatedly runs aground on other linguistic, denominational, and culturalist renderings of the word "church," yet across these differences is a common attribute: The local church and the global Church are always imagined to be in some kind of relationship.

Since the earliest Christian congregations formed in antiquity, Calder writes, "Christians have wrestled with the rightful relationship between those 'within' the community of the faithful and those it encounters as others, between the ecclesia and whatever is conceived to lie beyond it."[20] In his monograph on Bethlehem's Syriac Orthodox Christians, Calder il-luminates the condition of "rightful connectedness" that defines a distinctly Syriac sociality and belonging within the fraught political context of post-mandate Palestine, where ritual spaces are tightly regulated by Israeli state authorities. This is a situation where, for Bethlehem's Syriac Christians, questions of identity follow, rather than precede, acts of inclusion through liturgical practice: "The liturgy . . . provides a kind of centre, connecting these mundane border-crossings with an eternal, cosmic drama in the light of which, ultimately, they are to be made sense of."[21] Contrasted with a common Eastern Orthodox trope of Incarnational theology as "hospital-ity," in which room is made for the "stranger" as a guest at the Eucharistic feast, Calder observes, Syriac liturgical theology here enacts an ecclesiol-ogy based on a particular model of legal kinship: One is never a guest. Rather, liturgy transforms stranger into adoptee.[22]

Incarnational theology furnishes the interpretive framework through which this adoptive model of liturgical kinship is established: History is read Christologically. That is to say, present-day Syriac Christians look back at pre-Christian polities, whether Assyrian or Aramaean, and see them as having been transformed out-of-time by Christ's Incarnation, for after Christianity, there is no earthly government but the church. This point is only possible to grasp methodologically and epistemologically by engaging seriously with the ontological foundations of Syriac Christian Incarnational theology. "Our people," (in Syriac, '*amo dilan*) is a word that describes an interlocking set of material, affective, and ethical relationships continually reconstituted over time through liturgical acts. It refers to a set of civilizational myths refashioned at and by the miracle of Pentecost: the people called to a duty to the world, a duty enacted through an embodied relationship with the mystery of the Shepherd's Incarnation—with the mystery, that is, of history.[23]

Yet the chain of relations constituting Syriac liturgical identity also opens up a generative tension within its mechanics: On the one hand, participation precedes identification, a process of incorporation that is repeatedly tested at the borders, where others may become integral to the ethicopolitical body of the ecclesia and thus kin. On the other hand, liturgy is also a modality of reproductive power in the most physically incarnate sense. This is heard in specific historical memories inscribed in the very sound of a given liturgical performance. These historical memories are audible in the stylistic variations of the Syriac Orthodox Schools of sacred chant.

"School" is the name given to the eight distinct stylistic traditions of performing the Beth Gazo, the repertoire of chanted hymns and prayers that organizes the Syriac Orthodox Church's eight-week liturgical cycle.[24] Together, these eight schools constitute a sonic map of ancient migration and contemporary loss. No one I know speaks of their own school as the *truest or most original* school relative to any of the others because they understand these schools to reflect the diversity of the late antique and medieval Syriac world. What they do insist upon is correct pronunciation of classical Syriac within the conventions of their own school and of melodic lines reconstructed from their liturgical teacher's, or *malphono*'s, memory. The authorizing structure of the *malphono*'s memory demarcates the parish as a formation one might describe in English as "ethnic."

This ethnic formation is not exclusionary in practice (i.e., anyone can show up to participate by at least listening and praying silently), but it is exclusive in principle to those raised with a specific set of historical memories because the chant reproduces the emotional states associated with those memories. These parish-bound memories nest within the broader formation of the school's historical identity, in turn producing the social allegiances from which form political alliances connecting parishes throughout the diaspora. Learning to chant the Beth Gazo, and thus actively participate in liturgical prayers, is to be socialized and sensorially trained into a particular set of "right relationships": with priests and *mal-phone* whose role as sacrally authorized teachers is understood to generate a theologically mandated relationship with and among parishioners of "love and trust."[25] In practice, I have witnessed this distinctive liturgical relationship in public displays of an avuncular, almost casual, affection between ordinary parishioners and their priests, teachers, and monks in diasporic monasteries, churches, and cultural centers from the Netherlands to New Jersey.

I discerned the flipside of these relations when many of my friends in the women's choirs began to marry and leave their home parishes for their spouse's parish, where they would find their new parish's rendition of the hymns and prayers of the Beth Gazo just different enough that they could no longer follow along. My choir friends usually accepted this, understanding that their liturgical role in their community had shifted from that of a cantor to a congregant, whose responsibility for the spiritual well-being of the ʿamo now centered on their role as a mother or, if a woman was herself child-free, an extremely involved aunt. For the more expert of my choir friends, their new role often included teaching basic Syriac grammar to the youngest children at church (functionally equivalent to a Sunday school teacher, even if classes are not always held on Sunday) or Ṭuroyo to their children, nieces, and nephews. The distribution of their liturgical labor over their lifetime enabled the Syriac Orthodox women I worked with to manage the transition to a parish where the sounds of chanted prayers were audibly different from their childhood parishes' sounds.

Because musical notes are not transcribed, the chant's melodies reside in the body, trained from childhood. Picking up a variation of the same chant—intoned in a different register, at different speeds and timbres, incorporating different microtonal flourishes and structural arrangements, with subtly different pronunciations of the Syriac text—is not the trivial exercise it would be for a choir singer in a different tradition trained to sight-read sheet music. My friends and fellow choir singers Nahrin, Mariane, and Elizabeta each explained it to me, on different occasions, using a similar formulation: "The 'correct' sound of a chant is however your teacher taught it to you. That is *your* parish's sound, and it is correct on its own terms, regardless of what anyone else was doing in any other parish. You feel it in your body."

These stylistic variations, at the microscopic level of the parish as well as at the macroscopic level of the schools, inscribe a history of theologically meaningful relationships in the reproduction and transmission of liturgical knowledge. The sacrality of the sound is inseparable from the relationality of its production. Far from being abstracted from national, regional, and locally specific contexts, the variety of liturgical sounds among parishes enable diasporic Syriac Orthodox to embody "right relationships" with the villages, monasteries, and regions of their parents, grandparents, teachers, priests, and cloistered aunts and uncles. These attachments are often reinforced by associations and clubs through which parish members commemorate and celebrate their ties to their ancestral villages in Tur Abdin and by mundane practices like using their grandparents' village names for email addresses and social media handles. The power that flows through these relationships forms deeply felt affective and ethical attachments to "history" as a family affair in need of protection, weighted with the memory of great-aunts and uncles lost to the genocide of 1915 and witnessing grandparents continuing to suffer the psychological effects of unacknowledged trauma. It is to that chain of attachments to which Semela refers when she says, "my community has a history" to explain her work. This is not "history" in a naive primordialist sense, as her fluency in social constructivist theory makes clear; rather, it is a history of specific relationships, constituted sensorially, ethically, and affectively through a deeply personal mode of performing the liturgies of the West Syriac Rite.

The anthropology of global Orthodoxy enables this reading of liturgy as an intimate, theological, and sociopolitical force. It accounts for the dynamics of contention among Assyrians, Aramaeans, and "just Christians" in my fieldsite, especially when paired with Mark Calder's ecclesiological anthropology and its methodological sensitivity to thinking "history" Incarnationally. This is a major affordance for the anthropology of the Syriac world. But there is a point of friction here also, because anthropologists accountable to secular social science also approach history as "context." Historical context is that which both *explains* and *lies beyond* the spatiotemporal horizons of a given ethnographic situation. Where the ethnographer imagines their horizons will influence whether and how they attribute a particular past with any explanatory power for the present. The tension between history as Incarnation and history as context calls for more careful attention to how we construe narratives of the past as necessary context, lest we recapitulate early imperial techniques in service of a Chalcedonian ecclesiology at the expense of non-Chalcedonian ecclesiologies. It is to this problem I now turn.

History as Context

For the anthropology of the Syriac world, there are several ways a scholar might narrate its historical formation, depending on where the scholar is located institutionally, geographically, epistemically, and ideologically. For my research participants, how to approach history as "context" is a pressing political and existential problem, and Euro-American influenced scholarship both assists and disrupts their struggles for recognition in complicated ways.[26] My own understanding of Syriac history begins in the fourth century, in the years when Syriac-language writers begin to attest to a formalized practice of women's liturgical singing, the Bnoth Qyomo, or Daughters of the Covenant, unmarried women who took vows of celibacy in service to urban churches in and around Antioch and Edessa. By the time of the Council of Chalcedon (451 CE), this practice was already publicly associated with the hymnody of St. Ephrem the Syrian (c. 306–373).[27] While it is difficult to determine from the available textual evidence whether this gendering of liturgical voices was entirely unique to Syriac-speaking churches, the commemoration of St. Ephrem's role as a deacon, theologian-poet, and founder of the Bnoth Qyomo became central to the Syriac Orthodox Church's self-image in subsequent centuries.[28]

Only in the sixth century did Syriac-speaking churches' self-image, increasingly identified with a more exclusive sense of linguistic and regional difference, link up with emergent Christological distinctions formulated by anti-Chalcedonian theologians like Jacob Baradaeus (d. 578), St. Severus of Antioch (d. 538), and others as they revisited the texts of earlier theologians like St. Cyril of Alexandria to resolve certain questions of community practice in their own time. Cultural and liturgical practice, language, and Christology thus came to implicate one another in the process of ecclesiological boundary making, but this took place over the course of decades, if not centuries, *after* the great councils.[29]

The Contested Legacies of St. Cyril of Alexandria

While Christological distinctions are important for grasping communal self-understandings ethnographically, we need to be more careful in how we cite the ancient councils as context when we construct Orthodox Christianity as an object for scholarly inquiry. The Councils of Nicaea (325 CE), Constantinople (381 CE), Ephesus (431 CE), and Chalcedon (451 CE) were the culmination of long-running disputes over the relationship between the divinity and humanity of Christ; the ontic status, and thus gender, of the Holy Spirit; and the relationship between the Byzantine emperor and ecclesiastical authority. The Chalcedonian Definition spoke of "a single concrete existence that both unites but holds distinct the human and divine natures of Christ." Proponents of this definition won the debate in 451 CE and so became associated with the imperial Orthodox Church (with occasional interruptions by unsympathetic emperors), which centuries later schismed into the Latin "West" and the Greek "East." The dissenters (those now retroactively called *miaphysites*) objected to this definition because they felt it emphasized the duality of Christ too much (a theological orientation now called "dyophysite"). Those who dissented, while not a unified faction, came under pressure from imperial Byzantine authorities and, with the crackdown instigated in the sixth century by Justin I and Justinian I, sought refuge with their followers in Persian and Arab lands.

Anti-Chalcedonian writing was forbidden and suppressed in Greek but could be safely translated and circulated in Syriac and Coptic.[30] Over the course of centuries, through missions and the circulation of texts in western, central, and southern Asia, as well as eastern Africa, congregations reading these texts formalized their hierarchical structures to become what are now known as the Syriac Orthodox, Armenian Apostolic, Coptic Orthodox, Ethiopian Orthodox, and Eritrean Orthodox Churches, as well as the Mar Thoma Syrian Church of Malabar and the Malankara Orthodox Syrian Church of southern India.[31] Yet later Western Christian commentators have tended to characterize Chalcedon in terms of a preexisting Christological factionalism among three groups: Nestorians, Miaphysites, and Chalcedonians. This tendency, reproduced in *Praying with the Senses*, reifies and projects current ecclesiological divisions and interpretations onto a situation about which we in fact understand very little but which extant written sources suggest that dynamic human relationships were perhaps as or more fundamentally at stake than clear-cut Christological dispute.

Convened by the Byzantine empress Pulcheria and her senator husband Marcian, the Council of Chalcedon developed the Definition from the later writings of St. Cyril of Alexandria, a vehement polemicist who wrote broadly from his position as a member of the catechetical School of Alexandria. Just as with the competing catechetical School of Antioch, the School of Alexandria was not a homogenous Christological "faction" per se but rather an intellectual community animated by a diverse and dynamic current of thought. In 429 CE, Nestorius, briefly bishop of Constantinople and himself a Greek-speaking monk born in the province of Syria, delivered a sermon claiming that while he could refer to Mary as *Christotokos*, the mother of Jesus's humanity, he could not call her *Theotokos* because "no mother can bear what is not consubstantial to herself."[32] By implication, this called into question Jesus's identity: Could he be both consubstantial with God and with humanity? Cyril took exception to this sermon, publicly complaining that Nestorius's comment constituted a dualistic Christology that fragmented Jesus's identity and "led to the complete separation of the divine and human natures, and thus threatened the efficacy of salvation."[33] Yet the so-called Nestorian Crisis seems in this reading to be more a matter of Cyril's overinterpretation of a single, poorly thought-out comment by Nestorius, and by implication his teacher Theodore of Mopsuestia and the rest of the School of Antioch. The crisis culminated in the Council of Ephesus (431 CE), at which *both* Nestorius and Cyril of Alexandria were excommunicated. Cyril bribed his way back into office; Nestorius returned to his monastery, living just long enough to see his ideas, but not his name, vindicated by the Chalcedonian Definition twenty years later.[34]

The rub here is that much of Nestorius's writings, along with those of Theodore, whose Christology he formally shared, appears according to twentieth-century Chalcedonian theologians to be not particularly unorthodox.[35] This has been the claim of the Church of the East for centuries, the heirs of those congregations who rejected the Council of Ephesus in 431 CE, used Syriac in their liturgy, and fled to (or already lived in) the Persian Empire, which legally recognized them as an independent church. By refusing to repudiate Nestorius's name they were called by others "Nestorian," but they themselves consider this to be a pejorative term because the so-called dyophysite Christology attributed *by* Cyril *to* Nestorius does not accurately convey what they themselves believe Christologically. East Syriac difference appears as such now, from a Western Christian perspective, only through the lens of a long history of cultural, political, and linguistic separation from Greek Christianity's sphere of influence.

What of the so-called *miaphysite* position in all this? This is especially difficult to discern from a twenty-first-century vantage point. In the time of the great councils, ordinary people in the eastern provinces spoke Syriac while Greek remained culturally and politically dominant. Many elite families from whom ecclesiastical leaders were drawn were bilingual in Greek and Syriac. Mapping current ecclesiological boundaries onto debates that took place in a period of immense cosmopolitanism, linguistic diversity, regional mobility, and theological ferment does not make much sense.[36] What little generalization one can make across the diversity of so-called miaphysite writings, writers, and their followers of this period seems to be a thread of concern for the legacy of Cyril of Alexandria and whether the Council of Chalcedon dealt with his Christological thought appropriately. While a vast corpus of early non-Chalcedonian writing in Greek *and* Syriac remains untranslated and unanalyzed, several foundational theologians of the "orthodox" tradition, like Severus of Antioch, articulate the crux of their theology with reference to Cyril's earlier writings. The gap between positions, to the extent that there is one, appears to be between an anti-Chalcedonian "orthodox" attachment to early Cyril and a pro-Chalcedonian "Orthodox" attachment to late Cyril.

The bishops assembled at Chalcedon relied on Cyril's later writings to develop the Definition of Christ's nature, essence, and personhood. Decades and centuries afterward, theologians and bishops of the "orthodox" tradition, like Severus of Antioch, cited St. Cyril's *early* writings to argue that the Chalcedonian bishops had strayed from Cyril's true meaning. Specifically, in an early letter, Cyril used the phrase *mia physis tou theou logou sesarkomene* ("one enfleshed nature [*physis*] of God the Word") arguing *against* "the Syrians" of the School of Antioch, Diodore of Tarsus and his students Theodore of Mopsuestia and Nestorius ("the Syrians" seeming in this case to mark a regional identity rather than a linguistic or Christological one). With the term *mia physis* Cyril was not designating a communal position or doctrine but was rather describing "a metaphysical mystery of a vast cosmic order having taken place in the coming of the Word into history by means of an incarnation as a Man."[37]

As the grammatically feminine Greek word for "one," *mia* here modifies *physis*, meaning "nature." [38] However—and this is the crucial point—in later writings, Cyril shifted from using the word *physis* ("nature") to *hypostasis* ("being" / "essence" / "substance") to refer to "the underlying reality of a thing."[39] Early Cyril's *physis*, according to the Romanian Orthodox priest, theologian, and church historian John McGuckin, is semantically equivalent to late Cyril's *hypostasis*. If this is so, then to describe Severus of Antioch and his followers as espousing a "one-nature" Christology is to accuse Cyril of Alexandria himself of monophysitism.

To what extent, then, does a Christology founded upon early Cyril's conception of *mia physis* differ from a Chalcedonian position, on paper much less in practice? According to the theologian Eboni Marshall Turman, what is essential about the Chalcedonian Definition is the way it resolves the problem of the temporality and materiality of personhood—that is, the question of the relationship among history, identity, and embodiment posed by the birth, life, death, and resurrection of Jesus Christ—by allowing a *both/and* approach to complex identities. The Chalcedonian Definition affirms that a human is defined by more than what happens to her in her life because Jesus is defined by more than what happened to him living on Earth. In Cyrillian Christology, first the word *physis* and then the word *hypostasis* convey this integration of different parts into a cosmic, spiritually significant wholeness.

But, despite the fact that no one at Chalcedon called themselves a miaphysite, the term has become a commonplace self-designation among non-Chalcedonian Orthodox Churches in the twentieth and twenty-first centuries, as church leaders seek ecumenical reconciliation by finding common kinship through the texts of the Church Fathers. The grammatical gender of the word *mia* suggests a carefully modulated emphasis on *oneness* that distinguishes it from the accusation of being monophysites, who, as McGuckin wryly observes, "have largely existed between the covers of heresiology books."[40]

What I see in this history is less a clear-cut debate between polarized Christological factions than a broader set of linguistic, cultural, epistemic, and practical tensions about how to *think* or *do* theology at all. Even among Chalcedonians, there remains a tension between Greek and Latin conceptions of "personhood," whether human or divine, conveyed in Christological terminology, as the Greek *prosopon* maintains subtler distinctions than the Latin *persona*.[41] To which language, then, does an authoritative understanding of the connotations of and distinctions among Christological concepts belong? From an anthropological perspective, at least, this should remain an open and unanswerable question.

Given the backdrop of such indeterminacy, what we understand of the scribal tradition of the third through eighth centuries supports the view that Syriac-speaking Christians' emergent self-definition in opposition to Chalcedon was inflamed more by deeper problems of incommensurability among languages, and the publics these languages mediated, than by disagreement about whether Christ's personhood is composed of one nature or two. This is not to say that Christological differences do not matter to ecclesiology, nor that ecclesiastical hierarchs of later centuries did not rely on the authority of their precursors' writings to legitimize boundaries among their congregations. Rather, this is to say that nonelite Syriac-speaking Christians had different practices and forms of celebrating liturgy than Greek-speaking and bilingual elites, before and during the centuries of Christological controversy—indeed, from the very start of Christianity—and these practices and forms of liturgy did more to shape identities and subjectivities than actual Christological disagreement.

This history, which I render here as "context," reflects centuries of asking and answering different kinds of questions about the meaning of Christ's Incarnation. The later scribal tradition commemorating a Hellenized St. Ephrem, for example, is accessible to scholars, but to twenty-first-century practitioners that Hellenized St. Ephrem cannot compete with the daily commemoration of St. Ephrem the Syriac-speaking cantor, poet, and leader of women's liturgical participation, whose hymns and prayers voicing biblical women in the cosmic drama of salvation are sung weekly among congregations around the world. Many of the women I work with will speak proudly of their historical St. Ephrem as a poetic visionary, the first feminist and the first environmentalist, whose melodies made their church famous. Through their vocal practices of singing and chanting, twenty-first-century Syriac Orthodox women reproduce an embodied relationship with this history. In the modern Syriac Orthodox Church's efforts to seek social, political, and ecumenical recognition in contexts dominated by Chalcedonian theopolitical imaginaries, the twentieth-century adoption and transformation of the Cyrillian term *mia physis* into a collective noun may very well work to bridge a centuries-wide gap between incommensurable modes of *doing* theology. My fear, however, is that the word *mia*, with all its rhetorical connotations, exacerbates Orientalist stereotypes, racist prejudices, and accusations of heresy among the very pro-Chalcedonian Christians with whom many of my interlocutors seek reconciliation.

How the Roman and Greek churches remember the ecumenical councils, and thus how they remember their own Byzantine pasts, differs from what the heirs of early Syriac-speaking Christians remember, as these memories have been shaped and reshaped by their shifting position as subjects of other empires. The Syriac Orthodox with whom I work consider themselves Orthodox because they adhere to the Nicene Creed. They consider themselves non-Chalcedonian and in no way identify with the Byzantine past, not because they disagree with the substance of the Chalcedonian Definition of Christ's Incarnate identity but because they see Chalcedon as the political event that began Syriac Orthodox Christianity's historical troubles as a subjugated minority (if they think of it at all). The complexities of Christian history and identity, then, are a consequence not only of global migration, conquest, schism, and conversion but also of the generative problems of ontological pluralism, conceptual translation, and the embodied practices with which concepts always articulate. Just such a problem spurred the earliest tensions between Greek-speaking and Syriac-speaking Christianities, leading to a bifurcation of Greek and Syriac liturgical worlds that intersect at points yet do not neatly coincide. These were processes that took centuries.

In the simplest terms, I see my ethnographic subject not in terms of ecclesiological boundaries but in terms of a relatedness constituted through liturgical practice, which is a mode of doing theology. For Semela the Assyrian, this relatedness takes shape in adulthood as an attachment to the hymns of the Syriac Orthodox Church and in her Assyrian identity, because that intimate history of relations encompasses the Church of the East's liturgical identity within her sense of herself as a religious subject in a manner entirely consonant with the West Syriac tradition of embodying the truth of Christ's Incarnation through poetic, communal, liturgical practice.

Conclusion: The History That Makes Us Who We Are

Semela's self-ascription as an Assyrian Christian illustrates both the affordances and the limits of using a capital-O "Orthodox" ecclesiological imaginary, at least as constructed by twenty-first-century pro-Chalcedonians, to make ethnographic sense of Syriac Orthodox liturgical subjectivity and sociopolitical identity. On the one hand, the Orthodox frame offers tools to apprehend the sociopolitical potentialities of a liturgically ordered life. On the other hand, the Orthodox frame does not do justice to Syriac Orthodox Christians who feel strong kinship with Chaldeans, Syriac Catholics, and the Assyrian Church of the East, a kinship constituted through a shared historical relationship with classical Syriac language, literature, and liturgical memory but not with Byzantium.

For the Syriac Orthodox in my research, ethnonational belonging is linked to village identity. Village identity is linked to parish belonging, and the sound of the liturgy intoned in each parish materializes a specific regional identity, reproducing an embodied, intersensorial relationship with that history among successive generations. Each of these diverse renditions of the chant are *right* precisely because they embody a personal relationship. Who your teacher was and who your priest was matters to the rightness of the sound because the spiritual crux of the matter is right relationship, and that relationship defines who you are. This is embedded in a broader theological framework in which a right relationship with history is a matter and manner of relating to Christ's Incarnation.

Another way to say this is that culture—the history that makes us who we are—matters theologically, and this is a Christological insight conveyed and reproduced through practice. Does your history make you who you are? Or are you, as Eboni Marshall Turman argues, something other or more than what has happened to you (or your people)? This is as urgent a political and spiritual question today as it was in the late Roman Empire. And the answer may change, as a close reading of St. Cyril makes clear, depending on how you define your terms. If the answer is "yes, your history does make you who you are," then culture matters theologically because it is a living facet of the Mystery of Incarnation. But, I suspect, this is an uncomfortable notion for the heirs of a certain version of Chalcedonianism to grapple with, politically, socially, and emotionally, as well as theologically. (I will leave that grappling for another essay.) For now, my concern is with how an alternate approach to history, a history stripped of its Incarnational meaning, can yield a different set of problems: Certain narratives *of* the past, originating *in* the past, continue to shape the present in ways that go unmarked in ethnography.

My reflections on liturgy as practical theology, embodied historical memory, and sociopolitical formation lead me to argue for a both/and approach: an anthropology of the Syriac world unbound by Chalcedonian ecclesiological imaginations that can also attend methodologically to those power dynamics through which the Syriac world formed, at some times in response to imperial Christianity and, at other times, at a vast remove from its conversations and concerns. Such an anthropology would be sensitive to their areas of overlap *and* their incommensurabilities. It would approach a word like *miaphysite* not as "context" but as an ethnographic entity that does a specific kind of work to bridge a centuries-wide gap between different modes of thinking and doing theology. In facing up to the imperial legacies of Chalcedon, we can expand our sense of what is at stake theologically and politically in Christian thought and practice, which would in turn expand our grasp of how, for better or worse, Christianity shapes worlds beyond itself.

Notes

1. See also Vlad Naumescu, "Becoming Orthodox: The Mystery and Mastery of a Christian Tradition," in *Praying with the Senses: Contemporary Orthodox Christian Spirituality in Practice*, ed. Sonja Luehrmann (Indiana University Press, 2018); and Vlad Naumescu, "Pedagogies of Prayer: Teaching Orthodoxy in South India," *Comparative Studies in Society and History* 61, no. 2 (April 2019): 389–418. Naumescu has documented and analyzed the rigor and centrality of this learning process (what he calls "enskillment") to Syriac Orthodox Christian models of communal and individual personhood in the south Indian context, showing how class and colonialism have shaped its practical application in locally distinctive ways.

2. "Syriac" technically refers to the second-century variety of Aramaic spoken in Edessa (now Urfa in Turkey), capital of the Roman client state of Osrhoene, but then as now it also was commonly used to refer to several varieties of Aramaic spoken throughout the region. The Edessan variant became, throughout late antiquity and into the medieval Islamic world, a transregional Christian literary language, ensuring its longevity where other variants died out. Present-day congregational communities who trace their liturgical traditions to the ancient Syriac-speaking world include traditions of the West Syriac Rite—the Syriac Orthodox Church of Antioch, the Syriac Catholic Church, the Maronite Church, and various Malankara churches of India, as well as those of the East Syriac Rite—the Chaldean Catholic Church, the Assyrian and Ancient Churches of the East, and the Syro-Malabar Church in India. Both rites also continue to be used, with adaptations, among congregations who have adopted Protestant theologies, such as the Reformed Eastern Malankara Mar Thoma Church and the Assyrian Pentecostal Church. Generally speaking, I understand a congregation to be "Syriac" if it maintains a commemorative relationship with the language of ancient Edessa in its liturgical practices.

3. Sarah Bakker Kellogg, *Sonic Icons: Relation, Recognition, and Revival in a Syriac World* (Fordham University Press, 2025).

4. Chalcedonian Orthodoxy specifically refers here to those Orthodox churches (e.g., Greek, Russian, Balkan, Arabic) who follow Byzantine liturgical traditions and who recognize theology grounded in the decisions of the Council of Chalcedon in 451 CE. By non-Chalcedonian churches, I mean the Syriac, Coptic, Armenian, Ethiopic, and Eritrean Orthodox traditions, who followed a

different historical course while still sharing the historical and theological commitments of the first four Christian centuries, including the Council of Nicaea in 325 and its resulting creed.

5. See also Sarah Bakker Kellogg, "Ritual Sounds, Political Echoes: Vocal Agency and the Sensory Cultures of Secularism in the Dutch Syriac Diaspora," *American Ethnologist* 42, no. 3 (August 2015): 431–45; Tala Jarjour, *Sense and Sadness: Syriac Chant in Aleppo* (Oxford University Press, 2018); and Sonja Thomas, *Privileged Minorities: Syrian Christianity, Gender, and Minority Rights in Postcolonial India* (University of Washington Press, 2018).

6. Many Syriac Orthodox Christians who identify as Aramaean tend to focus on historical ties to Roman Syria in the "West," where Aramaic-speaking city-states like Antioch and Edessa were among the very first converts to Christianity. Assyrian Syriac Orthodox Christians, on the other hand, tend to emphasize the historical continuities connecting the Syriac speakers of ancient Edessa and Nisibis to the Mesopotamian "East" in what is now the borderland areas of Syria, southeastern Turkey, Iran, and especially northern Iraq, where the material remains of the ancient empires (Old Assyrian Empire, 2025–1364 BCE; Middle Assyrian Empire, 1363–912 BCE; and Neo-Assyrian Empire, 911–609 BCE) were rediscovered by British colonial archaeologists in the nineteenth century. There is considerable debate over whether Assyrian ethnicity is a modernist construct introduced by colonial powers to the neo-Aramaic-speaking Christians of northern Iraq in a deliberate effort to undermine pan-Arab nationalism; while this debate is too involved to explain here, the key point to understand is that Syriac Christians have been debating whether they are descended from ancient Assyria or the biblical city-states of Aram since at least the ninth century CE. The issue is not whether one or the other narrative is "correct" in naive primordialist terms but rather how imperial and state powers establish or transform the terms of political recognition through which minoritized communities are able to secure for themselves the space needed to reproduce socially. Irrespective of whatever name they are known by others in a given historical moment, Assyrians/Syriacs are "a people" in both an ethnic and a religious sense.

7. Daniel King, ed., *The Syriac World*, 1st ed. (Routledge, 2019). This approach accommodates the fact that the world in question could be understood in different terms depending on one's vantage point within it—just as with the Islamic or Roman or Black Atlantic worlds, local experiences and interpretations of the global can vary widely while nonetheless together constituting that world. My argument focuses on Syriac Orthodox, or West Syriac, understandings of their genealogical relationship with the broader Syriac liturgical family, while recognizing that this relationship is often understood quite differently among East Syriac liturgical traditions. See also Alda

Benjamen, *Assyrians in Modern Iraq: Negotiating Political and Cultural Space* (Cambridge University Press, 2022); Heleen Murre-van den Berg, "Syriac Identity in the Modern Era," in *The Syriac World*, ed. Daniel King (Routledge, 2019).

8. Mark D. Calder, *Bethlehem's Syriac Christians: Self, Nation, and Church in Dialogue and Practice*, Modern Muslim World 4 (Gorgias, 2017); Mark Calder, "Syrian Identity in Bethlehem: From Ethnoreligion to Ecclesiology," *Iran and the Caucasus* 20, nos. 3–4 (December 19, 2016): 297–323.

9. When I refer to liturgy's sociopolitical power, I mean the dialogical, intersubjective, and intersensorial processes through which liturgical practice can form a person's sense of themselves as a relational being—a daughter, a son, a Christian, a citizen, or any other identification that makes an ethical demand upon a subject.

10. To protect the anonymity of research participants, all names are pseudonyms unless otherwise indicated.

11. To be clear: The shift in terminology that I perceived from one summer to the next did not reflect a shift in actual usage among the Dutch Syriac community at that time. Assyrian and Aramaean factions had become firmly entrenched among the Dutch Suryoye through competing cultural associations and advocacy-activist organizations with roots in Turkey and Syria since the early 1980s. The shift reflected, instead, the fluctuating power dynamics among those factions with access to the recently installed bishop, whose arrival from the United States coincided roughly with mine. This in turn shaped their access to me and my access to them, as an interested outsider whose point of entry to the ethnic enclaves of the eastern Dutch cities of Enschede and Hengelo was initially through the monastery. What had changed was with whom I had the opportunity to speak under the eye of the diocesan governance board and, with that change, my understanding of where and how the boundaries of Syriac Orthodox sociality were drawn in a given time or place by different interlocutors.

12. As the majority of my research participants are second- and third-generation Dutch Suryoye, my primary field language is Dutch.

13. In some villages in northern Iraq, dialects of East neo-Aramaic (also called *Sureyt* or *Sureth*, but not to be confused with Central neo-Aramaic Surayt/Ṭuroyo) are still commonly spoken. These dialects are also often referred to as neo-Assyrian. See also Yasmeen S. Hanoosh, *The Chaldeans: Politics and Identity in Iraq and the American Diaspora*, Library of Modern Middle East Studies (I. B. Tauris, 2019).

14. See also Gil Anidjar, *Blood: A Critique of Christianity* (Columbia University Press, 2014); Sarah Bakker Kellogg, "A Racial-Religious Imagination: Syriac Christians, Iconic Bodies, and the Sensory Politics of

Ethical Difference in the Netherlands," *Cultural Anthropology* 36, no. 4 (November 18, 2021): 618–48; and Tomoko Masuzawa, *The Invention of World Religions; or, How European Universalism Was Preserved in the Language of Pluralism* (University of Chicago Press, 2005).

15. Sonja Luehrmann, ed., *Praying with the Senses: Contemporary Orthodox Christian Spirituality in Practice* (Indiana University Press, 2018).

16. Birgit Meyer, ed., *Aesthetic Formations: Media, Religion, and the Senses*, 1st ed. (Palgrave Macmillan, 2009). As Meyer explains, the term "aesthetic formation" clarifies that "a community is not a preexisting entity that expresses itself via a fixed set of symbols, but a formation that comes into being through the circulation and use of shared cultural forms and that is never complete" (4). My own research similarly builds upon this approach by asking about the kinds of relatedness that can be brought into being through these forms.

17. Talal Asad, *Formations of the Secular: Christianity, Islam, Modernity* (Stanford University Press, 2003) Talal Asad, *Genealogies of Religion: Discipline and Reasons of Power in Christianity and Islam* (Johns Hopkins University Press, 1993).

18. Andreas Bandak and Tom Boylston, "The 'Orthodoxy' of Orthodoxy: On Moral Imperfection, Correctness, and Deferral in Religious Worlds," *Religion and Society* 5, no. 1 (January 1, 2014).

19. Calder, *Bethlehem's Syriac Christians*, 280.

20. Calder, *Bethlehem's Syriac Christians*, 267.

21. Calder, *Bethlehem's Syriac Christians*, 260.

22. Calder, *Bethlehem's Syriac Christians*, 265–66.

23. Calder, *Bethlehem's Syriac Christians*, 266. This is one alternative answer to the skeptical question I directed at Semela that summer day in her office: For many Syriac Orthodox Assyrians, twenty-first-century Syriac Christian sociopolitical identity is linked to the pre-Christian Assyrian Empire retroactively through the miracle of Pentecost, which transformed humanity's relationship with the divine.

24. While similar melodic structures are detectable to the well-trained ear, the various schools of Syriac chant developed separately over centuries among congregations of the West Syriac Rite: the School of Tur Abdin in southeastern Turkey, exemplified in the sounds of the monks of Mor Gabriel Monastery; of ancient Edessa, now of the Urfalli parish of St. George's in Aleppo, Syria; of Diyarbakir, also an important center of Kurdish sociopolitical life, in southeastern Turkey; of Sadad, in southwestern Syria; of Kharput, the formerly Armenian town now called Elazig in eastern Turkey; of ancient Takrit, now sung in and around Mosul in northern Iraq; of Malankara in Kerala, India; and of Mardin, the Patriarchal School originating in the Monastery of Deyr el-Zafaran in Turkey but now located in Homs, Syria.

25. Baby Varghese, *The Early History of the Syriac Liturgy: Growth, Adaptation, and Inculturation*, Gottinger Orientforschungen, Band 62 (Harrassowitz Verlag, 2021); Baby Varghese, *West Syrian Liturgical Theology* (Ashgate, 2004), 43. *Teshmeshto*, the closest Syriac equivalent to the English word "liturgy," can refer to "all the ministries and offices of the church" as well as to specific services and celebrations. Varghese, *West Syrian Liturgical Theology*, 42–43. The verb form, *shamesh*, means "to supplicate or intercede," which refers to both the male diaconate specifically and to the vocation of priestly ministry generally. *Shamesh* also forms the basis of the word *mshamshonitho* (pl. *mshamshonithe*), the title given to individual women when they participate in the women's choirs, although the English word "choir" does not quite convey the sacramental role played by the historical Daughters of the Covenant in the West Syriac tradition. As Varghese explains, the Syriac conception of *teshmeshto* "denotes the disposition of availability, a proximity to the sovereign, an attitude of humble and loving readiness to obey and to fulfill his will. . . . *Teshmeshto* is an act of communion, a life in the presence of God, seeking and seeing his face" (43–44).

26. Adam H. Becker, *Revival and Awakening: American Evangelical Missionaries in Iran and the Origins of Assyrian Nationalism* (University of Chicago Press, 2015); Henry Clements, "Documenting Community in the Late Ottoman Empire," *International Journal of Middle East Studies* 51, no. 3 (August 2019): 423–43; Sargon George Donabed and Shamiran Mako, "Ethno-Cultural and Religious Identity of Syrian Orthodox Christians," *Chronos* 19 (April 11, 2019): 71–113; Su Erol, "The Syriacs of Turkey: A Religious Community on the Path of Recognition," *Archives de Sciences Sociales des Religions* 171 (September 1, 2015): 59–80; Shak Hanish, "The Chaldean Assyrian Syriac People of Iraq: An Ethnic Identity Problem," *Digest of Middle East Studies* 17, no. 1 (April 2008): 32–47.

27. Susan Ashbrook Harvey, "Revisiting the Daughters of the Covenant," *Hugoye: Journal of Syriac Studies* 8, no. 1 (February 1, 2011): 125–50; Susan Ashbrook Harvey, *Song and Memory: Biblical Women in Syriac Tradition* (Marquette University Press, 2010); Susan Ashbrook Harvey, "Women and Children in Syriac Christianity: Sounding Voices," in *The Syriac World*, ed. Daniel King (Routledge, 2019); Fergus Millar, "The Evolution of the Syrian Orthodox Church in the Pre-Islamic Period: From Greek to Syriac?," *Journal of Early Christian Studies* 21, no. 1 (2013): 43–92.

28. Cf. Varghese, *The Early History of the Syriac Liturgy*, 56.

29. For a detailed discussion of evidence of the gradual (and in some domains uneven) process of differentiation from 300–800 CE drawn from Syriac patristic writings, archeology, and religious-artistic production, see Bas ter Haar Romeny, ed., *Religious Origins of Nations? The Christian Communities*

of the Middle East (Brill, 2010); and for the same in Syriac-language hagiographical literature, see Jeanne-Nicole Mellon Saint-Laurent, *Missionary Stories and the Formation of the Syriac Churches* (University of California Press, 2015).

30. Susan Ashbrook Harvey, *Asceticism and Society in Crisis: John of Ephesus and the Lives of the Eastern Saints*, Transformation of the Classical Heritage 18 (University of California Press, 1990).

31. As Lois Farag points out, the formalization of the Chalcedonian churches was also a gradual, centuries-long process. Lois Farag, "Review of Missionary Stories and the Formation of the Syriac Churches, by Jeanne-Nicole Mellon Saint-Laurent," *Journal of Early Christian Studies* 25, no. 2 (2017): 329–30.

32. Eboni Marshall Turman, *Toward a Womanist Ethic of Incarnation: Black Bodies, the Black Church, and the Council of Chalcedon* (Palgrave Macmillan, 2013), 31.

33. Marshall Turman, *Toward a Womanist Ethic of Incarnation*, 32–33.

34. Frances M. Young, *From Nicaea to Chalcedon: A Guide to the Literature and Its Background*, 2nd ed. (Baker Academic, 2010).

35. Ben Green, "Nestorius and Cyril: Fifth-Century Christological Division and Recent Progress in Reconciliation," *Concept* 28 (2004).

36. Fergus Millar details this gradual binding in the formation of a Syriac-language "orthodox" scribal tradition, in which "orthodox" is the only consistent term these writers used for themselves to distinguish themselves from supporters of Chalcedon.

37. John McGuckin, "St. Cyril of Alexandria's Miaphysite Christology and Chalcedonian Dyophysitism," *Ortodoksia* 53 (2017): 38.

38. Millar, "Evolution of the Syrian Orthodox Church," 52. Millar notes that *miaphysite*, as a compound noun, is a neologism retroactively applied in the twentieth century to non-Chalcedonian Orthodox churches.

39. McGuckin, "St. Cyril of Alexandria," 38.

40. McGuckin, "St. Cyril of Alexandria," 33.

41. See Marshall Turman, *Toward a Womanist Ethic of Incarnation*. For example, in Latin *persona* means the Greek *prosopon* (the Greek literally meaning "face"), while the Latin *substantia* can mean *either* the Greek *ousia*, meaning "essence" (hence homoousios = of the same essence) *or* the Greek *hypostasis* (in Greek, literally "a distinct reality"). Here, Latin cannot make the subtle distinction between essence and hypostasis that Greek can make, and consequently the Latin version of Chalcedonian theology has, at times, lent itself to more heavily "dyophysite" readings.

THE LIVES OF PRIESTS IN THE COPTIC IMAGINATION

Aaron Michka

Priests can appear as the human face of the institutional church. For the faithful, these are the men—and among the Orthodox and Catholics, they are only men—who oversee liturgies and provide pastoral care. For anthropologists, priests are often the inescapable brokers of community access and sources of insider knowledge. Yet while both perspectives tend to locate priests at the center of church life, these clergymen do not remain there. In this chapter, I approach priests as ambulatory agents of the church, as men who interact with the laity within and, more importantly, at the periphery of the ecclesial domain. This reframing echoes the tendency in anthropology to study religion in both its official and popular registers. But my aspiration here is slightly different. Instead, I argue that studying priests beyond the church walls shows how the church is reproduced through social labor; that is, how priests, along with the laity, work together to expand or limit the reach of the church's authority. I will focus on Coptic Christians in Egypt, but this approach might be fruitful in other contexts where there is a clear division between priests and laity.[1]

Why study how priests extend the church and its authority in social contexts? For one, it helps us see how the priesthood as a form of religious authority is at least partially dependent on the recognition of the laity. One point I will emphasize in the following pages is how in the context of Egypt, the priest's authority is limited. Outside the church, the laity can demarcate when and where this authority applies. To make this claim is not to suggest that the interactions of priests and laity should be reduced to power struggles. The priesthood is a highly idealized office, and ideas about what priests should and should not do tend to flow from the theological foundation of the priesthood. One might say that, in this setting, the laity limit the authority of priests not out of disregard, but respect.

As anthropologists of Christianity have shown, studying members of the religious "elite"—the clergy, members of church hierarchy, vowed religious—helps us see how church leaders model and extend aspects of the religious community they serve.[2] For instance, in reflecting upon the repetitive nature of Catholicism, Maya Mayblin sees in the priesthood "the quintessence of repetition." (2019, 135). Through the rite of ordination, the priest assumes an identity that links him, via apostolic succession, not only to generations of fellow priests but to the original apostles, as well as to the person of Jesus Christ. The repetition baked into the priesthood reflects and draws validity from a characteristic of the broader Catholic tradition. For Mayblin, this recognition of repetition as part of the Catholic DNA perpetuated by the priesthood allows for her to explore how even dissidents, such as Catholics who advocate for female ordination, follow this style of thought. The priesthood, apart from being a church office, also provides a crucial reference point for thinking about the Catholic Church and what it means to be Catholic.

Mayblin follows clergy and lay activists who think and engage with each other in an explicitly theological way. Yet as this chapter will show, the laity encounter priests in many different settings, and theological discussion can be an afterthought. In examining the various ways priests and laity interact outside the church, I argue that we can see how the church is extended and, in a sense, reproduced in settings beyond the formal sanctuary. This argument hinges on a distinction that is important for Christians in Egypt and likely for Orthodox communities elsewhere: that is, the distinction between the church in its immediate, material form and the church as an interactive framework that extends across space and time. Theologians would find this point rather redundant, as membership to the Body of Christ is certainly not confined to church liturgies.[3] Social life, however, does not always conform to the strictures of theology. In my experience, Christians in Egypt most often use the word "church" (*kinisa*) in a physical sense: the building with fixed boundaries and where liturgies are celebrated, the most important being, at least for Orthodox and Catholics, the Divine Liturgy (Abdelsayed 2014). In the Durkheimian sense, the church building is a sacred place, a place set apart. This attention to the physical church also has a political dimension. Christians in Egypt are a religious minority, and the church in its material form reflects an ecclesial domain that is set up and against a civil society influenced, in complex ways, by Islamic and secular ideals (Asad 2003; Agrama 2012; Mahmood 2015).[4] The point I wish to emphasize is that commonplace talk about churches in Egypt tends to emphasize—but is not limited to—this physical, stable, and sacred place. It is where priests do their most important work. It is the threshold that priests cross when they enter into the daily affairs of the laity.

I come to this topic as an ethnographer and a Catholic priest. One might say that the priesthood located me at the center of the lives of the Copts that I studied in Egypt. I presented myself as a priest during fieldwork: I put on the black cassock, grew a beard, and always carried the handheld cross that is de rigueur for clerics in Egypt. Few of my contacts fully understood my work as an ethnographer. In this sense, I lived at their margins, always a step or two behind the action. But having merged the two identities through my stance in the field, I came to see how there is an uncanny symmetry to priests and ethnographers. Both are invested in observing, understanding, and even helping the lay members of these church communities. Both are insiders and outsiders, people, typically with advanced educations and outside funding sources, who come to the community out of personal interest but also professional obligation. They both have unusual and interesting insights but stand opposite each other in relation to the community they study or serve. Ethnographers have a myriad of experiences in the field, but many approach their subjects first as strangers, then with familiarity, but nonetheless as outsiders. Much of the magic of ethnography happens in this pull between familiarity and strangeness. The same occurs with priests, especially, I want to suggest, in these zones at the spatial and conceptual periphery of the church.

A Coptic Town in Upper Egypt

I conducted fieldwork from 2016 to 2018 in Upper Egypt, the part of the country that extends along the Nile valley south of Cairo. My focus was on the rural town of al-'Aziya, which is located on the western edge of the valley just north of Asyut, the largest city in the region and the capital of the Asyut Governorate. Unlike in previous generations, only a minority of the residents now farm for a living, with most working in small-scale business ventures, such as in carpentry, textile production, or refurbishing and reselling automobiles (by far the most lucrative industry in the town). The Nile valley in this middle part of Egypt is dotted with towns of similar size, all bound by an intense sense of community.

I was drawn to this town because I was interested in studying the relationship between different Christian denominations. This town is almost entirely Christian, a rarity in Egypt. Of its 55,000 residents, only two hundred are Muslim. The rest belong to a variety of denominations: Coptic Orthodox, Coptic Catholic, Evangelical, Pentecostal, and Baptist. Given the town's Christian majority, one might expect clergy to have more authority here than elsewhere in Egypt. In fact, the opposite is true. The clergy I knew seemed to encounter challenges to their authority at every step.

The multidenominational character of al-'Aziya influences the way that town residents understand and interact with priests and other clergy. In this sense, this town is a microcosm of the multidenominational nature of Christianity in Egypt. Whereas the large majority of Christians in Egypt belong to the Coptic Orthodox Church, there is a smaller number of Protestants, most of whom belong to an independent offshoot of the Presbyterian Church of the United States, known officially as the Synod of the Nile but referred to locally as the "Evangelical Church" (Sharkey 2008). The membership of the Evangelical Church in Egypt is now almost entirely Egyptian, and there is a small yet prominent Evangelical community in al-'Aziya. The roots of this local community can be traced back to the region's wealthy landowning families, some of whom, in the late nineteenth and early twentieth centuries, left the Orthodox Church to join the new Evangelical Church (Wissa 2000). There are also a growing number of Pentecostals in Egypt, a community that traces its origins in Egypt to the first half of the twentieth century (Nagib 2019). As elsewhere, it can be difficult to determine the size of this denomination's membership, in part because various official churches fall under the umbrella of Pentecostalism. In al-'Aziya, there is one established Pentecostal church, known as the "Apostolic Church," and three new branches of this church are currently under construction. Out of all the denominations present, these Pentecostal churches have the most fluid membership.

Alongside Evangelicals and Pentecostals in al-'Aziya, there are also Catholics. This community was the one that claimed me as their own, though my ecclesial commitments did not exactly match theirs. There are only roughly three hundred thousand Catholics in Egypt (Mayeur-Jaouen 2019), and most belong to the Coptic Catholic Church, a "uniate" church with its own liturgy and canon law that is in communion with Rome (Hamilton 2006). In terms of piety and worship, the Coptic Catholic Church resembles the Coptic Orthodox Church far more than the Latin Rite of the Catholic Church. Even some of the Catholics were confused over what exactly distinguished these two churches, and the Orthodox and Catholics would occasionally accuse each other of capitalizing on this ignorance. Yet at the end of the day, the Coptic Orthodox Church stands apart from the Catholic Church, and all other denominations, in terms of its deep historical and cultural reach in Egypt. This superiority is reflected in the local landscape. There are two Catholic churches in the town and six Orthodox—an extraordinary number for just one town.

An important feature of this multidenominational landscape is how the priesthood, as a social identity and status, takes on parallel forms in different churches. In other words, the priesthood is both a religious office and a specific and highly visible social class, a conceptual and semantic convergence that can result in slippage in ordinary social interaction. Catholic and Orthodox priests (*kahin* / p. *kahana*) wear similar outfits and are ministers of the sacraments: a responsibility that unites them with the priesthood of Christ and distinguishes them from the laity. When people talked about priests, they did not always make it clear whether they were referring to Catholics or Orthodox, and I will echo this ambiguity here. Matters are different for Protestant pastors (*qass* / p. *qusus*), who are easily recognized by their Western-style outfits: khakis, a button-down shirt, possibly a jacket, and the Bible always tucked under an arm.[5] While they are technically neither priests nor sacramental ministers, Protestant pastors celebrate weddings and baptisms that draw a wide range of people from the town and therefore enjoy broad sympathy and respect among the different denominations.

As priests and pastors are the representatives of their respective institutions, they also reflect the global nature of their churches. These various kinds of Christians know they belong to communities that extend beyond their town, region, and even country. The nature of these broader communities is a matter for expert opinion, so I found myself occasionally explaining how Italy, Russia, or the United States fit within the multidenominational landscape of Egypt. That I was never certain whether I was answering these questions as a priest or an ethnographer highlights another way that these two figures overlap. Even in a remote place like al-ʿAziya, where politics is very local, the presence of the priest, like an ethnographer, stands as a witness of the broader, if not somewhat ambiguous, social worlds to which town residents take themselves to belong.

Family Matters

What I want to explore in this section is how the authority of the priest operates in the realm of local politics. This topic is worth considering not just because it shows how church authority works in the rural setting of Upper Egypt but also because it demonstrates how the laity might play a determinative role in what priests can and cannot do. How do these laity-clergy interactions, particularly in the realm of politics, come to define the scope of priestly authority?

First, some background on Upper Egypt. This region is known for its conservative culture, one marked by attachment to religion, kinship, and "customs and traditions" (*'adat wa taqalid*) (Gran 2004). These core values are typically held by Copts and Muslims alike. Social identity is tightly connected to one's family (*'a'ila*), which includes one's household and the extended patriline. When one of the Catholic priests I worked with in al-'Aziya welcomed visitors from Cairo or another city in Egypt, he would emphasize this point: "Here there are *families!*" The clergy are not exempt from these kinship networks, though their relationship to families and family politics is complex.

The traditional model of priesthood for Copts is itself rooted in kinship. In al-'Aziya, there is a family named "the Priests" (*al-qusus*). This family has traditionally supplied the various pastors who have served the oldest Orthodox church in town, one whose history extends back to the founding of the town in the early nineteenth century. For many, the connection of kinship and priestly service reflects a simpler, more harmonious time. One elderly man who had grown up next to the old Orthodox church and attended it frequently throughout his youth, explained that this model had restrained the ambitions of priests. In those days, he said, priests were content to live like everyone else in the town. Payment would be expected from each family, some livestock or agricultural produce, or maybe even a single Egyptian pound.

Over the course of the twentieth century, however, the different Christian denominations in Egypt professionalized their clergy, resulting in a style of behavior that creates a buffer between the identity of priests or pastors and this traditional network of kinship relations. Evangelicals were already training future Egyptian clergy at Asyut College in the early half of the century (Sharkey 2008), as was the Coptic Catholic Church at that time (Mayeur-Jaouen 2019). It was only in the second half of the century that the Coptic Orthodox Church expanded its theological training such that even a remote town like al-ʿAziya might experience its effects (see Guirguis and van Doorn-Harder 2011). In fact, the Catholic church in al-ʿAziya even marks its origins with the refusal of the Orthodox bishop to ordain a young man who had been promised the priesthood but did not want to go to the Theological College. This young man was married with young children, and going off to the seminary would have placed financial strains on his family—evidence of the new clerical structure that was emerging. This new clergy, across denominations, would be more mobile, more educated, and more exposed to the broader world.[6]

Apart from explicitly religious signifiers, such as the distinct wardrobes of the clergy, this professionalization has also created various secular ways by which the clergy signal their distinction from the laity. A common complaint among the laity is that the clergy are always the first to obtain luxury goods: air conditioners, cars, and smartphones. While the items reflect the level of income a priest might expect, they also point toward the broader social network that priests enjoy, which would necessitate this increased ability to travel and communicate. A case in point would be the automobile. I sometimes wondered why priests tended to drive instead of walking when doing their house visits. But when I started to walk the town myself, I quickly learned why. Out of almost every house would emerge someone who would shout "Come in, Father!"—an invitation not intended to be taken literally but that would still slow my progress. As fifteen-minute walks started to take over an hour, I saw the car for what it offers priests: a means of streamlining social engagement in a place where demands on one's time abound.

This cultivated detachment is not just a byproduct of this new professionalism. It also has the practical, if perhaps unintended, effect of insulating priests from what one Orthodox subdeacon described to me as "occasions of honor." Concerns about honor cut across virtually every aspect of social life in Upper Egypt, from domestic affairs to everyday interactions on the street and in the workplace. What this subdeacon had in mind, however, were blood feuds between families: a perennial problem that has been aggravated by the recent arrival of military-grade weapons. I had asked this subdeacon if priests would ever use their authority to bring these feuds to a peaceful end. "Priests would never involve themselves in such a thing," he replied, adding that any intrusion by a priest would put him, and maybe even his family, at risk. Rather, priests can provide council and support, but only through the official channels of confession or pastoral visits. In every other way, the office of the priesthood both protected and restricted them from these affairs of honor.

I want to linger on this point because this sidelining of the priest from local politics might be understood as part of a broader effort at keeping the church sanctuary (to which the priest is closely linked) free from this kind of disruption. For instance, while people are keenly aware of ongoing feuds, this topic is never mentioned in homilies or in any public fashion. Only in confession will people speak about this topic. If feuding families belong to the same church, they might try to avoid each other, either by not attending services or switching to another church. In an exception that proves the rule, the only time I witnessed the clear intrusion of local politics was when a Catholic priest resigned his post as associate pastor. When word spread that this decision reflected long-standing disagreements between this priest and the priest who served as pastor, members of a politically influential family sprang into action: They placed a chain around the church's main doors, stationed an armed guard nearby, and declared that the church would only be reopened when either the two priests reconciled or the pastor left as well. People in the town murmured that it was unthinkable that two priests could bicker outside the sanctuary but then celebrate the Divine Liturgy together. This kind of conflict, while common in the everyday life of the town, did not belong in the church.

The consequence of this close attachment to a professional identity and the purity of the church is that, in the flow of actual politics, priests have very little authority. That said, there was one time when a priest in al-ʿAziya oversaw a reconciliation session (*sulh*), the customary way in which vendettas are brought to an end in Egypt. It was organized by a local Catholic priest. Town residents often complained about these blood feuds and how families were reluctant to participate in these reconciliation sessions.[7] When I would ask why this particular *sulh* was successful, residents would talk about how the priest in charge had recruited various prominent officials to serve as witnesses. In the words of one of those who had been present: "Then we made a truly great reconciliation [*sulh*] with the Director of Security and Director of Investigations. . . . Our Catholic priest invited all these people, all of them, important people, members of the Egyptian Senate and the like. And one among them was the Director of Intelligence. Lots of important people."

Perhaps the most obvious interpretation of this description is that the *sulh* succeeded because of the overwhelming presence of state authorities. Yet I think it is also true that it succeeded because these authorities, all of them Muslims coming from nearby regional hubs, had been recruited by a priest. In my experience, town residents prized their autonomy and would not be eager to invite outsiders to help sort out their affairs. But the priest, while lacking authority of his own in this "occasion of honor," could give legitimacy to this gathering and convene these different groups through his presence.

Regardless how the success of this *sulh* is interpreted, the fact that it is the only example of its kind hints at the difficulties a priest would face if he tried to curtail the violence of blood feuds. It takes being creative, politically savvy, and courageous to organize this kind of reconciliation. Given the professionalization of the priesthood, with its emphasis on cultivated detachment from local politics, these kinds of character traits are not likely to be encouraged or rewarded.

The Church-Adjacent

In reflecting on the life of the priest beyond the church, we might also ask: What exactly is the church? Here I want to argue that this question is not just theoretical but rather takes shape in the daily life of Christians in Egypt. The reason why this question is relevant is because church sanctuaries are, at least in Egypt, typically surrounded by several other buildings. For instance, one might find an older "historical" (*athari*) church, a courtyard where families can gather, and a residential building for priests in the church compound: zones peripheral to the church sanctuary I refer to as the "church-adjacent." The question of where the church begins and ends is therefore often not straightforward, and this touch of ambiguity is reflected in the different interactive frameworks that guide social behavior in these related but distinct settings: The sanctuary calibrates a embodied sense of reverence, for instance, whereas the courtyard facilitates an easygoing sense of play and security afforded by the watchful eyes of church members but clearly not a ritual space in itself. To draw on the work of Ilana Gershon, this church-adjacent space might be thought of as "porous";

that is, the boundaries that distinguish the ritual activity of the church and the everyday affairs of the world are "porous," such that "interweaving or moving between these two social orders forces people on the ground to become explicit analysts of the contradictions in their situation" (2019, 406). In following the priest's interactions with the laity in these church-adjacent sites, I argue, we can see how these porous boundaries are navigated and managed.

How porous boundaries create problems can be illustrated by a simple example: the priest's residence Orthodox priests typically live with their wife and children in a house in town. For Catholic priests, things are not as simple. All the Catholic priests in al-'Aziya during my fieldwork were celibate.[8] They tended to live in apartments adjacent to the church, which residents referred to as the rectory or priest residency. This household was different from all others in that there were no women or children. It is not a "house" in the traditional sense, yet neither is it part of the church. Given the proximity of this residency to the church, it is highly visible, and residents keep tabs of who comes and goes. But the priests—at least the Catholic priests in town—also considered this domestic space their own. These apartments are owned by the diocese, and the priests who lived in this church-adjacent zone felt like it was theirs to manage as they saw fit.

When I first arrived in al-'Aziya, the status of my residency was a major concern for the people in my town. They wanted to find me a house in town. For me, this issue was mostly a nuisance. It was something I wanted to move beyond so I could get on with my research. But nothing I did would put the issue to rest. Initially, I stayed with the Catholic priest who had built a house on the edge of town, but later, for security reasons, we decided it would be best for me to commute every day from a nearby city. My lack of a stable living arrangement grated on the town's residents, many of whom insisted that, as a priest, I should be allowed to stay in one of the properties owned by the church. A group of men from the town appealed to the local priests on my behalf. Having no luck, they even went to the Catholic bishop to see if he might allow me to reside in a place simply referred to as the "House of the Offering" (*bayt al-qurban*). This "house" is a small apartment located above the large room where the bread for the liturgy would be prepared. It is a space that the people in the town felt they had control over and could therefore offer to me, as a good host might do for a guest. But these attempts were stonewalled by the priests, who considered this building to be the property of the church (technically it is owned by the Catholic diocese). Tension over this issue continued for about a year, and it was fueled by competing interests: the obligation the towns-people felt to properly host me versus the hesitation of the pastors, who felt they could not deny me this space outright yet were reluctant to let me inhabit this church-adjacent space.

The priest's residence, the House of the Offering: Who controls these places that exist neither in the town nor squarely in the church proper? This concern was framed and addressed through the idiom of hospitality: a fa-miliar, slightly dated, yet always relevant theme in studies of the Middle East (Shryock 2008). The laity had approached me as a host might a guest for a reason, as this mode of interaction is how the laity expect to interact with priests outside the context of the liturgy. This attitude is anchored by a tendency among the laity to see the town's churches as belonging to the people of the town: These are their churches, and the priests and the dio-cese are the custodians and servants of this local patrimony. I make these claims not because families would speak of priests explicitly as guests of the town. Rather, it was through patterns of exchange that the laity solidi-fied this particular arrangement with their priests. People of goodwill from the town would often stop by to offer food at the priest's residence. Dur-ing visits I would occasionally be given small donations of money—not for the church, but for my own needs (feeling guilty, I would always turn down this act of generosity). If a lay person had a car, he would insist on providing transportation for a priest, as one would do if hosting a guest under one's roof. These displays of hospitality initiate a pattern of interac-tion: Hosts offer, guests refuse but then, out of respect for their hosts, relent, thus being freed of any accusation of greed (Pitt-Rivers 2017a, 179). Underlying this pageantry, however, is a clear power differential between host and guest, and outside the church, the laity attempt to outdo one an-other in their attempts at being good hosts to priests.

Hospitality serves as a powerful framework for priest-laity interactions, in a very different way, within the confines of the church sanctuary. In fact, themes of hospitality are woven into the Divine Liturgy itself. The church becomes a kind of domestic space in which people gather for a sacred meal. Subdeacons bake the Eucharistic bread (*qurban*) near the church, which is consecrated and is distributed by the priests to the faithful. After the service ends, bread that was not consecrated is given to families as they leave the church. In his account of the Eucharist among Orthodox Christians in Ethiopia, Tom Boylston notes that, as a ritual, the Divine Liturgy "is manifestly not the same as the hosting of a guest in one's home, but they draw on the same patterns and techniques—especially those of feeding—in order to produce organized, meaningful, morally charged power relations" (2018, 127). The same can be said about Orthodox and Catholics in Egypt, though one might add a further detail. Priests, in their ritual capacity, seem to exercise a role as host, though ultimately the church is a house of God, and it is God who, through the Divine Liturgy, feeds his people.

Outside the church, the laity host priests; inside the church, priests, along with God, host the laity. These relatively stable frameworks collide in spaces I have named as church-adjacent not just because these are liminal zones of interaction but also because there are lay people who have a foot in both worlds (and the same, of course, can be said of the clergy). To choose a most prominent example, lay ministers (*khadim* / p. *khudam*) are the young adults who administer—and have strong views about—parish activities beyond the official liturgies. They also oversee the finances of the church.[9] These lay ministers often do their work in the church hall, and their relationship with the clergy involves acts of hospitality. When the priests visited these events, the lay ministers would treat them as one might treat a guest. The priests would be ushered to a seat that had been reserved, and cold soda and snacks would appear. These gestures of hospitality always struck me as pedestrian, especially when considered in light of the importance of hospitality everywhere else in town. Perhaps this subdued form of hosting reflects the considerable tension that can take hold between the lay ministers and clergy. The separation of responsibilities over the church is not entirely clear, so there would be occasional jostling to control aspects of church life beyond the sacraments and liturgies. Once I even witnessed a public shouting match between two ministers and a priest in the middle of a gathering of ministers. In the midst of this instability, hospitality can become a more subtle, and therefore preferable, means of managing this ambiguous space.

By focusing on these church-adjacent spaces—the priest's residence, the church hall—I want to emphasize that the boundaries separating church from town are not always obvious, neither for the ethnographer nor for the people who inhabit them. They are porous boundaries; work is required to clarify how such boundaries should be maintained. In this section I have focused on the way that hospitality frames the interaction between laity and priests at these thresholds. The power of hospitality is that its salient themes—the morally charged role of guest and host, the importance of food—can be found in the most basic social interactions in Upper Egypt and are echoed in the elaborate rituals of the Divine Liturgy. In bridging the town and the ritual activity of the church, it is a useful way for people to clarify where the domain of the church ends, which is to say: when a priest ceases to be a host and becomes a guest.

Ecclesial Diplomacy

So far, I have treated church-related spaces in an abstract way, if only to isolate certain forms of interpersonal behavior. The reality is that churches in Egypt must also be understood in light of the status of Christians as a religious minority. The guiding legal principle in the state's relationship with the country's official religions is *nizam al-'amm*, or "the public order."[10] Concerns over managing this public order can justify state intervention in religious matters, which has the result of religious institutions relying on the state for recognition and support (Agrama 2012). For Christians, this arrangement has the consequence of granting them a collective status as "Christian," which appears on their government-issued identification. While matters are much more complex when it comes to family law, where denominational difference is very consequential, the state in practice tends to view Christians as an undifferentiated collectivity.

This legal framing in turn can motivate how members of the state work with and alongside the clergy. Angie Heo (2013) offers a useful case in this regard in her study of a miraculous icon of the Virgin Mary that had been put on display in a Coptic household in the Egyptian city of Port Said. For the Coptic Orthodox hierarchy and the Egyptian state, this placement of an object of public devotion outside the confines of the institutional church was problematic, and both ecclesial and state actors used their respective authority to move the image into a church sanctuary. What I want to emphasize in this example is the shared interest by members of the state and clergy in maintaining the integrity of official Orthodox sacred space. These same concerns can also be found among other denominations, as all Christians in Egypt must deal, at some level, with the state's investment in protecting, and also observing, the churches and other places where Christians gather. What I want to argue in this section, then, is that within this broader legal framework and investment by the state, a curious fellowship among the clergy of Egypt's different Christian denominations has developed.

To do so, I first would like to consider how this interdenominational fellowship plays itself out in public and private as priests and pastors move beyond their own church walls. While these relationships among clergy from different churches can unfold in numerous ways behind closed doors—I saw both deep friendships and animosity—this shared status as leaders of the country's Christian minority elicits a peculiar style of public diplomacy. In the rural communities of Upper Egypt, all priests and pastors will visit one another's churches if there is noteworthy event, such as the installment of a new pastor or the anniversary celebration of a church. Given the intensity of the theological debates that I would hear among some of the laity in al-'Aziya, I found that these visits introduced a bit of levity to the religious character of the town. When the Evangelical Church in al-'Aziya held a large event in commemoration of the five hundredth anniversary of the Protestant Reformation, I heard no complaints that all the Catholic priests had attended and been given seats of honor.

While the public-facing nature of this diplomacy emphasizes the unity of Christians in Egypt, I found that Catholic priests and Protestant pastors would pay these visits more often than their Orthodox peers. This openness is not surprising, since Catholics and Protestants are themselves minorities among Egypt's six million Christians. The Coptic Orthodox Church has much more political, social, and religious capital than other churches. It claims the many native Egyptian saints as its own, it has a vibrant network of historical monasteries throughout the country, and it has political clout through the central importance of the Orthodox pope, who represents all the nation's Christians before the Egyptian state. Outnumbered and eager for support among other Christians, these non-Orthodox clergy often include one another in different church activities and rituals. For instance, I learned to come prepared to preach when visiting Protestant churches in Upper Egypt, as the pastor would likely invite me, as a Catholic priest, to participate if a prayer service were taking place. The Orthodox do not have the same practice, and over time I had to master the delicate art of visiting Orthodox churches while not putting the clergy in the awkward position of explaining why I would not be invited to address the congregation.

This ecumenical diplomacy, while influenced by the state, is also motivated by the fact that Christian families can be split across churches. An important example in this regard is the typical Upper Egyptian funeral. As is the custom, the men from the deceased's family will sit in chairs that have been placed in the street nearest the house of the deceased. These chairs are covered by a large tarp; other chairs are available for men from other families who have come to mourn. The laity expect the clergy from all the town's churches to show up. When a priest or pastor arrives, he greets each person seated under the tarp and then moves to an empty chair in the middle of the gathering. Each clergyman will preach, sometimes while another is waiting his turn. I once sat through a lengthy sermon given by a young and zealous Evangelical preacher about the absolute necessity of faith (and the futility of works) for salvation. The Catholic priest I was with listened calmly and, when his turn came, delivered his own potted sermon, all while an Orthodox priest took a seat and started to wait his turn. The deceased was a Catholic, though this denominational identity seemed to matter little, as these proceedings occurred with virtually every death in town. This cooperation across denominations was never discussed or elaborated upon. No one among either the clergy or laity would have labeled it as ecumenism. It was rather something that was simply expected by the families of the town, and the clergy, for the most part, was happy to oblige them.

One conclusion that can be drawn from these observations is that the authority of priests and pastors depends not just on the laity from their own congregations. This point can be extended even further when considering the attention clergy receive from the security state itself. Through their pastoral work, including but not limited to confessions, clergy are privy to an incredible amount of sensitive information. It should not be surprising, then, that the agents from the security state paid close attention to the clergy. During my fieldwork, I learned that clergy from across the town's churches interacted with plainclothes officers from the intelligence service, who would regularly pay visits to the two Catholic priests I worked alongside. These priests considered these visits something that both sides benefited from. Over cups of tea, the agent, who would be known to the priest, would ask some questions about the affairs of the church and, in turn, would share some information about local politics. I never saw evidence that the clergy betrayed anything said in confidence, though I would occasionally hear concerns from residents about whether or not a particular priest or pastor was trustworthy. Priests and pastors have to walk a fine line when it comes to managing these relationships with agents of the state.

This clerical fellowship stems from both their shared status as leaders of Egypt's Christian community and a pervasive, homegrown sense of ecumenism. It is true that some members of the laity can be very zealous, even fanatical, in their denominational commitment. It was not uncommon for me to hear disputes about church doctrine aired in public during my fieldwork. But far more pervasive is a softer, quieter form of ecumenism, one that emphasizes the unity of Christians, especially in the face of the mounting political and social problems that they face. These simple acts of diplomacy, in other words, might have seemed pro forma for some of the clergy. But this movement beyond their own congregations is facilitated by the legal framework in which all Christians in Egypt live, and it is spurred by the laity, who themselves have conflicting views as to how their own denominational commitments relate to the more expansive, and ultimately mysterious, communion of Christians to which they belong.

The Priest's Body

Having considered the various layers of the priest's social life outside the church, here I consider a more intimate tension, one that flows from the priest's body. In order to develop this idea, I want to introduce a distinction between popular piety and the stance of the institutional church. My claim is that the priest's body is a point of focus for both perspectives since the priest celebrates the Divine Liturgy and, through his embodied presence, consecrates the Eucharist. It is not unusual, of course, for popular piety to diverge from what might be considered orthodox practice. Popular gatherings for a saint's feast days will involve both formal liturgies within the church or monastery and festive activities that range from tattoo booths, carnival games, and markets for religious knickknacks, all of which gets folded into the celebration of the saint.[11] What makes the priest's body exceptional is that, being both subject and object, he cannot easily distance himself from acts of piety he may find problematic. How his body is treated becomes an important and unavoidable site where laity and priests negotiate this relationship between popular piety and the institutional church.

The concept at the heart of popular piety is *baraka*, or God's blessing. For Coptic Christians, *baraka* can be accessed through physical contact with sacred objects, such as relics, icons, or water or oil that has been blessed (Heo 2018). Visits to churches or monasteries typically involve touching these objects, sometimes in rapid succession. The Orthodox and Catholic priests I came to know did not object to this style of worship, though they would want to sharpen the distinction between sacraments and sacramentality. In their view, it is the sacraments, and the Eucharist in particular, that serve as the most powerful form of God's blessing, which might better be understood as grace.[12] *Baraka* and sacramental grace might be thought to flow from two overlapping, somewhat interwoven, yet ultimately nonsynchronized channels that structure the practice of faith for many Upper Egyptian Copts.

Both *baraka* and sacramental grace flow through the priest. As a sacramental minister, the priest is a key node in the ecclesial economy of grace. But he is a dispenser of *baraka*, and the faithful seek *baraka* from him. For instance, it is customary for Orthodox and Catholic Copts to kiss either the hand-held cross or the actual hands of priests. Families are happy to have visiting priests hold their children in their arms. Occasionally on a visit someone would touch my black clerical robe and then kiss his or her hand—a sign that *baraka* has been "taken." One time, a mother had her son write a few prayer intentions on a scrap of paper. She then instructed me to put it in my pocket and walk around with it "on me" (*'alayk*). Some of these gestures can be attributed to signs of respect, though seeking *baraka* is itself a sign of respect: It is how one approaches and interacts with any holy person, living or dead.

Orthodox and Catholic priests have different reactions to this kind of treatment from the laity. I spent much more time with Catholic priests, all of whom were from small towns in Upper Egypt. They tended to distance themselves from these acts of piety. At a wedding reception, one Catholic priest washed his hands and tossed the water in the air toward some of the men in the room. He winked at me and laughed: He was gently parodying a part of the Divine Liturgy when the priest washes his hands and flings water into the assembly, at which point some pious worshipers, having felt some droplets coming from the priest's hands, will bow and cross themselves. Some of these Catholic priests viewed popular piety, especially as it pertained to the holiness of the priest, as an aspect of the Coptic Orthodox Church that Catholics did not share. As for the Orthodox priests I knew, they usually accepted these displays of reverence with magnanimity, as they tended to move through much of everyday life as if it were an extension of the liturgy. In short, the attitudes of priests toward their own ability to generate *baraka* could scaffold ideas about denominational difference, which also reflected the ways that these churches navigated the divide between piety and the integrity of the institutional church.

The issue of how the laity should relate to a priest as a privileged source of *baraka* is most apparent in the house visit. As mentioned earlier, many interactions between clergy and laity are framed by hospitality, and the people of al-'Aziya evaluate their priests and pastors in terms of the frequency of such visits. I learned and adopted the format of these visits during my fieldwork. The visit would involve the entire family, or at least everyone who was at home. Plentiful food and drink would be offered. The visit is an opportunity for direct contact with the priest. People would ask for advice and request prayers. The visit would go on as long as the priest desired. I learned that asking someone to bring out a metallic mug of water for me to bless would help bring the visit to an end. Then everyone would take my hand and kiss it, or kiss my handheld cross, and insist that I stay a little longer.

This visit seems straightforward, though this unique style of interaction depends on the singular distinction of the priest. His presence triggers different patterns of behavior. For instance, women can sit unaccompanied with priests—a privilege that would not be extended to any other man beyond her own family. As in liturgies, some of the expectations about the mixing of women and men are temporarily lifted when a priest is involved. This extension of church behavior into the home occurs in other ways as well. In the blessing of the house, the priest makes holy water, which is then sprinkled throughout the house. The common prayer with the family would be brief but solemn, and residents would participate with reverence similar to that of the Divine Liturgy.

While there is nothing controversial about these house visits, there is an important difference between the liturgies of the church and these informal house blessings. In the former, the priest, as a sacramental minister, is the means through which God works in the sacred liturgies; in the latter, his authority to generate *baraka* might be attributed to power inherent to himself.[13] This subtle distinction is reflected in the gentle back and forth that would take place between laity and clergy during these visits. Residents want priests to visit them in the home. Priests, on the other hand, want residents to attend church more faithfully (despite the overt religiosity of al-'Aziya, church attendance across the board was relatively low). It is of course easier to access *baraka* from a priest than to partake of the demanding liturgical life of the church, which requires fasting and regular confession to receive the Eucharist. Yet residents would also speak about these visits as something owed them. Being a priest means being available to channel God's blessings to his people. On occasion I would hear people say that "the priest is *baraka*," and I think some residents took that claim very seriously.

Further evidence of this view of the priest's body as a source of *baraka* can be found in the tendency among some Christians to objectify and evaluate different parts of the priest's body. A good example: the priest's voice. "Your voice is . . . fine," a subdeacon once told me, mercifully, before critiquing the voice of another priest in town. He was referring to the chanting that the priest performs in the Divine Liturgy, which would be amplified by loudspeakers directed out onto the streets in al-ʿAziya.[14] The voice of a holy priest can even cause miracles, an idea echoed, perhaps originating in the power of Jesus's voice as described in the New Testament (John 10:27, Acts 9:7). I heard a story of the healing of a lame woman, another of the miraculous protection of a church from a crowd of strangers set on violence, all through a particular priest's voice. This attention to the voice even extends beyond Catholics and the Orthodox. When I consulted with a female prayer leader (and part-time exorcist) from the Pentecostal church about what to do with a mother with a temperamental child, she faulted me for not having breathed on the child. "You must breathe on him," she instructed me, as the mouth is a part of the body that channels the Holy Spirit. The hands and the feet—especially for priests or monks who walked in old sandals or shoeless—also receive similar attention. One man even corrected my posture: "It's important for you as a priest to sit like a man."

In isolating these different parts of the body, we can see how the link between subjectivity and agency is liable to be disrupted, in the lives of priests, with their agency being "mediated by gods and other actors" (Johnson 2021, 9). Priests might be said to inhabit this hybrid self, containing both one's own agency and the agency of God. The point I wish to stress is that lay discussion and interaction with the priest's body raises questions about the various ways that God channels blessings through the church and its clergy. It should be remembered that the unity of the body is as ideational as it is physical (Merleau-Ponty 1962), and the unity and nature of the priest's body is produced through these interactions with the laity, both within the context of the liturgy and beyond. As in previous sections, this attention toward the priest's body can show how ideas about the church—such as its ability to generate and distribute God's blessing—are processed and discussed at the church's periphery.

Theology, Priests, and the Household

While the authority of priests tends to weaken in social domains beyond the church in Upper Egypt, there is one important exception: reforming moral concerns pertaining to the household and the immediate family. In what follows, I briefly explore why this might be the case.

Placed in the broader context of the anthropology of Christianity, this kind of reform is quite common. In parts of the world that have been recent recipients of missionary activity, for instance, the family and the household can be the locus of non-Christian rituals or concepts that church leaders try to uproot (Keane 2007, Schieffelin 2014). While this emphasis on a "rupture" from a pre-Christian past does not easily fit with Christians in Egypt—the Coptic Orthodox Church traces its origins all the way to St. Mark—the nature of family law in Egypt has linked questions of marriage and divorce more closely with the institutional church. As Saba Mahmood (2012) has shown, this modern arrangement of family law gives these domestic concerns a sectarian charge. Matters of the household, in other words, might not be subject to reform as in places where Christianity is a new arrival, but they still receive scrutiny and attention from church leadership, if only to avoid the damage of scandal or sectarian tension.[15]

While it is helpful to understand the broader legal framework that links Christian households with the institutional church, I found clergy in Upper Egypt to be less concerned about marriage and divorce. The cultural conservatism of the region means that divorce is almost never pursued, and norms around marriage remain very traditional.[16] Rather, when the clergy would offer pointed correction to family affairs, it tended to be directed toward practices concerning lifeways and deathways. During the 1970s, clerics from various churches in al-ʿAziya began to encourage families to abandon cultural practices that Christians had shared with Muslims, such as female circumcision or the practice of gathering for a meal at the family mausoleum to commemorate the dead. In the 1990s, church leaders began to focus on reforming the mourning rituals found in Upper Egypt. After the death of a relative, people will put their lives on pause for long periods of time, forgoing work or church. During holidays like Christmas and Easter, some men will sit outside the front door of their homes, refusing to participate in any festivities because any expression of happiness might suggest to watchful neighbors that the recently deceased (who may have died months previous) is not truly missed. Many residents found these practices to be embarrassing yet hard to overturn, since personal and family reputations are at stake.

A curious aspect of these reform efforts is its multidenominational character. At least in al-'Aziya, clergy from all the churches were united in this respect, even if they were quick to disagree on other matters. I am not sure what motivates this cooperation. In fact, early descriptions by Westerners tended to frame the Coptic Orthodox Church as itself being beholden to non-Christian customs, and I would hear echoes of this claim from Protestants I would meet. Perhaps these reforms, endorsed by the Orthodox priests in the region, were a means of responding to this criticism. Or as the clergy professionalized in the second half of the twentieth century, church leaders from all sides gained enough distance to take a critical stance on these questions of custom and culture. Whatever the case, I found that the Catholic priests I would accompany during house visits would sometimes have me instruct families to give up their mourning rituals. "Tell him he must attend church," one Catholic priest told me, tagging me into a conversation that, until that point, I had only been observing. Given how I was rarely invited to speak as directly on any other issue in such situations, I wonder if my authority as a Westerner was a useful asset for these local priests.

In sum, I suspect this attention to local customs is attributable to multiple factors: to an initial Protestant critique of local culture that was picked up by Catholic and Orthodox priests, to concerns by the clergy that such customs present an obstacle to attending church, and to the critical distance that comes with the professionalization of the clergy. There is also the possibility that priests used their authority here because they wielded far less authority elsewhere. At the same time, this presence of the priest in the household was genuinely welcomed. Residents tended to acknowledge that their ways of mourning their loved ones were outdated but were reluctant to change, fearing what their family and neighbors might say. A more pressing and intractable problem is addiction (to smoking but also to various narcotics). On this topic—which is also laced with fears about local gossip—the advice and support of priests was often sought out, usually in the context of a house visit. What these examples show is that even this exercise of priestly authority in the household occurs with the tacit support of the laity. Life has changed quickly for the people I came to know in Upper Egypt. Having the priest or pastor involved in these affairs—especially when neighbors or other family members might pose a challenge—is one of the few resources that many of these residents can turn to for help. Priests can offer important pastoral care, but largely on the terms set by the laity.

Conclusion

This chapter has explored how interactions between the laity and clergy play an important role in determining the extent to which church authority extends into everyday life. There is much more one could say on this topic. Fasting, for instance, is a central discipline in the lives of many Christians in Egypt. There is also some religious apathy among the younger generation, which cuts away at clerical authority. The interaction between priests and laity can take many forms, yet the fundamental status differential between these two groups of people—rooted in theology but interwoven in the cultural landscape—gives way to coded forms of boundary making that run throughout everyday life. Guarded professionalism, the idiom of hospitality, performative ecumenism, the body as a potent source of divine blessings: These are the frameworks that sharpen the distinction between the laity and the clergy and that clarify the nature of priestly authority and the reach of the church into everyday life.

These imaginative, locally informed attempts by the laity to shape, and even counteract, the influence of institutional churches have been treated before in the study of Orthodox. Working in the context of western Ukraine, Vlad Naumescu (2005) has examined how the laity appeal to an imagined religious unity that unites local Christians and operates as a check against the political maneuvers of the region's various prelates and religious institutions. In her study of Marian apparitions in nearby Transcarpathia, Agnieszka Halemba finds that the laity make use of history to manage the authority of contemporary Catholic and Orthodox priests. "The cult of underground priests," that is, Catholic priests who experienced persecution or even been killed during the Soviet era, produces "a counterbalance to the discourse of priests as service providers subordinate to their local communities" (Halemba 2015, 172). Given how the Catholic and Orthodox traditions have a particularly strong history and presence in the local landscape (Wanner 2022), Transcarpathia makes for an intriguing comparison to Upper Egypt. In fact, much of what Halemba observes in the village communities echoes my own findings. Orthodox and Catholic priests tend to have limited authority in village affairs. The local church is viewed as the possession of the laity. Priests celebrate the sacraments, but they have no clear role in society beyond their liturgical function. To exercise any authority outside of the church, they have to resort to various strategies, all aimed at winning over the support of the laity. The resemblance to Upper Egypt is strong.

These points of similarity, however, highlight a few critical differences. While there might be a widespread Orthodox style that informs lay-cleric interaction, the fact that Christians in Egypt are a religious minority alters the visibility of the internal politics of these churches. Compared to Orthodox settings in Europe, the Christian presence in Egypt is muted. Monumental displays of Christian faith tend to be restricted to monasteries or churches, and interaction across denominational lines—as we have seen—is shaped by state oversight. Naumescu's model of the "Orthodox imaginary," then, does not exactly fit the experience of Christians in Egypt. While there is evidence of ecumenism among the laity, the political exigencies of minority life have tied Christians most closely to their church institutions, with the clearest and most dominant example being the Coptic Orthodox Church (Guirguis 2017). There is less public and conceptual space for the laity to gain separation from their institutional churches, so these institutions, and the personalities that lead them, will loom large in any attempt at imagining, or reimagining, the ties that bind the various Christians who live in Egypt. Priests tend to be some of the most immediate and recognizable symbols of their churches. For the laity, interacting with priest can, in certain situations, be an opportunity to refashion their relationship with the church. Such is the role that priests can play in the Coptic imagination.

Works Cited

Abdelsayed, John Paul. 2014. "Liturgy: Heaven on Earth." In *The Coptic Christian Heritage: History, Faith, and Culture*, ed. Lois Farag, 143–59. Routledge.

Agrama, Hussein Ali. 2012. *Questioning Secularism: Islam, Sovereignty, and the Rule of Law in Modern Egypt*. Stanford University Press.

Asad, Talal. 2003. *Formations of the Secular: Christianity, Islam, Modernity*. Stanford University Press.

Badone, Ellen. 1990. *Religious Orthodoxy and Popular Faith in European Society*. Princeton University Press.

Boylston, Tom. 2018. *The Stranger at the Feast: Prohibition and Mediation in an Ethiopian Orthodox Christian Community*. University of California Press.

Bourdieu, Pierre, and Monique ce Saint Martin. 1982. "La Sainte Famille. L'épiscopat français dans la champ du pouvoir." *Actes de la recherche en sciences sociales* 44–45: 2–53.

Gershon, Ilana. 2019. "Porous Social Orders." *American Ethnologist* 46, no. 4: 404–16.

Gran, Peter. 2004. "Upper Egypt in Modern History." In *Upper Egypt: Identity and Change*, ed. Nicholas Hopkins and Reem Saad, 79–96. American University in Cairo Press.

Gruber, Mark. 2002. *Journey Back to Eden: My Life and Times Among the Desert Fathers*. Orbis.

Guirguis, Laure. 2017. *Copts and the Security State: Violence, Coercion, and Sectarianism in Contemporary Egypt*. Stanford University Press.

Guirguis, Magdi, and Nelly van Doorn-Harder. 2011. *The Emergence of the Modern Coptic Papacy: The Egyptian Church and Its Leadership from the Ottoman Period to the Present*. American University in Cairo Press.

Halemba, Agnieszka. 2015. *Negotiating Marian Apparitions: The Politics of Religion in Transcarpathian Ukraine*. Central European University Press.

Hamilton, Alastair. 2006. *The Copts and the West, 1439–1822: The European Discovery of the Egyptian Church*. Oxford University Press.

Hann, Chris, and Hermann Goltz. 2010. *Eastern Christians in Anthropological Perspective*. University of California Press.

Heo, Angie. 2013. "The Bodily Threat of Miracles: Security, Sacramentality, and the Egyptian Politics of Public Order." *American Ethnologist* 40, no. 1: 516–28.

———. 2018. *The Political Lives of Saints: Christian-Muslim Mediation in Egypt*. University of California Press.

Johnson, Paul C. 2021. *Automatic Religion: Nearhuman Agents of Brazil and France*. University of Chicago Press.

Keane, Webb. 2007. *Christian Moderns: Freedom and Fetish in the Mission Encounter*. University of California Press.

Lester, Rebecca. 2005. *Jesus in Our Wombs: Embodying Modernity in a Mexican Convent*. University of California Press.

Mahmood, Saba. 2012. "Sectarian Conflict and Family Law in Contemporary Egypt." *American Ethnologist* 39, no. 1: 54–62.

———. 2015. *Religious Difference in a Secular Age: A Minority Report*. Princeton University Press.

Mayblin, Maya. 2019. "The Ultimate Return: Dissent, Apostolic Succession, and the Renewed Ministry of Roman Catholic Women Priests." *History and Anthropology* 30, no. 2: 133–48.

Mayeur-Jaouen, Catherine. 2019. *Voyage en Haute-Egypte: Prêtres, Coptes et Catholiques*. CNRS Editions.

Merleau-Ponty, Maurice. 1962. *Phenomenology of Perception*. Trans. Colin Smith. Humanities Press.

Nagib, Tharwat Maher Nagib Adly. 2019. "A Historical Perspective on Pentecostalism in Egypt." PhD diss., Regent University.

Naumescu, Vlad. 2006. *Religious Pluralism and the Imagined Orthodoxy of Western Ukraine*. LIT Verlag.

Pitt-Rivers, Julian. 2017a. "The Law of Hospitality." In *From Hospitality to Grace: A Julian Pitt-Rivers Omnibus*, ed. Giovanni da Col and Andrew Shryock, 163–84. HAU.

———. 2017b. "The Place of Grace in Anthropology." In *From Hospitality to Grace: A Julian Pitt-Rivers Omnibus*, ed. Giovanni da Col and Andrew Shryock, 69–103. HAU.

Schieffelin, Bambi. 2014. "Christianizing Language and the Dis-placement of Culture in Bosavi, Papua New Guinea." *Current Anthropology* 55, no. 10: S226–37.

Sharkey, Heather. 2008. *American Evangelicals in Egypt: Missionary Encounters in an Age of Empire*. Princeton University Press.

Shryock, Andrew. 2008. "Thinking About Hospitality, with Derrida, Kant, and the Balga Bedouin." *Anthropos* 103: 405–21.

Wanner, Catherine. 2022. *Everyday Religiosity and the Politics of Belonging in Ukraine*. Cornell University Press.

Wissa, Hanna. 2000. *Assiout: The Saga of an Egyptian Family*. Rev. ed. Book Guild.

Notes

1. The term "Copts" typically refers to members of the Coptic Orthodox Church, though it can also signify the present-day descendants of pre-Islamic Egypt. Given how there are different kinds of Christians in Egypt—some of whom identify as "Coptic" in the ethnic but not denominational sense—I stick to the broader term "Christian," using "Copt" or "Coptic" only when referring to the Orthodox.

2. For ethnographic treatment of Catholic and Orthodox clergy and religious elites, see Gruber (2002) on Coptic monks, Lester (2005) on Catholic nuns in Mexico, Badone (1990) on European clergy, and Bourdieu and Saint Martin (1981) on the French Catholic Episcopacy.

3. Both Catholics and Orthodox share the idea that the church, as the Body of Christ, is composed of both an earthly and heavenly community. Differences between these two traditions appear in the way that local churches are integrated into the universal church (see Hann 2010). In this chapter, I treat questions of ecclesiology as I most often encountered them in my fieldwork: as

a matter of constant negotiation among the laity and, on occasion, with their priests.

4. All churches in Egypt are monitored by a police detail that is stationed near the entrance, which only underscores the idea that churches have discrete perimeters.

5. The Arabic terms for "priest" or "pastor" are multiple, though only the Orthodox and Catholics refer to their priests as *kahin*, where all denominations, Protestant and otherwise, would refer to their clergy as *qass*. The word for pastor, *ra'i*, was used strictly in reference to the priest or pastor in charge of a parish.

6. Though I was unable to get a clear sense of general trends regarding vocations to the priesthood, I heard from several priests that Orthodox and Catholic vocations now tend to come more from the countryside than the city, where religiosity tends to weaken. I found it telling that when the Catholic bishop and other priests from the Diocese of Asyut made appeals for vocations to the priesthood and religious life, they did so by visiting village churches.

7. In general, Christians in Egypt tend to be wary of reconciliation sessions, as they are thought to be weighed in favor of the country's Muslim majority (that is, when a feud breaks out between a Christian and Muslim family). In al-'Aziya, however, most of the feuds were among Christian families, and state officials, not fearing any escalating sectarian conflict, had far less incentive to get involved. It was this vacuum of authority that the priest in question tried to fill in organizing the *suln*.

8. Catholic priests are allowed to be married and have families, but they must marry before they are ordained. Still, most Coptic Catholic priests in Egypt are not married. One reason for this trend is the fact that marriage is an expensive endeavor (not to mention supporting children), and Catholic seminarians face years of study before ordination. Few have the resources to marry and to cover the expenses of their coursework, which is not always covered by the local diocese.

9. In the eyes of these church ministers, the parish was under their stewardship. Priests were present to celebrate the sacraments and to help the town grow in holiness. These attitudes have a long history in the Coptic Orthodox Church. For centuries, the lay elite (*arakhna*) exercised much control over church affairs, including the clergy. Similar arrangements can be found elsewhere in the world of Eastern Christianity (see Halemba 2015, 180).

10. What anthropologists tend to find interesting about "Public Order" are the complications that arise as the Egyptian state manages religious pluralism, especially in terms of Christian-Muslim difference. While this concept is an important feature of Egypt's legal system, it was a topic that almost never came up in conversation during my fieldwork.

11. The celebration of a saint or holy person's birthday, or *moulid*, is an Egyptian tradition shared by Christians and Muslims. More recently, Christians have tended to rename these celebrations as *mazar*.

12. My distinction between *baraka* and grace is a heuristic intended to distinguish the two overlapping economies of blessing (of popular piety and of the institutional church) that Egyptian Christians navigate when seeking divine assistance. Of the two, grace has received far more attention by theologians, especially given the emphasis that grace receives in Protestant theologies. *Baraka*, on the other hand, is the focus of popular, nonacademic forms of expertise. Alternatively, see Pitt-Rivers (2017b) on grace as an expansive category that, at least in Europe, bridges personal interaction ("doing so with grace") and divine blessing, both in its orthodox and heterodox expressions.

13. Both Catholics and Orthodox residents recognize that the priest on his own does not produce the sacraments but rather does so in concert with the Triune God. To clarify this point, Catholics with some theological sophistication would reference the Latin phrase *in persona Christi* (that is, Christ acts through the person of the priest in the Divine Liturgy, especially in the words of consecration), while the Orthodox preferred to talk about the participation of the priest in the priesthood of Christ.

14. Because al-'Aziya is mostly Christian, most church steeples amplify their liturgies and preaching through external loudspeakers, a privilege not afforded to churches in majority-Muslim towns.

15. Sectarian conflict can emerge out of family affairs if a Christian converts to Islam or if a young woman's reputation is at stake. These concerns peaked in 2011 with the widely publicized cases of Kamilia Shehata and Wafa Constantine, two wives of Coptic Orthodox priests (Mahmood 2012).

16. Marriage in Upper Egypt is tightly controlled through scripted customs and family input. Marriage is not "arranged," though it is seen as a matter of concern for the entire family.

PART II

SOCIAL TRANSFORMATION AND ORTHODOX THEOLOGIES

Hagiographic Emplacement

St. Servatius, the Armenian Community of Maastricht, and Oriental Orthodox Christians in Europe

Christopher Sheklian

Every year on May 13, the city of Maastricht, in the region of Limburg in the southern Netherlands, celebrates its patron saint, Servatius. On the first Sunday following the saint's day, a solemn Mass takes place in the Basilica of St. Servatius before a grand procession through the streets of the city. Bands perform, civic organizations march, and the Brotherhood of St. Servatius carries the golden shrine containing the saint's relics. Traditionally, St. Servatius was the Bishop of Tongres (Tongeren, in present-day Belgium), but he died in Maastricht on May 13, 384, preaching the Gospel. The site of his death quickly emerged as a pilgrimage site, and later bishops built the church that houses the saint's relics. As one of the earliest evangelists of the present-day Netherlands, Servatius is linked to the fate of the city, such that "without Servatius, Maastricht would probably have remained a place of little significance, a small fortress on the river Meuse protecting the bridge on the road from Tongres to Cologne."[1]

Among the residents of Maastricht who regularly participate in the celebrations and veneration of St. Servatius are a group of Armenian Apostolic Christians connected to the Surp Karapet Armenian Church in the city. The Armenian community, over two thousand strong and largely made up of recent immigrants from the Republic of Armenia, has embraced the patron saint of Maastricht. This saint of the Catholic Church has been associated with Armenia and Armenians since Heinrich von Veldeke penned the *Servaaslegende*, the *Legend of Saint Servatius*, at the end of the twelfth century, claiming that "his father lived in Armenia."[2]

By appealing to the idea that St. Servatius was an Armenian, the relatively recent Armenian population of Maastricht intimately connects themselves to the textured history and landscape of the city. Though Servatius has no official place in the hagiographic tradition of the Armenian Church, this emplacement happens through theological and liturgical practices related to the veneration of saints. For instance, on May 15, 2016, Armenians dedicated a *khach 'k 'ar*, the traditional Armenian cross-stone, outside the central Basilica of St. Servatius, to their "compatriot St. Servatius." Armenians thus connect the Catholic veneration of Servatius to themselves by deploying their own Oriental Orthodox theology of saint veneration and the liturgical practices of both the Catholic Church and the Armenian Apostolic Church.

Hagiographic emplacement is the name I will give to this concerted use of theological arguments and liturgical practices regarding saints to forge connections to place in the context of migration precisely by connecting multiple traditions of saint veneration. It offers a technique and mode of placemaking for contemporary Orthodox Christian migrants that is thoroughly enmeshed in the theology of the broader Orthodox Church. In this chapter, I articulate the notion of hagiographic emplacement by drawing on ethnographic material from Maastricht, the theology of the Armenian Apostolic Church, and anthropological work on saints.[3] Following Julie Chu's careful ethnography of Fuzhounese migrants and what it means to "be emplaced," I attend to "processes for emplacement in a world where 'place' and 'home' can no longer be assumed to be stable objects and points of anchorage."[4] I demonstrate ethnographically how the Armenians of Maastricht and other Oriental Orthodox Christians in Europe insert and inscribe themselves—both literally and metaphorically, as the inscription on the *khach 'k 'ar* demonstrates—into the history and contemporary landscape of Europe through the techniques of hagiographic emplacement.[5]

The Armenians of Maastricht thus make use of aspects of their Armenian Christian tradition and the local Catholic one to forge a sense of home and place in the context of migration. They build their presence in the city by creatively deploying the tools of their tradition. As such, hagiographic emplacement suggests a broader theoretical point for any minority migrant population: Forging a presence in the context of migration often happens precisely through such a deployment of elements within a migrant population's tradition that can connect to the local situation. This focus on the dynamic forging of presence through the minority migrant's own tradition has important consequences for how we think about the migrant experience.

At a time when unprecedented numbers of humans are fleeing violence, famine, or economic hardship, the ability to forge a sense of belonging and to assert a presence under conditions of migration and diaspora is crucial.[6] This is especially true because discourse about migration is often framed around questions of borders, law, and state power. Without underestimating the sovereign power of the state and the necessity to gain forms of legal recognition, migration is also always about placemaking, forging connections to a new location, and creating a sense of home.

In Europe, to the extent that this aspect of migration is attended to, discussion tends to focus on anxieties around migrant "integration," particularly what happens when integration is not "successful."[7] Success, in this context, often conflates integration with assimilation. In the United States, in part because of the association of the concept of integration with desegregation, both academic discourse and policy discourse around migration tend to eschew the language of integration, though the anxieties and public political focus are often similar. In these debates, the mechanisms of placemaking are often given less attention than the anxieties themselves. While many immigrant and minority communities speak about integration, there are also internal conversations and other starting points for thinking about migrant belonging. Attention to practices like hagiographic emplacement encourages a shift from focusing on anxieties around migrant presence to particularized forms of placemaking and the migrant's own modes of asserting presence grounded in their practices and traditions.

Abstract legal citizenship before the law, questions of national identity, or debates about the essence and limits of Europe do not disappear with this shift in analytic focus.[8] Often, Armenians and other migrants themselves participate in such debates and argue for their inclusion in Europe.[9] Hagiographic emplacement, rather than fully replacing these ways of thinking about and claiming belonging, brackets them in favor of efforts directed toward the local history of a place and the minority migrant tradition itself. One might, for instance, assert a European identity grounded in shared Christianity through the connection to a specific saint. Yet, as the dynamics of hagiographic emplacement suggest, it is not necessary to do so.

Decidedly local in its orientation, these practical, agentive modes of asserting presence and placemaking emerge at the limits of these other modes of belonging. As such, they function at least partially in ways that Mayanthi Fernando calls "indifferent" to the state, a mode "of intercommunal life that bypass[es] the legal and political architecture—and tentacles—of the state."[10] We will see that recognition by the state can be bolstered through the connections forged through hagiographic emplacement. However, as developed in this chapter, the initial deployment of these techniques of placemaking are directed not toward state recognition or ideas of national belonging but rather toward local actors and to the community's own sense of place in their new home. They thus demonstrate the importance of careful attention to the specific traditions of a minority migrant community in discussions of the dynamics of migration and possibilities for forging a sense of place and home in the context of migration and diaspora.[11]

For Armenians in Maastricht, as this chapter shows ethnographically, their ability to forge such a sense of place depends on specific aspects of Armenian theology, including ideas about saintly glory. At the same time, the chapter explores the extent to which the specific Armenian theological articulations and hagiographic practices might be shared across Oriental Orthodox and other Orthodox Christian traditions. In this way, the chapter intervenes into questions of a shared Orthodox Christianity and the extent to which theological differences matter for our anthropological understanding of various Orthodox Christian groups. While hagiographic emplacement will emerge as a dynamic available to various Christian denominations that have a practice of saint veneration, the specific ideas about saintly presence that each group has influence the way the emplacement happens in a specific situation. Thus, theological differences, especially Christological ones, between Oriental and Eastern Orthodox branches of Christianity, will come to matter for our textured ethnographic understanding of a particular Orthodox Christian migrant group. Just as the conceptions of presence and the tools of a minority tradition matter more broadly for migrant emplacement, the details of Christian theology shape the actual practices of hagiographic emplacement. Hence, the chapter asserts both that a shared Orthodox Christianity underpins much of the workings of hagiographic emplacement while also insisting on a closer attention to theological and ecclesial difference between Orthodox Christian groups studied anthropologically.

Through the ethnographic and theological unfolding of this specific mode of placemaking I am calling hagiographic emplacement, the chapter makes three interventions. First it argues for the specificity of hagiographic emplacement as a mode of presence assertion and placemaking that is grounded in the Orthodox Christian tradition. Second, it suggests that theological and historical differences between groups of Orthodox Christianity are relevant for our understanding of the actual experience of contemporary Orthodox groups. Finally, it argues more broadly that minority belonging in contexts of migration and diaspora is heavily dependent on the local, creative deployment of strategies and techniques already available in the "toolkit" of the tradition of the minority. To make these arguments, the chapter builds on the ethnographic encounter with Armenians in Maastricht, in the south of the Netherlands.

Saintly Connections in Maastricht

The Basilica of St. Servatius dominates the Vrijthof, the central plaza of Maastricht. This current church is a largely Romanesque building, with later Gothic adornments, and is one of the most important Catholic churches in the Netherlands. There has been a church in this location since perhaps the sixth century, when Bishop Monulphus (Monulf) built a church dedicated to his holy predecessor Servatius, whose grave, according to Gregory of Tours, never "became covered with snow" during the invasion of the Huns.[12]

Such early stories bolstered the status of St. Servatius, traditionally known in the fourth century as the bishop of Tongeren (in present-day Belgium). He preached in Maastricht, where he died on May 13, 384.[13] There are accounts of his attendance at fourth-century synods and councils, and there is "no doubt that legends grew up around a certain St. Servatius in the first two centuries after the bishop's death."[14] Over time, as the monastic order of St. Servatius grew in importance and influence, the stories about the saint proliferated. "In the course of the 11th century the canons of the Chapter of St. Servatius felt a growing need for a complete hagiography of their patron saint,"[15] and "the first 'official' hagiography" from that period included "the story of Charlemagne gaining a glorious victory over the Saracens on May 13 (St. Servatius day) thanks to the intervention of Maastricht's patron saint."[16] St. Servatius emerged from this Latin *vitae* of Jocundus officially a saint, one connected intimately to the Holy Roman

Emperor and the city of Maastricht. Hence, the fact that Maastricht "emerged as a key centre in a vast region is an indicator of the power of the saint. Even today Servatius is vital to the self-image and identity of the citizens of Maastricht."[17]

Visiting Maastricht on the weekend after May 13, the saint's day of commemoration, corroborates this assessment. There are various activities beginning on Friday, including a walking pilgrimage on Saturday to a well outside the city walls associated with Servatius and whose water is said to have healing properties. Sunday begins with Mass, the basilica overflowing with hundreds of people. Once services have ended, various groups—bands, local notables, centuries-old fraternal civic orders—regroup outside for the procession through the winding medieval streets of the city.

In 2023, attending the procession, I spotted about a half-dozen members of the Surp Karapet Armenian Church lining up outside, in rich purple robes with gold-thread trim. They carried a cross and banners that both simultaneously fit perfectly with the pomp of the procession that included the golden bust of St. Servatius but also distinguished them from the other groups. They lingered, perhaps simply by coincidence, on the side of the building that hosts an unusual feature, even for the layered architecture of the basilica: a reddish-orange stone carved as a cross. This element is an Armenian style cross-stone, a *khach'k'ar*, a characteristic feature of the Armenian Christian tradition and part of the practice of saint veneration. Under the ornate carvings, an inscription read: "to the city of Maastricht by the local Armenian community in memory of their compatriot Saint Servatius."[18]

In both the characteristically Armenian piece of Christian art dedicated to St. Servatius at the most prominent building in the city and their participation in the most important civic celebration of the year, the Armenian community has successfully emplaced themselves into the space and life of Maastricht. Crucially, they have done this by following a thread, a single detail from Heinrich von Veldeke's *Servaaslegende*, the *Legend of Saint Servatius*, penned in Limburgish Middle Dutch at the end of the twelfth century. According to von Veldeke, St. Servatius, whose father was Armenian, "had been born as a consolation to the Armenians, and as a chosen vessel of the Holy Spirit."[19] St. Servatius's link with Armenia was thus indelibly forged in the first vernacular account of his life.[20] Today, the Armenians of Maastricht use this historical and literary link between Servatius and Armenia as a starting point to connect the contemporary Armenian community to the history of Maastricht and to its self-image through the techniques of hagiographic emplacement.

There are about 2,500 Armenians today living in the area around Maastricht. Their presence in the city largely dates to the 1960s, concurrent with the broader trends of migration of Armenians and other citizens of Turkey to the Netherlands.[21] Though there was an earlier Armenian connection to the Netherlands through a network of early modern merchants, this community dissolved by the early nineteenth century as shifting trade routes and the emergence of British colonial rule in India sidelined them.[22] For one hundred years, there was no community of Armenians in the Netherlands to speak of. Even in the aftermath of the catastrophe of the Armenian Genocide in 1915, few Armenians moved to the Netherlands. Rather, it was in the 1950s and 1960s, through the guestworker program, which encouraged single male workers to fill in gaps in the postwar workforce, that Armenians migrated alongside other citizens of the Republic of Turkey.[23]

Today, Maastricht is one of three major centers of Armenian life in the Netherlands, after Amsterdam and Almelo. Many of the first Armenians in Maastricht and the broader region of Limburg had previously migrated to Almelo or Amsterdam, then moving to Maastricht in the 1980s. A core group of Armenian migrants from both the Republic of Turkey and the Republic of Armenia founded the Armeense Stichting Ani, or the "Ani Foundation," in 1999. While we will return to other activities of the Ani Foundation, the organization was crucial in the early support for a church. The Catholic Diocese of Roermond loaned a church, the Church of the Ascension, to the *stichting* for Armenian liturgical services beginning in 2012. On January 26, 2013, the church was consecrated as an Armenian church by Archbishop Norvan Zakarian, with the consent of the Catholic bishop of the diocese of Roermond.[24] In addition to the Ani Foundation and the Surp Karapet Church, there is a Sunday school, women's union, Armenian dance club, and football team in Maastricht. Especially through the leadership of the Ani Foundation and of the church, as we will see, these Armenians in Maastricht have worked to forge a connection to the city and the local Catholic Christians based at the Basilica of St. Servatius. They have done this precisely through the dynamics of hagiographic emplacement.

Hagiographic Emplacement and Other Forms of Saintly Placemaking

Hagiographic emplacement is an affective, intimate technique of placemaking that asserts a minority migrant presence by forging connections between new migrant communities and the local population through practices of saint veneration grounded in the traditions of both groups. As such, it is a subset of broader practices of placemaking through saint veneration that depend on the Christian "cult of the saints."[25] Such potential and possibility for deploying saint veneration as a mode of asserting presence and belonging in a particular place spans Christian denominations and even helps forge connections across religious boundaries. When the Armenians of Maastricht erect a *khach'k'ar* outside a Catholic basilica or join in a procession for a saint that is not officially venerated in the Armenian liturgical calendar, they are doing exactly that.

Connecting two traditions of saint veneration depends on a long and shared tradition of reverence for holy figures in Christianity. Though the veneration of saints in Christianity shares commonalities with other traditions, scholars such as Peter Brown argue that there is an important specificity to the Christian "cult of the saints."[26] This "cult of the saints" encouraged ethical edification through emulation of the lives of the saints since at least Athanasius's prologue to his *Life of Anthony*, which arguably set the parameters for the genre of Christian hagiography.[27] Another crucial element in the Christian conception of saints is the connection to particular sites or places, a connection often made through relics of the saint. As Wendy Mayer notes in her introduction to the homilies of St. John Chrysostom on *The Cult of the Saints*, the "sanctification of places became enhanced and extended. The relics, like the tomb, linked the commemoration of the martyr to a local holy place."[28] Through shrines, often holding relics that could still be "heavy with the fullness of a beloved person," "wherever Christianity went in the early Middle Ages, it brought with it the 'presence' of the saint."[29] Relics, which could move from the place while still being connected to it, helped foster pilgrimage to holy sites, such that there was a "rapid expansion of the network of holy places and sites of pilgrimage that occurred in the second half of the fourth century."[30] Saint veneration in Christianity was very early linked to the ability to forge connections between places and people.

Saint veneration thus forges connections between different groups of people through what the anthropologist Angie Heo, in *The Political Lives of Saints*, calls the "material aesthetics of saints." According to Heo, these material aesthetics of saints "forge social imaginaries and political horizons of belonging and action."[31] That is, the concrete practices—like pilgrimage—and the material instantiations—like relics—related to the veneration of saints are generative of social and political modes of belonging. Heo's book pays careful attention to the power of saints themselves, such as relics that do not decompose or fall apart, offering a "bodily aesthetics of extraordinary vitality [that] mediates the power of the resurrection to overcome earthly vulnerability."[32] Starting from the power of the saints themselves, Heo's argument offers a fine-grained look at the way that the power of the saints mediates Coptic Christian understandings of belonging in Egypt, including the apparition of the "Virgin of Zaytun" in 1968.[33] While the context of mediation is quite different from the diasporic minority experience of Armenians in Maastricht, Heo points us to the crucial ability of saint veneration to "forge social imaginaries and political horizons of belonging and action."

What makes hagiographic emplacement different from other modes of saintly placemaking is the concerted use of theological arguments and liturgical practices regarding saints by a migrant group to forge connections to a new place, asserting their presence by connecting their own saint veneration to the veneration of the local and regional majority already present. It is a technique that directs our scholarly attention to the encounter between a minority, migrant tradition and certain subsets of a local dominant tradition. Within traditions, there are specific ideas about presence that directly shape the dynamics of migrant emplacement, given that the very conception of what it means to be present depends on these tradition-internal discourses and practices. In any given encounter, the negotiation of two hagiological traditions reflects the specifics of the local encounter and the notions of veneration and presence in each tradition.

In the ethnographic case of Armenians in Maastricht that undergirds the conceptual development in this chapter, the specific history includes a longer Armenian connection to Europe, Dutch discourses of belonging and citizenship including autochthony,[34] and the Catholic heritage of the southern Limburg region of the Netherlands, which distinguishes it from much of the rest of the country.[35] Armenians in Maastricht, through the techniques of hagiographic emplacement, claim a presence in Europe generally and the Netherlands specifically that emplaces them locally and regionally in the continent. This form of presence and belonging in the continent exceeds mere "visibility."[36] It is not just that they are new migrants whose Christianity connects them to the main historical religion of Europe or only that they deserve recognition and visibility in a multicultural Europe. Rather, hagiographic emplacement insists on a specific form of presence and belonging to a place, one thoroughly enmeshed in the theology of the Orthodox Church.

The Orthodoxy of Hagiographic Emplacement

Relics and pilgrimage sites are profound material instantiations of presence. Saint veneration in general and hagiographic emplacement in particular, then, are intimately connected to broader discussions around materiality and presence in Christianity. Relics, especially, "raised the problem of the material" already "from the days of the early church."[37] Given the question of how the saint's presence does or does not reside in material such as relics or physical shrines, the question of presence is likewise connected to saint veneration. The presence of the divine in the saint, the often excessive "power" of material presence at shrines, and the efficacy of saints' relics suggest the conceptual interconnection between materiality, presence, and saint veneration.

Many of the academic discussions about Orthodox Christianity—both within and beyond the discipline of anthropology—have started from the question of materiality. In particular, there is a strong focus on the status of icons. As Caroline Walker Bynum notes, the anxiety over images in Christianity was never really (only) about the image, but rather, "the anxiety was over materiality itself."[38] While Bynum's characterization applies to the whole of ancient Christendom, the heavily iconic tradition of the post-Iconoclastic Eastern Orthodox Church has made it a generative site for thinking about the material instantiation of presence, in icons as well as in relics. Marie-José Mondzain's compelling *Image, Icon, Economy: The Byzantine Origins of the Contemporary Imaginary* has been an especially generative account of rich philosophical questions around icons, including the role of the Incarnation and Christology.[39] Yet, while the materiality of icons and questions of presence have become almost iconic of academic discussions of Orthodox Christianity, there is at present scant attention to the theological differences within Orthodoxy pertaining to these topics. Given that hagiographic emplacement works through the instantiation of presence that is tied to particular Christian traditions of saint veneration, it matters that most of the generative theological philosophizing about materiality and presence is deeply imbricated in a Christian theological genealogy that, while Orthodox, is not exactly identical to that of the Armenian Apostolic Church and the other Oriental Orthodox churches.

The autocephalous Armenian Church, the Hayots' Ekeghets'i, often called the Armenian Apostolic Church or the Armenian Orthodox Church, developed a distinct Christian rite.[40] Intimately linked to the long history of the Armenian people, the Armenian Church is the main Christian denomination of most Armenians in the small post-Soviet Republic of Armenia and among the vast worldwide Armenian diaspora. It is considered part of the Oriental Orthodox 'branch" of Christianity, which is actually a loosely affiliated "family" of churches composed of several autocephalous church hierarchies: the Armenian, Coptic, Eritrean, Ethiopian, Syriac, and Indo-Malankaran.[41] Today, these churches recognize one another's sacraments and are in "full communion" with one another. This sacramental unity distinguishes them from what are usually called the "Eastern Orthodox" churches as well as the Assyrian Church of the East. While all these churches fall under a larger umbrella of Orthodox churches, there are important elements that distinguish between them.

Both these differences and the similarities that justify a broader study of Orthodox Christianity are taken up in the Introduction to this volume. Crucially, as the Introduction points out, the imperial past of the Byzantine Empire and the official status of Eastern Orthodoxy therein, as well as the later official or semiofficial status of various churches in modern nation-states, has led to very different trajectories for the churches of the Eastern and Oriental branches of Orthodox Christianity. Moreover, there is a fundamental *theological* break, which Sarah Bakker Kellogg's chapter also crucially articulates in relation to imperial politics and history, that separates Eastern and Oriental Orthodox Christianity.

Specifically, Christological differences, the answer to the question of the relationship between the divinity and the humanity of Jesus Christ, separate the two branches of the Orthodox Christian family. A broadly "Miaphysite" Christology that insists that Jesus Christ is one person with one unmixed divine and human nature unites the Oriental Orthodox churches. Though each church has articulated their position in their own way, at some point in each church's history they reject the answer given at the Council of Chalcedon in 451. This council, on the other hand, is the authoritative starting point for the Christology of the Eastern Orthodox churches. While ecumenical efforts in the twentieth and twenty-first centuries have often downplayed this division, no church hierarchy fully denies the difference in emphasis and language for describing some of the most central theological concepts of the Christian experience. Without insisting on an unbridgeable theological-philosophical divide between Duophysite and Miaphysite Christologies, we can still attend to the nuances of theology and practice within the Orthodox world.

Attention to this level of specificity helps us rethink the place of Orthodox Christianity in the contemporary world and the extent to which "Orthodox" theological categories and liturgical practices inform the actual Orthodox experience in the world. Crucially for this chapter, concepts of presence and materiality central to saint veneration are related to Christological definitions. In other words, the dynamic of hagiographic emplacement that this chapter unfolds depends upon conceptions of presence intimately tied to Christology. Hence, Christological differences—as well as other nuances of theology—matter for the way that different groups of Orthodox Christians live in contemporary situations of diaspora and migration. This is true *not* because every Orthodox Christian is a theologian but because theological concepts suffuse the practices of those Christians in their daily lives and modes of engagement with the world.

From this perspective, the implicit starting point of Eastern Orthodox thought and categories for "Orthodox" Christianity writ large is a form of erasure of Oriental Orthodox specificity and the individual theologies of the churches. Even as sophisticated a take on saintly presence as Heo's discussion of Coptic Christians (Miaphysite, non-Chalcedonian Oriental Orthodox) relies implicitly on the theoretical and theological underpinnings of Eastern (Duophysite, Chalcedonian) Orthodox Christianity.[42] Similarly, there is a sophisticated philosophical discussion about sacramental presence that largely departs from Catholic theology or Eastern Orthodox positions.[43] In part, this is attributable to the availability of sources: Many Armenian and Oriental Orthodox texts remain untranslated or at least not easily available. Others have simply not entered broader theological and academic discussions. This is also a product of the scholarly interest around certain topics mentioned above. Yet, as anthropological and other scholarly interest in Orthodox Christianity continues to grow, as evidenced by this volume, the erasure—whether intentional or merely because of the paucity of easily available material—greatly diminishes our understanding of Orthodox Christian realities on the ground. To start from a theological category or idea that might actually be inimical to the thought of the members of the church under ethnographic consideration is clearly problematic. Even when certain practices, like saint veneration, seem to overlap, the justifications for and discourse around them might be very different. To fully grasp the possibilities for action and thought on the ground with specific Orthodox communities, we as anthropologists and scholars must pay attention to this specificity.

Armenian Conceptions of Saintly Presence

In the present chapter I am less concerned with the overarching theological question of Duophysite and Miaphysite Christology as alluded to earlier. Instead, I turn to Armenian Christian discourses and practices of saint veneration in order to make sense of the strategy of hagiographic emplacement deployed by the Armenians of Maastricht. In the case of Oriental Orthodox migrants to Europe, the capacious possibilities of Christian presence related to the materiality of saints, Incarnational theology, and liturgical practice point to a specific mechanism of emplacement in a new home in Europe. To develop these possibilities in some detail, I turn from the larger context of Christian saint veneration, clearly connected to placemaking, and the relationship of different "families" of Orthodox Christianity to the particularities of saint veneration and placemaking in the case of Armenian Christianity.

Armenian Christianity has long recognized the social and political implications of the "material aesthetics of envisioning saints," to use Heo's felicitous characterization. Two of the earliest pieces of Armenian literature, the *History of the Armenians* by Moses Khorenats'i and the *Buzandaran* (also known as the *Epic Histories*), suggest the social force of relics and saint veneration. According to the *History of the Armenians*, the first head or "Catholicos" of the Armenian Church, St. Gregory the Illuminator, purposely retired to a monastery before his death to make sure that his relics would not be immediately available for veneration, which might inadvertently lead recent Christian converts astray by focusing their worship on him rather than Christ. St. Gregory's relics were eventually revealed to an ascetic, who buried them near what would become one of the most important pilgrimage sites of Armenian Christianity—but only after "the faith had become firmly established in these regions [Armenia]."[44] Similarly, the power of bones as relics is demonstrated in the *Bu-*

zandaran, where we learn that the Persians stole the bones of the Armenian Arshakuni kings and that the Armenians then recovered them, "that the glory of the kings and the fortune and valor of this realm might go from here with the bones of the kings and enter into our realm."[45]

Both these early accounts describe the material instantiation of presence and power in saints and their relics. This power, attested to in other Christian traditions, takes a particular form in Armenian Christianity. *P'ark'*, translated as "glory," is precisely the power of the bones mentioned in the *Buzandaran*. This indwelling *p'ark'*, related to the ancient Persian concept *farr*, is a specifically Armenian conception of powerful presence, one that shapes Armenian Christian understandings of saintly power and the presence of God.[46] From the perspective of the church hierarchy, as long it is harnessed appropriately, this formidable power can encourage Christians to emulate those saints and provide narrative touchstones and collective practices that bind people together.[47]

One deeply material and physical mode of saintly presence that binds Armenians together across time and space is the creation a "sacred geography." Indwelling *p'ark'*, the glory of the saints, becomes a presence at a site of pilgrimage. Over time, as already attested to in Khorenats'i's account, these sites became crucial not only as individual sites of saintly presence but as manifestations of Armenian Christian presence more broadly on the landscape that was considered home. Such saintly geographies are attested up to the 1915 Armenian Genocide that wrenched Armenians from this native hagiographic landscape. Fr. Garabed Kalfayan, writing his memoirs in Yettem, California, later in the twentieth century, insisted on the importance of "Our Holy Places" in Anatolia and even linked his priestly name to his "dedication" by his mother at the Monastery of St. Garabed near his birthplace.[48] Relics, practices of veneration, and churches linked to the biographies of saints historically connected Armenian Christians to their homes in the Armenian Plateau and other portions of Anatolia where they had lived for centuries. In this case, intracommunal bonds are created through practices of saint veneration that unite Armenian Christians to the land and buildings around them—a form of emplacement through the creation of a saintly geography.

Armenian Christianity, then, has at its roots a "material aesthetics of envisioning saints" and practices of saint veneration that shape a conception of what "the church" is and who belongs to it. Saints, in the Armenian Church, are "canonized" precisely through their inclusion in liturgical practices of memorialization.[49] In addition to the full recognition of saint-hood in the liturgy proper, Armenian Christianity has quasi- or paraliturgical texts that encourage the emulation of saints, notably the Synaxarion known as the *Yaysmawurk'*.[50] Through this active memorialization in the liturgy and in the public reading of the *Yaysmawurk'*, saints become a part of the Christian community. A saint who is deemed worthy of emulation then shapes the virtues and sense of collectivity of the entire church. Inclusion in the liturgy is essentially membership in the church in its extension in time and place. In other words, these hagiographic practices influence the very contours of the Armenian Christian community.

Such practices shape the boundaries of communal belonging both through inclusion and exclusion. In the eighteenth century, the Armenian Catholic Mkhitarist order had printed their own liturgical calendar venerating saints who were outside the accepted pantheon of saints of the Armenian Apostolic Church. The success of their printing program rattled the eighteenth-century Catholicos Siméon Erewants'i, who responded by creating the first printing press in what is today's Armenia and then printing a liturgical calendar out of the headquarters of the church in Etchmiadzin.[51] That is, Erewants'i deployed liturgical practices of saint veneration to define the limits of communal belonging. These authoritative understandings of communal belonging come to bear on which connections can be forged and which figures and connections are possible for techniques of emplacement.

If the example of Erewants i exemplifies how practices of saint veneration have been used by the Armenian Church for boundary maintenance, shared hagiographies have also been the starting point for ecumenical outreach and activity. An earlier catholicos, Gregory II, who may have been the first hierarch to institute the readings of the lives of the saints in the liturgical context of the Armenian Church, was an ecumenist and collector of saints' vitae who earned the epithet "Vkayasēr," the "lover of the martyrs/witnesses."[52] The *Yaysmawurk'* itself "was a direct translation from an already-existing Greek liturgical collection."[53] Moreover, since the *Yaysmawurk'* is paraliturgical, it includes individuals who may not rise to a clear-cut status of "official" saint but are nonetheless commemorated and celebrated in the broader liturgical context of the Armenian Apostolic Church. Step'anos of Siwnik', an eighth-century Armenian polymath, is one such figure.[54] Like Step'anos, many Greek and Latin saints have also been venerable figures that the Armenian Church has deemed worthy of emulation even if they do not enter the formal liturgical canon. Saint veneration in the Armenian Apostolic Church, then, is precisely a location where ecumenical overtures can occur through practices that sit right at the boundary of official liturgical practice.

This flexibility of saint veneration—the ability to commemorate someone that is not explicitly a saint with forms of liturgical commemoration— is essential for the unfolding of the dynamic of hagiographic emplacement in contemporary Maastricht. As we will see, this flexibility, the specific conception of saintly presence of the Armenian Church, and practices that mark a sacred geography are all mobilized in the encounter with the Catholic tradition of saint veneration in Maastricht. Crucially, the long history of Western European, Catholic Christian use of saint veneration as a mode of power, what Brown describes as the way "the power of the bishop tended to coalesce with the power of the shrine," is key to the success of the techniques of hagiographic emplacement deployed by Armenians in Maastricht.[55] While our excursus into the practices of saint veneration of the Armenian Church challenges Brown's claim that this use of saints for the power of the church was a particularly distinct Western European phenomenon,[56] it is the combination of the flexibility of practices of saint veneration on the Armenian side and the deep association between saintly power and ecclesial power in the Catholic Church that makes the use of hagiographic emplacement by Armenians in Maastricht so potent.

Armenian Veneration of Servatius and Techniques of Emplacement

We are now able to return to the ethnographic material in Maastricht, to see how these Armenian Christian conceptions of saintly presence and the flexible understanding of canonization in the Armenian Church have been creatively deployed in the encounter with local Catholic practices venerating St. Servatius. From the outset of organized collective Armenian life in Maastricht, some members of the community have recognized the possibility of connecting to the city, to emplacing themselves there through a connection to St. Servatius. One of the first organizations founded was a *stichting*, a flexible Dutch form of corporate personhood that Armenians have wielded throughout the country to organize their activities. Officially registered as a foundation (*stichting*) with the Chamber of Commerce on November 25, 1999, the Armeense Stichting Ani (Armenian Ani Foundation) has placed the Armenian connection with St. Servatius front and center since its inception. Their website declares that "the city of Maastricht is connected to the Armenian community through Saint Servatius, the patron saint of Maastricht," and that today in large part thanks to the efforts of the foundation, "the city of Maastricht has now become known among Armenians at home and abroad, and the tomb of Saint Servatius has become a place of pilgrimage."[57] In addition to supporting Armenian language and culture and their efforts coordinating with the Surp Karapet Church, another important priority for the Ani Foundation is "the development, participation, and integration of our community in Dutch society." Participation and integration occur through involvement in civic events. The major mode of this involvement has been through the connection between Armenians and St. Servatius.

Since St. Servatius has no official cult following in the Armenian Apostolic Church, despite his position as a prominent Western bishop and revered saint of Limburg, the link between the Armenian community and the saint of the city must be actively forged through the creative deployment of Armenian hagiographic practices. This possibility is also dependent on the central place of St. Servatius in Maastricht and the long tradition of saint veneration in the Catholic Church. The following ethnographic instances demonstrate how members of the Maastricht Armenian community forged connections between the saintly presence of Servatius and their own recent presence in the city, instantiating material moments of presence in the city that link these two, the saint and the minority migrant community. Throughout, this section highlights how these ethnographic encounters exemplify the workings of hagiographic emplacement, in this case grounded in the encounter between the Armenian Christian tradition and the local Dutch Catholic one. Notably, these encounters are local and regional, generally directed to Catholic institutions and individuals, or to the civic life of Maastricht, rather than to the Dutch state. That is, for the most part, they remain "indifferent" to the "legal and political architecture—and tentacles—of the state," as Fernando put it.[58]

I saw this local and even personal element of forging connections around St. Servatius on one of my first visits to Maastricht for church services at Surp Karapet. Once coronavirus pandemic restrictions were loosened and both attending liturgy and socializing after services was again allowed, I met Vazgen. An active member of the Surp Karapet church community, Vazgen has been particularly involved in the effort to forge a connection between the existing memory and veneration of St. Servatius in Maastricht and the Armenian community. When we met and I told him of my interest in St. Servatius, not only was he immediately excited, but he also mentioned other Armenian connections to the region, including Macarius of Ghent.

Over the course of several visits to Maastricht, Vazgen traced out a sacred geography of the city for me. After the Divine Liturgy at Surp Karapet one Sunday, Vazgen drove us from the Armenian church, located on the outskirts of downtown, to park in the center of the city, pointing out Catholic churches and a statue of St. Servatius along the way. Nearly two years later, when I attended the 2023 walking pilgrimage to the St. Servatius Well on the outskirts of town led by the Catholic priest of the St. Servatius Basilica and other members of the Brotherhood of St. Servatius, they noted some of the same places. Just as Fr. Garabed Kalfayan had insisted for the "holy places" of Armenian Anatolia, Maastricht had its own sacred geography, with important sites linked to the city's patron saint. On that first Sunday tour with Vazgen, what distinguished the geography was Vazgen's emphasis on the efforts of the Armenian community to build physical and historical connections to points in that saintly civic geography. He coordinated a long-standing Armenian understanding of a geography of "our holy places" with the existing hagiographic landscape of the city of Maastricht.

After we parked, we walked to the Basilica of St. Servatius, which at that point I had only visited once before. We bought our tickets, since the basilica is both a working church and a historic site. In a demonstration of Vazgen's personal connections to the priest and the basilica, the priest tossed Vazgen the keys to the crypt of St. Servatius, which we visited while we waited for the priest to finish a baptism. We made our way downstairs, beneath the main altar to a smaller chapel that houses the remains of the saint. Opening the gate, we entered the crypt, where I immediately noticed a small wooden cross in a distinctly Armenian style sitting on the cenotaph. With a smile, Vazgen told me that he had placed it there on a previous visit. This small gesture, while not as grand as the physical presence of the *khach'k'ar* outside the basilica, marks a material assertion of presence at the heart of the hagiographic geography of the city. With the literal keys to the shrine in hand, Vazgen left a distinctive Armenian cross as a marker of Armenian presence at the crypt of the saint. Together, we said *Hayr Mer*, the Lord's Prayer in Armenian, and then left the crypt.

Outside the crypt, we spoke with the priest, who showed us around the sanctuary. We also toured the treasury museum that contains many relics of the beloved saint of Maastricht. At one of these relics, Vazgen stopped as a smile beamed across his face. 'Look," he told me, pointing to one of the artifacts in the treasury. "What does that look like to you?" In a flash of recognition, I exclaimed, "Armenian writing!" Vazgen nodded, telling me that on an earlier visit he had noticed the piece. While the provenance of the artifact isn't clear, Vazgen alerted the caretakers that the piece had been mislabeled as Syriac. Our visit was the first time the description of the piece noted that it was Armenian with Armenian writing. As with the *khach'k'ar* or the small cross, the description in the treasury museum marks a literal inscription in the landscape of the city, an assertion of presence precisely through the Armenian connection to the revered patron saint.

Beyond the connection directly to the Basilica of St. Servatius and the Catholic Church, the Ani Foundation has worked for over a decade to forge connections between the Armenian community and the city of Maastricht through St. Servatius. For instance, they organized the March 10, 2012, symposium "Saint Servatius the Armenian."[59] This symposium was the first major event to publicly emplace the Armenians of Maastricht into the city through an association with St. Servatius. Notably, the Surp Karapet Church was already on loan at that time but had not yet been consecrated as an Armenian Apostolic Church. While the Ani Foundation had already existed for over a decade, the community and church were moving into a new phase around 2012 and 2013. At the same time that a permanent church building was finalized, the Armenians of Maastricht made the connection between their community and the patron saint of the city explicit through the symposium. Literal emplacement in the city through the purchase of a physical church building went hand in hand with a symbolic emplacement connecting Armenians to the history of the city through St. Servatius—that is, hagiographic emplacement.

Present at the symposium were Archbishop Norvan Zakarian, the Armenian primate of the diocese of France, the Catholic bishops of Roermond and Hasselt, the Armenian ambassador to the Netherlands, and the Dutch minister of immigration, integration, and asylum. Speakers included a local church historian and deacon, the French Armenian historian Maxime K. Yevadian, and the Dutch Armenologists Theo van Lint (Oxford) and Joseph Weitenberg (Leiden).[60] The event emplaced the Armenians in

Maastricht and the Netherlands more broadly by emphasizing shared history and culture. All of this was done through the context of St. Servatius.

Maxime Yevadian, one of the authors of the book *Saint Servatius d'Arménie: Premier évaque de Maastricht*, through both the book and his presentation at the symposium, made the strategy of emplacement that uses St. Servatius explicit. In the talk and in the book, Yevadian and his coauthor, the late Georges K. Khayiguian, use Armenian historical sources to connect the name Servatius to an ancient Armenian noble family.[61] By offering this connection publicly, after a broader history of St. Servatius presented by a local historian and theologian, Yevadian connected the history of Maastricht to the history of the Armenians. Later in the day, Yevadian presented the book to the Dutch minister of immigration, integration, and asylum.[62] After literally writing the Armenians into the history of Maastricht, that written record was offered to a representative of the Dutch government, suggesting the full integration of Armenians into Dutch society and history through that inscription into history. This is an incredible instance of the simultaneous inscription and insertion of presence into the historical record while giving a material (and political) presence through the offering of the physical book to the Dutch minister.

Both the long history of Armenians in the Netherlands and their integration were the topics of other speakers at the symposium. Prof. van Lint traced the "social, cultural, and literary developments of the Armenians," and Prof. Weitenberg discussed the Armenians in the Netherlands. According to Leo van Leijsen, writing for the blog of the Katholieke Vereniging voor Oecumene (Catholic Association for Ecumenism), Weitenberg stressed that Armenians and Dutch belong to the same cultural circle. Van Leijsen found the "Western" sounds of the musical program later in the day a sonic confirmation of "the fact that Armenians are culturally European."[63] This event is notable in its direct engagement with broader discourses of European and Dutch identity, as well as integration, through the presence of the Dutch minister whose purview includes integration. Hagiographic emplacement, then, can be caught up in these larger discourses and is not exclusive of them. However, this event, while forging connections through St. Servatius, was also the furthest removed of several events and activities organized by the Ani Foundation from the actual practices of saint veneration of the Armenian Apostolic Church. At the same time, based on the attendance of Dutch politicians and the reaction of the Dutch Catholic Church, the use of St. Servatius as a springboard to help emplace Armenians in the history of the Netherlands and the city of Maastricht was highly successful.

It is the erection of the *khach'k'ar,* the Armenian carved cross-stone, on May 15, 2016, that marks the most dramatic and visible inscription or emplacement into the hagiographic landscape of Maastricht.[64] The Ani Foundation, along with the Surp Karapet Church, was crucial to this event, when, in a grand ceremony, the three-meter-tall orange-red tuff stone was erected and unveiled on the grounds of the Basilica of St. Servatius.[65] They dedicated the *khach'k'ar* "to the city of Maastricht by the local Armenian community in memory of their compatriot Saint Servatius."[66] By doing so, they made use of a common practice of Armenian Christianity, the establishment of memorial *khach'k'ars*, as a creative deployment of the kinds of saint veneration central to Armenian Christianity described in this chapter.

This is an especially appropriate use of the Armenian Christian tradition, as the dedication of a *khach'k'ar* includes a liturgical blessing and consecration by a priest. As such, it is properly part of the liturgical life of the Armenian Apostolic Church, an accepted practice. At the same time, *khach'k'ars* are dedicated for all sorts of reasons and to all kinds of people or events. They are not limited to the official saints of the Armenian Church who are commemorated during the Divine Liturgy or other regular liturgical services. For the Armenian Apostolic Church, sainthood is essentially a liturgical designation marked by inclusion in the liturgical calendar and certain portions of the liturgy. While not a remembrance in the official *Divine Liturgy,* the Mass of the Armenian Apostolic Church, erecting a *khach'k'ar* to St. Servatius does at least incorporate him into the liturgical life of the Armenian Church. Thus, hagiographic emplacement here is bidirectional: Armenians emplace themselves into the physical saintly geography of Maastricht through the veneration of St. Servatius while simultaneously elevating the status of the saint among Armenians.

Indeed, it is such practices like the erection of the *khach'k'ar* that begins a local veneration that might eventually be taken up by the Armenian Apostolic Church. As I have detailed elsewhere, the *Hokihankisd* memorial service of the Armenian Church, when conducted regularly for beloved public figures, appears much like the liturgical veneration of a saint.[67] Eventually, "canonization" might occur through incorporation into the liturgy. In the case of the 1.5 million Armenians massacred during the 1915 Armenian Genocide, they recently "became" martyrs and therefore official saints of the Armenian Church in 2015, when a full cycle of hymns and an official day of commemoration entered the liturgical calendar. Such an incorporation of St. Servatius into the full liturgical life of the Armenian Apostolic Church is indeed possible: There are currently discussions to bring relics of the saint from Maastricht to Armenia. Local practices of veneration, then, may eventually lead to official status within the Armenian Church for St. Servatius or other saints encountered by Armenians in Europe.

During interviews with members of the Surp Karapet Church, several people agreed on the importance of St. Servatius for their ability to emplace themselves in Maastricht. By linking themselves and their community to St. Servatius, these Armenians asserted that they belonged to the city of Maastricht, that they had a meaningful presence in the city not simply because they lived there or because the Netherlands had welcomed them or their parents as guestworkers in the 1960s. Rather than a contingent history and belonging built from claims to abstract citizenship or the political traditions of the country, Armenians in Maastricht asserted a deep and textured presence in the history and landscape of the city. "We tell our [non-Armenian] friends that Servatius is Armenian," one member of the congregation asserted. Many of the people I spoke to at the church had attended the ceremonial opening of the *khach ̔k ̔ar* or some portion of the Servatius symposium. While not as deliberate as the official events, these everyday conversations with non-Armenian neighbors and friends suggest that the strategies of hagiographic emplacement have a broader appeal. The connection between St. Servatius emerges not only through grand public rituals and ceremonies directed outward to the non-Armenian residents of Maastricht but also in quiet conversations with neighbors or even in the developing self-understanding that Armenians themselves have about their place in the city.

The inscription on the *khach ̔k ̔ar*, claiming the saint as a "compatriot," suggests how powerful emplacement through reference to St. Servatius can be. The *khach ̔k ̔ar* is a physical presence, a material incarnation of the Armenian hagiographic tradition on the grounds of the saint's basilica, at the geographic and symbolic heart of the city. Instantiated through Armenian liturgical practices that make use of the flexible understanding of sainthood in the Armenian tradition, this presence also partakes in the Armenian understanding of saintly glory, of *p ̔ark ̔*, that is an integral part of the Armenian theological tradition, one that resonates with the configuration of human and divine in the Miaphysite Christology of the Oriental Orthodox churches. This Armenian form of saintly presence emplaces the entire Armenian community in Maastricht, at the very heart of the city, precisely by coordinating with the long-standing tradition of the veneration of St. Servatius. Catholic and municipal practices, which include a local sacred geography that encompasses the basilica and healing wells, encounter the Armenian conception of saintly presence and an Armenian notion of "holy places." In this encounter, hagiographic emplacement works as a dynamic grounded in both local/regional practices and conceptions of presence in the minority migrant tradition. Minority belonging here does not work only through legal mechanisms like refugee status or claims of equal rights as citizens or residents but through the textured encounter between creatively deployed practices of the minority tradition that link to the religious, hagiographic history of the place in Europe where they live.

The techniques of emplacement exemplified in the veneration of St. Servatius by the Armenians of Maastricht are tentatively being applied elsewhere. The first time I met Vazgen, he eagerly argued for the Armenian background of Odo van Metz, an eighth-century architect who designed buildings for Charlemagne in nearby Aachen, and mentioned Macarius of Ghent in nearby Belgium. In the 1930s, Fr. Jean (Hovhannes in Armenian) Nalbandian, an Armenian Catholic priest, had declared St. Marcarius of Ghent the patron saint of his periodical, Հայ Աշխարհ / *Le Monde Armenien*. Fr. Jean, then, recognized the potential strategy of asserting presence and connection through hagiographic emplacement nearly a century ago, just as Vazgen and members of the Ani Foundation do today.[68]

In addition to these and additional Armenian cases of presence assertion through saintly veneration, contemporary efforts by other Oriental Orthodox churches suggest the broad applicability of hagiographic emplacement as a mode of forging a presence in the context of migration. For instance, the Coptic diocese for Austria and the German-speaking portions of Switzerland on their "Copts in Switzerland" page claim the saints Felix and Regula in the city of Zurich, forging a connection there similar to techniques deployed by Armenians in Maastricht.[69] These and other examples demonstrate the efficacy of hagiographic emplacement as a strategy generally available to Oriental Orthodox and Middle Eastern Christians. To conclude, I consider what this broader efficacy might mean for a shared Orthodox presence in Europe, for our ethnographic approach to Orthodox Christianity, and for how we conceive of minority belonging.

Oriental Orthodox Hagiographic Emplacement in Europe

From Zurich to Maastricht, London to Marseille, Armenian and other Orthodox Christians are making new homes across Europe. While there is a long Orthodox Christian presence in many of the countries that make up the European Union today, often these Orthodox Christians, like the Armenians in Maastricht, are recent migrants who must forge new connections to their homes. These Orthodox migrants are what Mayanthi Fernando calls "nonnormative subjects" from at least two perspectives: first, in their status as migrants and, second, as practitioners of a form of Christianity that is the minority in much of Europe.[70] As such, their presence in their new home is not a given but must in some way be forged. Emplacement strategies, like hagiographic emplacement, help recent minority migrants assert and build a presence in Europe, to forge these important connections to place necessary for making a home somewhere.

Claims of belonging, of course, often make recourse to the state, government bureaucracy, and law. Fernando asks if there might be ways "to achieve religious equality (and other forms of equality) without addressing the state."[71] Perhaps, as the attendance of the Dutch minister of immigration, integration, and asylum at the Servatius symposium suggests, the state ultimately does shape the possible forms of action. Liturgical practices like the dedication of a *khach'k'ar* depend on legal and bureaucratic permission from at least local government.

However, I have argued that the mechanism of hagiographic emplacement forges a form of material presence that in its immediate address and its specific techniques of placemaking does not, in the first instance, address the state. In a sense, it brackets the discourses of civic belonging and equal citizenship and avoids entanglement with the mechanisms of state recognition. This does not make it "beyond politics" or completely indifferent to the state. In fact, the presence claimed through hagiographic emplacement may very well form the basis for further claims, sometimes explicitly of legal or political rights. Yet through recourse to the practices of saint veneration, Oriental Orthodox Christians in Europe are building a presence in Europe that emplaces them in their local context, helping them build a new home using tools already available in their tradition. Hagiographic emplacement, as I have described it, is a broadly available strategy whose concrete success in the case of the Armenians of Maastricht works through its Christian and Orthodox particularity.

Some of the elements of this particularity are shared across all the ancient Christian traditions. Indeed, hagiographic emplacement as I have described it depends on forging links that assume some shared practices of saint veneration, such that the Armenian emplacement in Maastricht also depends on the Catholic veneration of St. Servatius. Some elements are common to all members of the "family" of Orthodox Christianity. These commonalities include liturgical and material emphases.

Yet the dynamics of emplacement, such as that of hagiographic emplacement, also require a fine-grained attention to the particularities of a given migrant minority tradition, notably the conception of presence that undergirds any emplacement. How, exactly, is presence formed and articulated for a migrant minority group? Here, the Miaphysite Christology of the Oriental Orthodox churches implies an idea of presence that differs from other Eastern Orthodox churches. Finally, there are also specific Armenian Apostolic Christian discourses and practices, crucially a conception of saintly glory that dwells in material objects and places and the dedication of *khach'k'ars*, that the Armenians of Maastricht deploy.

Hence, I urge attention to the specific theological discourses and liturgical practices of individual Orthodox churches in any ethnographic encounter with Orthodox Christians. Orthodox Christianity, in all its forms, shares important orientations to saint veneration and other practical expressions of Christianity that might influence the way Orthodox Christians emplace themselves in Europe. Hagiographic emplacement, as exemplified in the ethnographic example of the Armenians of Maastricht, emerges as a generally applicable Orthodox Christian strategy for forging connections, asserting presence, and cultivating a sense of belonging in a place. Yet at the same time, we will only fully understand the forms of action, the dynamics of emplacement, and the techniques available to the huge number of Orthodox Christians living in the context of migration by working through the specifics of their theology and liturgy. By doing so, we see that through the practices of saint veneration Orthodox Christians in Europe assert their presence as minority migrants, emplacing themselves through modes that would otherwise escape our attention.

Notes

1. Frans Theuws, "Maastricht as a Centre of Power in the Early Middle Ages," in *Topographies of Power in the Early Middle Ages*, ed. Mayke de Jong, Frans Theuws, and Carine van Rhijn (Brill, 2001), 155.

2. Kim Vivian, Ludo Jongen, and Richard H. Lawson, eds. and trans., *The Life of Saint Servatius: A Dual-Language Edition of the Middle Dutch Legend of Saint Servatius by Henrich von Veldeke and the Anonymous Upper German Life of Saint Servatius* (E. Mellen, 2006), 20. I follow their translation throughout.

3. This project has received funding from the European Research Council (ERC) under the European Union's Horizon 2020 research and innovation programme (grant agreement No. 834441 GlobalOrthodoxy).

See "Rewriting Global Orthodoxy," under the direction of Prof. dr. H.L. (Heleen) Murre-van den Berg, https://www.ru.nl/ptrs/research/research-projects /rewriting-global-orthodoxy/.

4. Julie Chu, "To Be 'Emplaced': Fuzhounese Migration and the Politics of Destination," *Identities: Global Studies in Culture and Power* 13 (2006): 399.

5. The metaphor here of "inscription" opens up different possibilities from the overarching concern with "emplacement" operative throughout the chapter. Inscription could be considered a subset of broader practices of emplacement, those that focus on placemaking through written efforts, which is largely how I consider it here. At the same time, given broader questions about writing, Jesus Christ as "the Word of God," and the Christological difference of the Oriental Orthodox Churches described in this chapter, there are different, generative metaphoric possibilities of inscription, which I largely leave to the side here.

6. The UN High Commissioner for Refugees says that the dramatic rise of displaced persons resulting from Russia's invasion of Ukraine has catapulted the number of forcibly displaced persons beyond 100 million for the first time, a "staggering milestone." Diane Taylor, "Number of Displaced People Passes 100m for the First Time, Says UN," *Guardian*, May 23, 2022, https://www .theguardian.com/globaldevelopment/2022/may/23/total-displaced-people-now -at-staggering-milestone-of-100msays-un.

7. The "Migrant Integration Policy Index," a collaboratively produced research tool, lists a number of areas and questions that aim to measure the success of integration. See Giacomo Solano and Thomas Huddleston, "Migrant Integration Policy Index," https://www.mipex.eu/. For more on the official governmental discourse and EU policy related to integration, see the official website of the EU, "The European Website on Integration," European Commission, https://ec.europa.eu/migrant-integration/home_en. Anxieties around migrants in Europe often revolve around Islam and constantly pose the question of whether "Islam" is "compatible" with European ideals. For nuanced and critical works that look at this anxiety, especially around Muslims, see, among others: Mayanthi Fernando, *The Republic Unsettled: Muslim French and the Contradictions of Secularism* (Duke University Press, 2014); and Martijn de Koning, "'No, I'm Not a Salafist': Salafism, Secularism, and Securitization in the Netherlands," in *Political Muslims: Understanding Youth Resistance in a*

Global Context, ed. T. Abbas and S. Hamid (Syracuse University Press, 2019), 75–99.

8. The literature on the debates over the limits of Europe and what constitutes European identity is vast, spanning historical arguments about medieval legacies to contemporary discussions about the inclusion of Turkey or post-Soviet countries into the European Union. For an introduction to discussions on the "idea" of Europe, see Brian Nelson, David Roberts, and Walter Veit, eds., *The Idea of Europe: Problems of National and Transnational Identity* (Berg, 1992). For a succinct and compelling discussion of the role of Christianity and religion in discourses on Europe, see Talal Asad, *Formations of the Secular: Christianity, Islam, Modernity* (Stanford University Press, 2003), 161–72.

9. A long history of Armenian diplomatic missions to Europe, hoping to gain support for various liberation projects, underscores the allure of claiming a European connection. Gerard Jirair Libaridian, "The Ideology of Armenian Liberation. The Development of Armenian Political Thought Before the Revolutionary Movement (1639–1885," PhD diss., University of California, Los Angeles, 1987, 9, 16–29, 33–36.

10. Mayanthi L. Fernando, "State Sovereignty and the Politics of Indifference," *Public Culture* 31, no. 2 (May 2019): 270.

11. Throughout, I refer both to migration and diaspora, knowing full well that the two concepts are disparate and that each has a full and expansive literature. While the chapter intends to intervene in questions of minority belonging in contexts of migration and diaspora, I keep the broader theoretical discussions of these two concepts at arm's length to focus on the specific mechanism of hagiographic emplacement at the heart of the argument. To move from one place to another, no matter for how long, requires some form of placemaking and development of attachment to the new place. It is this dynamic with which this chapter is concerned. Regarding the concept of diaspora, it sometimes seems to proliferate definitions beyond any practical use. Yet I continue to find value in the term, used with some specificity, as in the careful articulation in Khachig Tölölyan's work. See, for instance, Khachig Tölölyan, "Rethinking Diaspora(s): Stateless Power in the Transnational Moment," *Diaspora: A Journal of Transnational Studies* 5, no. 1 (Spring 1996): 3–36. I have dealt with many of these conceptual questions regarding diaspora and migration in a recent piece focusing on a different moment in the dynamic of migration: Christopher Sheklian, "The Liturgical Subject of the Armenian Apostolic Church: Recent Waves of Migration," in *The Armenian Diaspora and Stateless Power: Collective Identity in the Transnational 20th Century*, ed. Talar Chahinain, Sossie Kasbarian, and Tsolin Nalbantian (I. B. Tauris/Bloomsbury, 2023), 148–72.

12. Cited in Theuws, "Maastricht as a Centre of Power," 165.

13. For details on the identity and sources for the life of St. Servatius, see my earlier work on Armenian emplacement in Maastricht, on which this piece builds. Christopher Sheklian, "'Their Compatriot St. Servatius': Armenian Emplacement in Maastricht," in *Europe and the Migration of Christian Communities from the Middle East*, ed. Martin Tamcke (Harrassowitz Verlag, 2022), 111–24.

14. Vivian, Jongen, and Lawson, *The Life of Saint Servatius*, xx.

15. Vivian, Jongen, and Lawson, xxii.

16. Vivian, Jongen, and Lawson, xxii.

17. Theuws, "Maastricht as a Centre of Power," 155.

18. Translated by the author from the inscription.

19. Vivian, Jongen, and Lawson, *The Life of Saint Servatius*, 20.

20. While it is possible that Servatius's medieval hagiographers confused "the Latin word 'Aramaic' . . . as 'Armenian,'" the link between Armenia and St. Servatius stuck. Vivian, Jongen, and Lawson, *The Life of Saint Servatius*, 232n12. This tenuous link, first found in Jocundus and reiterated by von Veldeke, has been challenged by modern historians. However, the Armenian historians Kahyiguian and Yevadian argue that Servatius's name is connected to an Armenian noble dynasty mentioned in two ancient Armenian histories. George K. Khayiguian and Maxime K. Yevadian, *Saint Servatius d'Arménie: Premier évêque de Maastricht* (Sources d'Arménie, 2012), 27–33, 81.

21. Work on the early modern community in the Netherlands exists, including, among others, Sebouh David Aslanian, *From the Indian Ocean to the Mediterranean: The Global Trade Networks of Armenian Merchants from New Julfa* (University of California Press, 2011); and Aṛakʻel Saruhkhan, *Hollandan ew Hayeri: ZhZ–ZhTʻ darerum* [Holland and the Armenians in the sixteenth to nineteenth centuries] (Mkhitarist Tparan, 1926). Less has been written about the contemporary Armenian community. In an earlier work grappling with Armenian emplacement in Maastricht, I offer a brief overview of the history of Armenians in the Netherlands, encompassing both the early modern merchant community and the contemporary one. See Sheklian, "'Their Compatriot St. Servatius,'" 115–20.

22. Aslanian, *From the Indian Ocean to the Mediterranean*, 202–14.

23. Both the Netherlands and Germany relied heavily on "guestworkers" (*gastarbeider* in Dutch) from several countries after World War II. The Republic of Turkey, through bilateral agreements encouraging migration for work (an agreement was signed with the Netherlands on August 19, 1964), quickly became the largest country of origin for many of these migrant workers. Ahmet Akgündüz, *Labour Migration from Turkey to Western Europe, 1960–1974: A*

Multidisciplinary Analysis (Ashgate, 2008), 61. See also Rita Chin, *The Guest Worker Question in Postwar Germany* (Cambridge University Press, 2007).

24. "Onze Kerk," Armeens Apostolische Kerk Maastricht, https://www .surpkarapet.com/Home/.

25. Peter Brown, *The Cult of the Saints: Its Rise and Function in Latin Christianity* (University of Chicago Press, 1981).

26. Brown, *The Cult of the Saints*, 1. For a recent, largely anthropological look at sainthood across traditions in the Middle East, see Andreas Bandak and Mikkel Bille, eds., *Politics of Worship in the Contemporary Middle East* (Brill, 2013). Their "broad conceptualization of sainthood as a fragile set of relations," where "sainthood can be understood as particular nested relationships with extraordinary persons, living or dead, that function as models *of* and *for* action" (11–12) opens up a number of important possibilities for thinking about saints and sainthood.

27. Athanasius, *The Life of Antony and the Letter to Marcellinus*, trans. Robert C. Gregg (Paulist, 1980).

28. Wendy Mayer, "Introduction," in St. John Chrysostom, *The Cult of the Saints*, trans. Wendy Mayer and Bronwen Neil (St. Vladimir's Seminary Press, 2006), 18.

29. Brown, *The Cult of the Saints*, 11, 12.

30. Mayer, "Introduction," 19.

31. Angie Heo, *The Political Lives of Saints: Christian-Muslim Mediation in Egypt* (University of California Press, 2018), 21.

32. Heo, *The Political Lives of Saints*, 59.

33. Heo, *The Political Lives of Saints*, 102.

34. Sarah Bakker Kellogg, "A Racial-Religious Imagination: Syriac Christians, Iconic Bodies, and the Sensory Politics of Ethical Difference in the Netherlands," *Cultural Anthropology* 36, no. 4 (2021): 629. For more on the concept of autochthony in the Netherlands, see Paul Mepschen, "Everyday Autochthony: Difference, Discontent, and the Politics of Home in Amsterdam," PhD diss., University of Amsterdam, 2016.

35. The Dutch Reformed Church became the dominant strand of Christianity in the present-day Netherlands "in the course of the seventeenth century." Catholicism remained important in parts of the Netherlands, including portions of Gelderland and Overijssel, Brabant, as well as the Limburg province where Maastricht is located. There, "Catholics had more freedom" in part because the Dutch Republic "formally shared power with the prince-bishop of Liège." James C. Kennedy, *A Concise History of the Netherlands* (Cambridge University Press, 2017), 174–75. While Maastricht is not unique in the Netherlands in its continuing importance of Catholicism, the presence and

role of the Catholic Church is more apparent and consequential than in many other parts of the country.

36. For many Christians from the Middle East, misrecognition as Muslims makes visibility "not only a question of visual presence, but also a question of public recognition on the one hand and voices from minority groups speaking publicly on the other." Lise Paulsen Galal, Alistair Hunter, Fiona McCallum, Sara Lei Sparre, and Marta Wozniak-Bobinska, "Middle Eastern Christian Spaces in Europe: Multi-sited and Super-diverse," *Journal of Religion in Europe* 9 (2016): 20. My suggestion in this chapter is that the political possibilities stemming from visibility are different than those that start from presence.

37. Caroline Walker Bynum, *Christian Materiality: An Essay on Religion in Late Medieval Europe* (Zone, 2011), 178.

38. Caroline Walker Bynum, *Dissimilar Similitudes: Devotional Objects in Late Medieval Europe* (Zone, 2020), 133.

39. Marie-José Mondzain, *Image, Icon, Economy: The Byzantine Origins of the Contemporary Imaginary*, trans. Rico Franses (Stanford University Press, 2002).

40. For an excellent introduction to Armenian history, see George A. Bournoutian, *A History of the Armenian People*, vol. 1: *Pre-History to 1500 A.D.* (Mazda, 1993); and vol. 2: *1500 A.D. to the Present* (Mazda, 1994). For a wonderful primer on the history and doctrine of the Armenian Apostolic Church, including details about the conversion and hierarchy, see Malachia Ormanian, *The Church of Armenia: Her History, Doctrine, Rule, Discipline, Liturgy Literature, and Existing Condition*, trans. G. Marcar Gregory (A. R. Mowbray & Co., Ltd., 1955): 3–13.

41. Such an ecclesial division of Christianity differs fundamentally from another distinction, common in social scientific literature, about "Middle Eastern Christians." Middle Eastern Christians are grouped more by geography and history than by ecclesiology. Thus, most Oriental Orthodox Christians are Middle Eastern Christians, but Middle Eastern Christianity includes the Assyrian Church of the East, Eastern Orthodox, Catholic, and Protestant Christians who live in the Middle East. While there is important overlap between the categories, I emphasize here the theological (and hence liturgical as well as "theoretical," regarding topics like "presence") commonalities of Oriental Orthodox Christianity rather than the shared grounding in a specific geographic region—even if that shared geography leads to shared histories and shared experiences of migration.

42. "According to *Orthodox* teachings, the holy icon depicts a holy person." Heo, *The Political Lives of Saints*, 181, emphasis mine. Heo goes on to dispel the "essentializing dichotomies of 'aniconic Islam' versus 'iconophilic Orthodoxy,'" a trope more suited to the Eastern Orthodox than the Oriental Orthodox churches. In terms of theology and theory of the icon, Mondzain's *Image, Icon,*

Economy, which depends on Chalcedonian Byzantine theologians who were often involved in anti-Miaphysite polemics, has been the starting point for sophisticated and careful anthropologists of Oriental Orthodoxy like Heo and Sarah Bakker Kellogg in "A Racial-Religious Imagination" and her chapter in this volume. Both Heo and Bakker Kellogg draw as much as possible on thinkers from the churches that they study ethnographically and as there are many shared "Orthodox" elements to icon veneration, the paucity of work on the specifics of the Oriental Orthodox churches in this regard has led to the reliance on Eastern Orthodox theology to talk about images and icons in the contemporary Oriental Orthodox churches. In a forthcoming essay, I develop the philosophical implications of the Miaphysite Christology of the Armenian Apostolic Church with regard to contemporary theoretical debates about materiality. Christopher Sheklian, "'One Unalterable and Indivisible Nature' Through the 'Ineffable Union': Armenian Christology and Materiality," *Études arméniennes contemporaines* (forthcoming). See also Gaétan du Roy and Christopher Sheklian, eds., *Oriental Orthodox Visual Cultures*, forthcoming.

43. See, for instance, Jean-Luc Nancy, *The Birth to Presence*, trans. Brian Holmes et al. (Stanford University Press, 1993); and Lieven Boeve and L. Leijssen, eds., *Sacramental Presence in a Postmodern Context* (Leuven University Press, 2001).

44. Moses Khorenats'i, *History of the Armenians*, trans. Robert W. Thomson (Harvard University Press, 1978), 250.

45. P'awstos Buzand (attributed), *The Epic Histories (Buzandaran Patmut'iwnk')*, trans. Nina Garsoïan (Harvard University Press, 1989), IV:xxv.

46. Steven H. Rapp Jr., "The Early Christian Caucasus," in *Routledge Handbook of the Caucasus*, ed. Galina M. Yemelianova and Laurence Broers (Routledge, 2020), chap. 4.

47. On the emulation of the saints in the Armenian Church, see the collection of sermons attributed to St. Gregory the Illuminator, which includes *Homily 16*, "On the Edification from Teaching About the Martyrs." Grigor Lusaworich', *Hachakhapatum Chark' ew Aghôt'k'* [The oft-cited discourses and prayers] (Venice: I Tparani Srbots'n Ghazaru, 1838), 157–60. Khorenats'i's account suggests that the church hierarchy was worried about the "proper" veneration of saints, recognizing that the power of saintly presence might slip outside the bounds of acceptable Christian orthodoxy, as defined by the church itself.

48. Garabed Archpriest Kalfayan, *Sop'erk' Yetemagan* [The Yettem writings] (Donigian, 1962), 67–70.

49. For a short introduction to sainthood and canonization in the Armenian Church, see Michael Daniel Findikyan, *From Victims to Victors* (St. Vartan, 2015).

50. The title of the book derives from the phrase "On this day" in the plural, which is the first line of most entries. Dr. Edward Matthews is preparing a month-by-month translation of the *Yaysmawurkʿ*, publishing each as he finishes the translation. Much of the following information on the book comes from his introduction to the January translation. Edward G. Matthews Jr., *On This Day: Յայսմաւուրք; The Armenian Church Synaxarion (Yaysmawurkʿ), January* (Brigham Young University Press, 2014), xi–xx.

51. Sebouh Aslanian, *Dispersion History and the Polycentric Nation: The Role of Simeon Yerevantsi's Girkʿ or Koèi Partavèar in the 18th Century National Revival* (S. Lazarus, 2004), 32–35. See also his recent *Early Modernity and Mobility: Port Cities and Printers in the Armenian Diaspora, 1512–1800* (Yale University Press, 2023), especially pages 332–49.

52. Matthews Jr., *On This Day*, xiv–xv.

53. Matthews Jr., *On This Day*, xv.

54. Findikyan, *From Victims to Victors,* 48.

55. Brown, *Cult of the Saints*, 9.

56. Brown, *Cult of the Saints*, 10.

57. "Over de Stichting," Armeense Stichting Ani, https://www.animaastricht .nl/.

58. Fernando, "State Sovereignty and the Politics of Indifference," 270.

59. "Sint Servatius (Servaas)," Armeens Apostolische Kerk Maastricht, https://www.surpkarapet.com/Sint-Servatius/. Some of the details regarding the symposium have been deleted in a recent update. See the version of this page from the Wayback Machine: https://web.archive.org/web/20140812115418 /http://www.surpkarapet.com/sint-servatius.html.

60. Leo van Leijsen, "Sint Servaas de Armeniër," *Katholieke Vereniging voor Oecumene*, March 20, 2012, https://www.oecumene.nl/nieuws-blogs/blogs/71 -sint-servaas-de-armenier.

61. Khayiguian and Yevadian, *Saint Servatius d'Arménie*, 27–33, 81.

62. Leo van Leijsen, "Sint Servaas de Armeniër."

63. Leo van Leijsen, "Sint Servaas de Armeniër."

64. There are many works about the artistic tradition of *khachʿkʿars*. See, for instance, Facoltà di architettura del Politecnico di Milano and the Accademiá delle scienze di Yerevan, *Documenti di architettura armena/Documents of Armenian Architecture*, vol. 2: *Khatchkar* (Edizioni Ares, 1977).

65. The dedication of the *khachʿkʿar* is available to view on the YouTube channel of the Ani Foundation: https://www.youtube.com/watch?v=msEFwo -MBrY&t=247s.

66. Translated by the author from the inscription.

67. Christopher Sheklian, "Venerating the Saints, Remembering the City: Armenian Memorial Practices and Community Formation in Contemporary

Istanbul," in *Armenian Christianity Today: Identity Politics and Popular Practices*, ed. Alexander Agadjanian (Ashgate, 2014), 145–70.

68. Jean Nalbandian, *Hay Ashkarh Parperat῾ert῾/ Le Monde Arménien: Revue Mensuelle Historique Culturelle* 1, 2, 3 (April 1937). In his periodical, Nalbandian recognized that teaching Armenian Christians about the Catholic saints in the region who had connections to Armenia was a way of helping displaced Armenians who had been forced from their historical homeland to establish their new home in the context of migration. Each issue contained a section dedicated to "historic episodes from the lives of saints and select Armenians" (4). In later issues, in fact Fr. Nalbandian detailed the life of St. Servatius. My thanks to La Bibliothèque Nubar de l'UGAB in Paris, where Nalbandian's periodical was shown to me.

69. "Die Kopten in der Schweiz," Coptic Diocese of Austria and German-Speaking Switzerland, https://www.kopten.ch/lokale-geschichte. This example was brought to my attention by fellow researchers in the Rewriting Global Orthodoxy project.

70. Fernando, "State Sovereignty and the Politics of Indifference," 261.

71. Fernando, "State Sovereignty and the Politics of Indifference," 261.

Dynamic Honor

How Ethiopian Orthodox *Keber* Mediates the Secular, the Islamic, and the Religiously Plural

John Dulin

On Good Friday in Gondar, a historical town in northwestern Ethiopia, the faithful fill Ethiopian Orthodox Church courtyards and engage in swift, repetitive prostrations. They begin in an upright standing position, then quickly move to their knees, then lower their forehead and arms to the ground. Some perform this intensely aerobic act of worship throughout the day, sweating profusely, all the while abstaining from food and drink. The Amharic word for prostration is *sigdet*, "'obeisance' or 'surrender' . . . it is the bodily show of deference, rather than the uttering of words, that is highlighted."[1] One can find people intensely performing *sigdet* like this on Good Friday throughout Ethiopia. However, Gondar is unique because it is a particularly religious town in a particularly religious country, so, unlike elsewhere in Ethiopia, the people who remain in neighborhood parishes throughout the day, hungry and prostrating, represent a sizable mass of Gondar's residents. Gondar is home of the famed forty-four churches built by the kings when the city served as Ethiopia's seat of power. These churches sit in the shadow of the yet more famous castle ruins. These castles evoke what Cressida Marcus calls "imperial nostalgia," serving as a conspicuous reminder that Gondar was once the capital of Ethiopia and has a central place in old Abyssinia's religious and political history.[2]

Consistent with this heritage, Gondar has a reputation for strict Christian commitment. For example, Gondare are said to pester their relatives from other regions for not observing fasts and feasts well enough. I've spoken to students from Addis Ababa attending Gondar University who said they hide their relaxed approach to Orthodoxy to avoid censure from their Gondare friends. During the COVID-19 pandemic, Gondare Orthodox Christians mounted particularly strong resistance to social distancing rules from the secular government that curtailed religious gatherings, to the point where police had to station themselves outside of churches during the initial lockdown to prevent Christians from entering the church.[3] Some Orthodox Christians interpreted lockdowns as a secular denial of God's capacity to free Ethiopia from the pandemic. Hence, the way that the secular was imagined in relation to the religious shaped and motivated resistance to government-mandated lockdowns.

In this chapter, I discuss the ways in which Orthodox Christian practice in Gondar, like *sigdet*, forge links between social imaginaries of Christianity, the secular state, and Ethiopia's interreligious milieu. Charles Taylor writes that his concept of a social imaginary includes a "normative and factual . . . sense of how we all fit together" and understandings of "how we got to where we are, how we relate to other groups."[4] Theology serves as an important backdrop for legitimizing social imaginaries. Just as the great chain of being underpinned "premodern" social imaginaries of hierarchical complementarity, theologies of human rationality as the expression of the divine image underpin what, Taylor claims, is modernity's more instrumentalized vision of society. The rapid changes Ethiopia faced over the last fifty years has put into flux the question of how different sectors of society fit together, such as the historical relationship between church and state institutions and between Orthodox Christians and Muslims. Ethiopian Orthodox Christian theologies provide potential answers to this state of flux, generating imaginative links between the Orthodox Christian community, the secular state, and religious others. However, these links are not frozen in a state of unquestioned normativity. A look at the intersection of theology and practice highlights a particular dynamism at work in the forging of Christian social imaginaries in Gondar.

I examine the theology-practice nexus with a focus on the concept and practice of *keber*, an Amharic term translated to English as "honor" or "respect." *Sigdet* is just one of the many ways Ethiopian Orthodox Christians extend *keber* to God. Fasting, observing the ritual calendar, kissing the church gate, bowing, and prostrating during the liturgy all demonstrate *keber* for God and the saints. Also, outside of ritual spaces, *keber* serves as an important value frame in everyday social interactions: Greetings, commensality, and attendance at weddings and funerals express *keber* for neighbors, family, and friends. Muslims and Orthodox Christians extend *keber* to each other through such quotidian practices, which gives *keber*, as a value, interreligious legibility. Hence, *keber* provides a frame for evaluating religious others, e.g., "Are they respectful or not?" The inverse of *keber* is *nek'at*, the Amharic word for "denigration," "disrespect," or, as some of my interlocutors translate it into English, "underestimation." The perceived performance of *nek'at*, such as declining to return a greeting or leveling insults, can disrupt cycles of respectful mutuality. The potential for reversal inflects the performance of *keber* with fluctuating dynamism. Here I argue that because *keber* within Orthodoxy has dynamic affordances—to reinforce as well as invert existing hierarchies, to create asymmetries and level them out—its performance gives impetus to dramatic shifts in orientation, putting it at the center of a triad of conflict and rapprochement between nation, Christian, and Muslim.

Narratives of *Keber*, Narratives of the Nation

It is not uncommon to hear Christians preach the importance of "honoring God." Orthodox Christian acts of honoring—whether extended to God, scripture, priests, relics, spaces, or icons—often acknowledge symbolic hierarchies between divine and human, sacred and profane. Theologies of divine transcendence and immanence find a real-world footing in practices of honoring God, in their forms and their directionality. They find a footing in conceptions of spaces, words, and practices that represent the set-apart nature of divinity and allow honor to be pointed upward. Timothy Ware, speaking of Orthodox thinking in general, says, "The Holy Liturgy is something that embraces two worlds at once, for both in heaven and earth the Liturgy is one and the same."[5] This theology of presence underpins an Orthodox blending of the sacred and mundane in everyday life, as well as an intertwining of divine hierarchies with mundane status hierarchies of wealth and political influence, which sometimes provokes critique. For example, in the fifteenth century, a faction of the Russian Orthodox Church known as "the possessors" was supportive of monasteries owning a third of Russia's land and using the coercive powers of the state to punish heretics. The nonpossessors mounted an opposing faction, arguing that monks must fully detach from the world, which meant ridding themselves of entanglements with wealth and state.[6] The nonpossessors could make their case because Christian narratives contain the potential for dramatic reversals, inversions of the honored and those obliged to extend it.

One such inversion framed a Palm Sunday sermon at the Abo Church in Gondar. The Ethiopian Orthodox priest spoke to a massive crowd over a loudspeaker in the church's unusually large courtyard, saying: "Jesus was riding on the back of a donkey. Donkeys are unloved, but he chose that animal to ride into Jerusalem, to show that he loves those who are unwanted. . . . He could have chosen a horse, but he chose a donkey because he loves those who are forgotten and unloved . . . the denigrated are honored." Biblical commentators interpret Jesus's act of riding a donkey as a symbol of meekness and peace. They contrast Jesus's actions with those of a conqueror who rides to battle on a horse.[7] This Ethiopian Orthodox priest, though, emphasized how the act of riding a donkey extended honor to people of low status, a gesture offered as his disciples honored Jesus with shouts of praise and the waving of palm leaves. He added, "When Jesus came into Jerusalem, the educated did not want to praise him, but all the children were praising him."

This story could have special meaning to him as a member of the Ethiopian Orthodox clergy—because he would have experienced life on the margins of society, only to achieve honor once officially ordained. *Tamari*, or students training for the clergy in traditional church schools, go through a period of poverty as part of their early education, "not necessarily because they are needy, but as part of spiritual discipline and a means of 'disowning' their souls from this world."[8] I often heard *tamari* in their early teens shouting from outside my host family's compound, chanting the words "*sele mariam*" "for the sake of Mary," begging in the name of Mary in a stereotypic intonation. The maternal head of the household would either tell him "God will give it to you" (which is to say, "I will not give it to you") or hand the *tamari* leftover, often stale, injera bread. During this period of their training, the *tamari* are intentionally grouped with nonclerical mendicants[9] and treated as marginal members of society. The spatial organization at my host family's Christmas feast put this marginal status on display. As a successful businessman and landowner, Ato Telahun threw a massive Christmas feast, which included the slaughter of several cows and oxen. Relatives poured in from the countryside, and neighbors frequented the feast throughout the day. The compound was organized into two levels. The honored guests ate on the top level, feasting on unstained injera and fresh meat from the pot. When the honored guests finished their meal, they dropped their leftovers in a large barrel. These scraps were fed to those eating on the lower level—these included the very poor who beg for food and money and young *tamari*. While many of my Orthodox neighbors expressed disdain for this practice, asserting that all guests should be given fresh food, it is notable that, unlike *tamari*, adult priests sat at the top level as honored guests. The *tamari*, who in Gondar mostly come from rural villages, are already marginal because of their country-boy accents. Some are thought to be so undesirable that young women fear *tamari* might slip them love magic because, they assume, it's their best chance to find a wife. However, these marginal persons come to assume a place of honor in Gondare society as they advance in their training. One could say the life of a priest enacts the classic Christian reversal of the honored and dishonored.

The priest at the Abo Church provided one of many possible interpretations of Jesus's entry to Jerusalem. As I learned later that day, the palm leaf symbolism can also turn attention to Ethiopia's theocratic history. Because of the ubiquity of palm leaves in Gondar on Palm Sunday, it would be impossible to step outside without being constantly reminded of how Jesus's followers welcomed him to Jerusalem. Palm leaves proliferated not just on church grounds but on Gondar's streets, shops, and taxis. Some Orthodox Christians fashioned their palm leaves into a hat; others created a palm-leaf cross that they wore around their necks. Many wore palm rings around their fingers, which, Qes Abraham told me, symbolized their marriage to God. On that Palm Sunday, I had a lengthy conversation with Qes Abraham at the Taklah Haymanot Church in Gondar's Piassa (city center). He emphasized, "We use palm leaves to honor God and recognize he will rule for eternity." This statement was nestled within a larger lesson, wherein he quoted scripture verses providing examples of when biblical actors used palm leaves to show respect to prophets and leaders. In quoting these verses, he tied this Orthodox practice to patterns of deep time, rooting them in the history of God's chosen. His Orthodox Christian theological orientation attuned his sensibility to see in ritual objects vectors of continuity between sacred worlds of the past and sacred practices of the present. Yet as I stood to leave, this foray into the mythical roots of Ethiopian Orthodoxy suddenly turned to the present temporality of states, territories, and constitutions in the priest's explosive parting statement: "Ethiopia is not ruled by the constitution. It is ruled by the law given to Moses and the things Jesus did. Only God judges Ethiopia. He does so by the Ten Commandments, which rest in Axum. No other laws can rule Ethiopia. We do not accept the laws of non-believers." The visions the two priests express seem to conflict. One focuses on the plight of the marginal peoples, the other on matters of government and state. Yet, in the context of present-day Ethiopia, both discourses imply a challenge to the prevailing metrics of honor: the first honoring the poor over the rich, the second honoring the imperial theocracy of the past over the secular constitution of the present.

The constitution Qes Abreham referred to was ratified in 1994, when the Ethiopian People's Liberation Front came to power, ousting the Derg regime. This constitution provided "a government-independent framework for religious plurality,"[10] introducing "religious freedoms . . . at an unprecedented scale."[11] Article 27 of Ethiopia's constitution states: "Everyone has the right to freedom of thought, conscience and religion. This right shall include the freedom to hold or to adopt a religion or belief of his choice."[12] As Winifred Sullivan argued in *The Impossibility of Religious Freedom*, to codify religious freedom is also to codify what counts as religion.[13] This, inevitably, prioritizes some formulations of religion over others. The line quoted here focuses on religion as "conscience," as a form of "thought," and as "a belief of . . . choice," which deprioritizes religion as a taken-for-granted obligation, hierarchical network, vector of intergenerational continuity, and sign of territorial and national belonging. It is not surprising that Orthodox Christians in Ethiopia who are suspicious of religious-freedom provisions worry that it facilitates the spread of Pentecostalism and Salafism, whose evangelizing activities presuppose that religion is a chosen belief. Qes Abreham's rejection of the constitution likely had less to do with the document's language and more to do with his perceived contrast between presently observed secular regimes and Ethiopia's past religious regimes remembered in history and scripture—the latter of which Qes Abreham evoked in his allusions to Israelite history.

Politics, Historical Theology, Religious Practice

In the fourteenth century, a new dynasty came to power in Ethiopia that claimed descent from King Solomon and thus the mantle of Israelite Kingship. Their right to rule was bound up in a story about the Queen of Sheba and her son Menelik. A few short passages in the Old Testament give an account of the "Queen of Sheba" visiting King Solomon, showering him with gifts, seeking wisdom, and testing "him with hard questions" (1 Kings 19:1). An Ethiopian holy book dating at least to the fourteenth century called the Kebra Negest (The Glory of Kings) elaborates upon this story, giving it an Ethiopian twist. It claims the Queen of Sheba was an Ethiopian queen. It recounts that during the queen's visit, Solomon tricked her into sleeping with him, and she conceived a child. On her journey home to Ethiopia, she gave birth to Solomon's child, Menelik, who grew up to rule Ethiopia. In adulthood, Menelik traveled to Jerusalem to visit his father, the king of Israel. Solomon bequeathed Menelik with riches and an entourage to take back with him to Ethiopia; however, some of his new servants were upset about having to leave Jerusalem, so they stole the Ark of the Covenant from the temple without Menelik's knowledge. Upon learning of the Ark's removal, King Solomon sets out in pursuit of his son, but according to the *Kebra Nagast* tradition, God thwarts his efforts by miraculously returning Menelik, his entourage, and the Ark to Ethiopia—in some tellings by hastening their journey beyond natural possibility, in others by carrying them through the air. This divine intervention indicated that God's favor had passed to Ethiopia and that Ethiopia had superseded Israel as God's covenant people.[14] Ethiopian Orthodox Christians believe that the original Ark of the Covenant rests in a church in Axum, and once a year, on a holiday called Mariam Ṣion, Ethiopian Orthodox Christians make a pilgrimage to Axum to honor the original Ark. As I observed when I took this pilgrimage with my local parish in 2013, the Ark is fastidiously protected and never taken out of the inner sanctum of the large church that houses it.

The holy object of the Ark, or Tabot, is one of the unique features of the Ethiopian branch of Oriental Orthodoxy in the way it forges an indexical link between Ethiopian Orthodox liturgy and a particular narrative of the nation—a narrative that justifies particular claims to power and forms of state government that trace the right to imperial succession to the Israelite monarchy. The Ark's central place in Orthodox ritual sustained a link between the dominant political ideology and religious practice for centuries. Every Ethiopian Orthodox church houses an Ark, consecrated with the same powers and divinity of the original that rests in Axum. Though the Ark functions ritually as an altar for the preparation of the Eucharist, the Ark's presence in the church is a precondition of a church's sanctity. When priests temporarily remove the Ark from a church and move it to a tent or castle compound, as they do on the holiday of Epiphany, the sacred qualities of the church are transferred to their new, temporary abodes. Though technically the Solomonic dynasty remained in power from the fourteenth century to the day that the last emperor was deposed 1974, kings had to deal with rebellion from conspiring nobles and warlords that weakened their power and sometimes killed them.[15] However, rebellions transpired and succeeded without undercutting the Solomonic narrative, for there was always a surplus of people who could make a claim to Solomonic heritage. Monarchs continued to reign symbolically even if they exercised limited power. According to the Ethiopian philosopher Messay Kebbede, the rise and fall of the powerful in Ethiopian history expresses a particular Ethiopian metaphysic that all powers and positions are reversible, that God dispenses fortunes as he pleases.[16] Despite this history of rebellion, when the Derg deposed the last emperor, Haile Selassie, in 1974 it was unprecedented not because they deposed an emperor but because they instituted an avowedly secular regime inspired by a Marxist-Leninist political philosophy hostile to religion.

The Derg was no friend to the Ethiopian Orthodox Church, confiscating its land and detaining church officials.[17] They also repressed minority religions. The Derg followed a pattern that Saba Mahmood observed in Egypt: that secular regimes take a particular interest in the religious sphere not despite their secularism but because of it.[18] Following suit, the Derg systematically persecuted Protestants, including Pentecostals, as enemies of the state. To weaken the power of the Orthodox Church, they initially took steps to establish parity between Islam and Orthodoxy by, for example, recognizing some Islamic holy days as official government holidays.[19] Nevertheless, they eventually banned the importing of Muslim literature, restricted mosque construction, and severely restricted pilgrimages to Mecca.[20] In 1991, the Tigrayan People's Liberation Front (TPLF), leading a multiethnic coalition known as the Ethiopian People's Liberation Front (EPRDF), defeated the Derg and took their place at the helm. The chairman of the TPLF, Meles Zenawi, became the prime minister in 1993 until his death in 2012. The EPRDF took an overtly pluralistic approach to governance. Their constitution, ratified in 1994, divided the provinces according to ethnicity and put each ethnicity on an equal legal footing. The EPRDF's "Ethnic Federalism" recognized each ethnicity as a semiautonomous "nation" or "nationality" with some limited rights to self-governance. Functional ethnic pluralism required religious pluralism as well because the hegemony of Orthodoxy went hand in hand with Amhara dominance, and religious identity in Ethiopia "often coincides with membership of a particular ethnic group."[21] Therefore, along with ethnic federalism, the 1994 constitution provided explicit provisions for religious freedom. These constitutional shifts had an immediate practical impact on Ethiopian Muslims. They afforded Muslims press freedoms to print magazines and books, allowed for public celebration of Muslim holidays in stadiums and public spaces, and, compared to previous regimes, were more liberal in permitting mosque construction.[22]

Many of my Gondare Orthodox interlocutors remember early opposition to the EPRDF in Gondar as a reaction to Gondar's increasing religious plurality. I often heard about Abba Am'ha Eyesus, a charismatic monk-priest who preached against the spread of Pentecostalism and expansion of Islam over a loudspeaker at the Baal Egzīyaber Church. The Baal Egzīyaber Church is notable for its central location adjacent to the castle on the south side, set along the main road running through Piassa (the city center). The events surrounding Abba Am'ha are important in Gondare Orthodox imaginaries, as they signal Orthodox Christian resistance to the EPRDF's brand of secularism. I heard many mentions of Abba Am'ha from younger people who would not likely have much first-person recollection of the events.

My most detailed account comes from an interview that my Orthodox Christian research assistant, Diborah, conducted with Abba Gabrielle Yohannes, an elderly priest who claimed to be friends with Abba Am'ha.[23] According to his account, Am'ha Eyesus was involved primarily in opposing Pentecostals, whom he called *menafek'* (heretics). The priest and his associates concluded there was a government conspiracy to expand Pentecostalism in Gondar and accused the mayor of Gondar of secretly converting. In response to this accusation, the government accused the priest and his followers of associating with Moa Ambassa, an illegal Ethiopian political movement seeking to reinstate the monarchy. Eventually, the followers of Abba Am'ha clashed with the federal police. According to Abba Gabriel's account, the police entered the churches with their shoes on (an act of desecration) looking for Abba Am'ha. They also, in this telling, at one point opened fire on unarmed youth singing hymns and carrying an icon of the Virgin Mary. A woman asked the police officers what they were up to, and one answered, "We are looking for the followers of Haile Selassie." By the time the state had completed its intervention, forty youth had been killed, and Abba Am'ha was given a seven-year prison sentence. Diborah said she heard that the rebellious priest was released early because he had miraculously escaped from his shackles while in prison. In her account, his escape struck fear into his captors, who took it as a sign from God that he should be released. Following Abba Am'ha's release, the then head of the Ethiopian Orthodox Church, Abuna Paulos, pardoned him and asked that he start preaching again. Abba Am'ha responded, "I will not preach a single day under the EPRDF government."[24]

Key details from this account reveal how many conservative Gondare Christians construct the secular state and its relationship to religious minorities. Opposition to the EFRDF was framed in terms of church-level mobilization to protect the Orthodox hegemony of Gondar and, by extension, Ethiopia. The belief that the local EPRDF government was carrying out a secret Protestant conspiracy suggests a link between Protestantism and their brand of secularism. When they entered the church wearing shoes, they performed a clear act of *nek'at* (disrespect) toward the divine, an inversion of *keber*. The government accused the religiously inspired opposition to the EPRDF of supporting a return to the old imperial order, which the Derg had already dismantled in 1974. Gondar was a known hotbed of resistance to the Derg,[25] but, of course, the present shapes popular memory as much as, or more than, the past. My interlocutors criticized the EPRDF for issues of election integrity, espionage, government repression of opposition, taxes, uneven economic development, and the privileging of Tigray networks in politics. However, one of my Orthodox Christian interlocutors' more common criticisms of the EPRDF echo the critiques of Abba Am'ha: They alleged the EPRDF fostered unchecked religious pluralism, compromising Gondar's Orthodox character.

A picture of Meles Zenawi—the then recently deceased prime minister and founding member of the EPRDF government—that hung in a café in Gondar provoked one such criticism. I drew attention to it while eating lunch with a group of Orthodox men. One of the men noted, proudly, that American politicians honored Meles at his death in 2012, calling him "a great man." His friend Abebe retorted that Meles was not good; he was "all bad," even suggesting that the Derg leader, Mengistu Haile Mariam, was preferable. It's true that under Mengistu people went hungry, but at least he "feared God." By contrast, Meles "did not fear God." I pressed him about this claim, pointing out that Meles was a practicing Orthodox Christian. He responded that when Mengistu was head of state, there were only a few Muslims, yet when Meles came to office "Muslims grew, and now they are everywhere." Because of this, Abebe concluded that Meles only "pretended" to be Orthodox. Abebe here evokes the idiom of *keber*—to not fear God is to disrespect him. Abebe frames the government's permissiveness with non-Orthodox religions as an act of *nik'at*—disrespect marking an illicit subversion of status hierarchies.

Likewise, Qes Abreham's stance against the constitution could be seen as a reassertion of sacred hierarchies against a state hierarchy that subordinates the church to secular governmentality and places Orthodoxy on a more equal plane with minority religions. In Gondar, this shift required the church to compete with alternative faiths instead of governing with a taken-for-granted, state-sanctioned authority. For context, it is worth noting that Qes Abreham's church is in a neighborhood near Arada, the market area of town, which has a burgeoning Muslim population. Up until the early twentieth century, Muslims had been more or less confined to living in a village called Addis Alem, located on a slope outside of town, since Emperor Yohannes's decree of religious segregation in 1668.[26] The Italian occupiers allowed Gondar's Muslims to build a mosque just outside of Addis Alem near the Saturday market.[27] Since then, throughout the twentieth century, Gondare Muslims and their worship spaces have moved closer and closer to the city center, until now the minaret of the Ergeber Mosque can be seen from Piassa—a few blocks from Qes Abreham's church. His advanced age would have given him firsthand experience of changes in religious demographics taking place over the twentieth century. During his lifetime, he had, like Jesus, and like all *tamari* who had come before him, won spiritual esteem by adopting the mantle of the socially dishonored. No matter the power, wealth, and education a member of the Orthodox laity may possess, they can only access the higher levels of the sacred through him or men like him. However, he had also observed the surrounding neighborhoods become more and more populated with people who worship in nearby mosques, which are highly visible and sonorous sites of vibrant religious activity.

Qes Abreham did not directly criticize Muslims or religious plurality. He expresses *nek'at* toward the secular state, but he even does that somewhat indirectly, through an expression of *keber* for God. This is an example of how *keber* and *nek'at* can be performed together because one can interpret *keber* pointed in one direction as also gesturing *nek'at* to what falls outside its field. This potential duality—a duality conditioned upon the performance's directionality—is one thing that gives *keber* its leveling potential. This performative duality also helps explain how government actions that Muslims see as respectful, such as permission to build a mosque in a new neighborhood, some Orthodox Christians interpret as an act of *nek'at*. In the following two sections, I argue that the potential of an act of *keber* in one direction to be received as an act of *nek'at* in another depends on what the anthropologist Edward Hall calls "proxemics."[28] Proxemics refers to "people's perception and use of interpersonal distances to mediate their interactions with other people."[29] As I show, through proxemics, some of the discourses described in this section become instantiated in practice. Moreover, the proxemic norms of Orthodox worship spaces create potential for shifts and reversals of honored and dishonored that implicate entities outside Ethiopian Orthodox ritual regimes.

Keber and the Proxemics of Ethiopian Orthodox Worship

The practice of honoring fellow humans, divine mediators, and God can reinforce existing hierarchies, such as that between clergy and laity or emperor and subject. Ethiopian Orthodox Christian practices of honoring contain the potential to offset hierarchies as well. Some of these leveling acts are subtle. They are ambiguous enough to soften asymmetries without challenging the status quo. Anita Hannig argues that the emphasis on commensality infuses Amhara society with practices of mutuality and care,[30] which scholars of Ethiopia have often overlooked when arguing that all of Amhara social life is run through with competitive hierarchy.[31] Tom Boylston notes that the practice of mutual hospitality in Amhara, between feeding and being fed, lends itself to an alternating hierarchy. Reflecting on the relationships he formed in the field, he suggests that the act of offering food to a guest has the potential to "offset . . . asymmetry" that may prevail outside the host's home, while also instilling "a sense of obligation" to reciprocate in some fashion.[32] The Ethiopian Orthodox Christian practice of *ziker*, a feast held in the saint's name on their monthly or annual holiday, expresses a similar logic. Holding the feast in the name of the saint, like most hospitable acts, sustains a relationship of reciprocity. In this case, it helps ensure that the saints protect and bless the host. The point is not that commensality and hospitality reverses hierarchy per se. However, it foregrounds care and "mutuality of being"[33] consistent with *keber*, putting into the background other dimensions of hierarchy, such as differentiation, domination, and separation. Even distinctions in purity status may be experienced as mutuality. Malara found that some Ethiopian Orthodox parents assert that their fasting provides spiritual benefits by proxy to their children, who may take a more lackadaisical approach to the fasting calendar.[34] While technically this places them in a hierarchy of more pure/less pure, the result is one of mutuality: Parents fast for children and care for children, and children obey and respect their parents. In fact, in this case, the children have more autonomy than their parents over what and when they can eat.

By contrast, the organization of worship in Ethiopian Orthodoxy foregrounds purity hierarchies in a way that limits mutuality through distance. That is, worship in the church separates people based on their level of purity. The presence of the Ark at the center of the church's holy of holies helps justify this spatial distribution. Priests bless the Eucharist upon the Ark, so it functions like an altar in other Orthodox churches. However, the Ark is unique because Ethiopian Orthodox Christians see it as a holy object constituting the divine presence. The Arks that sit in every church are, like the Old Testament Ark of the Covenant, considered the "dwelling place of divinity."[35] Arks are also named after distinct saints, like Mary, Gabriel, and Michael. Many Orthodox Christians in Ethiopia see the Ark as a physical instantiation of these saints. Because of the Ark, the church "ceases to be a meeting hall for a congregation of believers. . . . It becomes a holy site, with that holiness made present and real in an object."[36] Because of the presence of God housed at its center, the Ethiopian Orthodox worshiper must be sensitive to their words, bodily position, dress, adherence to purity standards, and their proximity to the church's sanctified core. Ethiopian Orthodox Christians have choices to make when positioning themselves in a church. They can enter the church building. They can stand outside the church building in the church courtyard. They may even choose to stand at the gate of the church compound, outside the wall that surrounds the church grounds. To enter the church building to partake of the Eucharist presupposes the highest levels of purity, what some have called "containment":[37] fasting, premarital virginity, no menstruating, no seminal emissions the previous night. Some even see a runny nose as disqualifying.

In Gondar, most worshipers at church do not enter the church building proper. They worship in the courtyard because they rank their purity below exemplary status. Many spend most of their lives worshiping in the courtyard because they lost their virginity before marriage. Others may worship outside the gate on occasion because they are menstruating or had eaten breakfast that morning (others may simply be in a hurry, so they need to leave mid-liturgy). The worshiper who stands further afield than others does not experience shame. An Ethiopian Orthodox Christian honors God when they calibrate their distance to their level of purity. Spatial position synchronizes with other signs of deferential virtue in the liturgy: prostrations, bowing when a chant references the Virgin, and standing attentively at the appropriate times. The link between where a person stands and the performance of *keber* are among the "embodied dispositions of Orthodox believers"[38] in Gondar. The rhythms and synchronies of worship train habits for perceiving ethical rightness of *keber* and the transgression of *nik'at* in bodily proxemics. This proxemic disposition is so well embedded in habitual ways of thinking and feeling that worshipers choose to keep a distance even after priests assure them that they are worthy—or can become worthy to partake of the Eucharist if they confess their sins and perform restitution.

This proxemic disposition not only conditions one to discipline the self but motivates and normalizes disciplining others who violate spatial norms. For example, at my local parish, the Ark was taken out of the holy of holies for an annual saint day. Clergy were parading the Ark in procession around the church when a young adolescent boy moved too close to the holy object. A guard, who was following the Ark, blowing a horn to honor it, stopped for a moment and hit the boy multiple times with this horn for violating proxemic norms.[39] Some laughed, but few seemed to take much notice of the occurrence. It seemed like a nonevent, even though the discipline took place in open view, at the backend of the procession that held the audience's attention. Most Orthodox worshipers attending the Ark's procession clap and sing and bow to honor the Ark, but they do so at a safe distance. My Orthodox interlocutors tended to agree that nearing the Ark without the proper purity and authority is dangerous. This danger does not come from the aggressions of guards with weaponized horns but from the Ark's tendency to mete out its own discipline. The Arks at the center of Ethiopian Orthodox churches have the sanctified properties of the original. Readers of the Old Testament know that God has a history of meting out capital punishment when the wrong person touches or looks at the Ark.[40]

A ritually fine-tuned disposition—that is, a way of feeling, attending, responding, perceiving—can be transposed into "different practical domains, forming the basis for . . . improvisation in everyday life."[41] I have observed children lightly struck or pinched for standing too close to adults without permission or invitation. Teddy, one of my Orthodox Christian interlocutors, explained that, unless invited, it's considered disrespectful for a child to approach adults who are not kin. Physical discipline enforces a proxemic norm that signals respect. (However, children approaching adults within their family tend to be met with warmth and delight.) There is likely not a one-to-one mapping between ritual practices and this pattern of disciplining children, but it is worth noting that a similar pattern crosscuts the proxemics of ritual and quotidian domains. Some ways of improvising these overlapping domains do not always meet widespread approval. For example, a priest was explaining the meaning of the Day of the True Cross to me in the church courtyard, gesturing to the large, beautifully latticed wooden cross he held up as a prop. Mid-lesson, he swiftly struck a boy in the head with this same cross. The boy bunched his face and moved away with his hand on his head; nearby young men erupted in laughter. Without missing a beat, he returned the cross to its original position and continued his explanation. The boy, who looked about twelve years old, was a *tamari* who had approached out of curiosity and stood inches from me. The priest exacted swift discipline as soon as he noticed him. Most of my Ethiopian Orthodox Christian interlocutors disapprove of his use of a cross for physical discipline. When I told Mesquelow, my lay Orthodox Christian neighbor, about it, he was visibly disgusted. He called the disciplinarian "a devil priest" for disrespecting the cross. Of course, this act of discipline responded to a transgression in the heat of the moment; it is not a routine disciplinary strategy. This example highlights the ambiguities of *keber* outside a "tightly controlled"[42] liturgical context, at what we might call the ritual edges. At these edges, the range of signs that index *keber* intersect with proxemic signs in ways that can turn one person's *keber* into another's *nek'at*. This is also prone to happen when the ritual edges intersect with Muslims, who carry their own signs for honoring their God and their neighbors. In the next section, I argue that these signs can index *keber* or *nek'at* to the Orthodox majority depending on the proxemics of interreligious semiosis.

The Proxemics of *Keber* in Mixed Spaces

Thus far, I have alluded to tensions between the Orthodox majority and Muslim minority in Gondar. These tensions are real, but if you ask most

Gondare, most will tell you that Muslims and Orthodox Christians in Gondar get along very well. It's not hard to find Muslims and Christian individuals that claim to be best friends, holding hands and expressing love for each other, as platonic friends tend to do in Ethiopia. My Orthodox Christian and Muslim interlocutors told me that *mechachal* characterizes the relationship between Muslims and Christians. The literal translation of *mechachal* is "accommodation,"[43] but many Amhara English speakers translate it as "tolerance" or "balance." "Balance" was the translation one Gondare Muslim taxi driver preferred. He explained that *mechachal* refers to a balanced circulation of *keber* between Muslims and Christians: "He is a Christian [pointing to a passenger]. I am a Muslim. He respects me. I respect him." Gondare tie this respect to everyday practices of conviviality. Gender sometimes conditions these convivial practices. Many women in Gondar often spend hours visiting and receiving visitors, sharing coffee and food. Muslims and Christian women routinely visit one another as part of these social routines. Muslim and Christian men may work together as business partners, and they often purchase gifts for neighbors and business associates. For example, Ato Telahun had purchased a sheep before his Christmas feast. He did not intend to feed it to his guests. He told me the sheep was "*le Islam new*" ("for Islam"), meaning it was his Christmas gift to Muslim neighbors, who would slaughter and prepare it in a halal fashion. This allowed him to include his Muslim neighbors as guests at his Christmas feast while respecting their religious dietary restrictions. Practices of Muslim-Christian respect are also on display at Muslim festivals. For example, in 2015, an Orthodox Christian man sat in a seat of honor during the Madrasa students' performance at Gondar's major Mawlid[44] festival because of the sizable donation that he had made to help fund the celebration. One of my Orthodox Christian interlocutors speculated that the Christian man must have many Muslim business partners. Overall, mutual donations to buildings and festivals were common between Muslims and Orthodox Christians. Each of these examples of Muslims and Christians extending *keber* to one another operates within the bounds of proxemic norms. The Christian gives his Muslim neighbors a sheep to hold a separate Christmas feast. Muslim organizers of the Mawlid festival gave the Orthodox Christian a seat of honor in the meeting hall within the mosque compound, but he never entered the mosque itself.

Granted, some religiously mixed practices in Ethiopia involve crossing religious boundaries. Meron notes that in different parts of Ethiopia

Muslims and Christians participate in each other's healing rituals.[45] Seeking blessings, Christians visit Sufi shrines, and Muslims visit holy water springs. Both holy water springs and Sufi shrines are relatively peripheral ritual spaces within each respective ritual order, which makes them more accessible to the religious other. These spaces also often lack the sonic (loud prayers, liturgy) and visual qualities (large buildings, distinctive architecture) that conspicuously mark them as Christian or Muslim territorial centers.[46] This boundary-crossing practice is also common in Gondar, but I never heard them included in common narratives about Muslim-Christian tolerance. Conservative Christians like the idea of Muslims seeking healing from the Virgin and holy water but disapprove of Christians seeking healing from Muslim sheikhs. Many conservative Muslims express similar disapproval of fellow Muslims seeking blessings from Christian saints and spaces. Because of these asymmetries of approval, in Gondar these practices are not widely seen as emblematic of tolerance and mutual respect. Rather, many of my interlocutors emphasized signs of respecting the boundaries of religious spaces as a key sign of interreligious *keber*.

My research team conducted dozens of audiorecorded interviews with Muslims and Orthodox Christians about this topic. When asked the question "How do Muslims and Orthodox Christians get along in Gondar?" several Muslim and Christian respondents evoked the same stereotypic narratives. One of these narratives emphasizes proxemic respect for religious boundaries. It told of Muslims and Christians spending hours passing the day together, having coffee, and chatting in cafes. Otherwise inseparable, these friends would only part when it was time for a Muslim to go to their mosque or for a Christian to go to their church. One friend prays in their worship space, while the other waits patiently outside. Once religious obligations have been fulfilled, they continue passing the day together. Another stereotypic narrative focuses on Muslim and Orthodox attendance at each other's funerals, which, admittedly, often results in Muslims entering an Orthodox church compound. However, Muslim comportment when they attend Christian funerals indicates their sensitivity to proxemic signs of *keber*. I observed many Muslims join Orthodox funeral processions in my neighborhood. During one such event, I remember a Christian and Muslim neighbor walking in front of me, side by side, holding hands. For Orthodox funerals in Gondar, neighborhood boys carry the body of the deceased from their homes. Clergy lead the procession carrying ritual umbrellas, while funeral attendees follow. Funerals are considered an acceptable occasion for Muslims to enter a church courtyard; nevertheless, many of them left the procession before entering the church gates. Others removed conspicuous Muslim attire before entering. Likewise, when I observed Orthodox Christians attend Muslim funerals, they walked with their Muslim neighbors to the cemetery but left before the prayers began. In medieval Ethiopia, Richard Pankhurst notes, funeral attendance was "virtually obligatory."[47] Likewise, based on his recent fieldwork with Orthodox Christians in the Amhara region, Boylston states, "Attending funerals becomes the most significant indicator, for locals, that a person is a member of their group."[48] By attending each other's funerals in this way, they meet the most basic requirement for positive social relations while also making subtle adjustments that demonstrate respect for the other's religious boundaries.

Because of their mutuality, these practices perform an egalitarian image against a larger-scale backdrop of interreligious hierarchy. These displays of *keber* do not merely accrue to the religious majority. Each side has its parallel honorific emblem, which they routinely reciprocate without fanfare. The leveling image appears consistent with the gentleness of a God who chooses to ride a donkey over a horse. It is consistent with an ecclesiastical system that expects the rich and powerful to bow to rural men who grow up begging for food and often walk barefoot as a sign of humility. However, Gondare enact these performances of egalitarian respect in the wake of a hierarchical imaginary. At the scale of the city, Orthodox Christians have the numbers and state influence to give local hegemony an outsized Christian inflection. One can see the Christian inflection in the presence of police officers with crosses hanging from their necks, patrolling Eid celebrations in Gondar's stadium, where the Christian mayor of Gondar gave an opening address. This hegemony assumed a more violent form when, for example, Muslims constructed a minaret on top of what was once a discreet house-mosque indistinguishable from its neighborhood surrounds. Its two-hundred-meter proximity to St. Gabriel Church outraged local Orthodox Christians, some of whom hurled stones at the edifice. Some Orthodox Christians felt this was justified in part because, as one neighbor put it, "All of that land belongs to Gabriel!" This violent reaction appears less consistent with the God riding a donkey and more consistent with the practice of disciplining trespassers using crosses and musical instruments. It is more consistent with Emperor Yohannes's decree of religious segregation discussed earlier, which exiled Gondare Muslims to Addis Alem.

From these descriptions, it should be clear that there are similar prox-emic patterns both within Orthodoxy and between Orthodox Christians and Muslims. Routines of honorific mutuality sometimes harden into po-liced hierarchical boundaries of separation when the proxemics of sacred space is at play. I lived in a neighborhood belonging to St. Gabriel parish between 2013 and 2015. During this time, a mosque with a minaret erected within two hundred meters of the church was an ongoing point of con-sternation. A house had functioned as a mosque for some time before the construction of the minaret, but it was indistinguishable from surround-ing residences. Before they built the minaret, Christians could ignore the discreet house-mosque. The discretion also gave an air of respect, like the men who remove Muslim attire as they enter church grounds. Chris-tians saw the construction of the minaret, which put the top of the mosque at a higher point than the church, as a sign of *nek'at*. While Orthodox youth took up stones, the mosque's Christian neighbor responded with a building project. He built a hotel in his compound, which towered higher than the mosque, and he placed three crosses on top of the building. The hotel made it so one could not view the mosque from the main road. It was common for my Christian neighbors to express annoyance and anger about the mosque followed by smiles and laughing when talking about the retaliatory counter-construction.

The perceived *nek'at* of the mosque provoked what some interpreted as the leveling discipline of vandalism and the protest construction. These actions focus on the buildings themselves and do not disturb the quotid-ian mutuality I have discussed. However, one interaction I observed shows that buildings that some interpret as violating proxemic norms can affect quotidian Muslim-Christian interactions. I was walking to the St. Ga-briel Church with my Orthodox neighbors Addisu and Thomas, at about 10 PM on Easter Eve. As good Orthodox Christians are supposed to do, we were setting out to spend the night in the church compound. At the church, we would lie half-asleep on the concrete floor outside the church building while absorbing the blaring liturgy. As we walked up the steep dirt road that leads to the church, a Muslim young man left the place he was standing on the side of the road and introduced himself to me while walk-ing beside me. Under most circumstances, this act of friendliness between adults would be seen as a sign of *keber*. However, Addisu and Thomas grabbed him and pushed him to the side of the road. They had a heated argument I could not quite hear. At the end, the Muslim young man tried to smooth things over, "*Salam now?*" (Is it peace?). Addisu answered harshly, "Salam aydelem!" ("There is not peace!"). These are fighting words: something you only say in very serious situations when anger is strong and justified.[49] I asked Addisu that night why he became so upset at what appeared to me as benign behavior. He said, "He's a Muslim! He should not be around the church!" Addisu is a person I regularly see laughing with Muslims, affectionately holding hands with Muslim young men, and trusting Muslim young men to guard his music kiosk. The main issue that night was not his general problem with Muslims but the particular placement of *that* Muslim during an Orthodox holiday. It was enough of an offense to justify a breach of the peace, if you will, in order to discipline the Muslim young man into keeping a respectful distance from the church. When this confrontation came up in a conversation a few months later, Addisu explained that he had assumed the young man was being intentionally disrespectful because of the mosque recently built near the St. Gabriel Church. The Muslim young man became a proxy for the mosque that offended so many Orthodox Christians, while Addisu acted as a proxy for Gabriel, disciplining the young man for his insolence toward a mediator of God. This example suggests that the value of interreligious *keber*—performed through practices of mutuality and proxemic respect— also lays out conditions for its undoing. When Addisu saw the Muslim's actions as a proxemic sign of *nek'at*, his routine stance of mutuality gave way to a hierarchical, disciplinary stance focused on enforcing separation. His explanation suggests that the backdrop of perceived proxemic violations, which the new mosque represented, justified his refusal of mutuality even after the individual Muslim attempted to declare peace.

At the beginning of this chapter, I stated that the performance of *keber* can lead to dramatic reversals of orientation. While the value framework of *keber* allows for egalitarian practices in daily interactions, it can also enforce asymmetry at the larger scale because many Orthodox Christians view mosque construction within parish boundaries as a breach of proxemic norms—an act of *nek'at* that breaks the flow of mutuality. The perceived *nek'at* that follows the construction of mosques does not just lead to rival construction and vandalism. It can lead to spontaneous *nek'at* between individuals, like that of Addisu. Were Muslims to comply with Christian expectations, however, their public presence would be significantly curtailed because, in the eyes of many Orthodox Christians, churches have already claimed nearly all of Gondar.

I also claimed at the beginning of this chapter that *keber* is at the center of a triad of conflict and rapprochement between Muslim, Christian, and nation. How so? The state has made these kinds of conflicts its concern. They exercise power to offer permits and restrict mosque construction—and, according to my interlocutors, they often deny permits because they fear provoking the ire of Orthodox Christians. They also revoke permits when backlash erupts.[50] They jail those who vandalize religious buildings and punish those who incite interreligious conflict. Government officials give speeches at major Orthodox and Muslim festivals extolling Ethiopian norms of religious tolerance and championing national unity. At Muslim holidays, I observed that government speeches include extra exhortations for them to keep the peace, implying that Muslims have more potential to foment tensions.[51] Likewise, Orthodox Christians often blame the government for the changing sounds and sights of Gondar, as heard in regular prayer calls and seen in proliferating minarets and vivid Islamic dress. As the examples detailed in this chapter indicate, resentment toward an expanding Muslim community can easily fold into resentment toward the secular government, which many Orthodox Christians see as supporting Muslim expansion. When there is a religious conflict, Orthodox Christians sometimes blame both Muslims and the government.

In early 2009, a three-day Muslim-Christian conflict transpired in connection with the Epiphany procession. The local government had given Muslims permission to build a mosque on a large open field that serves as a resting place for an Ark once a year. In the days leading up to Epiphany, on that field Muslims had constructed a small, makeshift mosque out of tin corrugated sheets. As the Ark approached, Orthodox Christians gathered in the field, shouting inflammatory chants like "this year we will segregate" and "our blood will flow."[52] In the three days that followed, there were several incidents of violence. Christians threw stones at mosques and Muslim shops, and a Muslim shot one Christian in the hand.

Gebre, an Orthodox man in his late twenties, claimed to be involved in the upheavals on Timket in 2009. Gebre is a Gondare man raised in Piassa: bald, serious, furrowed expression, often wearing jeans with a polo shirt and sneakers. One of my first encounters with him was on Good Friday. He was in the church courtyard, prostrating, sweating. In a conversation a day later, I asked for details about 2009. Of course, he did not want to provide details about his involvement, but he took the conversation as an opportunity to explain his understanding of the state's role in Muslim-Christian conflict. He said *"yemengist Orthodox ychenetal"* ("The government's Orthodoxy forebears/tolerates it"). The current regime, he says, "does not give [the church] much freedom" because they are afraid that the clergy will speak out against the government. Behind the scenes, the government pressures the clergy to preach their approved message. This explains the church's tolerant attitude toward Muslims in the wake of the events of 2009. He sees Islam as the primary danger, which the state supports by promoting religious pluralism and pressuring the church to countenance Muslim ascendance. On another occasion, I sat with Gebre and some friends at a café as he elaborated his view of rising religious tensions in Gondar. Echoing common tenets of global Islamophobia, he asserted, "Everything ISIS does, Ethiopian Muslims would like to do in order to spread Islam. . . . Shariah says if you change to Christian, you die. They want to institute Sharia in the entire world." He referenced a recent case in Sudan in which a woman was sentenced to death for converting to Christianity. His friend Anbassa clearly disapproved of Gebre's ideas. "You are complaining too much about Muslims!" Anbassa asserted that it was the government's fault that Muslims and Christians do not get along. He said that since the current government came to power, the relations between Muslims and Christians have deteriorated. In his view, they spread propaganda to keep different religions and ethnicities fighting to extend their power.

This difference between Gebre and Anbassa suggests that whether one blames interreligious conflict on a violent Muslim essence or on external manipulations, they imagine the government as a key player mediating relations and pursuing their own designs. The proxemic norms of *keber* empower Gondare like Gebre to boost their narrative about the evils of Islam. It also gives them a framework to make a case for conflict with Muslims. However, the narratives that circulate about conflict events are unstable. They fit uneasily with the routine practices of mutual *keber* that enact a daily image of *mechachal*. Some Orthodox Gondare prefer narratives that place blame not on Muslims but solely on the state. It is not Ethiopian Muslims but the secular government that needs to be put in its place. In sum, I have argued that as much as *keber* underpins quotidian practices of Muslim-Christian mutuality, it also justifies disciplinary conflict that reinforces the hierarchy of Christians over Muslims. Moreover, I have shown that both modes of Muslim-Christian relations implicate the state. The state publicly embraces mutuality as a performance of "tolerance," or *mechachal*. The state claims it as a key element of national identity and precondition of development. Conversely, some Orthodox Christians also imagine the state as an evil manipulator that has forsaken God or fomented conflict to amplify its power.

Finally, there are times in which the performance of *keber* directly challenges state power. Elsewhere, I discussed the response in Gondar to a viral film that documents ISIS soldiers beheading Orthodox Christian migrants in Libya.[53] In the wake of the video's release, the local government organized a "demonstration" that culminated in a government speech in the auditorium near the Fasilides bath castle compound—a restored ruin of the vacation residence of Emperor Fasilides, who reigned in Gondar in the seventeenth century. Government speakers stood at a podium, while Muslim and Orthodox Christian leaders in religious clothing were seated visibly behind the speaker. Leaders from both faiths sat on benches parallel to each other, suggesting unity and symmetry. This placement also signified their encompassment by the secular government, whose representatives gave the final speeches. Government officials decried extremism and emphasized that terrorists did not represent the Islamic faith. They asserted that extremists seek to divide Ethiopia and halt its economic development. In the middle of one official's speech, a large group of Orthodox Christian young men burst onto the scene, singing a hymn that declares that they would never abandon their faith. Their singing drowned out the speaker. They walked directly in front of the speaker, then continued past the stage and faced in the direction of the castle compound, lowering to their knees to pray. Like Qes Abreham's statement in the first section of this chapter, this act exploited the deictic potentials of *keber* to imply *nek'at*. By pointing one's *keber* to persons or entities in one direction, one also points away from other potential recipients of honor. In doing so, they performed a reversal of a scene that foregrounded respect for government officials. In this case, they pointed *keber* to God and, in facing the castle, to the old, nonsecular political order—pointing away from the current government in an act of implicit *nek'at*. This also performed a placement of the religious over the secular state, indicating that one deserves more honor than the other. As one Orthodox Christian interlocutor put it, "They came to interrupt the government. They wanted them to be quiet because a speech is worthless; the only useful thing is to pray to God."[54] *Keber/nek'at* performances unfold against an Ethiopian Orthodox Christian theological backdrop, with its imaginaries of a divinely chosen Ethiopian monarchy. These imaginaries crystallized in holy ritual objects (Arks), which serve as a nexus for honoring God. These elements enhance the potential of *keber*—as performance and discourse—to evaluate the church against the state, Christian majorities against Muslim minorities. It allows embodied practices to forge multipronged links between (plural) religious and secular spheres while enacting reversible frames of value.

Conclusion

Heo argues that in Egypt, Mary the mother of Jesus can serve as a symbol of national unity because both Muslims and Coptic Christians love and respect her.[55] This emblem of Muslim-Christian similarity turns into a source of conflict when reports circulate of Mary appearing at Coptic churches in neighborhoods experiencing demographic changes and interreligious tension. To some, Mary's proximity to a church suggests she gives Christians special recognition, one might say honor, which makes these visions fertile ground for Muslim-Christian polemics. Likewise, in Gondar, a shared value of *keber* serves as a basis for Muslim-Christian "tolerance," which, in Ethiopia, also serves as an emblem of national unity. However, the shared value of *keber* can turn into a source of conflict because of its proxemic dimension: The placement of people and buildings can create a situation of contested *keber*. Any performance has a deictic element, which gives them dynamic affordances to draw together elements of a context in ways that shift.[56] I have argued that proxemics are central to how the performance of *keber* creates social effects. There is a tendency in Orthodox Christianity to claim spaces not just for religious activity but for the sacred—treating lands, buildings, and other material forms as divine incarnations.[57] Because of this, proxemic signs carry a particular force, imbued with far-reaching, value-potent significance—hence the great potential of proxemic signs in Gondar to provoke interreligious conflict.

Moreover, as the secular state in Ethiopia asserts itself as the administrator of lands and buildings, it positions itself as the custodian and arbiter of large-scale proxemics. While Asad argued that secular and religious are discursively inseparable, one dependent on the other for significance,[58] in Orthodox Christian–majority regions of Ethiopia, secular and religious *action* sometimes seems inseparable, either supporting or subverting the other. This applies at least to the domain of state-orchestrated proxemics: permitting and restricting construction projects or permitting and restricting movement. While Christian narratives tell of dramatic reversals between honored and honoree, Ethiopian Orthodox proxemics of *keber* facilitate dramatic reversals in practice. Distinctions between sacred and profane space give proximity the power to transform honor into dishonor and mutuality into conflict. On the other hand, the clear boundaries and rich semiotic forms of Ethiopian Orthodoxy also create a map for regular practices of interreligious *keber*, which enables mutuality to define Muslim-Orthodox relations most of the time—this despite the tensions fueled by rapid social change.

Notes

I am grateful to Sarah Riccardi-Swartz and Candace Lukasik for the invitation to contribute to this volume and for their comments on several drafts. Thanks are also due to Diego Malara for providing valuable feedback on an earlier draft. I also appreciate the reviewers for the time and attention they dedicated to this chapter.

1. Tom Boylston, "Sharing Space: On the Publicity of Prayer, Between an Ethiopian Village and the Rest of the World," in *Praying with the Senses: Contemporary Orthodox Christian Spirituality in Practice*, ed. Sonja Luehrmann (Indiana University Press, 2018), 165–82, 167.

2. Cressida Marcus, "Imperial Nostalgia: Christian Restoration and Civic Decay in Gondar," in *Remapping Ethiopia: Socialism and After*, ed. Wendy James, Donald L. Donham, Eisei Kurimoto, and Alessandro Triulzi (James Currey, 2002): 239–56.

3. Terje Østebø, Kjetil Tronvoll, and Marit Tolo Østebø, "Religion and the 'Secular Shadow': Responses to COVID-19 in Ethiopia," *Religion* 51, no. 3 (2021): 339–58, 449.

4. Charles Taylor, *Modern Social Imaginaries* (Duke University Press, 2003), 23–24.

5. Timothy Ware, *The Orthodox Church* (1963; Penguin, 1997), 264.

6. Ware, *The Orthodox Church*, 104.

7. Carl Greg, "Jesus' Subversive Donkey Ride (A Progressive Christian Lectionary Commentary for Palm Sunday)," *Patheos*, March 23, 2012, https://www.patheos.com/blogs/carlgregg/2012/03/jesus-subversive-donkey-ride-a-progressive-christian-lectionary-commentary-for-palm-sunday/.

8. Girma Mohammad, "Cultural Politics and Education in Ethiopia. A Search for a Viable Indigenous Legend," *Journal of Politics and Law* 5, no. 1 (2012): 117–25, 118. See also Christine Chaillot, *The Ethiopian Orthodox Tewahedo Church Tradition: A Brief Introduction to Life and Spirituality* (Inter-Orthodox Dialogue, 2002), 97.

9. Amharic speakers tend to be sensitive to the demeaning nature of begging and avoid referring to them using the Amharic work for beggar, *leman*. Instead, they opt for the term *yuneybeetey*, which they translate as "like me."

10. Jorg Haustein and Terje Østebø. "EPRDF's Revolutionary Democracy and Religious Plurality: Islam and Christianity in Post-Derg Ethiopia," *Journal of East Africa Studies* 5, no. 4 (2011): 722–55.

11. Haustein and Østebø, "EPRDF's Revolutionary Democracy and Religious Plurality," 756.

12. Federal Negarit Gazeta of the Federal Democratic Republic of Ethiopia 1st Year No. 1 ADDIS ABABA—21st August, 1995 Proclamation No. 1/1995, https://www.ethiopianembassy.be/wp-content/uploads/Constitution-of-the-FDRE.pdf.

13. Winnifred Fallers Sullivan, *The Impossibility of Religious Freedom* (Princeton University Press, 2018).

14. Sir E. A. Wallis Budge, trans., *The Queen of Sheba and Her Only Son Menyelek (Kebra Nagast)* (In Parenthesis Publications, Ethiopian Series, 2000).

15. Harold Marcus, *A History of Ethiopia*, updated ed. (1994; University of California Press, 2002), 30–47.

16. Messay Kebede, *Survival and Modernization: Ethiopia's Enigmatic Present: A Philosophical Discourse* (Red Sea 1999), 184–85.

17. Oyvind M. Eide, *Revolution and Religion in Ethiopia: The Growth and Persecution of the Mekane Yesus Church 1974–85* (James Currey, 2000), 111.

18. Saba Mahmood, *Religious Difference in a Secular Age: A Minority Report* (University of California Press, 2015), 3.

19. Hussein Ahmed, "Islam and Islamic Discourse in Ethiopia (1973–1993)," in *New Trends in Ethiopian Studies: Papers of the 12th International Conference of Ethiopian Studies*, ed. H. G. Marcus (Red Sea, 1995), 785.

20. Ahmed, "Islam and Islamic Discourse in Ethiopia," 790–91.

21. Terje Østebø, "The Question of Becoming: Islamic Reform Movements in Contemporary Ethiopia," *Journal of Religion in Africa* 36 (2008): 416–46, 435.

22. Ahmed, "Islam and Islamic Discourse in Ethiopia," 791.

23. This interview was recorded, transcribed into Amharic, and translated. The oral history comes from the transcript.

24. This quotation is from the account of Abba Gabriel Yohannes; however, other interlocutors told me a ban was imposed on his preaching activities as a condition of his release.

25. Christopher Clapham, "Controlling Space in Ethiopia," in *Remapping Ethiopia: Socialism and After*, ed. Wendy James, Donald L. Donham, Eisei Kurimoto, and Alessandro Triulzi (James Currey, 2002), 16.

26. According to Emperor Yohannes's decree, non-Christians were barred from owning land in Gondar and from hiring or marrying Christians. Abdussamad Ahmad, "Muslims of Gondar, 1864–1941," *Annales d'Ethiopie* 16 (2000): 161–72.

27. Ahmad, "Muslims in Gondar," 171.

28. Edward T. Hall, "Proxemics," *Current Anthropology* 9, no. 2 (1968): 83–108.

29. Nicolai Marquardt and Saul Greenberg, *Proxemic Interactions: From Theory to Practice* (Morgan & Claypool, 2015), 3.

30. Anita Hannig, *Beyond Surgery: Injury, Healing, and Religion at an Ethiopian Hospital* (University of Chicago Press, 2017), 44.

31. C.f. Alan Hoben, *Land Tenure Among the Amhara of Ethiopia: The Dynamics of Cognatic Descent* (University of Chicago Press, 1973).

32. Tom Boylston, *The Stranger at the Feast: Prohibition and Mediation in an Ethiopian Orthodox Christian Community* (University of California Press, 2018), 120.

33. Marshall Sahlins, *What Kinship Is, and What It Is Not* (University of Chicago Press, 2015); cited in Hannig, *Beyond Surgery*, 44.

34. Diego Malara, "The Alimentary Forms of Religious Life: Technologies of the Other, Lenience, and the Ethics of Ethiopian Orthodox Fasting," *Social Analysis* 62, no. 3 (2018): 21–41.

35. Ralph Lee, "Symbolic Interpretations in Ethiopic and Ephremic Literature," PhD diss., University of London, 2011, 99.

36. John Binns, *The Orthodox Church of Ethiopia: A History* (I. B. Tauris, 2017), 100.

37. See Anita Hannig, "The Pure and the Pious: Corporeality, Flow, and Transgression in Ethiopian Orthodox Christianity," *Journal of Religion in Africa* 43, no. 3 (2013): 297–328. See also Boylston, *Stranger at the Feast*.

38. Vlad Naumescu, "Becoming Orthodox: The Mystery and Mastery of a Christian Tradition," in *Praying with the Senses: Contemporary Orthodox Christian Spirituality in Practice*, ed. Sonja Luehrmann (Indiana University Press, 2018), 29–54, 37.

39. John Dulin, "Value-Dense Indexes and the Escalation of a Muslim–Christian Conflict," *History and Anthropology* 32, no. 1 (2021): 47–63, 57.

40. For example, God struck down seventy men because they looked in the Ark (6:19) and killed Uzzah because he touched the Ark (1 Samuel 6:2–7).

41. Tom Csordas, *The Sacred Self: A Cultural Phenomenology of Charismatic Healing* (University of California Press, 1994), 11.

42. Joel Robbins, "Ritual, Value, and Example: On the Perfection of Cultural Representations," *Journal of the Royal Anthropological Institute* 21, no. S1 (2015): 18–29.

43. Dereje Feyissa, "Mechal or Mechachal? The Politics of Representing Ethiopia's Religious Past," *Ethiopian Journal of Religious Studies* 1 (2014).

44. Mawlid is a celebration of the birth of the prophet Muhammad. Most Sunnis and Shias observe the practice, though Salafis condemn it as *bida*, or innovation.

45. Meron Zeleke, "'We Are the Same but Different': Accounts of Ethiopian Orthodox Christian Adherents of Islamic Sufi Saints," *Journal for the Study of Religion* 27, no. 2 (2014): 195–213.

46. Compare with Andreas Bandak, "Of Refrains and Rhythms in Contemporary Damascus: Urban Space and Christian-Muslim Coexistence," *Current Anthropology* 55, no. S10 (2014): S248–61.

47. Richard Pankhurst, *A Social History of Ethiopia: The Northern and Central Highlands from Early Medieval Times to the Rise of Emperor Tewodros II* (Red Sea, 1992), 196.

48. Boylston, *Stranger at the Feast*, 108–9.

49. "Salam now," "it is peace," is among the most conventional greetings in Amhara-speaking regions of Ethiopia. The person almost invariably responds with a reciprocal "salam now." According to my interlocutors, to break this convention with the response "there is not peace" indicates a serious conflict. The directness makes this response all the more striking, as it's common for Gondare to express social tensions indirectly through tone of voice or through ignoring overtures.

50. As I detail elsewhere, government officials allegedly revoked the permit for mosque construction on land known as "Lideta's field," following religious conflict that erupted in 2009. They compensated Muslim petitioners with a permit to build elsewhere. See Dulin, "Value-Dense Indexes."

51. Yefet argued that in discourses of Coptic-Muslim unity, the emphasis on national identity as the basis of this unity served to delegitimize attempts to assert minority rights and protections. See Ficquet Bosmat Yefet, "Defending the Egyptian Nation: National Unity and Muslim Attitudes Toward the Coptic Minority," *Middle Eastern Studies* 55, no. 4 (2019): 638–54. There has been a similar pattern in Ethiopia.

52. Dulin, "Value-Dense Indexes," 52.

53. John Dulin, "Transvaluing ISIS in Ethiopian Orthodox Christian-Majority Ethiopia: On the Inhibition of Group Violence," *Current Anthropology* 58, no. 6 (2017): 785–804.

54. Dulin, "Transvaluing ISIS," 793.

55. Angie Heo, *The Political Lives of Saints: Christian-Muslim Mediation in Egypt* (University of Chicago Press, 2018).

56. Michael Silverstein, "Shifters, Linguistic Categories, and Cultural Description," in *Meaning in Anthropology*, ed. Keith Basso and Henry A. Selby (UNM Press, 1976): 11–55.

57. Clayton Goodgame, "Custodians of Descent: The House, the Church, and the Family Waqf in the Orthodox Patriarchate of Jerusalem," *Jerusalem Quarterly* 89 (2022): 32–50.

58. Talal Asad, *Formations of the Secular: Christianity, Islam, and Modernity* (Stanford University Press, 2003).

THE STATE OF GRACE

OLD BELIEVERS' DETERMINATIONS OF CORELIGIOSITY AND MORAL LIFE IN THE DAYS BETWEEN THE MYSTERIES

Amber Lee Silva

Toward an Ethnography of God's Grace

"*Stay here, in this state of grace*," Fr. Simon beseeched his Old Rite Russian Orthodox (ORRO) congregation in Erie, Pennsylvania, after many, *but not all*, attendees shared in the gift of the Eucharist.[1] The phrase resonated with to me. I had recently embraced grace as a central to my work on the congregational schisms (microschisms) that took place in Erie, Pennsylvania, and Nikolaevsk, Alaska (1980–1983), after years of circumventing soteriological and ecclesiological matters by treating them as historical details. Fr. Simon's plea was a common marker of his post-Paschal sermons—as blaring a symbol of the season as the moment when, as the bells ring long at midnight on Easter Sunday, women and girls exchange their dark or colored head scarves for white ones, in a striking collective symbol of redemption. A few days earlier, he shared that he always feels wistful at the end of this "Spirit-filled season," seeing their souls, like their white robes, grow dingy over time without conscientious prayer and their close connection to God and "illumination" lost as they "slide further into darkness, and blindness."[2]

Old Believers, or Old Ritualists, are named for their rejection of the Russian Orthodox Church's (ROC) mid-seventeenth-century liturgical, textual, and ritual reforms.[3] For this dissent they were persecuted and anathematized, which is to say excommunicated (denied the Eucharist and other rites) and cursed ("a negative grace").[4] They scattered worldwide and repeatedly divided in their struggle to maintain their states of grace and ORRO continuity amid ever-changing circumstances of time and place. Divergent ORRO groups agreed on one point—the ROC had fallen to heresy and therefore "lost grace." From this premise emerged two branches of Old Belief: the *bezpopovtsy* (priestless), who considered the hierarchical institution of the church and the rites performed by priests (e.g., Eucharist) irrevocably lost, and the *popovtsy* (priested), who converted "New Rite" priests and searched for a bishop to revitalize the church. The two communities where I conducted fieldwork (2007, 2012–3) were *bez-popovtsy* (from different branches, as their ancestors disagreed on several points regarding priestless life and worship)[5] until a faction in each reconsidered this narrative of lost grace and became *popovtsy*. To further complicate matters, the *popovtsy* factions in Erie and Nikolaevsk did not join the same hierarchies.[6] As a people who "regarded themselves as the only true bearers of authentic Christian belief and practice,"[7] Old Believers' identities and ethnohistorical narratives cannot be separated from ecclesiology and soteriology—a thechistorical analysis is needed.

ORRO group making and breaking is essentially tied to the perceived place of God in history, from the Old Testament prophesies to the apocalyptic expectations of Revelations. Did the fall of the ROC catapult humanity to the end of the eschatological timeline? Can any institutional hierarchy legitimately claim to be the body (or bride) of Christ on earth and the authority to distribute the sacraments (or, mysteries)? Or is the church a decentralized, disembodied collective of "true" Christians? How are considerations of God's will and commandments a conscious force in Christians' day-to-day decision making? These questions underline the theoretical (if not ontological)[8] premise that the divine is not an otherworldly concern outside anthropologists' quest to understand human behavior. Recently, the anthropology of Christianity has shifted toward greater theological engagement to better understand our Christian interlocutors' motivations, actions, and relationships.[9] This volume is a necessary addition to this effort given the subfield's current deficiency in Orthodox representation. This chapter explores the role that considerations of grace play in American Old Believers'[10] individual (salvation, everyday morality), congregational (local ritual and social participation), and institutional (ecclesiastic authority, distribution of grace through the sacraments) decision making and social (non)relationships.

Douglas Davies, whose *Theology and Anthropology* (2002) led the way to an interdisciplinary dialogue on several shared topics of interest, analogized that the centrality of grace is to theology as culture is to anthropology.[11] As conceptual foundations of their respective fields, "grace" and "culture" are similarly burdened with the weight of numerous definitions too heavily entrenched and entwined to be abstracted from other key concepts like "salvation" or "society." Grace variously refers to God's gift of mercy, redemption, and salvation to his believers (e.g., 1 Peter 1:8–11); the dispensation of this gift through Jesus Christ's bodily sacrifice (Acts 15:11; Rom 5); and the relative state or standing of an individual's soul to receive that unmerited pardon.[12] Grace, as a conduit of God's relationship with believers and between believers, presents several avenues of interdisciplinary as well as cross-cultural conversation, as evidenced by a recent *Cambridge Journal of Anthropology* volume dedicated to the subject.[13] I concur with its introductory declaration that grace is a "decidedly social phenomenon" and seek to further the authors' efforts to counter the anthropology of Christianity's preoccupation with individualism by "considering how ideas about salvation emerge from and animate the collective character of Christian life."[14] Ethnographies of Roman Catholic and Orthodox Christianities are particularly valuable in this endeavor, for if the congregational life of Christians has been neglected, then the institutional church has been forsaken, if not conscientiously dismissed as a worldly necessity antithetical to the ideals of the faith.[15]

Nearly every Epistle begins with a salutation of grace (and peace); God's blessings appear as a uniting force of coreligiosity—the Spirit which binds the church. The Epistles also advised Christians how to "live by the Spirit" by avoiding "obvious" works of oppositional flesh (e.g., fornication, impurity), for "those who do such things shall not inherit the kingdom of God" (Gal 5:16–21; NRSV throughout). The Ephesian congregation was furthermore instructed to not be "associated with them" who commit these acts (5:7), positing a social duality between those of the flesh and those of the Spirit. For the American Old Believers, perceptions of others' states of (dis)grace demarcate this social duality between those who one can (the coreligious) and cannot (the noncoreligious) worship, or even socialize, with. For the older (earliest immigrants in the 1890s) and far more "Americanized"[16] Old Believer community in Erie, these demarcations are only found in worship. For the intentionally physically and socially segregated Alaskan (and more recently immigrated, in the 1960s) enclaves, grace, as a categorical marker of belonging, has wide-ranging social implications. Yet for all four congregations in my study, how and where God's grace may be experienced and obtained was integral to their ecumenical evaluations during their microschisms. Grace alone may be sufficient for salvation (2 Cor 12:9), but the genesis and continuous theme of ORRO historical group making and breaking has been the ease with which grace may be lost.

Ethnographies of American Old Believers typically portray their socioritual and material lives utilizing well-worn pure/impure, sacred/profane dichotomies and analyses of "boundaries."[17] This is fitting, even scriptural (e.g., 1 Pet 1:22; 1 Jn 3:3). I argue that grace, specifically the perceived haves and have-nots of this divine gift, provides a more ethnographically relevant conceptual tool of social distancing as a third element of coreligiosity, the mutually recognized belonging of individuals to one faith based on shared practices and dogma. Without reference to grace, the sociocultural categories and theohistorical lens that determine Old Believers' inter- and intrareligious delineations of association, considerations of God as an actor in human history—and how the four congregations discussed here share historical, national, linguistic, ritual, and dogmatic legacies yet remain *noncoreligious*—cannot be understood.

The anthropology of Christianity's development as a "self-conscious" subfield was stalled by anthropology's general unwillingness to address the complicated relationship between early ethnography, colonization, and mission work; disinclination to engage with theology;[18] and blind eye to what Fenella Cannell termed the "Christianity of Anthropology."[19] The etymological relationship between theological grace and a vocabulary of appreciation and exchange (e.g., gracious, grateful), or the "Grace of Anthropology,"[20] is an example of the embedded Judeo-Christian orientations of Western European language and thought.[21] This embedment complicates the analytical work of addressing the theological components of anthropological categories (e.g., overlaps between flesh/Spirit and body/mind) but makes it all the more necessary to understand the lives of the Christians with whom we work. As Carroll argued, "theology—as a set of cultural categories of understanding and practice of and with God—is an active element within the value judgements, decision-making processes, and mode of life of many Orthodox Christians."[22] Soteriology, for example, shapes Old Believers' everyday sociomoral lives, identities, relationships, choices, and worldviews—aspects of lived Christianity inextricably tied within Scripture, which concludes with tell of an eternally significant record of deeds (Rev 20:12–15).

Richard Niebuhr's *Social Sources of Denominationalism* (1929) guided nearly a century of socioanthropological studies of schism away from the theological rationale given by the factioning parties themselves.[23] The historical accounts of the ROC schism that engaged with ORRO apologetics (rather than simply blaming illiteracy, fanatical traditionalism, or an ignorant conflation of rite and dogma) largely focus on the canonical and textual arguments of Nikon's dissenters devoid of broader theological concerns.[24] The imperial motivations of Tsar Alexis (r. 1645–1676)[25] are covered but seldom why the dissenters believed that making the sign of the cross with three fingers (representing Trinity) rather than two (representing the duality of Jesus Christ) was heretical ("Jesus alone was on the cross").[26] Similarly, Douglas Rogers's exemplary ethnohistorical account of two microschisms in the Urals (in 1880s and 1990s) provides an excellent picture of the political landscape, societal change, ethical complexities, and personal conflicts involved but was relatively quiet on their Eucharistic and ecclesiological motivations.[27] The *popovtsy* in Erie and Nikolaevsk also situated their return to the priesthood in the complexities of the late Soviet period, but above all they stressed the vitality of the Eucharist, the chance to truly *commune* with God, as their primary motivation for breaking with their *bezpopovtsy* neighbors and family.

As Courtney Handman argued, the anthropology of Christianity was long disserved by a tendency to characterize the denominations that arose from intrareligious ruptures as ethnically, politically, or otherwise socially motivated. While the subfield's focus on the individual over Christian group making cannot be solely blamed on Weber's or Niebuhr's pen, the latter's argument "that a church as an institution amounts to little more than a stultifying sedimentation of earthly social categories and traditions that keeps Christian practice from being authentic, free, and universal"[28] must be actively countered by greater attention to the forms of Christianity that posit the institutional church as a divinely ordained, Holy Spirit–directed, Christ-wedded essential component of the faith. In focusing on the "religious" rather than "social" causes of ORRO denominationalism, I considered my work to be a more theologically attuned intervention. Yet I too pored over the Erie's Church of the Nativity's detailed microschism records and initially ignored how their coreligiosity decisions reflected their relationships with God. I was more comfortable looking at canonical laws than the "mysterious" (Eph 5:32) relationship between God and the church. In my defense, asking people what they thought about Christian Others' (including their siblings, former friends, and even ex-spouses) shot at redemption *was* extremely uncomfortable.

Most Old Believers I spoke to were quick to emphasize that the divine calculus of faith, works, and repentance was unknowable. However, our discussions about schisms, whether those of the ROC centuries ago or their own congregational rifts, often implied the opposite. ORRO studies offer keen insights into the complex relationship between dogma and Christian social groupings given its genesis in schism, many subsequent intrareligious ruptures, and self-proclaimed status as the adamant defenders of the most (or *only*) authentic, true, *pravoslavnye* (right belief *and* right worship, or "Orthodox") church. The paradox of ORRO Christianity is that there have always been variant versions of "correct" continuity, the results of tense debates, negotiations, and schisms regarding how to (ironically enough) *adapt* to their new position outside the institutional church they had hoped to save. I found the subject of grace, its perceived presence and absence, a common feature of American Old Believers' critiques of Christian Others.

In 1983, the majority of the *bezpopovtsy* in Erie's Church of the Nativity followed Fr. Simon's recommendation to join the Russian Orthodox Church Outside Russia (ROCOR),[29] which especially ordained a new bishop according to the Old Rite for their benefit. The erstwhile *bezpopovtsy* founded the Church of the Holy Trinity a couple of blocks away, close enough that their bells compete during calls to prayer. Coincidentally, at the same time a minority of Nikolaevsk's *bezpopovtsy* Church of St. Nicholas joined the priested Belaya Krinitsa (BK), based in Romania.[30] The majority either remained in the small village with hostile neighbors or moved to newly founded communities elsewhere on the Kachemak Peninsula. Setting aside the four congregations' many ritual, linguistic, historical, ecumenical, and socioenvironmental differences, I observed that they shared similar doubts about whether there was a limit to God's grace and forgiveness, whether heterodox rites were "life saving" or salutary, and whether a church hierarchy could irrevocably damn itself and lose authority. These conundrums have oriented ORRO Christians' internal and external social relationships for centuries. This study of the ways in which the four congregations *agreed* on the individual, congregational, and institutional significance of grace provides a more complete anthropological understanding of contemporary ORRO

On the individual level, perhaps the most critical consideration of grace as it pertains to salvation, the maintenance work of one's "state" and relationship with God is personal, as are the socioritual and eternal consequences of everyday morality. On the congregational level, those perceived to be "out of good standing" or "out of grace" from other (or no) faiths as well as noncoreligious Old Believers are barred from participation in the Eucharist, common prayer, and/or entrance into the nave and may face social exclusion. The inclusivist/exclusivist constructions of a person's or church's access to grace has been a sensitive and divisive issue throughout Christianity from the earliest laws of the church. On the institutional level, the *pravoslavnye* ("rightness," orthodoxy) of a doctrine or practice is judged by its continuity with Scripture, the early Church Fathers, and canon law.[31] The church must also stand in rightness and not deviate into wrong teachings (heresy). Dissenters argued that through its "wrongful reform,"[32] the ROC lost apostolic succession and the evangelical mandate that Jesus gave to the Apostle Peter that is passed through ordination to subsequent priests (Mt 16:18). The "priesthood question" (whether the hierarchical church exists after the ROC's fall) has been a recurrent, divisive topic at the center of numerous ORRO schisms, including those in Erie and Nikolaevsk.

American Old Believers' categorical distinctions between states of grace reveal complex convergences between soteriology and sociality, or, between potential salvation and permissible degrees of social interaction. The social and ecumenical implications of an individual's or hierarchy's perceived state of grace, as a divinely ascribed status and metaphysical boundary between the saved and the doomed, indicates the essentiality of considerations of salvation in Christians' everyday moral decision making and socioreligious determinations of "what we believe and who belongs." Understanding the ecclesiological foundations of Christian group making is essential to the anthropology of Christianity as we continue to find common theoretical ground and lines of inquiry among the multitude of Christianities[33] in the world today.

Everyday Morality and Purity: Individual Considerations of Grace

The definitional aspect of grace as an unreciprocated, free, inalienable gift already exists as a point of exchange between anthropologists and theologians.[34] Themes of grace, Jesus's sacrifice in exchange for sins, and the "good deeds" of his believers to spiritually qualify themselves in hope of meriting salvation frequently overlap in Scripture (e.g., Titus 2:11–14). Beyond critiques of the applicability of reciprocity language in soteriological discussions (Christian or otherwise), dogmatic interpretations of the un-equal relationship between saviors and humanity influence believers' ac-tions and interactions. The general idea that grace is an *unmeritable* pardon (Eph 2:8–9) does not negate the common conceptualization of this rela-tionship in terms of an exchange or negate believers' efforts to be "wor-thy" (Eph 4:1). A "debt" (Mt 6.12; Lk 11:4) is owed whether it can ever be "repaid" (Rev 18:6, Isa 59:18). ORRO economies of grace indicate that to achieve a state of grace one must act in accordance with God's will, con-fess, repent, pray, and "live by the Spirit." But they must do so *correctly*, an aspect of ORRO Christians' lived religion and morality that anthropolo-gists and theologians alike may find thought provoking.[35] The theologi-cal crux of the matter—one's ability to commune with God—is as much a subject for the anthropologist of Christianity's observation as the ways in which Christians endeavor to follow these prescriptions.

Anthropological studies of ORRO are convincingly framed through pure/impure, sacred/profane dichotomies as Old Believers use *poganyi* (un-clean) to refer to natural (e.g., tobacco and dogs) and social (noncoreli-gious) contaminants.[36] The application of sanctuary purity laws to routine daily life was a hallmark of the Zealots of Piety movement, whose mem-bership included both Patriarch Nikon (†1681) and leading Old Rite de-fenders like Avvakum (†1682)[37] Old Believers have been characterized as possessing an "excessive emphasis on the observance of the canonical rules, especially regarding diet and ritual,"[38] a form of puritanical control Mary Douglas's seminal *Purity and Danger* associated with groups (like the long-persecuted Old Believers) experiencing ambiguity and "pressure" on their "external boundaries."[39] For example, "plants from beyond the sea" popu-larized under "the Great Modernizer" Peter I (e.g., coffee and tobacco) were damned by association, given the long-standing correlation between the ROC schism, social change, and foreign influence.[40] Furthermore, *pomi-eschanie* (mixing up) with noncoreligious, or *mirskie* (worldly), people is "one of the gravest infractions an Old Believer can be guilty of"[41] in con-servative ORRO enclaves. Like noncoreligious outsiders, those "guilty" are barred from group worship and use the *poganyi* dishware ("dog dishes").[42] Similar to Douglas's assessment that an unclean animal may not be offered as sacrifice (or eaten), an "unclean" (out-of-grace) individual may not be offered Christ's Eucharistic sacrifice (or eaten with).[43]

In Nikolaevsk, I only noted the distinction, variously observed, in *bezpopovtsy* households. For example, Anna served amazing salmon and vermicelli pierogies on paper plates, and Nadejda made a greater point of puritanical compliance when her elder brother was present or when we shared "clean" *braga* (homemade wine)[44] rather than "forbidden" coffee. Categorical im/purity is far more applicable to the conservative Old Believer communities on the West Coast (Oregon, Alaska, Alberta) than to the "assimilated" East Coast urban enclaves. Linguistic evidence (non-Russian vocabulary) and elders' memories of a "high degree" of contact with non–Old Believers indicates that the late-nineteenth- and early-twentieth-century ORRO immigrants to Pennsylvania did not practice material and social prohibitions to the same degree as contemporary Alaskan Old Believers.[45] In Erie, earlier practices of socially shunning the *hahli*, a broad term for "Others" (other religious and ethnic groups, as well as those who left the church or married outside the faith),[46] have long since vanished.

Popovtsy elders in both fieldsites dismissed these practices in similar terms—their respective congregations moved away from sociomaterial prohibitions as they became "more educated" and "less brainwashed"; "they read Scripture rather than relying on what their grandfather said." A couple of *popovtsy* elders offered a more nuanced explanation, one supporting David Scheffel's "sacramental deprivation hypothesis" that rigid socioritual puritanism compensates the *bezpopovtsy* for their lack of hierarchical assurances of *pravoslavnye* and Eucharistic communion with God.[47] They explained that with access to the full rites and blessings of the church their former methods of assuring individuals' states of grace (e.g., restricting *pomieschanie*) had become "unnecessary." In Erie, purity rituals common to other American Old Believers, like using the *banya* (sauna) before services, that theoretically function to delineate and separate the "dangerous" margins of their socioreligious lives[48] waned the generation before their microschism. Current analyses of ORRO Christians' social duality do not account for their theological motivations or the vast degree of variation within their diaspora. For despite the differences among my four congregational fieldsites' purification practices, they shared the desire to protect the spiritual well-being of their (congregational and church) members and mission to maintain (their version of) ORRO, the ancient way of worship passed down from the Apostles, and the mystical body of Christ on Earth—the "true" church. Simply, they share the pursuit for God's grace.

Jeanne Kormina skillfully noted the overlap between anthropological concepts of purity and theological considerations of grace in her discussion of ritual bathing (including triple immersions, mimicking baptism), which is a common feature of Russian Orthodox Christians' pilgrimages.[49] One of the most central, widely practiced "purity" rituals of ORRO worship can easily be reframed as a measure of ensuring grace—the Proschaneeye (also, "Entrance Bows" or "Remission Prayer"). This confessional prayer that demarcates pure/impure, redeemed/sinner, graced/graceless, Spirit/flesh dualities is recited at the margins of days and nights, before and after meals, and as entering and departing sacred spaces and "Christian homes."[50]

> God be merciful to me a sinner (cross, bow to waist)
> Thou hast created me; Lord, have mercy on me. (cross, bow to waist)
> I have sinned immeasurably Lord, have mercy and forgive me a sinner
> (cross, and bow to waist)[51]

Theoretically, purity rituals not only protect but punish transgressions of the social order.[52] As I will discuss, temporarily "excommunicated" penitents in Nikolaevsk (as was once done in Erie) recite the Proschaneeye in front of their congregation before they may rejoin them in prayer. A purity/pollution theoretical framework misses the key ingredient—the "sinner" is attempting to reestablish their relationship with God through confession and atonement. Over the course of four centuries, *bezpopovtsy* groups ruptured over how to sacramentally mediate between divine redemption and human frailty without priests, but they all agreed that the rite of confession brought "some particular Grace of God" without which "no Christian life was possible "[53] In Old Believers' social lives, purity and grace are similar conceptual qualifiers of an individual's merit, but grace goes beyond collective evaluations of an individual's status. Grace makes this status matter.

Without descending too far into a crude reductionism, salvation is an undeniable motivation to keep one's state of grace. This concern is clear from Erie's Fr. Smolakov's (*nastavnik*[54] from 1953–1973) *Sunday School Weeklies* (*SSW*, over 750 issues) published in English to aid his congregation's limited understanding of their Church Slavonic services. His prolific writings were an influential, posthumous source of spiritual authority[55] during Erie's microschism. Most of my *SSW* sample (79 percent, 75/95 that I examined) referenced positive and/or negative afterlife consequences of individuals' faith and actions, often using the terms "grace" and "salvation" interchangeably.[56] The consequences are unknowable but are a conscientious consideration in contemporary Christians' lives. Congregational determinations of an individual's state of grace are categorical markers of status and merit in anthropological terms, yet these are predicated on Old Believers' theological considerations of one's spiritual ability to commune with God. Fr. Smolakov described the Proschaneeye in puritanical language: "the Remission Prayer represents a short confession of our daily sins, committed since the last Common prayer in the church. It is needed as our purification from the sins, before we join the Common prayer. We are supposed to pray Proschaneeye every time when we feel that we have violated the God's laws and the rules of the Church."[57] And while the clean/unclean dichotomy was a common theme of my *SSW* sample (25 percent, 24/95), this is not the full picture; confession is a pre-requisite to access grace and union with God.

Eastern Orthodox theology posits a closer relationship between God and humanity than that depicted by the common sinful flesh/grace-filled Spirit dichotomy. Erie's Fr. Simon preached about the centrality of theosis (deification) to their understanding of salvation, humanity's existential dualism (or, Christian anthropology),[58] and the purpose of Christian life. An Orthodox Christian, he advised to his *popovtsy* congregation, aims to be "illuminated" and to "change ourselves from the fallen, dark creatures. . . . To raise ourselves up and reach the state of *theosis*, of deification, that is the goal of Christianity. To raise ourselves up, so that we can be in God's image and likeness."[59] Fifty years earlier, his *bezpopovtsy* predecessor, Fr. Smolakov, similarly described human existence, created "of the perishing body and of the immortal soul, which was breathed into the lifeless body by God's Divine breath: therefore, the purpose of this life is our test of fitness for the coming life, and for the return to the Giver of life, the Almighty God."[60] American *bezpopovtsy* and *popovtsy* disagree about ecclesiology and the necessity of puritanical segregation, but they share an understanding that the "purpose" and "goal" of Christianity is to unite with the spirit of God's grace through a ritual life of prayer, confession, and communion with God (with or without the Eucharist).

All the American Old Believers with whom I spoke were united in their lament that it was becoming increasingly difficult to "raise themselves up" out of darkness and that attendance and interest were declining (already a concern in mid-twentieth-century Erie, 25/95 of my *SSW* sample). Perhaps there are too many days between the mysteries now and fewer chances of illumination, as contemporary life has made it that much harder to be grace-filled "living saints, people who consecrated their whole lives to Christ,"[61] and harder to attend Sunday (let alone midweek) services. They share this concern for "authentic" religious continuity and desire for divine communion with "New Rite" Russian Orthodox Christians who seek to "replenish" their personal "stock of grace" via pilgrimage.[62] These concerns are certainly not reserved to the Orthodox world; the role of grace in Christian relationships (divine, ecclesiastical, social) is a fruitful area of interdenominational and interdisciplinary conversation. To this end, I expand Douglas's claim that "purity is the enemy of change, of ambiguity and compromise,"[63] to incorporate the ORRO's exacting emphasis on spiritual unanimity—the unified integrity of its congregational and institutional bodies required for an effective transmission of God's grace to congregants.

Congregational States of Grace and Belonging

In advising his congregation to guard their state of grace, Fr. Simon did not fail to explicitly remind them that no one knows how much time they will be afforded to seek redemption. Or, as Fr. Larry, his *bezpopovtsy* counterpart at Erie's Church of the Holy Trinity three blocks away once joked, "Your shirt is close, but death is closer." Ethnographies of American Old Believer enclaves on the West Coast commonly frame individuals' permitted level of socioritual participation as "controls" designed to protect community boundaries and ensure congregants' compliance with religious and moral laws. The East Coast congregations have largely not retained the linguistic, material, and ethnoreligious culture such as long beards and antiquated dresses expected of *Russian* Old Believers and have subsequently received limited anthropological attention—a critique Fr. Simon repeatedly raised to me as a limitation of our field's ability to understand ORRO. "And I told you before you came here . . . if you're looking for some sociological type of Old Believers, who you know, everybody's walking around with their *rubashkas* [men's shirt], you're not going to find it here. That's gone. It was gone before I was a child." But their concern for grace is not gone. Fr. Simon's congregation's position as outliers, as simply "American people, living American ways of life who still happen to be Orthodox Christians who follow the Old Rite,"[64] draws into focus the fundamental features of ORRO Christianity.

Analytical frameworks of "purity" and "community boundaries"[65] fail to incorporate the shared theological underpinnings and great variation of

Old Believers' conceptualization of their place in the world and constructions of coreligiosity. I had to look beyond the social effects of congregational evaluations of an individual's im/meritorious state to observe the
ways in which all Old Believers sought God's grace. The common ORRO
requirement that ritual participants are affirmed coreligious and uphold
prescribed moral and religious standards is motivated by the desire to maintain the sanctity and efficacy of their services. Similarities between otherwise disparate ORRO congregations' determinations of coreligiosity and
morality are readily apparent when the research focus shifts to their shared
dogma. On one point the four congregations agreed: I could observe
but not participate (receive no blessings, perform no genuflections) at
services. The social duality of ORRO groups illustrates the complex entanglement of belief and belonging that can only be understood within
the theohistorical context of their categorical division between *pravoslavnye* and heresy.

The exclusion of Christian Others and out-of-grace coreligionists from
sacred spaces, asceticism, and long penances are practices firmly rooted in
early Russian Orthodoxy. Excommunication practices predate Russian Orthodoxy (988) by centuries and are codified in the earliest laws of the
church, the Apostolic Canon, which also details the actions for which a
hierarch or priest may be considered ineligible to administer the sacraments.
The tenth has been especially formative to ORRO: "If any one shall pray,
even in a private house, with an excommunicated person, let him also be
excommunicated."[66] The basic premise of heretical contamination is that
prayer with those disgraced (heretics and *poganyi*) invalidates "true" believers' rites and prayers, making them *not* salutary. Or, in the words of
one Alaskan (*bezpopovtsy*) elder, like the sign of the cross made with three
fingers instead of two, it "doesn't count."

The history and internal struggles of ORRO exemplify the paradox of
grace as both a unifier and medium of distinction. The first dissenters argued that church law morally obligated them to separate from leaders who
preached heresy or proved themselves unworthy.[67] Beyond the fine points
of doctrine, ecclesiology is central to analyses of Christian denominationalism. Orthodox theological conceptions of belonging, particularly the
strict division between the (presumed) graced and graceless found in
ORRO practice, are significant because "puritanical boundaries" are merely
the methods set in place to ensure the spiritual health and oneness of believers with God, the very being and mystery of the church.[68]

Breaking coreligiosity through schism or the exclusion of disgraced individuals is considered necessary to those who believe that heresy damns
by association. The sociological and soteriological overlap in ORRO Christianity is most apparent in the ways in which segregation serves to protect
the faithful from deviation from union with one another and with God's
will and grace to ensure their prayers may "count." In ORRO thought, collective *pravoslavnye* and spiritual unanimity is necessary for efficacious
group prayer and salutary communion with God; the state of grace of the
congregation as a whole is vital. This aligns with anthropological thought
on puritanical boundaries as mechanisms that protect a group's "social self-
integrity"[69] and "wholeness."[70] This principle of a congregation wholly
united is phenomenologically exhibited in Old Believers' "one voice" (*edi-
noglassie*) prayers chanted and punctuated by bows and signs of the cross
made in unison, a characteristic of ROC worship lost by Patriarch Nikon's
detested "reforms."[71]

Analyses of boundaries, or the social lines through which those who belong and those who do not traverse, incompletely encapsulate how ORRO
Christian's determinations of coreligiosity intend to account for the (inclu-
sivist or exclusivist) dispensation of God's grace and people's desire to be
united in his Spirit.[72] The malleability of boundaries over time, place, and
social setting is precisely what makes them anthropologically valuable as exemplary of people's negotiations between religious ideals and their practical
application. For example, the *bezpopovtsy* who settled in Oregon constructed
coreligious boundaries discouraging intermarriage and joint worship between individuals from different regions abroad until their council (1967)
resolved that their differences in dress, dialect, and other "details" were not
matters of dogma.[73] The East Coast congregations once held annual councils
where they discussed and debated questions of practice, canon, dogma, and
history to maintain their coreligiosity with one another. Fr. Smolakov edited
a Q&A-format review of the conferences held between 1953 and 1966,[74] a
marvelous educational tool for his (and subsequent) congregations. It also
serves as a testimony of social change; actions that once barred people from
ritual participation are now commonplace. The invisible line between the
vestibule and nave is illustrative of the boundary between acceptable and
nonacceptable behavior but also between who may or may not be spiritually
able to be illuminated by God's grace. The line of acceptable deviation has
moved in every American Old Believer community, which indicates not
only social change but a reimagining of the extent of God's mercy.

In the early decades of the Erie Old Believer enclave (1920–1950s), those out of grace remained in the vestibule and bowed to the floor as others entered the nave. Monthly meetings were once full of the business of temporary ritual banishment, penances, and pleas for community forgiveness. The offenses that caused one to "lose grace" ranged from shaving (men), cutting hair (women), smoking, poor church attendance, and "too much time with outsiders."[75] ORRO's traditional prohibitions against shaving one's beard, which alters the image of a man made in God's likeness, is no longer a boundary against common worship in Erie—they depend on God's merciful understanding of contemporary occupational pressures. However, their desire to remain in his likeness in Spirit has not changed. Ideally, retired men are expected to regrow their beards, but there is no "deferred ritual practice" until they have become *nimirskie* (unworldly).[76] Both sides of Erie's and Nikolaevsk's microschisms have experienced an increased latitude regarding social sanctions and excommunicable offenses—but religious leaders' shared concern for their parishioners' states of grace and the spiritual health and continuity of their congregations has not changed.[77]

In all four congregations I was directed to not participate in any way, but the degree to which I could enter the nave varied. In Erie, I stayed in the back to minimize any distraction I may have caused (especially if my toddler was present); I was invited several times in both churches to approach further within. In Nikolaevsk, spatial segregation was present in both churches. For the most part, I did not know why another was in the vestibule with me. To question another's presence there is too intimate not only for spiritual reasons; a woman may simply be menstruating. In one case where I was aware of the cause of a *bezpopovtsy* congregant's exclusion, it was because of her visit to an ORRO community her own considered heretical (over their divergent forms of making the sign of the cross).[78] To rejoin the congregation in the nave and participate in prayer, penitents must recite the Proschaneeye as both a confession to God and the group and an appeal for mercy. Douglas Rogers described a similar process in the Urals when an ORRO individual (most often after retirement) becomes *nimirskie*, for whom participation in group worship and more stringent moral separations are reserved.[79]

Restrictions on who may dine with a family or use their dinnerware are extensions of the restrictions over who may receive communion or participate in common prayer. Mary Douglas argued that there is an increased conceptual insecurity in the uncertain and unstructured areas of social life where formalized social controls are wanting, and it is here that we see an increased vigilance against suspected pollutants.[80] A more theological explanation is that because the *bezpopovtsy* have no Eucharist to ritually confirm the community of believers or hierarchical determinations of authenticity, puritanical social markers of belonging in day-to-day life became especially critical.[81] In this way, segregation from people and things categorized as *poganyi* helps guard an individual's state of grace and the congregation's spiritual unanimity in lieu of the redemption from sin and reception of mercy enacted through the sharing of Christ's body and blood.

Fr. Simon went as far as calling the relegation of the noncoreligious to the foyer as "unchristian."[82] But in all four churches I was instructed personally, or by a written notice "For Non-Russian Guests," in the case of Nikolaevsk's priested church: "Do not perform external acts of worship." Both Erie churches have similar notices of correct dress and behavior for outsiders. The priestless Nikolaevsk chapel has no such sign; it expects no visitors. If a member of one congregation in my study were to visit any of the other three, the same restrictions would apply. This is social duality and noncoreligiosity in practice. The first question the East Coast Conference of 1953 asked was, 'Should people of other faiths be allowed in our church?" They agreed that outsiders could "stay within" as long as their behavior and clothing did "not conflict with the rules of our Church." But "they must not pray."[83] The experience of not praying with the congregation is jarring, as everyone else joins in the unified and physically active (numerous genuflections and bows to the waist and floor) prayers that characterize ORRO worship. You must remain still, an othered unholy statue. The limits of coreligiosity and ritual exclusion must not be conflated with the dubious existence of limits to God's mercy or with future damnation. As many people and the prolific writings of Fr. Smolakov on the subject were quick to remind me and one another, a Christian should not judge.[84]

The concept of human fallibility, the theological construction of humanity as composed of flesh and Spirit vacillating between the sin of former and redemption of the latter, has wide relevance to Christian anthropology. The daily life of this dichotomy and assumption that human error requires conscientious and constant self-correction was most apparent in the Old Believers' plea, "Lord have mercy," that repeatedly punctuates their services. The Proschaneeye is another such plea. It is also an act of separation between the world of flesh and the sacred space of prayer (in churches and homes) where one hopes to commune with God and "to cleanse them-selves from the pollution of non-Old Believer society."[85] Other times I have heard it said as an atonement to both God and the congregation to (re)achieve the individual state of grace and "good grace within the com-munity"[86] required of ritual participation and the reception of God's gifts.

Old Believers reject their characterization as a "sect" (or *raskol'niki*, "schismers," as they were once derogatorily labeled), outside of the "church" that is both an earthly institution and mystery of God's relationship with humanity. In their perspective, they remain *pravoslavnye* Christians; they are the church. As I became struck by the apparent paradox of a limit to God's grace, I began to gingerly prod whether this meant that members from one congregation doubted noncoreligious Christians' states of grace. While Old Believers discussed God's grace as unlimited and unknowable, they have repeatedly ruptured over conflicting perspectives about individ-uals' (hierarchs and laypersons) and institutions' ability to give and receive that grace.

The Institutionalization of Grace and Its Limits

Ecclesiology is essentially anthropological because it concerns Christian group making, yet the anthropology of Christianity has paid little atten-tion to the institutional church as a subject. What "church" means to di-verse ORRO groups is central to their identities and practices. Contemporary ORRO Christians' determinations concerning which church holds apos-tolic succession, who belongs to a church or congregation, and who can worship together are predicated on considerations of grace. These questions have framed Old Believers' delineations of belief and belonging since the seventeenth century. And these questions split the Erie and Nikolaevsk congregations when congregants' ecclesiological narratives of Old Belief diverged to the point that they could no longer be one coreligious commu-nity. Simply, Old Believers who do not believe the same thing *about* the church cannot *belong to* the same church.

According to *bezpopovtsy* ecclesiology, "the holy fire of the Apostolic Suc-cession was once extinguished, and there was none capable to rekindle it,"[87] when the only Old Rite–defending bishop, Paul of Kolomna (†1656), was burned at the stake. Because a priest must be ordained by a bishop,[88] they concluded that the hierarchical church was lost. In the early 1980s, *popovtsy* factions in Erie and Nikolaevsk questioned this ecclesiological

narrative and the legitimacy of centuries of their forebears' priestless practice. In Erie, even the original Nikonian dissenters' mandate to leave the
ROC came under review (an especially grave matter because it is an excommunicable office to leave one's bishop without just cause).[89] Erie's
Church of the Nativity's "Restoration Study Group" (RSG, forty members, the selection of whom was contentious) documented this shift in
theohistorical narrative. During ten sessions, Fr. Simon presented the history of Christianity, the preschism ROC, and the development of distinct
ORRO continuities before concluding that the move to priesthood would
be a true and *pravoslavnye* blessing. In the ninth session, the congregation's former *nastavnik* (from 1946–1952), Fr. Yokoff, defended the *bezpopovtsy*'s position and fielded the RSG's questions, creating an important
record of the priested/priestless debate on the church's state of grace. At
the tenth session, the majority of the RSG (60 percent in favor)[90] agreed
with Fr. Simon; the rest of the congregation voted (75 percent) a month
later to accept rapprochement with ROCOR.[91]

There are few records of Nikolaevsk's *popovtsy* faction's unification with
the Belaya Krinitsa of Romania. Fr. Nikola, who converted from *bezpopovtsy* to *popovtsy* a decade after the microschism and currently leads the
Church of St. Nicholas, told me that the very suggestion of priesthood
immediately sparked the rupture. There were no formal discussions and
study groups; he said sadly, "it wasn't that civilized." People decided well
before the faction leaders first visited (1980/1981) Romania, where their first
priest (Fr. Fefelov) was ordained. Fr. Nikola also suggested that perhaps
the leaders of the *popovtsy* movement had been too forceful and hurried
with this great change.[92] There is undoubtedly a personal component
behind microschisms; how congregants view the states of grace and religious knowledge of faction leaders informs their decisions.[93] Members of
each congregation commented on the opposition leaders' ages, education,
and/or previous moral failings. Giuseppe Tateo's work on the Romanian
Orthodox concept of *har*, which "condenses ideas of grace, charisma, gift,
and gratuity in one word," demonstrates how congregants' perceptions of
priests' and monks' relative amounts of *har* influence their religious commitment and participation. The relationship between grace and charisma
represents a theologically engaged theoretical bridge between the anthropology of Christianity's focus on individuals and Weberian priestly/char-
ismatic dichotomies of religious authority and institutional ecclesiologies
with "routinized," hierarchical mediations of God's blessings.[94]

Two additional dichotomies have long held sway over anthropological discussions of Christian denominationalism and schism, Augustine's visible (whole membership of church) and invisible ("elect") churches and the distinction between the concept of "church" (open membership; an institution) and "sect" (closed, "ecclesia pura," "community of the religiously qualified . . . called to salvation").[95] ORRO studies offer a nuanced critique of these inadequate models of understanding the dynamics of mediated grace and religious authority in institutional Christianities. The difference between the priested and priestless branches, or between the New and Old Rite Russian Orthodoxies, is not a matter of members' moral construction but of where God is worshipped "correctly" (and how this is authenticated)[96] and where God's blessings may fall. The church is an open institution, yet participation is limited. The "invisible" grace-filled (as determined by their clergy or congregation) are those visibly active. God will sort the rest.

Furthermore, the difference between the priested and priestless branches of Old Belief was not caused by a radical theological shift to an anti-institutionalism, individualist, or "sectarian" "priesthood of all believers" but rather a difference in theohistorical narratives concerning the post-ROC schism existence of institutionalized grace. The hierarchy was lost, not rejected. Nevertheless, several *popovtsy* converts *did* make comparisons to me between *bezpopovtsy* practice and Protestantism as a negative of their former church life, "without a clergy, anyone can say I don't like this *nastavnik* or church, I will start a new one." Other branches of Christianity have fractured over issues pertaining to individual moral judgment and institutionalized grace. For example, whether individuals have the moral obligation to leave the Anglican Church divided the Puritans between the Separatists, who rejected the Church of England's moral mandate to lead, and the anti-Separatists, who felt that they "had no right or authority to take the law into their own hands."[97] Maya Mayblin discussed a similar distinction between "being a dissenter and being with dissent" in her research on female Roman Catholic priests who reject gendered exclusions of apostolic succession but do not seek schism.[98] But to Separatists and Old Believers, schism was a necessary evil to keep the spiritual church (i.e., not a "sect") safe from contaminating heresies and associations. Further work on Christian groups' distribution of grace and moral authority is an important topic of conversation between theologians and anthropologists of

Christianity because both fields seek to understand the complex relationship between God and human organizations (congregational or institutional) united in shared beliefs and practices.

The idea that a church hierarchy could lose grace predates the ROC schism. According to an early-sixteenth-century prophecy, the "First Rome" lost apostolic succession and legitimacy in the Great Schism (1054), as did the "Second Rome" (Constantinople) when it fell to the Ottoman Empire (1453). Old Believers did not create the theory of Russian exceptionalism—in a sense, it created them, for "in the context of the mystical doctrine of Moscow as the Third [and Last] Rome holding fast to a faith which was indivisible, the [schism] was not only understandable, but inevitable."[99] Or, in Fr. Smolakov's theohistorical narrative relayed to those assembled at the East Coast Conference of 1959:

> Only in Russia, the holy Orthodox faith was kept pure and unchanged until the 17th century, when it became reformed by the patriarch Nicon, infected with the New Greek ideas. The church service books were altered according to the New Greek books, and also the church customs and rites were changed, so that they could become identical with the Greek customs, which were already wrong before. Therefore we cannot have anything common with the today's Greeks, for they, like the Niconians, have lost their old correct faith.[100]

New and Old Rite Russian Orthodox Christians mutually spurned each other[101] based on the same "puritanical" construction of church belonging that operates on the congregational level—the righteous community must excise unorthodox and amoral persons and practices or risk heretical contamination. The giver (church, priest, or *nastavniki*, as a conduit or container[102] of the sacred gifts) and receiver must both be within a state of grace for the salutary transmission of God's blessings. ORRO Christians' identities and polarization of the "pure and unchanged" against the "wrong," "altered," and "infected" belong within preexisting conversations in the anthropology of Christianity concerning themes of rupture and continuity.[103] These discussions are of the utmost importance to Christian groups who hold that the stakes of being "wrong" and losing "their old correct faith" might be salvation.

The one thing that Old Believer groups have held in common was the conviction that the ROC lost grace by accepting Nikon's heretical reforms.

In the early 1970s, ROC (1971) and ROCOR (1974) resolved that the pre-Nikonian rites were not heretical but "Orthodox and salutary" and declared the 1666–1667 anathemas against the Old Believers "null and void and rescinded."[104] Immediately after the ROC's anathema reversal, Erie's Fr. Smolakov explained to his congregation that "if a bishop puts curses not according to God's will, then God's punishment does not follow the curse. This is the reason why the curses and anathemas of the Niconians' and Greeks' Councils were not feared by Old Believers, nor regarded as effective at any time."[105] Or, as his predecessor Fr. Yokoff more concisely argued to the RSG, "What right did they have to damn us? They were the persecutors." They could not accept ordination from ROCOR, he continued, "because they are in heresy and you would be one of them. If you do not accept them, you are still maintaining the true faith. Once you accept a dirty work, you are the dirty one too."[106] In this formulation, "heresy," "dirtiness," and "change" are synonyms substantially incompatible with "true" Orthodoxy. If the ROC practiced heresy, it was no longer *the* church, its councils could no longer define dogma, and its priests could no longer sanctify others' lives.[107]

The Erie and Nikolaevsk *popovtsy* revised this narrative of church loss, but they too are noncoreligious; they do not accept each other's claim to apostolic succession.[108] Their evaluations of each other's legitimacy speak to the nature of the transmission of grace and its possible limits in ORRO theology. For Erie's Fr. Simon, the anathema reversals were the first step toward reconciliation, and the primary challenge of his effort to unify with ROCOR was to convince his congregation that the New Rite was not heretical. This was a running theme of the RSG meetings. Other American Old Believers questioned whether the ROC's persecution of *pravoslavnye* Christians *was* forgivable. When the East Coast *nastavniki* met to draft a united position paper regarding the anathema reversals to their congregations, they resolved "to forget all harms and unjustness." But it was well noted that neither the ROC nor the ROCOR hierarchs apologized (confessed) or even condemned the persecutions and therefore lacked the key prerequisite to redemption.[109] Nearly a decade later, redemption theology fueled the *bezpopovtsy* faction's polemic: "These same people who tortured us in 1666, trying to make us give up our religion and join their church. Since they could not beat us into submission, these past 300 years, they now want us to forgive and forget."[110]

To most Old Believers the decrees merely proved what they already knew and had spent their lives defending. They were right.

> Anyhow, we are to thank, and say our Christian "Спаси, Господин" to all Russian New Orthodox hierarchs, the partakers of the Council of 1971, for their good will to heal the breach between two brotherly Churches. But we must declare, too, that no reunion is possible. . . . Let us stay in our Old faith, my dear Old Orthodox Christians, receiving one more proof of its correctness and having the saving Grace of the Holy Spirit![111]

For Nikolaevsk *popovtsy* and *bezpopovtsy* alike, the anathema reversals did not reverse their view that Nikon's reforms *were* indeed heretical. During one of my first services there, an elder demonstrated to me the "right" and "wrong" methods of making the sign of the cross that mirrored the sign hung in his church's vestibule. The simple drawing depicted a man using the three-fingered sign, crossed out with a big X, and labeled "Nikonian." The fact that Nikolaevsk's founders (or their parents) fled Soviet persecution undoubtedly affected their response. The general element of distrust in American Old Believers' interpretations of the anathema reversals "reflected the historical Old Believer position that the dominant Church would go to any ends to ensnare Old Believers into the New Rite."[112] Fifty years later, Erie's Church of the Nativity is the only North American Old Believer congregation affiliated with ROCOR[113] and the only to acknowledge that the New Rite might also be salutary.

American Old Believers are by no means agreed on how one gains or loses grace. A conversation I had with Fr. Simon was illustrative of the relationship between coreligiosity and grace. Attempts at ecumenicism with the West Coast *popovtsy* failed for canonical reasons but also because they fundamentally disagreed about whether God's grace falls on the Old Believers alone.

> That's what an Old Believer believes. You understand? That's the basic concept. There is no grace in the entire world of Christianity other than the Old Believers who follow the books of the Russian Orthodox ritual, the pre-Nikonian ritual. That's the thing that I accepted myself as a kid growing up . . . and as I got older, there's no way I'm going to ever agree to that because I think it's wrong. It's just wrong.[114]

Conversely, when a member of the RSG asked the fervently *bezpopovtsy* Fr. Yokoff, "You are saying that we are the only ones right? Our little group here?" He simply answered, "Yes."[115] I heard other Old Believers echo this sentiment, but most left the answer to God. The crux of the difference between these four congregations, beyond divergent ecclesiologies and variants of *pravoslavnye*, was a fundamental disagreement about the possible limits of God's grace.

Conclusion

The theologian John Meyendorff argued that the "fundamental differences" of dogma between Roman Catholic and Eastern Orthodox Christianities (e.g., papal primacy) "can only be resolved if there is a common understanding of what makes one a Christian, of the doctrine of salvation."[116] Salvation, and by extension grace, is central to Christianity as a whole and central to the theological boundaries of coreligiosity. At what point does an individual or branch of Christianity lose "what makes one a Christian"? At what point does one lose grace and forfeit salvation? Grace is a mystery not only because it is divine but because on earth, this unifying theological concept paradoxically plays a fundamental role in Christian distinctions of belonging.

"Grace" is a conceptual bridge between the theology of humanity's relationship with God and the anthropological study of Christians' social (non)relationships with one another. Old Believers' variant theohistories and modes of ORRO continuity illustrate the numerous overlaps between their negotiations of divine and human relationships. On the individual level, the gift of grace finds its opposite in the curse of damnation just as purity finds its opposite in the unclean. Both conceptual pairs operate on a generalized good/evil binary that categorizes individuals into social categories based on their perceived moral qualifications (e.g., *mirskie/nimirskie*). On a congregational level, an Old Believer out of grace must confess before their congregation before joining them in common worship, just as they must confess to God before seeking his redemption. In fact, it is the same prayer. This is the dual meaning of excommunication that operates on the institutional level: Those deemed to be outside God's grace are simultaneously excised from the Christian community (church) and denied Communion.

If, as Meyendorff claimed, the doctrine of salvation is the common de-
nominator of Christian groups, does it follow that soteriology is at the root
of Christian group making? The answer depends on the extent to which
God is believed to be lenient and forgiving about issues from orthopraxy to
everyday moral lapses; it depends on another dichotomy: law and mercy.[117]
Are there *any* salvation deal breakers? Or is God's mercy, like his power,
unlimited? Belief is a requirement for salvation (famously, John 3:16), but is
this contingent on the form and specificity of a Christian's beliefs? Or, as
the title of one missionary leaflet I purchased at Erie's Church of the Nativity Bookstore asked, "Will the Heterodox Be Saved?"[118] These questions affect all levels of social relations and ritual participation and have triggered
(micro)schisms and anathemas. Ironically, the emphasis on the *oneness* of a
spiritual body has often led to division within ORRO, for if each individual
must possess the *right* spirit to worship and have their rites and prayers
"count" as sanctifying, then those outside the Spirit must be excluded.

Doctrines of soteriology and ecclesiology are at the root of Old Believer
schisms, whether the specific debate is a matter of the sign of the cross,
forgiveness, or apostolic succession. Orthodox Christianities are ripe for
inquiry into the intersections of dogma and group identity because heretical threats to God's mercy preclude coreligiosity. If the dispossessed of grace
have always been Othered, how do we then reconcile the linguistic, ethnic,
and theopolitical dynamics of autocephaly[119] to economies of grace?
American Old Believers' conscientious consideration of this divine gift;
how they hope to earn the "unmerited pardon" through daily works, faith,
love, humility, and prayer; and where and how they seek to "replenish" their
state of grace present a unique window into the lived sociotheological con-
structs of belief and belonging.

Notes

1. Simon, Sermon, Erie, PA, Church of the Nativity, June 13, 2021.

2. Simon, Sermon, Erie, PA, Church of the Nativity, June 9, 2013.

3. For a detailed account, see Paul Meyendorff, *Russia, Ritual, and Reform:
The Liturgical Reforms of Nikon in the Seventeenth Century* (St. Vladimir's
Seminary Press, 1991).

4. Julian Pitt-Rivers, "The Place of Grace in Anthropology," *HAU: Journal of
Ethnographic Theory* 1, no. 1 (1992; repr. 2011): 423–50, 426, as a call for
damnation.

5. Amber Lee Silva, "Selective Modernity of a Global Enclave: Unity, Duality, and the American Old Believers," PhD diss., McGill University, 2022, 72–86, 95–115. The West Coast Old Believers in Alaska, Alberta, and Oregon are/were Chasovennye, originally from Siberia, and the East Coast Old Believers in Pennsylvania, Michigan, and New Jersey are/were primarily Pomortsy from Poland and Baltic regions.

6. Silva, "Selective Modernity of a Global Enclave," 207–12.

7. Robert O. Crummey, "Old Belief as Popular Religion: New Approaches," *Slavic Review* 42, no. 4 (1993): 700–12, 701.

8. J. Derrick Lemons, "An Introduction to Theologically Engaged Anthropology," *Ethnos* 86, no. 3 (2021): 401–7, 405.

9. Timothy Carroll, "Theology as an Ethnographic Object: An Anthropology of Eastern Christian Rupture," *Religions* 8, no. 7 (2017); J. Derrick Lemons, *Theologically Engaged Anthropology* (Oxford University Press, 2018); Joel Robbins, *Theology and the Anthropology of Christian Life* (Oxford University Press, 2020).

10. My fieldwork is limited to North American Old Believers; however, several members of the Nikolaevsk congregations were born and/or raised in the South American communities in Brazil and Bolivia, who remain a part of the *bezpopovtsy*'s coreligious diasporic network.

11. Douglas J. Davies, *Anthropology and Theology* (Berg, 2002), 54.

12. List not exhaustive. See Davies, *Anthropology and Theology*, 56–66; Pitt-Rivers, "The Place of Grace in Anthropology."

13. *Cambridge Journal of Anthropology* 40, no. 1 (2022).

14. Michael Edwards and Méadhbh McIvor, "Introduction: The Anthropology of Grace and the Grace of Anthropology," *Cambridge Journal of Anthropology* 40, no. 1 (2022): 1–17, 7.

15. Courtney Handman, "Becoming the Body of Christ: Sacrificing the Speaking Subject in the Making of the Colonial Lutheran Church in New Guinea," *Current Anthropology* 55, no. S10 (December 2014): S205–15, 206; Courtney Handman, *Critical Christianity: Translation and Denominational Conflict in Papua New Guinea* (University of California Press, 2015), 3–4, 9–18, 41–45.

16. Jeffrey David Holdeman, "Language Maintenance and Shift Among the Russian Old Believers of Erie, Pennsylvania," PhD diss., Ohio State University, 2002, 33, 79.

17. E.g., Michael James Smithson, "Of Icons and Motorcycles: A Sociological Study of Acculturation Among Russian Old Believers in Central Oregon and Alaska," PhD diss., University of Oregon, 1977; Michael A. Colfer, *Morality, Kindred, and Ethnic Boundary: A Study of the Oregon Old Believers* (AMS Press, 1985).

18. Carroll, "Theology as an Ethnographic Object," 2; Jon Bialecki, Naomi Haynes, and Joel Robbins, "Anthropology of Christianity," *Religion Compass* 2, no. 6 (2008): 1139–58, 1139.

19. Fenella Cannell, "The Christianity of Anthropology," *Journal of the Royal Anthropological Institute* 11, no. 2 (2005): 335–56.

20. Edwards and McIvor, "Introduction."

21. Pitt-Rivers, "The Place of Grace in Anthropology," 423–26.

22. Carroll, "Theology as an Ethnographic Object," 7.

23. Richard H. Niebuhr, *The Social Sources of Denominationalism* (1929; Shoe String, 1954).

24. Meyendorff, *Russia, Ritual, and Reform*; Georg Bernhard Michels, *At War with the Church: Religious Dissent in Seventeenth-Century Russia* (Stanford University Press, 1999).

25. Meyendorff, *Russia, Ritual, and Reform*, 222–23.

26. Vladimir Smolakov, *Review of the Twelve Annual Conferences of the Old Orthodox Parishes in the USA, Held in the Time from A.D. 1953 to 1966* (Erie, PA, n.d.), 1957, question 2.

27. Douglas Rogers, *The Old Faith and the Russian Land: A Historical Ethnography of Ethics in the Urals* (Cornell University Press, 2009).

28. Handman, *Critical Christianity*, 11.

29. Rapprochement with ROC in 2007.

30. Noncoreligious with the BK based in Russia. A faction in Oregon also became *popovtsy*.

31. Caroline Humphrey, "Schism, Event, and Revolution: The Old Believers of Trans-Baikalia," *Current Anthropology* 55, no. S10 (December 2014): S216–25, 216; Carroll, "Theology as an Ethnographic Object."

32. Vladimir Smolakov, *Sunday School Weeklies* [*SSW*], July 1955–June 1973 (Erie, PA, July 1955–July 1973), 6 (August 14, 1955).

33. Robbins, *Theology and the Anthropology of Christian Life*, 8–10.

34. Pitt-Rivers, "The Place of Grace in Anthropology," 429; Davies, *Anthropology and Theology*, 53–55, 195–98; Cannell, "The Christianity of Anthropology," 337–38; Edwards and McIvor, "Introduction," 2–6. Marcel Mauss's *The Gift* (1924) is universally referenced.

35. Andreas Bandak and Tom Boylston, "The 'Orthodoxy' of Orthodoxy: On Moral Imperfection, Correctness, and Deferral in Religious Worlds," *Religion and Society* 5, no. 1 (2014): 25–46.

36. David Scheffel, *In the Shadow of Antichrist: The Old Believers of Alberta* (Broadview, 1991), 168–69, 172; Holdeman, "Language Maintenance and Shift," 50.

37. Michels, *At War with the Church*, 3.

38. Irina Paert, *Spiritual Elders: Charisma and Tradition in Russian Orthodoxy* (Northern Illinois University Press, 2010), 83.

39. Mary Douglas, *Purity and Danger: An Analysis of Concepts of Pollution and Taboo* (1966; Routledge, 2002); George A. De Vos, "The Dangers of Pure Theory in Social Anthropology," *Ethos* 3, no. 1 (1975): 77–91.

40. Colfer, *Morality, Kindred, and Ethnic Boundary*, 29–30; Scheffel, *In the Shadow of Antichrist*, 51, 169, 198–201.

41. Scheffel, *In the Shadow of Antichrist*, 61.

42. Colfer, *Morality, Kindred, and Ethnic Boundary*, 48; Scheffel, *In the Shadow of Antichrist*, 51, 201–2.

43. Douglas, *Purity and Danger*, 51–71.

44. Scheffel, *In the Shadow of Antichrist*, 176–79.

45. Holdeman, "Language Maintenance and Shift," 49–50.

46. Roy R. Robson, "The Other Russians: Old Believer Community Development in Erie, Pennsylvania," BA thesis, Allegheny College, 1985, 187n12.

47. Scheffel, *In the Shadow of Antichrist*, 204–5.

48. Douglas, *Purity and Danger*, 27, 150–58, 172.

49. Jeanne Kormina, "Avtobusniki: Russian Orthodox Pilgrims' Longing for Authenticity," In *Eastern Christians in Anthropological Perspective*, ed. Chris Hann and Hermann Goltz (University of California Press, 2010), 274–75.

50. Hieromonk German Ciuba, trans., *Old Orthodox Prayer Book*, 2nd ed. (Russian Orthodox Church of the Nativity of Christ [Old Rite], 2001), 21.

51. Dennis Fefelov, ed. and trans., *Old Believers Prayer Book: Morning and Evening Prayers* (Nikolaevsk, AK: n.p., 2000). The prayer is repeated eleven times in the twenty-eight-page compilation.

52. Douglas, *Purity and Danger*, 5–6, 47–50, 166–70.

53. Smolakov, *Review* 1956, question 8; *Review* 1963, question 2.

54. "Teacher," a *bezpopovtsy* leader.

55. Paert, *Spiritual Elders*; Silva, "Selective Modernity of a Global Enclave," 284–90, on the role of spiritual elders. All my gratitude to *Lola (*bezpopovtsy*) for sharing her vast collection.

56. Silva, "Selective Modernity of a Global Enclave."

57. Smolakov, *Review* 1955, question 4.

58. See Maya Mayblin, "Containment and Contagion: The Gender of Sin in Contemporary Catholicism," in *Anthropology of Catholicism: A Reader*, ed. Kristin Norget, Valentina Napolitano, and Maya Mayblin (University of California Press, 2017), 142–48, on debates regarding humanity's dual nature and the ordination of women.

59. Simon, Sermon, Erie, PA, Church of the Nativity, June 9, 2013.

60. Smolakov, *SSW* 356 (August 2, 1964).

61. Simon, Adult Sunday school class, Erie, PA, Church of the Nativity, January 27, 2013.

62. Kormina, "Avtobusniki," 276–77.

63. Douglas, *Purity and Danger*, 200.

64. Condensed. Fr. Simon, interview with author, Erie, PA, January 31, 2013.

65. See Robert O. Crummey, *Old Believers in a Changing World* (Northern Illinois University Press, 2011), 99–118, on Old Believer community paradigms.

66. Apostolic Canon (Henceforth AC) 10. See Bishop Gregory Grabbe and Archbishop Gregory Afonsky, "The Canon of the Apostles," in *Book of Canons*, trans. Eugene Zaharov, http://www.holytrinitymission.org/books/english/canons_apostles_grabbe.htm.

67. For example, simony (AC 29).

68. See Davies, *Anthropology and Theology*, 126–30, on similarities between V. Turner's communitas and *koinonia* (communion between believers with each other and with the Holy Spirit).

69. De Vos, "The Dangers of Pure Theory in Social Anthropology," 86.

70. Douglas, *Purity and Danger*, 64–66.

71. Michels, *At War with the Church*, 36, 165–69.

72. Silva, "Selective Modernity of a Global Enclave," 122–41.

73. Smithson, "Of Icons and Motorcycles," 163, 217; Colfer, *Morality, Kindred, and Ethnic Boundary*.

74. Smolakov, *Review of the Twelve Annual Conferences*.

75. Robson, "The Other Russians," 76–79, 90–93; Roy R. Robson, "Old Believers in Erie, Pennsylvania: Exhibition Catalog," Erie County Historical Society, Erie Maritime Museum, and the International Conference "Old Belief in Traditional Russian Culture," October 15–18, 1998, 5; Holdeman, "Language Maintenance and Shift," 74.

76. Rogers, *The Old Faith and the Russian Land*, 45–50, 56, 94, 154–58.

77. Silva, "Selective Modernity of a Global Enclave," 142–69.

78. See Silva, "Selective Modernity of a Global Enclave," 295–99, on this more recent microschism.

79. Rogers, *The Old Faith and the Russian Land*, 47.

80. Douglas, *Purity and Danger*, 5, 127–28, 162–63, 172.

81. Scheffel, *In the Shadow of Antichrist*, 204–5.

82. Fr. Simon, interview with author, Erie, PA, December 27, 2012.

83. Smolakov, *Review* 1953, question 1.

84. Smolakov, *Review* 1958, question 10.

85. Smolakov, *Review* 1961, question 8; Robson, "Old Believers in Erie, Pennsylvania," 6, 15.

86. Robson, "The Other Russians," 77.

87. Smolakov, *Review* 1956, question 8.

88. AC 1, 2. Two bishops are required to ordain a bishop. The majority of American Old Believers (and their ancestors) rejected the BK hierarchy's legitimacy because it was founded (1846) by the conversion of a single bishop (Ambrovsii). Church of the Nativity, *Restoration Study Group Minutes* 5 (1982): 6–8 (henceforth, *RSGM*).

89. AC 31.

90. *RSGM* 10 (1982).

91. Holdeman, "Language Maintenance and Shift," 103; Silva, "Selective Modernity of a Global Enclave," 244–51.

92. Fr. Nikola, interview with author, Nikolaevsk, AK, August 18 and 22, 2013; Silva, "Selective Modernity of a Global Enclave," 251–58.

93. See Rogers, *The Old Faith and the Russian Land*, 71–103, for a detailed historical example.

94. Alice Forbess, "The Spirit and the Letter: Monastic Education in a Romanian Orthodox Convent," in *Eastern Christians in Anthropological Perspective*, ed. Chris Hann and Hermann Goltz (University of California Press, 2010), 131–33; Paert, *Spiritual Elders*; Giuseppe Tateo, "The Orthodox Charismatic Gift," *Cambridge Journal of Anthropology* 40, no. 1 (2021): 68–83, 68.

95. Niebuhr, *The Social Sources of Denominationalism*, 18–19; Ferdinand Toennies, Georg Simmel, Ernst Troeltsch, and Max Weber, "Max Weber on Church, Sect, and Mysticism," *Sociological Analysis* 34, no. 2 (1973): 140–49, 141–42; Handman, *Critical Christianity*, 43, 73–74, 216, 240–41.

96. Bandak and Boylston, "The 'Orthodoxy' of Orthodoxy"; Silva, "Selective Modernity of a Global Enclave," 273–90.

97. Patrick Collinson, "Cohabitation of the Faithful with the Unfaithful," in *From Persecution to Toleration: Glorious Revolution and Religion in England*, ed. Ole Peter Grell, Jonathan I. Israel, and Nicholas Tyacke (Clarendon, 1991), 58–59.

98. Mayblin, "Containment and Contagion"; Maya Mayblin, "The Ultimate Return: Dissent, Apostolic Succession, and the Renewed Ministry of Roman Catholic Women Priests," *History and Anthropology* 30, no. 2 (2019): 133–48.

99. Michael Bourdeaux, *Opium of the People: The Christian Religion in the USSR* (Bobbs-Merrill, 1966), 28–29.

100. Smolakov, *Review* 1959, question 19.

101. Smolakov, "The Old Orthodoxy," in *Review*, n.d., 51–56.

102. Mayblin, "Containment and Contagion."

103. Joel Robbins, "Continuity Thinking and the Problem of Christian Culture: Belief, Time, and the Anthropology of Christianity," *Current Anthropology* 48, no. 1 (2007): 5–38; Carroll, "Theology as an Ethnographic Object."

104. Metropolitan Philaret, "Concerning the Old Ritual: The Decision of the Council of Bishops of the Russian Church Abroad," *Orthodox Life* 5 (September 25, 1974; repr. 1983): 39–41, 39–40.

105. Vladimir Smolakov, *1973 Calendar*, Erie, PA, 32.

106. *RSGM* 9, questions 15, 23.

107. Vladimir Smolakov, *1976 Calendar*, Erie, PA, 26.

108. Silva, "Selective Modernity of a Global Enclave," 188–93.

109. Smolakov, *1976 Calendar*, 30–34.

110. Association of Old Believers. "Resolution Passed by the Conference of Priests Held in Marianna, PA, Church of St. Nicholas, on September 14, 1975," redistribution Fall 1982.

111. Smolakov, *1973 Calendar*, 34. The phrase of thanks "Lord, save you" corresponds with the etymological discussion in Pitt-Rivers, "The Place of Grace in Anthropology," 423–26. For more on the ORRO response to councils, see Anton S. Beliajeff, "The Old Believers in the United States," *Russian Review* 36, no. 1 (1977): 80.

112. Robson, "The Other Russians," 129.

113. Holy Trinity Monastery. "Directory of the Hierarchy, Clergy and Parishes of the Russian Orthodox Church Abroad," 2020, https://jordanville .org/files/2021-Files/Spisok_2021_Gratis_v5.pdf.

114. Simon, interview with author, Erie, PA, January 2, 2013.

115. *RSGM* 9, question 39.

116. John Meyendorff, *Rome Constantinople, Moscow: Historical and Theological Studies* (St. Vladimir's Seminary Press, 1996), 4.

117. Smolakov, *Review* 1955, question 2; Smolakov, *SSW* 116 (March 23, 1958); Pitt-Rivers, "The Place of Grace in Anthropology," 428–30.

118. Metropolitan Philaret, ROCOR Missionary Leaflet #L213 (2290), n.d., 3–4.

119. Jeanne Kormina and Vlad Naumescu, "A New 'Great Schism?': Theopolitics of Communion and Canonical Territory in the Orthodox Church," *Anthropology Today* 36, no. 1 (2020): 7–11.

PART III

THEOLOGICAL ANXIETIES AND CULTURAL CONSTRUCTIONS

THE HERESY OF EASTERN *PAPIZM* IN RUSSIAN ORTHODOX ONLINE DISCOURSE

Jacob Lassin

T
he ecumenical patriarch's decision to grant autocephaly to the Orthodox Church of Ukraine stands as the most consequential act in recent Eastern Orthodox history (Denysenko 2018; Shchotkina 2019). Perhaps the most drastic of its effects can be seen in the Moscow Patriarchate's decision to break communion with the Ecumenical Patriarchate, creating a deep schism in Eastern Orthodoxy. The issue of autocephaly in Ukraine has been the primary flashpoint in the long-standing conflict for primacy and authority within the global Eastern Orthodox communion as Moscow and Constantinople both claim ecclesiastic authority over Ukraine.

The Russian Orthodox Church enjoys the support of the Russian state and has been a stalwart ally of the Putin regime. As such, these battles over autocephaly must be understood within its geopolitical context. The fight over ecclesiastic authority in Ukraine is a proxy for Russia's conflicts against the West. Moscow's decision to break communion with one of the other constituent churches of the Eastern Orthodox Church was always going to gain a great deal of attention and would need a well-developed rhetorical strategy to inform believers and outsiders alike as to why Moscow chose this dramatic course of action. In this chapter, I will explore a particular rhetorical strategy that the Russian Orthodox Church and its allies have used across media as a theological justification for why it was necessary for Moscow to take these steps: accusations of what they refer to as the heresy of Eastern *papizm*.

What does the charge of Eastern *papizm* entail? What is the history of this term? What is the intended effect of using this term within Russian and global Orthodox contexts? These questions guide the chapter. I focus on the online discourse surrounding Eastern *papizm*, looking there because of its centrality in shaping public opinion, its ubiquity in contemporary social life, and its accessibility for a wide range of people that other media and methods simply do not rival. I specifically analyze websites and publications that are associated with the Moscow Patriarchate as well as the statements of officials from the Moscow Patriarchate that are published in secular sources. Focusing on these sites will help elucidate how those with close ties to the institutional Russian Orthodox Church look to frame the issue of Ukrainian autocephaly and to explore the theological ideas and tools that they implement to make their case to the wider Russian Orthodox community.

The question of Eastern *papizm* and how it is addressed in Russian Orthodox online media offers a case study that, following in the example of Chris Hann's (2007, 405) research, foregrounds the importance of institutions for the larger anthropology of Orthodox Christianity. I focus on how the conflict between ecclesial institutions has led to the formation of a particular online discourse that is designed to question the legitimacy of both the newly autocephalous Orthodox Church of Ukraine and the Ecumenical Patriarchate. These ecclesial conflicts are imbricated with conflicts between various states. I argue that the online rhetoric surrounding Eastern *papizm* acts as a reflection and refraction of the ongoing media wars between the Russian and Ukrainian states (Pantti 2016). In addition, Eastern *papizm* is now a key topic of discussion that Russian Orthodox media uses to demonstrate the church's relevance to the contemporary Russian and Ukrainian populations.

Online discourse also gives the Moscow Patriarchate a tool in dealing with what Catherine Wanner (2014, 436) terms "syncretic secularism," a "blending of belief, doubt and non-belief with the desire to belong and the refusal to be coerced by institutions" that is predominant in post-Soviet countries. I contend that it is through online discourse regarding Eastern *papizm* that the Russian Orthodox Church attempts to regain some of its own authority by casting aspersions on the authority of the Ecumenical Patriarchate and the Orthodox Church of Ukraine.

In addition to these dedicated Orthodox websites and outlets, another important source of the discourse concerning the question of Eastern *papizm* is from interviews and comments that members of the hierarchy, clergy, or lay employees of the Moscow Patriarchate make to the secular media. Russian Orthodox media can have a limited impact, given its focus on issues that relate to the church and the faith. Thus, when secular media asks for a comment or offers an opportunity for someone working within the church to speak it can become an important moment to allow those within the church to reach wider audiences and have a greater impact on society at large.

I will expand upon some of the rhetorical strategies and tropes used in Russian Orthodox online media. These include the role of the United States in the granting of the tomos, the issue of converging Roman and Eastern papisms, charges of racism and ethnophyletism, feelings of betrayal, and the threat of other autocephalous movements emerging. Attending to these recurring themes demonstrates not only the Moscow Patriarchate's approach to the issue of Ukrainian autocephaly but also reflects how the church attempts to connect its own issues and concerns with ones that are pertinent in all aspects of Russian and Ukrainian life. Ultimately, I argue that the online discourse surrounding Eastern *papizm* frames Ukrainian autocephaly as a tangible example of the threats that the West poses to the Russian nation, its faith, and its culture. This discourse brings abstract theological concepts together with quotidian life to create a Russian Orthodox political subjectivity that sees the Russian Orthodox Church and the Russian state as the only possible forces that can oppose these threats and safeguard the nation.

In this chapter, I conduct critical discourse analysis of Russian Orthodox online media sources. I highlight the various media strategies that Russian Orthodox outlets and organizations use to communicate the potential repercussions the patriarchate envisages occurring from the formation of an autocephalous Ukrainian Church. I also investigate how readers and viewers of this content react to these ideas through their online comments to this material. I also note that the online discourse is not limited to the conflict between Russia and Ukraine but also includes the United States, other countries variously seen as part of the West, and almost every other country that has its own autocephalous Eastern Orthodox Church. Because of the presence of this discourse around the world, I also offer examples of how representatives of the Russian Orthodox Church present their views on Ukrainian autocephaly to members of other autocephalous churches. This is part of a strategy to present an image of the Russian

Orthodox Church as a defender of the canonical norms of Eastern Orthodoxy in the face of what they construe as heresy.

It is imperative to understand that the Russian Orthodox community, both online and off, is not monolithic. There are various tendencies and camps within it that span the ideological spectrum (Richters 2013; Verkhovsky 2002; Knox 2005; Mitrofanova 2005; Papkova 2011). Given the great volume and range of material present in the Russian Orthodox online space, it is not possible to cover all aspects of how the concept of Eastern *papizm* is discussed. This chapter includes sources that are affiliated with the institutional church and those that are fully independent. I include both in order to present a fuller view of the ways that the question of Eastern *papizm* is discussed across the Russian Orthodox online space while also centering the role that the institutional church plays in this debate.

"Eastern *papizm*" is not a common term. Many Russian speakers, even within the Orthodox fold, are most likely unfamiliar with it and thus it is worthwhile to understand its constituent elements before proceeding. Within the Eastern Orthodox context, "*papizm*" invokes one of the major ecclesiological rifts between the Eastern Orthodox Church and the Catholic Church, a highly visible sign of the differences between the churches (Demacopoulos 2013; Vgenopoulos 2013). In the Russian case, there is a long history of distrust of the institution of the papacy (Dunn 2004). Thus, to accuse a fellow Eastern Orthodox Church of emulating the actions of Rome presents the Ecumenical Patriarchate as continuing the work of schism that has divided the church. This exploration of schism at a global level offers a complement to Amber Lee Silva's localized study of the nature of schism in her contribution to this volume.

For the Moscow Patriarchate and the Russian state, the power on the international stage displayed in the Ecumenical Patriarchate's Eastern *papizm* presents a direct threat to Moscow's claims of spiritual supremacy in the eastern Orthodox world and the state's use of the ROC to accomplish foreign policy goals (Curanović 2007). The claim that Moscow is the "third Rome" has long been part of Russian national historiography, religious and secular. This myth has been reinvigorated in the post-Soviet period to promote Russian imperialist aims. The war with Ukraine and its aftermath has intensified its uses, especially among Russian nationalist thinkers and writers (Østbø 2016, 231–38). The ecumenical patriarch's taking on a papal role within Orthodoxy undercuts the idea that Moscow maintains a special place in the spiritual leadership and geopolitical order of the world. Russian Orthodox online media develop a discourse of Eastern *papizm* that actualizes this threat for Russian Orthodox believers by offering a concrete example of how the Ecumenical Patriarchate is fusing political and theological power. To begin this analysis, it is necessary to define what these sites mean when they invoke the term "Eastern *papizm*."

Defining Eastern *Papizm*

"Eastern *papizm*" is a term designed to elicit a strong, negative response from a Russian-speaking audience. Its widespread use in Russian Orthodox media, such as on the official websites of the Moscow Patriarchate, popular Russian Orthodox websites such as *Pravoslavie* and in the secular Russian and Ukrainian press, is a relatively new phenomenon within Russian Orthodoxy and plays upon a long history of negative connotations with the papacy within Orthodoxy. Previous research finds that the use of the term "Greek papism" was used in the Russian context among the church abroad in the aftermath of World War II and that, with time, the Moscow Patriarchate took to referring to "Eastern papism" to encompass the actions of the patriarchates of the Middle East (Kalkandijeva 2015, 324–25). As we shall see, in the present moment, there is a great deal of blurring between the use of "Eastern" and "Greek" or even "Constantinople" when describing this form of papism, in which they have become synonymous.

The potential for confusion has led some Russian Orthodox online outlets to offer content that provides a definition and genealogy of the term such as in an interview given by Archbishop Silvester (Stoichev) of Bilhorod, a vicariate archbishop of Kyiv and the rector of the Kyiv Theological Seminary and Academy of the UOC, for the official site of the Patriarchate of the Serbian Orthodox Church, that was translated into Russian and Ukrainian and posted on the official website of the Moscow Patriarchate. Silvester makes the claim that "in the nineteenth century, there were a number of Russian Orthodox canonists and historians of the Russian Orthodox Church that used the expression 'Eastern *papizm*' in relation to the Patriarch of Constantinople" (Sapsai 2021).

Silvester goes on to say that those who used the term in the past hoped that the ecumenical patriarchs would abide by certain rules and not cross what he refers to as "red lines," but that through his actions in Ukraine, Patriarch Bartholomew has broken these conventions, placing the entire

Orthodox world in a state of crisis, with many of the local autocephalous churches breaking Eucharistic communion with one another to an extent that exceeds previous moments of discontent within the eastern Orthodox Church (Sapsai 2021). This interview offers a historical pedigree to the term, explaining to readers that the threat of Eastern *papizm* has been a concern within the Russian Orthodox Church for centuries and that this is not some new slogan that the Moscow Patriarchate has developed for the current political moment. The ROC refers to the historical record as a justification of its actions, demonstrating that it is, in its own view, merely following the canons of the universal church and opposing what it sees as the Ecumenical Patriarchate's consistent violation of these norms. This is not mere pedantry: The ROC is attempting to establish, both for its own members as well as audiences in eastern Orthodox churches around the world, that Moscow is abiding by the canons and that Constantinople is breaking with the laws that govern the Eastern Orthodox Church. The Moscow Patriarchate does this to counter the narrative present in Ukraine and the West that it is unilaterally breaking communion.

While Bishop Silvester's comments on the origins of the term work to establish its alleged centuries-old use, much of the contemporary invocations of Eastern *papizm* in the Russian context reference the thought of Fr. Sofronii (Sakharov), a Russian priest who lived most of his life in the West and was canonized by the Ecumenical Patriarchate in 2019. The fact that Sofronii is a saint in the Ecumenical Patriarchate supplies his thoughts and prescriptions on these matters with added weight and importance that could not be matched by a priest who was always subordinate to Moscow. Russian Orthodox sources often use the writings of Sofronii, in particular his 1950 article "The Unity of the Church in the Image of the Unity of the Holy Trinity" (*Edinstvo tserkvi po obrazu edinstva Sviatoi Troitsy*) to demonstrate the long-standing problems of Eastern *papizm*. The example of a saint of the Ecumenical Patriarchate commenting on these issues and believing that they were equivalent to the heresy of Roman papism adds a higher degree of authority to the condemnation of the Ecumenical Patriarchate. Sofronii wrote in his article against the trend he saw in the Constantinople Patriarchate of "neo-papism moving extremely quickly from a theoretical phase to a practical one."

Sofronii claims that the "Russian adherents of this papism are almost all found in France." This is in reference to the highly influential cohort of Orthodox theologians such as Alexander Schmemann and Vasilii

Zenkovskii active in Europe in the mic-twentieth century. Sofronii himself was living in France at the time he wrote this article. Sofronii's claim that it is this geographically proscribed group of theologians that are the main proponents of papism allows him to build his case that such thinking is foreign to what he sees as the true Orthodox tradition and is influenced and tainted by proximity to Catholic theological thinking and modern intellectual trends that were sweeping across the West. Moreover, stating that these opinions are almost entirely limited to those thinkers working in France allows Sofronii to dismiss this support of papism as a distinctly minority position within the Orthodox world that in no way reflects the predominant thinking within the Eastern Orthodox communion.

Sofronii asserts that this sort of thinking "confuses the idea of 'autocephaly' with that of 'nationalism' in order to reject both in the name of 'universalism,' destroying the very principle of the structure of the Universal Church." He quotes Zenkovskii's statement that "'Christianity went wrong in allowing the formation of so-called 'national' Churches'" to support his interpretation of their position. It is interesting that Sofronii centers the importance of autocephaly as a principle in his opposition to these theological views when contemporary, Russian Orthodox uses of his thinking see the Ecumenical Patriarchate's decision to grant Ukrainian autocephaly as a key example of papist action. The explanation for this lies in who, from the point of view of the Moscow Patriarchate, has canonical authority over Ukraine. In its view of the situation, that Constantinople is circumventing Moscow, an equal autocephalous church, presents a perfect illustration of the threats to Eastern Orthodox ecclesiology introduced in this form of papism that Sofronii accused the Ecumenical Patriarchate of seventy years ago.

This digression into Sofronii's thinking is not a simple historical aside but represents a cornerstone of how the contemporary ROC conceives of Eastern *papizm* as a threat to both canonical Orthodoxy and Russia's ecclesiastical and cultural traditions. Metropolitan Hilarion (Alfeev), who at the time was head of the Moscow Patriarchate's Department of External Church Relations, quoted Sofronii's forceful conclusion to the article. There he stated: "'We reject Roman, or Constantinopolitan, or Muscovite, or London, or Parisian, or New York, or any other form of papism, as ecclesiological heresy, which distorts Christianity" during a speech to a conference of the Synodal Biblical-Theological Commission, providing a full articulation of the ROC's understanding of papism and its categorical opposition to it and its proponents.

Sofronii raises Eastern *papizm* to the level of heresy because he believes that it "introduces subordinationism [the theological idea that the Son is subordinate rather than co-equal to the Father] into the Church," demonstrating his view that it poses a serious threat to dogmatic orthodoxy. Within the Eastern Orthodox tradition, only a very small number of teachings have explicitly been pronounced as heresies by either an ecumenical council or by another major church council (Ladouceur 2017). However, this formal definition does not stop people within the Orthodox Church from deploying the term to castigate the actions of their opponents for anything that they believe violates the teachings of the church. As George Demacopoulos (2018) observes, "the question of Ukrainian independence has nothing to do with the dogma of the Church, the category of heresy is not applicable." This technicality does not stop the Moscow Patriarchate from using this term given its potency. To accuse the ecumenical patriarch as well as many Ukrainian clergy and faithful of taking part in heresy is perhaps the harshest condemnation that can be leveled by interjurisdictional actors. The use of this inflammatory term also rhetorically excommunicates the ecumenical patriarch and its followers and creates a clear division between the sees of Moscow and Constantinople.

Moving to more contemporary conversations, Fr. Georgii Maksimov in an article titled "The Heresy of Constantinople Papism" (*Eres' Konstantinopol'skogo Papizma*) offers a rather comprehensive accounting of the elements that bring the issue of Eastern *papizm* to the level of heresy. Maksimov is a professor of religious studies at the Moscow Theological Academy, an author, and a member of the working group on interreligious relations of the Russian Orthodox Church. His academic background and the tenor of the article makes it clear that he is speaking to those with similar interests and concerns, especially other clergy and particularly dedicated believers. Moreover, given that this is published on *Pravoslavie*, the website of the conservative Sretenskii Monastery, it is meant for a more traditionalist audience and one that would be staunchly against Ukrainian autocephaly. Calling these actions a heresy offers an example of how the term is being weaponized in the contemporary moment. In this article, he lays out the canonical issues surrounding the Ecumenical Patriarch's granting the tomos that established the Orthodox Church of Ukraine in 2019.

This historical genealogy is necessary so that the charge of heresy retains its rhetorical power. The audience reading this article knows that heresy has an important and well-defined theological meaning. To convincingly and effectively deploy the term for the imagined public of Russian Orthodox online media, Maksimov must address this history. Moreover, Maksimov strives to offer a historical understanding of the present actions of the Ecumenical Patriarchate to demonstrate its errors and provide evidence of how similar events have been dealt with in Orthodox tradition. This genealogy serves to provide support that the Moscow Patriarchate's assessment of the situation and its actions are the correct course.

From the outset, Maksimov's (2019) article is marked by its use of rather belligerent language. He refers to the actions of the ecumenical patriarch as an "invasion" or "incursion" (*vtorzhenie*), a word he repeats throughout the article. This term is complemented with the use of other bombastic language, such as references to Constantinople's "capturing" (*zakhvat*) of parishes from the Moscow Patriarchate, all of which are done to leave no doubt in the minds of readers that the Ecumenical Patriarchate is the aggressor. The militaristic framework that this rhetoric creates works to heighten the notion that the threat of Ukrainian autocephaly is not limited to the arcane realm of church canons but has consequences on the ground over where and how individual believers can worship and who can serve in these parishes. The issue is framed as one where the very future of Orthodox communities and traditions in Ukraine are at stake.

In addition, this rhetoric also links the specific situation among Orthodox believers with the larger military actions of the Russian and so-called separatist armies in the region. This type of language was mirrored in Putin's (2022) speech before the wide-scale invasion of Ukraine, where he asserted that "Kiev continues to prepare the destruction of the Ukrainian Orthodox Church of the Moscow Patriarchate. . . . The Ukrainian authorities have cynically turned the tragedy of the schism into an instrument of state policy." The theological issues over autocephaly are used as justification for the geopolitical actions of the Russian state.

Being part of the Moscow Patriarchate is a symbol of connection with centuries of religious tradition as well as with the Russian nation and its culture. Through the language of military threat, the author stresses the potential repercussions of these actions. Maksimov goes on to note that it is not just in Ukraine where the ecumenical patriarch has taken similar tactics. To convince his readers of the gravity of the issue and to make the case that it rises to the level of heresy, Maksimov (2019) offers an exacting historical record that delineates opposition to papism within Orthodox tradition. He draws on examples such as that of Patriarch Herman II of Constantinople in the thirteenth century decrying the schism of Rome as implemented "by a daring hand seeking predominance and leadership in the Church" and cites the 1848 Encyclical of the Four Patriarchs, which states, "The dignity [of the see of Rome] does not consist in dominance and not in primacy, which Peter himself never received, but in fraternal eldership in the universal Church," all to demonstrate that the Catholic position on the issue is incorrect.

Maksimov (2019) follows his discussion of the threats to other churches' sovereignty and authority with an investigation into the benefits that the Ecumenical Patriarchate sees in taking these steps. He takes issue with claims from Constantinople that the Ecumenical Patriarchate acts as the "yeast" that enlivens the body of the Orthodox Church, arguing that in fact the Orthodox Church can survive without the patriarch of Constantinople and going even further to claim that "in its history heretics have occupied the throne of Constantinople more often than any other ancient ecclesiastical seat." With such a statement, Maksimov attempts to make his case that the claims of Constantinople's centrality, primacy, and importance for global Eastern Orthodoxy are overstated. Moreover, making the claim that so many of the patriarchs of Constantinople have been heretics reinforces his point that there is nothing particularly special or necessary about the Ecumenical Patriarchate for the whole of the Orthodox communion. He dismisses the notion that the Ecumenical Patriarchate ought to enjoy a privileged position within Orthodoxy and makes the connections between Constantinople's current policies and its historical record to convince readers of the propensity of the Ecumenical Patriarchate to veer into heresy. These comments are designed to erode any pretensions that, because of the historical role of the Ecumenical Patriarchate, deference ought to be given to the institution. By presenting a predilection toward heresy through the ages, Maksimov aims to dislodge this historical fealty from the minds of his readers. The theological justification for historical revisionism seen here is a repeated theme seen across Orthodox online media. This instance is in line with other Russian and global examples where specific historical narratives are activated for nationalistic political purposes (Valencia-Garcia 2020; Laruelle 2021; Sullivan 2022; Mandaville 2023).

He goes on to describe what he calls the racist tendency of the Ecumenical Patriarchate in its dealings with Moscow, quoting from a speech of the Ecumenical Patriarch where Bartholomew states, "'Our brothers the Slavs cannot tolerate the primacy of the Ecumenical Patriarchate and our nation in Orthodoxy.'" Here, Maksimov (2019) offers a succinct example of a common accusation seen across Russian Orthodox online media that the Ecumenical Patriarchate privileges Greeks over other ethnic groups and that it strives for Greek supremacy across the Orthodox Church. The Russian Orthodox Church in the post-Soviet period, by virtue of its having the largest membership of any of the autocephalous churches, views itself as the leader within the global eastern Orthodox communion. In addition, it plays an important geopolitical role as the Russian state promotes the ROC on the international stage and uses it to help assure that its foreign policy objectives and preferences are met (Curanović 2007). The supposed ethnic prejudices that motivate the Ecumenical Patriarchate's actions are taken to be just another example of the idea of global Russophobia that the Russian state claims motivates the opposition to its actions and goals on the international stage (Robinson 2019). Maksimov's comments help link the more general discussion of a Russophobic international order with the spiritual realm, in an effort to have the Russian Orthodox reading public see the actions of the Ecumenical Patriarchate as part of larger anti-Russian processes.

The digital publications that address Eastern *papizm* represent only one part of the impact of this discourse in Russia and Ukraine. It is important not only to see what sort of rhetoric these publications tied to the institutional church hope to advance but also to investigate how they filter down to average believers to see how they might affect loyalty to the Moscow Patriarchate and support for the Russian state. This will help us better ascertain the efficacy of this discourse and its impact on not only religious sentiments but also on the political questions facing Russian Orthodox believers. A potential way to explore this question is through the comments readers post to these articles.

Previous research into internet comments has found that comments sections can be places for the formation of networked counterpublics. Much of this research focuses on the ways that marginalized groups can organize, strengthen identities, and counter hegemonic discourses (Lowenstein-Barkai 2022; Kaiser 2017; Wonneberger et al. 2021). Jeff Tischauser and Kevin Musgrave's (2019) work on the white nationalist website VDare provides a useful extension of the possibilities for digital counterpublics. They argue that VDare presents an example of "*imitated counterpublicity*" where "far-right media articulate a collective white racial identity as one under threat of extinction by the state" (3). In a similar vein, these Russian Orthodox websites display similar tendencies. The comments sections of these sites present examples of how readers engage in this imitated counterpublicity as they offer ritualistic responses that support the original content, which itself is designed to foster "a collective conscious, which orients the understanding of the world and maintains a collective identity" (Sik 2015, 151).

The first comment to the article from a reader using the name "Grigorii" offers a succinct encapsulation of how an average reader might see the article. He writes, "Many thanks for this wonderful article! At one time the second Rome gave us the light of the Christian faith. But now, it sows discord between peoples who are brothers in the faith, in blood, and in history" (Grigorii, January 12, 2019, 10:38 PM). His comment on shared "blood" is particularly interesting and likely refers to ethnic connections between Russians and Ukrainians that the commenter believes are being damaged because of the Ecumenical Patriarchate's actions in Ukraine. Another potential interpretation of his comments concerning blood could refer to the Christian conception of the Eucharist that links believers in the body and blood of Christ, underscoring the idea that the Ecumenical Patriarchate's actions are disrupting unity in the Body of Christ. This response offers a glimpse into how the rhetoric concerning the ecumenical patriarch's actions are received and filters into the thinking of readers.

Two issues raised by Maksimov's article are worth highlighting here: first, the question of sovereignty for individual autocephalous churches, which is a crucial element in Orthodox ecclesiology, differentiating the eastern Orthodox Church and its emphasis on conciliarity from that of the Catholic Church; and second, the fact that concerns over ethnic prejudice and racism are among the most salient elements in Russian Orthodox media decrials of the Ecumenical Patriarchate's Eastern *papizm*. These themes can be seen in headlines such as "We Value It: Dumenko Thanked the USA for Its Support of the Tomos of the OCU," which focuses on the West's perceived role in the establishment of the Orthodox Church of Ukraine; "The Legalization of the 'Macedonians': The Phanar Continues to Split Orthodoxy," which deals with the supposed threat of spreading autocephaly movements; and "Why Did Patriarch Theodore II Recognize the

OCU, or the Judas Syndrome and the Power of Christ," which centers on feelings of betrayal that the actions of the Ecumenical Patriarchate have engendered among Russian Orthodox Christians. Before expanding on these themes, I will first discuss the role and importance of online discourse within the Russian Orthodox Church today. I highlight some of the most important sources for the dissemination of Eastern *papizm* discourse to provide readers with an overview of its role in the Russian Orthodox online mediascape.

The Importance of Online Discourse in the Russian Orthodox Church

The centrality of the internet in guiding and disseminating news and information across the Russian Orthodox community cannot be overstated (Suslov 2016; Stähle 2021). The Russian Orthodox Church has not been immune to the changes in communication and the spread of information that the internet has brought to nearly every aspect of life. The internet can be seen as an invaluable tool for the Russian Orthodox Church, which must be understood as a transnational organization operating not only in the countries of the former Soviet Union but around the globe. The possibilities that the internet can provide in reaching wide audiences also is beneficial for the church's explicit mission to bring the Gospel to all people. Moreover, within Russia, given rather moribund church attendance numbers and the fact that online information is much easier and quicker to access than traditional, church-affiliated print publications, it is no surprise that the internet now plays a large role in the intellectual and informational life of the Russian Orthodox community (Pew Research Center 2017). The wide-scale affordances of spreadability and visibility inherent in internet media allows the church to circumvent national borders and create an online space that reflects its own vision of canonical territory, the area over which it is the sovereign spiritual authority. Not only does the Russian Orthodox Church consider Ukraine as part of its canonical territory, but this notion also extends to include Belarus, Moldova, as well as Orthodox believers in the Baltic countries, Central Asia, and diasporic Russian communities around the world. The Russian Orthodox Church considers Ukraine as part of its canonical territory. The question of canonical territory stands at the heart of any debate surrounding Ukrainian autocephaly and Eastern *papizm*. As Jeanne Kormina and Vlad Naumescu (2020, 9) show, the Moscow Patriarchate has worked in recent years to "globalize the logic of canonical territory and alter the current arrangement of sovereign rights and institutional structures in the Christian world." Online media provides the perfect vehicle for this reconceptualization and expansion of canonical territory to take place as the ROC can now reach what it views as its full flock in a way that is far less encumbered by states and governments. This new approach to canonical territory allows the Moscow Patriarchate to take a more assertive position within the Eastern Orthodox communion as it uses online media to influence Orthodox Christians across the world.

The Moscow Patriarchate can potentially gain credence and support by providing a reason to come together as a community to oppose an external institution. Moreover, the diffuse nature of online materials can help obfuscate some of its connection with the institutional Russian Orthodox Church, thus making it more appealing to an audience that might be suspicious of clerical power or religious institutions.

Orthodox Journalism

There are a number of central players in this online debate, and it is useful to spend some time exploring their roots and connections with the Moscow Patriarchate. Understanding these connections will allow us to chart the formation and dissemination of the discourse surrounding Eastern *papizm* and its relationship with the institutional church. One of the most prominent sites for this discourse is that of the Union of Orthodox Journalists (UOJ). The UOJ appeared rather suddenly in 2015, following Russia's invasion of eastern Ukraine. Inquiry into the origins of the UOJ finds that it was registered by the Donetsk businessman Viktor Vishnevetskii, the founder and owner of a coal company creatively named Coal Energy (*Relihiia v Ukraini* 2016). He is now one of the richest people in Ukraine. Vishnevetskii has long been a prominent supporter of the Russian Orthodox Church in Ukraine and Russia and has been awarded and recognized on multiple occasions by the patriarch for his largesse and commitment to the faith. In addition to his charitable giving to the church, he has also been implicated in supporting separatist fighters in Donetsk (*Relihiia v Ukraini* 2016).

The fact that Vishnevetskii is a strong supporter of the church but is not a member of the hierarchy or employed by the church directly is a central aspect of the branding surrounding the UOJ. This site allows the

Moscow Patriarchate to maintain a sense of plausible deniability concerning its actions. In addition, the rather anodyne name, the Union of Orthodox Journalists, allows it to present itself as a nonpartisan organization that is simply bringing together journalists who want to identify with their faith. Through these tactics, the UOJ can appear as an "objective" source for the average internet user that is not immediately traceable to having origins within the Moscow Patriarchate. At the same time, the UOJ's distance from the official church allows it to inject some more incendiary and bombastic rhetoric into these debates, language that would seem out of place for "official" publications to use.

Among the more subtle rhetorical elements that are present on the site of the Union of Orthodox Journalists are attempts to fully discredit both the Ecumenical Patriarchate and the clergy of the Orthodox Church of Ukraine. The UOJ often dismissively refers to the Ecumenical Patriarchate as simply the Phanar, a reference to the Istanbul neighborhood where its official headquarters is located. This choice downplays Constantinople's place in Eastern Orthodox history and tradition and reminds the reader of the small size, relative to the Moscow Patriarchate, of both the canonical territory and the membership of the Ecumenical Patriarchate. Moreover, it also speaks to the marginalized and precarious position of the Ecumenical Patriarchate within the Turkish state. For instance, the Turkish government has closed the Theological School of Halki, the central seminary of the Ecumenical Patriarchate. In addition, the Turkish government requires that any future patriarchs be natural-born Turkish citizens, which limits the potential candidates to an ever-shrinking pool. Calling the Ecumenical Patriarchate the Phanar emphasizes its limitations and small size, providing the UOJ with a direct way to undercut what it sees as the EP's pretensions toward temporal power and influence. At the same time, it helps inflate the importance of the Moscow Patriarchate as it attempts to take on the mantle as the leader of global Eastern Orthodoxy. Superseding the Ecumenical Patriarch in terms of size and prestige is part of the long intellectual tradition within the Russian Orthodox Church of viewing Moscow as the "third Rome." This idea dates to at least the sixteenth century and is premised on the idea that now that Rome is in schism and Constantinople has fallen to the Ottomans, authority has passed to Moscow (Østbø 2016). The dismissal of the Ecumenical Patriarchate is a key element in constructing Russia as a new Orthodox empire from the ruins of the former one.

In addition, the UOJ makes some rather pointed stylistic choices in order to discredit the new Orthodox Church of Ukraine. Perhaps the most visible of these is the frequent use of quotation marks around their hierarchs' ecclesial titles, "Metropolitan," "Archbishop," etc., such as in the headline "In Khorov, Supporters of the OCU Came With a 'Bishop' to a Sealed-Up OCU Church." The editorial decision to consistently apply these quotation marks has the effect of immediately calling into doubt the reality of their roles and to make them appear to be pretenders or usurpers who are challenging those who have legitimate rights to those titles and honors. Such a tactic also draws an important distinction between the hierarchs of the newly autocephalous Orthodox Church of Ukraine and the Ukrainian Orthodox Church, which remains an integral part of the Moscow Patriarchate.

Metropolitan Epifanii, the head of the Orthodox Church in Ukraine, receives some of the most pointed negative treatment on the site. Unlike the hierarchs of the Moscow Patriarchate and in what the ROC determines as other canonical churches whose last names are always put in parentheses, in reference to their dying to the world upon the taking of monastic vows, Epifanii is typically referred to along with his last name, Dumenko, or even by his full secular name, Sergei Dumenko, without any reference to his monastic name and no parentheses. The result of such a decision is a subtle yet pointed way of dismissing Epifanii's monastic vows as fake, given his not being part of what Moscow considers a canonically valid church, and suggests that his claims to apostolic succession and leadership of Ukraine's Orthodox faithful are false.

Another of the important sites that has been one of the generators of this discourse has been *Pravoslavie* (the name of the site is the Russian word for "Orthodoxy"). One of the oldest and most popular Russian Orthodox websites on the internet, *Pravoslavie* is based at Moscow's Sretenskii Monastery, which for about two decades was headed by the powerful and influential Metropolitan Tikhon (Shevkunov). Metropolitan Tikhon has close ties to the highest echelons of the Russian government and allegedly, though not definitively, serves as Vladimir Putin's spiritual confessor (*dukhovnik*) (Pertsev 2017). *Pravoslavie* is known as a bastion of conservatism and traditionalism within the Moscow Patriarchate and has been a staunch opponent of Ukrainian autocephaly (Zelenskiy 2017).

The online content related to the question of Eastern *papizm* is not limited to textual material. The use of videos has grown in prominence to communicate these messages with wider audiences and attract those who do not have the time or patience to sift through dense theological condemnations of the Ecumenical Patriarch's actions. *Vitrazhi* ("stained-glass windows," in Russian) is one such project that uses video to disseminate the Moscow Patriarchate's views on these issues. This project also shares an email address with the website Pravlife, the UOC-MP's official online portal. *Vitrazhi* produces engaging videos that use many of the elements common in internet memes as well as the presentation style that is seen in videos for secular websites. Through this style and approach, the producers at *Vitrazhi* aim to live up to their own tagline, that they create content "about the faith in color" (*O vere v kraskakh*), that is, present a vibrant and vital faith. As of late November 2021, *Vitrazhi*'s YouTube channel, which began in December 2019, has forty-seven thousand subscribers and nearly five million views on its videos (*Vitrazhi* 2021a). *Vitrazhi* is based in Ukraine, not Russia, allowing for Ukrainian believers to gain the sense that they are hearing from people that truly understand the situation in the country, rather than a source that is coming from outside, trying to influence the situation. Of course, the UOC-MP remains an integral part of the Moscow Patriarchate, but in its internal governance it is autonomous. Thus, the creation of media projects like *Vitrazhi* on the part of the UOC-MP attempts to provide a uniquely Ukrainian perspective on these issues to gain credibility with a Ukrainian audience but at the same time offer unwavering support of the actions of the Russian Orthodox Church and its opposition to Ukrainian autocephaly.

Denis Lapin, the founder of *Vitrazhi* and the host appearing in the videos, is a native of Donetsk in eastern Ukraine, which Russia invaded in 2014 and is now part of the largely unrecognized Donetsk People's Republic. Previously, Lapin produced videos that offered views into the history and culture of Donetsk and the surrounding area and had a decidedly more secular outlook. In addition to his videos on *Vitrazhi* he has also written several articles for the nationalist website *Russkaia Narodnaia Liniia*.

Lapin clearly sees his role as protecting the faithful from misinformation and the noise of contemporary media. He closes every video with the same exhortation: "Beware of dubious, unverified news. Read classical literature and watch *Vitrazhi*: concerning faith in color" (*Osteregaites' somnitel'nykh sobranii neproverennykh novostei. Chitaite klassiku i smotrite kanal Vitrazhi: o vere v kraskakh* (*Vitrazhi* 2021b). This ending is not just a simple signoff; it helps create a particular brand identity for *Vitrazhi* to distinguish it from other sources and the multitude of videos available on YouTube. It first instructs the viewer to be mindful of the "dubious, unverified news," seemingly taking the approach of trying to fight the "misinformation" and "fake news" rampant in the contemporary world. Lapin makes the case that it is only from sources like *Vitrazhi* that news consumers can be certain they are not being fed false information. The second part of the signoff, which calls upon people to read classical literature, is a more subtle attempt to curate the information consumption of viewers, guiding them toward reading the Russian classics. In online Russian Orthodox media, there has been a strong push to draw people to read Russian literature. Attempts by these Orthodox media outlets to stake a claim on the literary canon for Orthodoxy is a way of demonstrating the faith's foundational importance for all of Russian culture and its function as an antidote to influences from Western culture and other "ills" present in the contemporary world (Lassin 2019). Together, these two aspects of the signoff can be seen as an explicitly religious version of the recent Russian development of the concept of "political technology," a euphemistic term describing well-developed techniques of informational manipulation (Wilson 2011; Kemper 2019). Russian Orthodox online media outlets like *Vitrazhi* understand the difficult task they face in being able to make an impact on audiences faced with an overwhelming and constantly novel volume of content. Lapin instructs viewers to limit themselves to these activities to have his audience avoid other opinions and views; it is also a recognition of the limitations of using online platforms to persuade audiences of particular moral, theological, and political opinions.

The Ecumenical Patriarchate and the US Government

Throughout online discussions of Eastern *papizm* there is an attempt to cast the Ecumenical Patriarchate's actions in Ukraine as the work of the US State Department. These Russian Orthodox websites are taking part in a broader trend on the Russian internet that relies on conspiratorial framing (Yablokov 2017). As Robert Saler demonstrates in this volume, this conspiratorial thinking has been a prominent feature across Orthodox life. The internet is a prime site for the development and launching of conspiracy theories (Goldberg 2001). In the Russian context, conspiracies concerning the State Department and its support for Ukraine has become a well-established trope in Russian state media, such as *RT* (Yablokov and

Chatterje-Doody 2022, 45). The same is true in Russian Orthodox online media. Many articles that condemn the idea of Eastern *papizm* make the claim that former Secretary of State Mike Pompeo and the US government were instrumental in the decision-making process to grant the Ukrainian Church autocephaly (Filatova 2021a, 2021b; Konstantinova 2021; Golovko 2021). The results of such insinuations help feed into wider anti-American and anti-Western sentiments that are popular in Russia and that both highly placed government and church officials have supported. These are fueled by decades of Soviet and now Russian state news that views the West as an existential threat to Russia's existence. The popularity of these anti-Western sentiments "could be interpreted as a manifestation of the inequality in relations between Russia and the USA after 1991" (Yablokov 2018, 47). The invocation of the State Department and the US government in these online articles is typical of the conspiratorial thinking across Russian media concerning the war in Ukraine (Borenstein 2019, 204).

Vitrazhi's videos often invoke the US government's involvement in the granting of autocephaly. One, titled "Will the Visit of the Head of the Fanar to the USA Be Disrupted? The Role of the Friend from the Oval Office" (*Sorvetsia li vizit glavy Fanara v SShA? Rol' druga iz Oval'nogo kabineta*), shows a creative and confrontational approach to these questions for an online audience. In the video, Lapin speaks of Joe Biden as the Ecumenical Patriarchate's "friend in the Oval Office," helping engineer this perceived attack on the Russian Orthodox Church. The language and imagery used throughout the video borders on the level of conspiracy theory, with Lapin looking to find the source of Biden's long-standing fealty to the Ecumenical Patriarch (*Vitrazhi* 2021b). He finds his answer in a speech by Archbishop Elpidophoros, of the Greek Orthodox Archdiocese of America, back to Biden's early political career gaining the support of the Greek-American community in Delaware. The insinuation here is that the Ecumenical Patriarchate is not shy to boast of its strong ties to Biden and the highest echelons of the American government and that this relationship explains US support for the Ecumenical Patriarchate's actions in Ukraine.

Throughout the video, several images accompany Lapin on the screen. The most striking of these takes the image of Biden squeezing the shoulders of Stephanie Carter, the wife of former Defense Secretary Ash Carter, which has been the subject of much criticism and lampooning given its suggestive nature. The image present in the video from *Vitrazhi* replaces

Carter with Patriarch Bartholomew, whose *kalimavkion* bears the words "just a friend" (*prosto drug*) in Russian, offering a visual representation of the "intimacy" that Lapin references between the Ecumenical Patriarchate and the US government. The photograph introduces homophobic overtones designed to demean both men in the eyes of the Russian-speaking audience and to impugn the libertine values that Russian media accuses the United States and the West of exporting to Russia.

Posting these videos to YouTube allows viewers to comment and create a sense of community on the channel. Reading through these comments, just as we saw with the comments to articles on sites like that of the Union of Orthodox Journalists, provide insight into how the messages of these texts are being received among some of its viewers. A look at the comments on a video concerning whether or not Orthodoxy needs an "Eastern Pope," one sees a number of expressions of thanks to Lapin for his video. In addition, one user by the name of "Pravda zhizni" (Russian for "the truth of life"), writes in with a very simple message: "Neopapism. Cool term" (Pravda zhizni, October 2021). While this comment is only three words long, it expresses a great deal. It appears that through the video, the commenter learned of the term and concept of Eastern *papizm*, thus demonstrating the educative power of these videos for the general population. Through learning this term and describing it as "cool," the commenter now has language that they find appealing, which they can use to discuss the issue in a succinct and understandable manner. Calling something "cool" demonstrates its purchase on a more popular level. The comment indicates that through its popularization in online media that the discourse surrounding Eastern *papizm* is not only reserved to the realm of theologians and political thinkers but something that everyday believers can deploy and find useful in their own conversations and interactions.

Converging Papisms

Naming the Ecumenical Patriarchate's actions in Ukraine "Eastern *papizm*" creates a direct connection with the better-known term "Western papism." From the Russian perspective, the use of this term establishes that the actions of the Ecumenical Patriarchate are neither Orthodox nor Russian. Developing this notion of Otherness allows Russian Orthodox online media to more effectively frame the Ecumenical Patriarchate's decisions as something to be opposed and feared.

Adding to this understanding is the fact that Ukraine is home to a sizable Catholic community, the majority of which are members of the Ukrainian Greek Catholic Church. The Ukrainian Greek Catholic Church's history is complicated and multifaceted, and its relationship to Rome is not simple to characterize (Skinner 2009; Wolff 2019; Avvakumov 2016). Nevertheless, the rhetoric surrounding Eastern *papizm* and the coverage of Ukrainian autocephaly uses the presence of this large Catholic population to help it make the claim that the creation of the Orthodox Church of Ukraine is merely paving the way for a formal integration with the Catholic Church. The constant recourse to such a threat relies on long-standing cultural fears largely stemming from the era of the Petrine reforms and fully developing during the nineteenth-century debates over Russia's future and fears of domination by the West (English 2000, 19–25). Russia's loss in the Crimean War was a major factor in the growth of these conspiracy theories and fears of the West in the country (Yablokov 2018, 15).

Curiously, the granting of the tomos, the move that is seen as the ultimate expression of Constantinople's Eastern *papizm*, also functions in Russian Orthodox online media as a signal that Ukrainian Orthodoxy's union with Rome is a clear threat on the horizon. An article, poetically titled "Unia with Unia: To Be or Not to Be," from the Union of Orthodox Journalists, uses Patriarch Bartholomew's visit to Ukraine and his meetings with Catholics there as a sure sign of the looming potential for union (Aleksandrov 2021b).

Viewing Eastern *papizm* as a waystation to full communion with Rome seems paradoxical. Is not the point of having an "Eastern pope" that a Roman one is not necessary? But in Russian Orthodox online discourse, the threat of Roman Catholicism and the Ecumenical Patriarch's cooperation creates a scenario where the two papisms work in tandem. Fear of the Vatican has an important potency in contemporary Russia, where figures such as Nataliia Narochnitskaia, a conservative Russian public intellectual with a prominent media presence, often says things that depict "the Vatican as Russia's permanent adversary since it has always wanted to conquer Russian territory" (Yablokov 2018, 39). Papism then is deployed as both a historical and political category that represents opposition and antipathy to Russia and its culture and a proxy for Westernness and its connoted values and aims. It also aims to create a feeling of Western chauvinism and superiority over Russia. These sites play upon the fears built by the circulation of conspiratorial thinking as a key element in unifying their publics. These fears need only be based in discourse to have an effect, given the existential and civilization-shattering threats that are ascribed to them.

Another article, titled "Specter of a Third Union with Rome Is No Longer a Specter," uses the language of ghosts and the otherworldly to literally scare readers about the possibility that Orthodoxy in Ukraine will be subsumed into the Catholic Church. The article, which analyzes an interview that Patriarch Bartholomew gave to an Italian newspaper, makes it a point to mention that there has been talk from the Ecumenical Patriarch that the 1700th anniversary of the First Council of Nicaea in 2025 would present a great opportunity for restoring unity in world Christianity (Aleksandrov 2021a). This is an example of the scholar John Oddo's (2018) understanding of propaganda as an "intertextual" process that involves a "mass-recontextualization." This article is intertextual in that it draws from centuries of commentary on the Great Schism and the notion that the Catholic Church is aiming to take authority over the Orthodox churches. Placing a concrete time horizon on an issue that has been circulating for a millennium allows the Moscow Patriarchate to reenliven the topic for a contemporary Russian Orthodox public. This form of propaganda also enables the Moscow Patriarchate to link the theological issues of papism with the larger political notion that the West is attempting to diminish the standing and power of the Russian Orthodox Church and by extension the Russian state. Creating the explicit link between the theological and the political is an essential element in the ROC's development of the political subjectivity that I argue it forges through its online discourse concerning papism.

This propagandistic process continues through other examples that invoke the threat of union with Rome, especially when mentioning the Vatican and its representatives. In one instance, the UOJ relays the thoughts of Ivan Datsko, a theologian of the Ukrainian Greek Catholic Church, who remarks that the creation of the OCU offers many positive changes and developments for unity between the Catholic and Orthodox Churches in Ukraine and that communion between the two churches in the next twenty-five years is the main goal (Filatova 2021c). The comments from readers to Datsko's wishes are exceedingly harsh. A reader using the name "Aleksandr Marasanov" writes, "Van'ka Datsko, go unite with the OCU-niks, the sooner the better, according to the well-known expression, 'Proletarians (heretics and schismatics) of all countries, unite!'" This comment is loaded with meanings that demand unpacking. First, one sees that he refers to the theologian as Van'ka, a diminutive of his first name, Ivan. This rhetorical move works to discredit him and make him seem like an unserious and naïve commenter. In addition, the second half of the comment recontextualizes the official motto of the Soviet Union, adding "heretics and schismatics" along with the proletariat. Such a comment speaks to a number of important political issues. First, it makes the claim that the push to unite the Catholic and Orthodox Churches in Ukraine is akin to the forced unification of territories that the Soviet Union undertook. Second, the Soviet Union was of course known for both antireligious oppressions and authoritarian rule. Thus, invoking its motto in connection with the tomos equates the actions of the Ecumenical Patriarchate with those of the Soviet Union. This reader's comment can be seen as a direct instance of average believers making the discourse surrounding Eastern *papizm* promoted in Russian Orthodox media their own.

Charges of Ethnophyletism and Racism

Related to the threat of Western dominance that the "specter" of Roman papism is coming on the heels of Eastern *papizm*, Russian Orthodox online sources also levy the charge of another heresy against the Ecumenical Patriarchate concerning its actions in Ukraine, that of ethnophyletism. Ethnophyletism is the placement of national or ethnic concerns above those of the Gospel and the canons of the Orthodox Church and was condemned in a synod in Constantinople in 1372 (Vovchenko 2016, 178–79). In an article by Andrei Vlasov, published on the website of the Union of Orthodox Journalists, a reader sees how charges of ethnophyletism are responded to and weaponized in Russian Orthodox online discourse and its role in the larger discussions over Eastern *papizm*. Vlasov (2019) wrote this article in response to Patriarch Bartholomew accusing Russian monks of St. Andrew's Skete on Mount Athos of engaging in ethnophyletism. The claim here is that the actions of Constantinople signal an attempt to assert Greek dominance over the entirety of the Eastern Orthodox Church. When speaking out against this perceived trend, many sources in Russian Orthodox media often quote from Metropolitan Chrysostom (Dimitriu) of Zakynthos, who in a 1947 article claimed that the Slavic peoples needed to remember that the "Greeks gave them culture . . . and that therefore they should give their due respect and favor to the Greek race that educated and enlightened them and not show themselves as low and ungrateful enemies, the pan-Orthodox consciousness will sweep away all of their dark and treacherous plans" (Chrysostom [Dimitriu] 1947, quoted in Vlasov 2019).

This strong language elicits, not undeservedly, a rather heated response in Russian Orthodox online media. In one article on the website of the Union of Orthodox Journalists, the author sums up this quotation by writing that "it turns out that there is a great, Greek race and second-class, non-Greek peoples, who must serve this race and obediently fulfill its wise commands" (Vlasov 2019). He goes on to note that even though this was written in 1947, it has gone on to become the explicit policy of the Ecumenical Patriarchate, drawing from a 2018 speech where Patriarch Bartholomew stated, "Our brothers, the Slavs cannot tolerate the primacy of the Ecumenical Patriarchate and our people in Orthodoxy" (Patriarch Bartholomew 2018, quoted in Vlasov 2019). Vlasov, the author of the piece, knows that quoting this segment of Bartholomew's speech will be incendiary for his Russian Orthodox audience and uses it to offer evidence of some long-standing, nefarious intentions on the part of Constantinople. These moments help build the case that Constantinople is an aggressor moving to impinge upon the sovereignty of the Moscow Patriarchate and its parishioners. This full accounting of the Ecumenical Patriarchate's perceived ethnophyletism helps deflect attention from Moscow's attempts to further its notion of the "Russian world," or *Russkii mir*, which claims that Russia has a right and obligation to defend ethnic Russians anywhere they may be in the world. Russian, in the case of *Russkii mir*, is an expansive term that includes not only Russians but also subsumes Ukrainian and Belarusian national identity under the Russian nation and provides another example of the sort of imperial tendencies that the Ecumenical Patriarchate is displaying that are reminiscent of the Roman pontiff (Gorham 2011; Curanović 2012; Suslov 2016).

While it may not be expected, the charges of ethnic prejudice and the idea that Constantinople is promoting Greek supremacism within the Orthodox communion offers an interesting foil against which Russian Orthodox online media can condemn the granting of autocephaly to the Orthodox Church of Ukraine. Another article on the same site speaks of "Greek chauvinism" as one of the leading causes of this inter-Orthodox crisis (Shemliuk 2019). The author claims that it is the desire on the part of the Greeks to reestablish the lost glory of the Byzantine Empire and that they believe that Orthodoxy is their gift to the Slavs, repeating some of the same ideas that we saw in the previous example. The idea that the Slavic peoples should be more grateful to the Greeks for bringing them Christianity helps underscore the complaint from Russian Orthodox online media that the Ecumenical Patriarch is trying to strong-arm the rest of the autocephalous Orthodox churches into following its lead. This trope's connection with the discourse surrounding the idea of Eastern *papizm* elucidates how Russian Orthodox online media tries to fuse theological questions related to the granting of the tomos with questions of nationalism and community identity, authority, and value.

Feelings of Betrayal

One of the outgrowths of this alleged Greek supremacy within the Orthodox communion is the Greek Orthodox Church of Alexandria's decision to recognize the Orthodox Church of Ukraine, leading to feelings of betrayal within the Russian Orthodox community. In one of the more flowery articles on this topic, titled "Betrayal, Papism, and Us," the author, Fr. Valerii Dukhanin (2009) begins, "betrayal is always pain. And the meanness of a loved one is a wound in the heart." The article was written in the wake of the Greek Orthodox Church of Alexandria recognizing the Orthodox Church of Ukraine. The title attempts to make these rather abstract and often distant theological ideas and concepts personal to the average believer, invoking the idea of a shared "us." Dukhanin spends a great deal of time in the article recounting the history of the Patriarchate of Alexandria and how, in his view, it has fallen from its previous glory over the centuries into a husk of its former self. The article is suffused with lamentations over the actions of Alexandria and the pain and sadness this is causing for the Russian Orthodox Church. The author goes on to ensure that his readers understand what he sees as a major fundamental difference between the Russian Orthodox Church and the other Eastern Orthodox churches around the world: the fact that it was never subordinated to the Ottoman Empire. In the article he exclaims, "Russia—what a miracle!—remained the only Orthodox country that was not conquered by the proud Ottomans," insinuating that the other Orthodox jurisdictions owe a debt of gratitude to the Russians for maintaining their independence and helping bring an end to Ottoman rule, noting that "the Turks were defeated more than once by the Russian army and navy and gave way to other powers."

This sentiment in particular seems to connect well with readers, as evidenced in the article's comments section. A commenter by the name of "nataliia" writes that "the Ottomans were everywhere in the Orthodox Slavic and Asian-African world, only Russia was preserved! My God, what joy!" (nataliia, December 2, 2019, 8:41 PM). This comment gives the appearance that the writer believes that it was through divine intervention and favor that Russia avoided the fate of the other Orthodox churches. In a similar, albeit much less triumphalist vein, another commenter, using the name "Andrei," offers his own thoughts on the notion that the Ecumenical Patriarchate is attempting to subsume the entirety of the Eastern Orthodox communion under its authority. He writes, "We already adjusted to the Greeks for the sake of the unification of world Orthodoxy, it brought nothing good for the Russian Church. Just schism and misfortune" (Andrei, November 29, 2019, 10:08 PM). The user demonstrates a sense of woundedness and a desire to simply disengage from the Ecumenical Patriarchate and the other Greek churches. In doing so, he casts the actions of Constantinople as treachery perpetrated against Russian Orthodox believers.

In the article, Dukhanin (2019) asserts that "the temptation of *papizm* is a temptation, by and large, for all of us." In making this statement, he is claiming that the desire for power and egotism that many individuals— from the head of a family to a boss at work to a patriarch—might feel are forms of *papizm*. Dukhanin brings the issue of *papizm*, which is associated with a theological and technical register, down to the level of the quotidian. His examples of the potential other appearances of *papizm* in people's lives allows him to make this issue more immediate to his readers and demonstrate how seemingly distant and esoteric debates should be understood as examples of human pride and failings. He continues this line of thinking, writing, "*Papizm* is building the Tower of Babel, but the climber will never be satisfied." The connection with a well-known biblical story of vain human ambition underscores the spiritual folly that the author sees in the actions of the Ecumenical Patriarchate. Moreover, the story of the Tower of Babel is one that results in disunity and confusion, the exact opposite of what the Ecumenical Patriarch claims is the purpose of granting the tomos to the Orthodox Church of Ukraine, namely, overcoming division and schism and bringing unity to the Orthodox community of the country. This emotional appeal to other believers in which Dukhanin delineates what he sees as the dangers and false hopes of Eastern *papizm* and Ukrainian autocephaly shows us a different dimension of the online discourse surrounding these issues. Rather than solely relying on denunciations and attacks on the Ecumenical Patriarchate, which this article also does, Dukhanin adds emotional appeal to illustrate what a great wound these actions are inflicting across the Body of Christ.

Archbishop Feodosii (Snegirev), in an interview with the Union of Orthodox Journalists, draws a clear line showing who is still part of the "true" Orthodox fold and who is betraying it. He characterizes the debate over whether to recognize the tomos within the different autocephalous Orthodox churches as one between "devotees (*podvizhniki*) of the faith, adherents of the canons of Orthodoxy on the one hand and ecumenists, religious liberals, and Greek ethnophyletists on the other" (Chaika 2019). He castigates the supporters of the Ecumenical Patriarchate, leveling some of the most unflattering epithets that can be used in a traditional, religious setting against them. His goal seems to be one of completely and totally discrediting the Ecumenical Patriarchate and its allies by dismissing them as mere heretics, liberals, and innovators who have, in his view, drastically parted from the true path of Orthodoxy. Further in the interview, Feodosii makes clear his ultimate faith that in time Christ will triumph and correct these errors within the church. The "heresy of Eastern *papizm* will have sunk into the Lethe," he predicts, leaving no doubt for the reader which side they ought to support and laying out the potential consequences in no uncertain terms.

Perceived Threats of Spreading Autocephaly

In addition to decrying the Ecumenical Patriarchate's direct affronts to the ROC, Russian Orthodox online media also attempts to warn other autocephalous churches that they might suffer similar fates. Many invocations of Eastern *papizm* are quick to mention the other threats to Orthodox ecclesiological stability around the world, often noting that allowing for Ukrainian autocephaly will lead to a chain reaction of other breakaway groups attempting to gain autocephaly. As discussed earlier, the Russian Orthodox Church in the post-Soviet period has been vying to become the leading force in global Orthodoxy, taking what it sees as its rightful place in the Eastern Orthodox communion as the largest autocephalous church (Curanović 2007). In taking on this self-given role as leader within world Orthodoxy, the ROC finds it necessary to oppose what it perceives as infringements in the jurisdiction of other Eastern Orthodox churches from the Ecumenical Patriarchate. The official websites of the Moscow

Patriarchate and the words of the members of the hierarchy on this topic offer a view into how the ROC uses the potential threat of the Ecumenical Patriarchate meddling in the affairs of other autocephalous churches as a diplomatic tactic to assert its leading role in global Orthodoxy.

An illustrative example of this process is seen on *Patriarchia*, the Moscow Patriarchate's official website, which republished an interview with Metropolitan Hilarion (Alfeev), the Russian Orthodox Church's head of external church relations and one of the most prominent and well-known members of the hierarchy, that he gave to a Serbian newspaper. It is important to note that Maksimov's article, mentioned at the beginning of this chapter, starts by offering an account of the times that the Ecumenical Patriarch has succeeded and failed to have other Orthodox churches leave certain territory for Constantinople. Maksimov (2019) notes that while Patriarch Bartholomew was considering the question of granting autocephaly to the Ukrainian Church, he was also mulling the same issue for the Macedonian Orthodox Church–Ohrid Archbishopric. Through this example, Maksimov makes the case that Constantinople's intentions are to repeat this process across the Orthodox world. While at the time that the article was written, plans for Macedonian autocephaly had seemed to have slowed, Maksimov claims that it is only a matter of time and that the Ecumenical Patriarchate will not stop there, with threats to Romania, Bulgaria, and Georgia looming. Thus, a reader sees the importance of making these comments to a Serbian newspaper. The move allows the Russian Orthodox Church to offer its full support for the Serbian Orthodox Church, creating an alliance of Slavic nations in the face of Greek power grabs.

The newspaper *Vechernje Novosti* is nationalist and conservative in outlook and is often friendly toward the position of the Moscow Patriarchate. This friendliness is seen most clearly in the lines of questioning by its journalists. One interviewer asked Metropolitan Hilarion a question that began by stating that "Patriarch Bartholomew has shown even more that he wants to be an Eastern Pope" (Alfeev 2021b). Asking this type of leading question creates a biased environment in which Hilarion might share and expound upon the idea of Eastern *papizm*. Hilarion responds by noting that the ecumenical patriarch's actions are counter to Orthodox teaching and that if such actions continue, it will not be a divide between Moscow and Constantinople, nor even a divide between Greeks and Slavs, but between "bishops, clergy, and believers who are faithful to the holy canons and the patristic tradition and those who trample on it," reiterating some of the language seen in this chapter concerning drawing lines between these two camps.

Here, Hilarion cuts to the heart of the debate. Yet instead of focusing on Ukrainian autocephaly as a power play between Moscow and Constantinople arising from ethnic tensions within the larger communion, Hilarion moves to quash those sentiments, instead focusing the debate on questions of canonical law and following the Church Fathers and the councils. In making this the center of his argument, he casts his opponents as being in theological opposition to the teachings and traditions of the Orthodox Church. Using the word "trample" to characterize the actions of those who support Ukrainian autocephaly, Hilarion communicates the Moscow Patriarchate's utter rejection of this move and the Ecumenical Patriarchate's policies in general. In addition, translating the article into Russian and placing this article on the patriarchate's official site presents this powerful rebuke of the Ecumenical Patriarch to a Russian audience as well as showing, through the pointed question of Hilarion's interviewer, that it is not just Moscow that sees the actions of Constantinople as constituting an attempt at creating an Orthodox papacy but that it has been noted and is feared in other Orthodox-majority countries as well.

Overall, this interview and its dissemination to Russian-speaking audiences demonstrate how the online media associated with the Russian Orthodox Church attempts to communicate the global nature of the conflict between the Moscow and Ecumenical patriarchates. Both to Orthodox communities around the world and its own parishioners, the Russian Orthodox Church aims to portray itself as holding to "true" Orthodoxy and remaining within the bounds of canon law while Constantinople looks to innovate and make politically expedient moves. Stating this in a Serbian newspaper helps reify in the other majority-Orthodox countries the image of Moscow as the true protector of the rights of autocephalous churches against the alleged pretensions of the Ecumenical Patriarch to take a "papal" role.

Conclusion

In analyzing how Russian Orthodox online media develops, frames, and disseminates the concept of Eastern *papizm*, we gain a fuller understanding of how ideas emerge and circulate within Russian Orthodox intellectual circles in the present moment. The autocephaly for the Orthodox Church of Ukraine presents one of the biggest challenges to the Moscow Patriarchate and has led to both a schism within the Eastern Orthodox Church and an existential crisis within the Russian Orthodox Church over its own position and future. By deploying the label of Eastern *papizm* and calling it a heresy, online sources associated with the Moscow Patriarchate offer a strategy for melding theological concepts with the political and the personal.

The sources of and the reasons for Constantinople's engagement in Eastern *papizm* in Russian Orthodox online media offer a reflection of broader Russian concerns and neuroses. The granting of the tomos to the Orthodox Church of Ukraine circulates in these online outlets, drawing in conspiratorial ideas about the US government playing a role in both ecclesial and political affairs in Russia and Ukraine. Playing upon latent anxieties of Russian inferiority, such articles and interviews offer a reason why the Russian Orthodox Church needs to become more assertive within the global Eastern Orthodox communion.

The Russian Orthodox Church uses the threat of Eastern *papizm* to regain some of the authority that the institutional church has lost in the post-Soviet era from cynicism concerning the church's leadership and a wide-scale distaste for the institution. By presenting the actions of the Ecumenical Patriarchate as an egregious attempt to take undeserved power and prominence within the larger Orthodox communion, Russian Orthodox online media deflect criticisms from the Moscow Patriarchate and present the Russian Orthodox Church as the only force that is viable for opposing this new, insidious *papizm* and all the concomitant ills that it brings through its association with the West. Examining Russian Orthodox digital media discourse and the worlds it creates demonstrates the utility that seemingly remote and arcane debates over ecclesiology can have in the present moment. Ultimately, certain political beliefs are imbued from the beginning with theological connotations, which can make them very effective in both the political and theological fields.

Disclaimer: The conclusions and opinions expressed in this research paper are those of the author and do not necessarily reflect the official policy or position of the US Government, Department of Defense, or Air University.

Works Cited

Aleksandrov, Kirill. 2021a. "Prizrak tretei unii s katolikami uzhe ne prizrak." *Soiuz Pravoslavnykh Zhurnalistov*, February 17. https://spzh.news/ru/zashhita-very/77665-prizrak-tretyjej-unii-s-katolikami-uzhe-ne-prizrak.

———. 2021b. "Uniia s uniei v Ukraine: byt' ili ne byt'." *Soiuz Pravoslavnykh Zhurnalistov*, September 13. https://spzh.news/ru/zashhita-very/82551-unija-s-unijej-v-ukraine-byty-ili-ne-byty.

(Alfeev), Ilarion. 2021a. "Vlastnye pritiazaniia Konstantinopola kak ugroza edinstvu Tserkvi." *Patriarkhiia*, September 16. http://www.patriarchia.ru/db/text/5843718.html.

———. 2021b. "Vosstanovlenie edinstva v nashei obshchei pravoslavnoi sem'e vozmozhno tol'ko putem otkaza ot lozhnoi ekkleziologii." *Patriarchia.ru*, February 2. http://www.patriarchia.ru/db/text/5764914.html.

Avvakumov, Yury. 2016. "Ukrainian Greek Catholics, Past and Present." In *Churches in the Ukrainian Crisis*, ed. Thomas Bremer and Andrii Krawchuk, 21–44. Palgrave Macmillan.

Borenstein, Eliot. 2019. *Plots Against Russia: Conspiracy and Fantasy After Socialism*. Cornell University Press.

Chaika, Tat'iana. 2019. "Ierarkh UPTs: Veriu, chto so vremenem eres' vostochnogo papizma kanet v Letu." *Soiuz Pravoslavnykh Zhurnalistov*, October 23. https://spzh.news/ru/news/65873-ijerarkh-upc-veryu-chto-so-vremenem-jeresy-vostochnogo-papizma-kanet-v-letu.

Curanović, Alicja. 2007. The Attitude of the Moscow Patriarchate Towards Other Orthodox Churches." *Religion, State and Society* 35: 301-18.

———. 2012. *The Religious Factor in Russia's Foreign Policy*. Routledge.

Demacopoulos, George E. 2013. *The Invention of Peter: Apostolic Discourse and Papal Authority in Late Antiquity*. University of Pennsylvania Press.

Denysenko, Nicholas. 2018. *The Orthodox Church in Ukraine: A Century of Separation*. Northern Illinois University Press.

Dukhanin, Valerii. 2019. "Predatel'stva, Papizm i My." *Pravoslavie.ru*, November 26. http://pravoslavie.ru/125852.html.

Dunn, Dennis J. 2004. *The Catholic Church and Russia: Popes, Patriarchs, Tsars, and Commissars*. Ashgate.

Filatova, Ekaterina. 2021a. "Glava OVTsS MP: Raskol v Pravoslavii inspiriovali vlasti SShA." *Soiuz Pravoslavnykh Zhurnalistov*, January 18. https://spzh.news/ru/news/77104-glava-ovcs-mp-raskol-v-pravoslavii-inspirirovali-vlasti-ssha.

———. 2021b. "V SShA patriarch Varfolomei vstretitsia s Baidenom i glavoi Gosdepa." *Soiuz Pravoslavnykh Zhurnalistov*, September 30. https://spzh.news/ru/news/82932-v-ssha-patriarkh-varfolomej-vstretitsya-s-bajdenom-i-glavoj-gosdepa.

————. 2021c. "Bogoslov UGKTs: Esli my seichas ne ob'edinimsia s PTsU—
eto budet bol'shoi grekh." *Soiuz Pravoslavnykh Zhurnalistov*, October 27.
https://spzh.news/ru/news/83542-bogoslov-ugkc-jesli-my-sejchas-ne
-obedinimsya-s-pcu--eto-budet-bolyshoj-greh.

Geraci, Robert. 2009. *Window on the East: National and Imperial Identities in
Late Tsarist Russia*. Cornell University Press.

Goldberg, Robert Alan. 2001. *Enemies Within: The Culture of Conspiracy in
Modern America*. Yale University Press.

Golovko, Nazar. 2021. "Virtual'naia real'nost' Dumenko i real'naia zhizn PTsU."
Soiuz Pravoslavnykh Zhurnalistov, October 18. https://spzh.news/ru/zashhita
-very/83329-virtualynaja-realynosty-dumenko-i-realynaja-zhizny-pcu.

Gorham, Michael. 2011. "Virtual Rusophonia: Language Policy as 'Soft Power'
in the New Media Age." *Digital Icons: Studies in Russian, Eurasian, and
Central European New Media* 5: 23–48.

Hann, Chris. 2007. "The Anthropology of Christianity *per se*." *European
Journal of Sociology* 48, no. 3: 383–410.

Ivanov, Andrei. 2021. "Ierarkh UPTs—zhurnalu Serbskoi tserkvi: deistviia
Fanara v Ukraine nekanonichny." *Soiuz Pravoslavnykh Zhurnalistov*, May 13.
https://spzh.news/ru/news/79832-ijerarkh-upc-zhurnalu-serbskoj-cerkvi
-dejstvija-fanara-v-ukraine-nekanonichny.

Kaiser, Jonas. 2017. "Public Spheres of Skepticism: Climate Skeptics' Online
Comments in the German Networked Public Sphere." *International Journal of
Communication* 11: 1661–82. https://ijoc.org/index.php/ijoc/article/view/5557.

Kalkandijeva, Daniela. 2015. *The Russian Orthodox Church, 1917–1948: From
Decline to Resurrection*. Routledge.

Kemper, Michael. 2019. "Religious Political Technology: Damir Mukhetdinov's
'Russian Islam.'" *Religion, State, and Society* 47, no. 2: 214–33.

Knox, Zoe. 2005. *Russian Society and the Orthodox Church: Religion in Russia
After Communism*. Routledge.

Konstantinova, Elena. 2021. "My tsenim eto: Dumenko poblagodaril SShA za
podderzhku Tomosa PTsU." *Soiuz Pravoslavnykh Zhurnalistov*, October 7.
https://spzh.news/ru/news/83094-my-cenim-eto-dumenko-poblagodaril-ssha
-za-podderzhku-tomosa-pcu.

Kormina, Jeanne, and Vlad Naumescu. 2020. "A New 'Great Schism'?
Theopolitics of Communion and Canonical Territory in the Orthodox
Church." *Anthropology Today* 36, no. 1 (February): 7–11.

Ladouceur, Paul. 2017. "On Ecumenoclasm: Anti-Ecumenical Theology in
Orthodoxy." *St. Vladimir's Theological Quarterly* 61, no. 3: 323–55.

Laruelle, Marlene. 2021. *Is Russia Fascist? Unraveling Propaganda East and West*.
Cornell University Press.

Lassin, Jacob. 2019. "Sacred Sites: The Russian Orthodox Church and the Literary Canon Online." PhD diss , Yale University.

Lazarenko, Taisiia. 2022. "V Khorove k opechatoannomu khramu UPTs priekhali storonniki PTsU s 'arkh ereem.'" *Soiuz Pravoslavnykh Zhurnalistov*, July 12. https://spzh.news/ru/news 89500-v-khorove-k-opechatannomu -khramu-upc-prijehali-storonniki-ocu-s-arkhijerej.

Lowenstein-Barkai, Hila. 2022. "'Write It Down! I Am an Arab': The Role of Reader Comments in the Formation of Networked Counterpublics." *New Media & Society* 26, no. 6: 1–20.

Maksimov, Georgii. 2019. "Eres' konstantinopol'skogo papizma." *Pravoslavie. ru*, January 10. https://pravoslavie.ru/118507.html.

Mandaville, Peter, ed. 2023. *The Geopolitics of Religious Soft Power: How States Use Religion in Foreign Policy*. Oxford University Press.

Mitrofanova, Anastasia. 2005. *Politicization of Russian Orthodoxy: Actors and Ideas*. ibidem-Verlag.

Novikov, Andrei. 2021a. "Patriarkh Varfolomei i novyi mirovoi poriadok." *Patriarchia.ru*, March 1. http://www.patriarchia.ru/db/text/5780681.html.

———. 2021b. "IV Vselenskii Sobor i Teoriia Vostochnogo Papizma." *Patriarchia.ru*, May 14. http://www.patriarchia.ru/db/text/5809285.html.

Oddo, John. 2018. *The Discourse of Propaganda: Case Studies from the Persian Gulf War and the War on Terror*. Penn State University Press.

Østbø, Jardar. 2016. *The New Third Rome: Readings of a Russian Nationalist Myth*. ibidem-Verlag.

Pantti, Mervi. 2016. *Media and the Ukraine Crisis: Hybrid Media Practices and Narratives of Conflict*. Peter Lang.

Papkova, Irina. 2011. *The Orthodox Church and Russian Politics*. Oxford University Press.

Pertsev, Andrey. 2017. "President and Patriarch: What Putin Wants from the Orthodox Church." Carnegie.ru December 19. http://carnegie.ru /commentary/75058.

Pew Research Center. 2017. "Religious Belief and National Belonging in Central and Eastern Europe." Religion and Public Life, May 10. https://www .pewforum.org/2017/05/10/religious-belief-and-national-belonging-in-central -and-eastern-europe.

Putin, Vladimir. 2022. "Address by the President of the Russian Federation." En.Kremlin.ru, February 21. http://en.kremlin.ru/events/president/news /67828.

Relihiia v Ukraini. 2016. "K sozdaniiu 'Soiuza pravoslavnykh zhurnalistov' prichasten donetskii biznesmen, podozrevaemyi v finansirovanii terrorizma." *Relihiia v Ukraiini*, January 5. https://religion.in.ua/news/ukrainian_news

/31456-k-sozdaniyu-soyuza-pravoslavnyx-zhurnalistov-prichasten-doneckij
-biznesmen-podozrevaemyj-v-finansirovanii-terrorizma.html.

Richters, Katja. 2013. *The Post-Soviet Russian Orthodox Church: Politics, Culture, and Greater Russia*. Routledge.

(Sakharov), Sofronii. 1950. "Edinstvo tserkvi po obrazu edinstva Sviatoi Troitsy (pravoslavnaia triadologiia kak osnova pravoslavnoi ekkleziologii)." *Vestnik Russkogo Zapadno-Evropeiskogo Patrairshego Ekzarkhata* 2–3: 8–33.

Sapsai, Nikolai. 2021. "Episkop Belgorodskii Sil'vestr: Deistviia Konstantinopolia v otnoshenii Ukrainy–bespretsedentnyi primer narusheniia kanonicheskikh norm." *Patriarchia.ru*, May 14. http://www.patriarchia.ru/db/text/5809227.html.

Serebrich, Andrei. 2020. "Fenomen vostochnogo papizma." *Ezhenedel'nik Zvezda*, March 3. https://zvezdaweekly.ru/news/20202281453-KlZnF.html.

Shchotkina, Kateryna. 2019. *Khroniki Tomosu*. Vivat.

Shemliuk, Konstantin. 2019. *"Pochemu patriarkh Feodor II priznal PTsU, ili Sindrom Iudy i sila Khrista."* *Soiuz Pravoslavnykh Zhurnalistov*, November 11. https://spzh.news/ru/zashhita-very/66290-pochemu-patriarkh-feodor-ii -priznal-pcu-ili-sindrom-iudy-i-sila-khrista.

Sik, Domonkos. 2015. "The Imitated Public Sphere." In *Digital Media Strategies of the Far Right in Europe and the United States*, ed. Anne Simpson and Helga Druxes, 141–60. Lexington.

Skinner, Barbara. 2009. *The Western Front of the Eastern Church: Uniate and Orthodox Conflict in Eighteenth-Century Poland, Ukraine, Belarus, and Russia*. Northern Illinois University Press.

Soiuz Pravoslavnykh Zhurnalistov. 2019. "Pochemu Patriarkh Feodor II priznal PTsU, ili sindrom Iudy i sila Khrista." *Soiuz Pravoslavnykh Zhurnalistov*, October 11. https://spzh.news/ru/zashhita-very/66290-pochemu-patriarkh -feodor-ii-priznal-pcu-ili-sindrom-iudy-i-sila-khrista.

———. 2021. "My tsenim eto: Dumenko poblagodaril SShA za podderzhku tomosa PTsU." *Soiuz Pravoslavnykh Zhurnalistov*, October 7. https://spzh .news/ru/news/83094-my-cenim-eto-dumenko-poblagodaril-ssha-za -podderzhku-tomosa-pcu.

———. 2022. "Legalizatsiia Makedontsev: Fanar prodolzhaet raskalyvat' pravoslavie." *Soiuz Pravoslavnykh Zhurnalistov*, May 12. https://spzh.news/ru /zashhita-very/88325-legalizacija-makedoncev-fanar-prodolzhajet-raskalyvaty -pravoslavije.

Stähle, Hanna. 2021. *Russian Church in the Digital Era: Mediatization of Orthodoxy*. Routledge.

Sullivan, Charles J. 2022. *Motherland: Soviet Nostalgia in the Russian Federation*. Palgrave Macmillan.

Suslov, Mikhail. 2016. "The 'Russian World' Concept in Online Debate During the Ukrainian Crisis.' In *Eurasia 2.0: Russian Geopolitics in the Age of New Media*, ed. Mark Bassin and Mikhail Suslov, 295–316. Lexington.

Tischauser, Jeff, and Kevin Musgrave. 2020. "Far-Right Media as Imitated Counterpublicity: A Discourse Analysis on Racial Meaning and Identity on Vdare.com." *Howard Journal of Communications* 31, no. 3: 282–96.

Valencia-Garcia, Louie Dean, ed. 2020. *Far-Right Revisionism and the End of History: Alt/Histories*. Routledge.

Verkhovsky, Aleksandr. 2002. "The Role of the Russian Orthodox Church in Nationalist, Xenophobic, and Antiwestern Tendencies Today: Not Nationalism, but Fundamentalism." *Religion, State & Society* 30, no. 4: 333–45.

Vgenopoulos, Maximos. 2013. *Primacy in the Church from Vatican I to Vatican II: An Orthodox Perspective*. Cornell University Press.

Vitrazhi. 2021a. "About." YouTube video. https://www.youtube.com/channel /UCju5tmBe0zLUhl65El-mM-Q/about.

———. 2021b. YouTube video. https://www.youtube.com/watch?v=Q9tlr P4v_9E.

Vlasov, Andrei. 2019. "Fanar i etnofiletizm: v chem patriarch Varfalomei pytaetsia obvinit' afonitov." *Soiuz Pravoslavnykh Zhurnalistov*, October 24. https://spzh.news/ru/zashhita-very/65901-fanar-i-etnofiletizm-v-chem -patriarkh-varfolomej-pytajetsya-obvinity-afonitov.

Vovchenko, Denis. 2016. *Containing Balkan Nationalism: Imperial Russia and Ottoman Christians, 1856–1914*. Oxford University Press.

Wanner, Catherine. 2014. "'Fraternal' Nations and Challenges to Sovereignty in Ukraine: The Politics of Linguistic and Religious Ties." *American Ethnologist* 41, no. 3 (August) 427–39.

Wilson, Andrew. 2011. "'Political Technology': Why Is It Alive and Flourishing in the Former USSR?" *OpenDemocracy*, June 17. https://www.opendemocracy.net /en/odr/political-technology-why-is-it-alive-and-flourishing-in-former-ussr/.

Wolff, Larry. 2019. *Disunion Within the Union: The Uniate Church and the Partitions of Poland*. Harvard University Press.

Wonneberger, Anke, Iina R. Helsten, and Sandra H. J. Jacobs. 2021. "Hashtag Activism and the Configuration of Counterpublics: Dutch Animal Welfare Debates on Twitter." *Information, Communication & Society*, 24, no. 12: 1694–1711.

Yablokov, Ilya. 2017. "Social Networks of Death: Conspiracy Panics and Professional Journalistic Ethics in the Post-Soviet Russia." *Quaderni* 94: 53–62.

———. 2018. *Fortress Russia : Conspiracy Theories in Post-Soviet Russia*. Polity.

Yablokov, Ilya, and Precious N. Chatterje-Doody. 2022. *Russia Today and Conspiracy Theories: People, Power, and Politics on RT*. Routledge.

Zelenskiy, Mikhail. 2017. "Meet Bishop Tikhon, Vladimir Putin's Rumored Confessor." *Meduza.io*, December 1. https://meduza.io/en/feature/2017/12/01/meet-bishop-tikhon-vladimir-putin-s-rumored-confessor.

UFOs, Conspiracy, and American Eastern Orthodoxy

Narrative Performance of the "Patristic Mind"

Robert C. Saler

We live near the end of this fearful age of demonic triumph and
rejoicing, when the eerie "humanoids" (another of the masks of the
demons) have become visible to thousands of people by their
absurd encounters and take possession of the souls of those men
whom God's grace has departed. The UFO phenomenon is a sign
to Orthodox Christians to walk all the more cautiously and soberly
on the path to salvation, knowing that we can be tempted and
seduced not merely by false religions, but even by seemingly
physical objects which just catch the eye. In earlier centuries
Christians were very cautious about strange and new phenomena,
knowing of the devil's wiles; but after the modern age of "enlightenment" most people have become merely curious about such
things and even pursue them, relegating the devil to a half-
imaginary realm. Awareness of the nature of UFOs, then, can be a
help in awakening Orthodox Christians to a conscious spiritual life
of a conscious Orthodox world-view that does not easily follow
after the fashionable ideas of the times.

—Seraphim Rose, *Orthodoxy and the Religion of the Future*

What, then, if they are not advanced beings from other planets,
are these alien abductors? Ultimately, one cannot escape the
conclusion that they are demons or phantoms created by demonic
power. In the first place, they look like demons. They appear to be
material creatures, and yet have a transparent character. According

to the teachings of the Church, demons are spiritual beings; that is, they are fallen Angels. But because they are corrupt and degenerate, they thrive on the human passions—feed on them. . . . The spiritual effects of abductees' contacts with aliens, as we have pointed out, are anti-Christian. Abductees are drawn away from the universal teachings of Orthodox Christianity and towards the demonic delusion that underlies modern New Age philosophies. Human transformation ceases, for these victims of alien visitation, to be a God-oriented, Grace-mediated process, but becomes part of a personality-dissolving return to the "elemental" universals upon which the pagan notion of Paradise is predicated.

—Archbishop Chrysostomos of Etna, *Orthodox Tradition*,
Vol. 19, no. 1

To study US Orthodoxy with an eye toward the methodological and substantive intersections of theology and the social sciences is to, at first, engage what may seem to be a "fringe" movement. Yet these seemingly esoteric phenomena are charged with affective and theological energy that is often outsized based on the prima facie plausibility of the ideology or worldview. Such is the case with the theologoumenon (that is, a theological opinion not defined by dogma) that this chapter considers. Largely stemming from the writings of Fr. Seraphim Rose (1934–1982), a highly influential American convert to Eastern Orthodoxy whose polemical writings against what he took to be the pernicious forces at work in modernity have been influential upon certain sectors of the US Orthodox Church, this belief emphasizes the idea that UFO/"extraterrestrial" sightings relate to real events but are indicative not of extraterrestrial visitors but of demonic forces. Moreover, these events or encounters are the occasion for collusion (witting or not) between the demons and conspiratorial humans bent on forming a New World Order as a preparation for the Antichrist.[1]

My claim is not that Rose invented this opinion; indeed, while a historical survey of the context of the paranormal in the US imaginary is beyond the scope of this chapter, paranormal attribution of extraterrestrial encounters has been a feature of US Christianity (and the American psyche more generally) for many years in multiple theological traditions. Rather, this work demonstrates that within US Orthodox and (increasingly) Russian Orthodox circles, Rose is given credit as the key source for the idea that otherworldly encounters have a demonic countenance. However, it is not Rose as virtuoso author but Rose as champion of "the patristic mind" (*phromena*) that is given this authority. In other words, Rose's authority as expositor of the connections among UFOs, demons, and conspiratorial governments depends, I will argue, on his credibility in enacting a sort of patristic reinscription, a performative recasting of anxieties relating to extraterrestrials, the paranormal, and conspiracy that, crucially, lend themselves to being updated and recapitulated in ways that make their deployment all the more fraught in our time. The "patristic mind," in Rose's hands and on this topic, is a foundation on which can be built a whole range of associations with conspiracies, and the matter of UFOs is a helpful test case to see that in action.

Shifting Narratives

My method in what follows is a combination of theological analysis and narrative sociology.[2] "Narrative" sociology has multiple advantages as a tool of cultural analysis. When focusing solely on "frames" or discrete ideas (or even whole ideologies) in and of themselves, it can be challenging to understand how certain ideas not only hang together without cognitive dissonance but actually reinforce one another with affective force. In the case of conspiracy theories as elaborate as the Rose narrative, to reconcile these various frames or ideologies at a purely conceptual level can have two unfortunate effects. It can, in some cases, place the onus almost exclusively upon cognitive dissonance reduction (which has a venerable history but does not, in my view, get us very far in understanding what motivates certain confluences in the first place). Or, it can prompt a psychologization of the individual believer that runs the risks both of portraying as mentally aberrant what is in fact quite coherent from within the logic of the narrative and of being inattentive to the broader social structures within which individual believers are socialized (and within which they can plausibly improvise/augment/expand upon the narrative in their own settings).[3] Narrative analysis, for my purposes, is useful sociologically because in tracking a given narrative logic in its sociocultural outworkings we can perceive it as both a mechanism of constraint and of creativity; in other words, it forces us to realize that a given narrative's trajectory in social contexts depends upon keeping some degree of faithfulness to the original narrative logic, which itself draws upon specific repertoires of themes, characters, and emplotment devices for its plausible resonance with that social system. In other words, narrative tells us as much about the boundaries of individual and collective creativity as it does about creativity's exercise.

While my primary theoretical influences in the use of narrative come from sociology, for this chapter I also did research using methods more characteristic of anthropology, specifically ethnographic observation of online textual sources (blogs, social media posts, etc.).[4] All of the online data that I accessed is publicly available, which is important both for ethical reasons and as evidence for my contention that the particular outworking of the narrative that I am tracing is not a fringe or marginal feature of US Orthodoxy. Were I to stay only within the realm of analysis of published texts or "official" speeches that reflect Rose's influence, I could not as effectively make the case that the Rose narrative has real (and perhaps increasing) purchase among nontrivial segments of the US Orthodox population. My ethnographic method here is heavily influenced by William H. Sewell's oft-cited understanding of cultural frameworks as eliciting a "thin" coherence among those practicing in a given semantic or symbolic realm; in the case of the Rose narrative, it is imperative to see how the narrative is adapted, updated, or "practiced" in bounded yet improvisatory ways by different actors across varied contexts.[5] Because I wish to showcase how the narrative logic plays itself out through the reception and transmutation of the Rose narrative, I will quote fairly extensively and at length from the online textual sources especially.

I will conclude with a brief theological reflection on what might be at stake if the phenomenon that I am outlining is indeed a significant (and growing) force within US Eastern Orthodoxy. My main interest will be to demonstrate the ways in which gradual shifts in theological narratives, taking advantage of ambiguity, open up space for marshalling significant affective energy around otherwise seemingly arcane phenomena in religious discourse. This will, I hope, also provide insights into how theology as an analytic discipline can pair well with the social sciences in tracking both the durability and mutability of religious narratives as they are operationalized across time.

Epistemic Invasions and Inversions: The Rose Narrative

Why has Rose's voice been so influential on the topic of Orthodox engagements with UFOs and other "paranormal" phenomena? Partly because, as we will see, Rose himself saw the question of extraterrestrials as inextricably tied to broader questions around Orthodox spiritual survival in what he took to be an age of widespread apostasy. Rose believed that history is getting worse and worse and that much of what goes under the auspices of "spirituality" in his time and ours are symptoms of that decline:

> In the Christian apocalyptic view, we can see that the power which until now has restrained the final and most terrible manifestation of demonic activity on earth has been taken away (II Thess. 2:7), Orthodox Christian government and public order (whose chief representative on earth was the Orthodox emperor) and the Orthodox Christian world view no longer exist as a whole, and Satan has been "loosed out of his prison," where he was kept by the grace of the Church of Christ, in order to ' deceive the nations" (Apoc. 20:7–8) and prepare them to worship Antichrist at the end of the age. Perhaps never since the beginning of the Christian era have demons appeared so openly and extensively as today. The "visitors from outer space" theory is but one of the many pretexts they are using to gain acceptance for the idea that "higher beings" are now to take charge of the destiny of mankind.[6]

At St. Herman of Alaska Monastery in Platina, California (cofounded by Rose in 1969), I visited the cell in which Rose spent the latter decades of his life producing his prodigious literary and theological output. The contents of the modest bookshelves have been preserved by the monks at St. Herman's since Rose's death in 1982. When I visited the monastery in the summer of 2021, my monastic guide made a point of showing me that, amid the various spiritual and theological texts on the shelves, copies of the novelization of George Lucas s *Star Wars* movie, a similar novelization of the film *Close Encounters of the Third Kind*, and a book about Bigfoot sightings had a prominent place. "He always wanted to keep an eye on the world," the monk told me. This comment is significant because, even as much of Rose's legacy relates to his spiritual writings and testimonies about his personal charisms, much of his most famous published work consists of polemics about the history of Western culture and what he saw as its contemporary degeneracy. If, as his biographer said about him, he was "not of this world" spiritually, as an author he was very much in the world.

While Rose is revered by US and Russian Orthodox, especially for his personal sanctity and his insistence on the "otherworldly" character of

Orthodox faith, many of his most famous writings find him with his gaze fixed squarely on his own setting. Both in his highly influential text *Orthodoxy and the Religion of the Future* and in his regular public lecture series "The Orthodox Survival Course" (a lecture genre that many followers of Rose today have revived as a way of spreading conservative teachings), Rose offers a declension narrative of Western civilization as a gradual slide first into moral relativism, then nihilism, then (in his view) a coming totalitarian age of a dawning New World Order (which is the secular preparation for, and instrument of, the spiritual Antichrist). Characteristic of Rose's historical method is to interweave diagnoses of human prelest (spiritual delusion), conspiracy (particularly in its famous guises connected to the Illuminati and the Protocols of the Elders of Zion, the latter of which Rose defends even as he acknowledges the scholarly consensus of the text's being a forgery),[7] millennialist ambition, and spiritual warfare into signature events of what he sees as the West's apostasy stemming from the East/West schism, the Renaissance, the Enlightenment, and cognate historical movements; having told that story, Rose levies a similar mix of charges upon what he sees as harmful currents of spirituality and culture in his own time, including the increasing popularity of "Eastern" religions in the West, the "charismatic revival" in churches, Christian acceptance of theories of evolution, and nascent transhumanist currents. What is crucial to understand about this catalogue of ills, from Rose's perspective, is that it is relentlessly and linearly apocalyptic: Each current of presumed self-improvement of humanity or "new" spiritual gesture is another step toward the coming reign of the Antichrist as seeded by nihilistic, posthuman theologies characteristic of the intellectual development of the West.

Within this declension arc, UFOs play a prominent role. On the one hand, for Rose, the growing popularity of UFO sightings, accounts of abduction, and pop-culture depictions of aliens (as in the previously mentioned films) are further evidence of humanity's desire for spiritual experience beyond the mundane grind of disenchanted secularity (likely tied to the West). More significantly, however, Rose also argues that UFOs do exist, but not as extraterrestrial visitors from other planets; instead, he claims that they are demons who utilize abduction, prelest, and spiritual torment to advance evil ends:

UFOs are but the newest of the mediumistic techniques by which the devil gains initiates into his occult realm. They are a terrible sign that man has become susceptible to demonic influence as never before in the Christian era. In the 19th century it was usually necessary to seek out dark séance rooms in order to enter into contact with demons, but now one need only look into the sky (usually at night, it is true). Mankind has lost what remained of basic Christian understanding up to now, and now passively places itself at the disposal of whatever "powers" may descend from the sky.[8]

As mentioned previously, the notion that aliens are demons was not invented by Rose; ties between extraterrestrial and paranormal/supernatural ascriptions go deep into Western thought.[9] However, within the context of Rose's teleology and reading of history as the steady gathering of the Antichrist's forces in concert with nihilistic and posthuman philosophy's ascension, this theologoumenon alien demonology takes on additional layers of significance. The historical emplotment of both *Orthodoxy and the Religion of the Future* and the "Orthodox Survival Course" is one of dialectical entanglement between human nihilists/chiliasts and demonic agency; thus, throughout both texts demonic conspiracy is narratively packaged with human collaboration, all with an eye toward both of them setting the scene for an apocalyptic, nihilistic, and ultimately totalitarian future of Antichrist rule. Such a rule would presumably be prior to Christ's return, although it should be noted that the eschatological triumph of Christ—a key feature of Orthodox Christian eschatology—plays a comparatively small role in Rose's narrative compared to the suffering of the faithful under the Antichrist's ascent and rule:

The conscious Orthodox Christian . . . knows that man is not to "evolve" into something "higher", nor has he any reason to believe that there are "highly evolved" beings on other planets; but he knows well that there are indeed "advanced intelligences" in the universe besides himself; these are of two kinds, and he strives to live as to dwell with those who serve God (the angels) and avoid contact with the others who have rejected God and strive in their envy and malice to draw man into their misfortune (the demons). He knows that man, out of self-love and weakness, is clearly inclined to follow error and believe in "fairy tales" that promise contact with a "higher state" or "higher beings" without the struggle of Christian life—in fact, precisely as an escape from the struggle of Christian life. He distrusts his own ability to see through the deceptions of the demons, and therefore clings all the more firmly to the Scriptural and Patristic guidelines which the Church of Christ provides for his life. Such a one has the possibility to resist the religion of the future, the religion of antichrist, in whatever form it may present itself; the rest of mankind, save by a miracle of God, is lost.[10]

For Rose, the "patristic mind" or "patristic guidelines" laid out here pertain to discernment of when demons have engaged in temptation, assault, or other modes of spiritual warfare. Rose was an avid reader of (firsthand) accounts of extraterrestrial encounters and abductions, and based on that evidence he concluded that only an Orthodox mind trained in both the hagiography of saints engaged in such warfare and in the spiritual disciplines designed to help discern and combat demonic influence could be effective in sustaining the faithful in the face of a UFO's diabolic threats.[11] Only an Orthodox mindset can recognize "aliens" for what they are (demons), what they are not (extraterrestrials), and why it matters (resisting the harbingers of the Antichrist). The irony, of course, is that this "Orthodox mind" is in fact a reinscription of the same suspicions around UFOs and government characteristic of multiple evangelical currents in the United States—the "ancient mind" looks suspiciously modern to those who know their Hal Lindsey!

Rose himself seems somewhat ambivalent as to whether the deception that UFOs are extraterrestrial visitors as opposed to demons is being consciously and ironically perpetrated by human actors or whether such collusion is unwitting. However, many of the Orthodox thinkers who take up his narrative are more willing to elaborate on their suspicions of conscious collaboration by chiliastic human conspirators. If we think of narrative as a cultural apparatus in Sewell's sense, and if we follow Sewell's insistence that every creative exercise within a cultural field brings the field itself into crisis by testing the boundaries of its coherence, then such flexibility within Rose's own narrative logic can be seen as a strength rather than a weakness of his narrative. To anticipate the theological discussion in what follows, the slippage between human and demonic agency, while a feature and not a bug of Rose's narrative, creates an opportunity for the afterlife of the narrative to become even more enmeshed in conspiratorial accusation and "immanent" demonization of human actors than anything seen in Rose himself. This matters not only for theology but for those interested in how Orthodox rhetoric of the kind offered by Rose might cohere with—and perhaps incentivize—Orthodox participation in conspiratorial thinking.

The "Rose narrative" can be summarized as follows:

(1) UFO encounters are real, but the malevolent entities behind them are not extraterrestrials but rather demons.

(2) The pernicious activities of these demons—abduction, spiritual torment, encouragement of delusion (prelest), etc.—are meant to advance the march of history to the arrival of the Antichrist, either through inspiring worship or persecuting believers (or both).

(3) Powerful forces within the government are prone—wittingly or not—to misleading people about the nature of these demonic forces in order to advance misguided ends and usher in a "new humanity" and in so doing become collaborators with the demons (wittingly or not) in establishing the Antichrist's reign.

(4) Discernment of and resistance to these forces can only come about from those with a specifically Orthodox frame of mind (*phronema*).

We should emphasize again that, for Rose, human collusion with the demonic is not yet human conspiracy (at least in the case of UFOs); however, the total sweep of his writings provide plenty of grist for the online conspiratorial mill in the reception of his narrative.

Reception and Recapitulation of the Rosian UFO Narrative

How has the Rose narrative fared in more recent times? The following textual examples are drawn from social media, blogs, parish lectures, and a prominent conservative Orthodox voice and will serve as a snapshot of how the "thin coherence" of the Rosian narrative's parameters offer theological and politico-discursive possibilities for recapitulating, expanding upon, and "performing" the reinscription of conspiracism as "patristic *phronema*" in the late monk's work. This performance, as we will see, encompasses more contemporary conspiracist worries such as the "Great Reset," anti-COVID vaccination, and (supposed) Marxism.[12]

Much of this conspiratorial performativity can be found on the internet. Even a casual perusal of "Internet Orthodoxy" reveals the particularly virulent character of Eastern Orthodox debates in US-based social media platforms such as Facebook; in particular, more conservative strands of Eastern Orthodoxy are well represented (and easily findable) in online

Orthodox Facebook groups. As a participant-observer in these groups, I regularly had occasion to pose questions about UFOs, demonology, and conspiracy in public settings (phrased often, using Rose's common honorific, along the lines of: "Are Blessed Seraphim Rose's warnings about UFOs still relevant?"). Affirmative responses often quote Rose verbatim or else paraphrase him, such as in the following: "Absolutely 100% thats why the media outlets keep saying aliens are coming. Because Church Fathers explain that when Antichrist comes, the army of demons will be in physical form on earth to assist him in his deception. The media will convince people that they aren't demons but aliens."[13] Other responses pointed me to Father Spyridon Bailey's writings or would produce quotations from such high-profile UFO writers such as Jacques Vallee or Whitley Strieber, who similarly have questioned whether the US government is occluding the fact that UFO activity is reminiscent of accounts of paranormal beings.

Within the blogosphere, the Orthodox artist and writer Jonathan McCormack (who blogs and posts regularly on social media concerning the intersection between theology and the occult), while quoting Rose often and approvingly, has resolved the narrative ambiguity in Rose concerning human/government agency in a decidedly conspiratorial direction:

> But the truth is the UFO ideology has been strategically seeded by government sponsored programs in the media and movies, and indeed has changed the way we think about ourselves, replacing God with the greater ET's. As Jung said, UFOs are our technological angels, and inspires a vision of man evolving into a new being all together with a planetary mindset. The UFO mythology provides a new symbolic vocabulary to shape the way we imagine who we are for the new space age. . . . If I may go all woo for a moment, personally, I believe there is an even more nefarious goal, perhaps from forces playing these folks like chess, in a gambit to destroy the image of the Divine in man through transhumanism.
>
> Transhumanism is one of the major stated goals both of the World Economic Forum, and in Klauss Schwaub's book Corona and The Great Reset, WEF has lectures about When Humans Become Cyborgs. They predict within 10–15 years there will be trillions of nanobots swimming in our blood stream, and indeed the biological species called "human" will disappear by 2050, as our bodies will have merged with technology and AI to such a degree as to create a

new being where man and machine is permanently blurred and indistinguishable.

Many, from Christians to more esoteric spiritual practitioners believe this might sever the soul from the body, or prevent God from entering and acting naturally through our hearts. Darker, many believe this AI will incarnate a demonic spirit, whether the Anti-Christ or Rudolf Steiner's Ahriman, to block out God's presence on earth and bring literal Hell on Earth.

So we must decide, will we be the body of God, or Satan?[14]

We should note here that the notion of a "Great Reset," originally used as an innocuous (albeit perhaps ill-advised) title of a series of World Economic Forum deliberations on rebuilding a sustainable economic future after the COVID-19 pandemic, has become in the conspiracist lexicon shorthand for the total domination of society by conspiratorial actors who perpetrated the COVID-19 pandemic (either as a hoax, by some accounts, or as a biological false-flag operation, according to others). Vaccine denial, suspicions of biohacking (e.g., Bill Gates directing the implantation of microchips via the vaccine), QAnon-adjacent concerns over military coups against corrupt elites, and so on are all easily assimilable within the frame that McCormack is appending to Rose's narrative.

McCormack, as well as many of the social media interlocutors I encountered on this topic, are Orthodox laity; thus, turning attention to how these narratives have been taken up and promulgated by Orthodox clergy either in the United States or featured prominently on US-based Orthodox outlets provides another important vista. One such clergy is Father John Valadez, whose platform is significant because he is the current (sole) curator and distributor of the influential magazine/apparel company *Death to the World*, which has become an Orthodox lifestyle brand deeply indebted to the theology and aesthetic of Rose. In 2020, Fr. Valadez offered an updated version of Rose's "Orthodox Survival Course" as a series of lectures in his own parish in Lompoc, California. When he came to the section on UFOs, he too amplified the role of potential government conspiracy in dealing with (and benefiting from) the UFO mythos, even as he hewed more closely to Rose's restraint on the question than McCormack. What follows are excerpts from Valadez's recorded lectures:

So, Netflix put out a thing about them [UFOs]. Another very popular YouTube podcast is, um, the *Joe Rogan Experience*, who, he's interviewed people who have either worked at Area 51 or have had contact with, quote unquote, extraterrestrials, so this still pervades it, it still pervades it.

Government agencies have also led full investigation into these sightings and encounters and abductions. So the US Department of Defense released this just, just in August, August 14, 2020, um, the establishment of unidentified aerial phenomena task force—apparently UFO is too, um, you know, uh, too much, uh, funny, uh, hot-button type of a name, so they renamed it to identify aerial phenomena—uh, they just declassified several videos of military aircraft pursue—pursuing, uh, unidentified flying objects, which was a picture. The very first picture that I had on the slide was a picture of one of those videos. And also numerous government agencies and reputable scientists began to investigate UFOs. Ever since the 1950s, there are big waves of the late '40s and early '50s, and these, these, these lasted for many years, these exp—these different experiments, and also projects, one of which was the Blue Book, which is one of the most popular ones, um, that was conducted by the Air Force. So, there are scientists looking into this, government agencies looking into this. And there's also, this is also pervasive in modern media.

So it's something we cannot ignore or just sweep it away under the rug as being, um, completely conspiracy theory. It has somehow captivated the minds of modern man, and so it's important for us to know why, why has mankind become so obsessed with this, quote unquote, extraterrestrial life or these unidentified flying objects in the air? And also in USS—in, in, in the Soviet Union, they also put together force, uh, uh, government forces to investigate UFO phenomena, in order to try to harness the power of these, quote unquote, alien beings, so that they might be able to use it to conquer the world, right? And this is not science fiction, this is real-life government agencies working to try to harness, you know, what is seen or believed as extraterrestrial life, um, in order to use it physically as, um, a political tool of power.

So, there are too many reported cases and findings to discard them and sweep them under the rug, um, just as I think, I think you could kind of look at it this way: Just as many mediums, psychics, and all these kinds of things could be frauds, nevertheless the spirit behind them is something that is very real and very sinister. And there are many mediums that are real, and there are people in the occult who are real, and there are demonic appearances, and there are, um, encounters with spirits of another of another realm, quote unquote, right? So, some of these people obviously can have weird stories and might be a bunch of frauds, but nevertheless there are people who have these real encounters and, um, they're sometimes numbered in the thousands of them. And so we have to take a look at what is actually happening through an Orthodox perspective.[15]

Throughout 2020 and 2021, Valadez has utilized his *Death to the World* platform to sharply criticize the California legislature for lockdowns that curtail religious gatherings, although he has insisted that his motivation for doing so is tied to concern for Orthodox faithful's spiritual health and not politics per se.[16] Thus, even as some could see his work as participating in and fostering a conspiratorial spirit, some key aspects of his rhetoric mirror Rose in directing attention away from human actors and toward metaphysical/demonic ones.

If Valadez is a clergy who is largely restrained in his linkage of UFOs and conspiratorial tropes, the same cannot be said of Fr. Spyridon Bailey, a convert priest based in the United Kingdom but with a large US following thanks to his platform on the popular US-based Orthodox outlet Ancient Faith Radio as well as his substantial social media following. One of Bailey's most popular self-published texts, 2017's *Orthodoxy and the Kingdom of Satan*, is also essentially an updated version of Rose's "Orthodox Survival Course" but with much of the historical content replaced by an extensive cataloging of what he takes to be contemporary government conspiracies toward a New World Order (although, again, one that is the "secular" counterpart to the diabolical Antichrist).[17] In 2021, Bailey self-published *The UFO Deception: An Orthodox Christian Perspective*, which is largely an updating of the Rose narrative but with a characteristic conspiratorial bent. I cite sections at length here to highlight how Rose's themes are recapitulated:

The fact that governments have been deliberately concealing and misrepresenting the UFO phenomenon is something UFO researchers have recognised for a long time. It is a constant theme in their books and on their websites. The conclusion they have drawn from this is that political leaders have some corrupt motivation for keeping their contact with aliens a secret. This has been the argument from the likes of Steven Greer. As a consequence, UFO believers invest a great deal of psychological energy in the hope that one day the truth will be revealed, that "disclosure" will finally come.

In the post-Christian West, the promises of Humanistic materialism are proving empty. Men are searching for the truth of personal experience and so exposing themselves to a variety of occult practices. Meditation and yoga classes are available in schools, prisons, work places and even non-Orthodox places of worship, and the acceptable face of witchcraft is found on chat-shows and in movies. Along with the spirit of the age, many western Christians are willing to experiment with practices that would once have been judged as satanic and avoided. It should be of no surprise that UFOs, once the interest of a few fringe groups, has now entered the mainstream, and the possibility of a dramatic sign from the heavens comes closer. As Saint Gregory the Great writes: "The spiritual world is moving closer to us, manifesting itself through visions and revelations." As we have seen, extraterrestrials are an accepted reality for western man because science fiction has provided the fantasies and imagery, technological advances have given him the reasoned expectation that space flight could happen, and evolution has built the philosophical foundation for believing that it makes sense. The myth-making has been presented with the assurance of a pseudo-science, convincing many that fanciful speculation is fact. The nature of the UFO deception is such that as visions of strange lights and shapes in the skies become more common, they appear to bring with them proof of theories and beliefs about the universe that contradict Christian doctrine. If men can be convinced that the planet is being visited by extraterrestrials, then belief in evolution and a rejection of the teaching of Genesis is inevitable. In this confusion of ideas, we witness not a move to repentance and prayer, but to a willingness to embrace mystical traditions of the East as men seek to move deeper into the UFO experience. Orthodoxy stands alone in its warning about UFOs. Both Roman Catholic and Protestant leaders have spoken warmly of alien visitors. This is to be expected, as Father Seraphim Rose explains: The reason for this credulity is clear: Roman Catholicism and Protestantism, cut off for centuries now from the Orthodox doctrine and practice of spiritual life, have lost all capability for clear discernment in the realm of the spirits. Those currently attempting to examine the UFO phenomenon are not equipped to do so. It is something that can only be examined and understood from within the Orthodox Christian tradition. Those who attempt to apply scientific methods will only be further deceived; we already see this in the way some areas of scientific research have moved into occult practices such as telepathy and telekinesis. Belief in UFOs also promotes the ideas of global unity, which may have a superficial attraction. However, those seeking to globalise their interests have shown their willingness to suppress cultural diversity and enforce a single ethical code: for example the European Union has repeatedly punished Poland and Hungary for their traditional stances on issues such as abortion and marriage. Like the threat of environmental disaster, anticipation of extraterrestrial attack may result in a move to the idea of a single humanity defending itself under a single world government. This threat has been explored in numerous publications. For the Orthodox Christian, the assurance is very clear. There is nothing to fear in this phenomenon, UFOs are merely a further manifestation of demonic presence.[18]

Bailey's Rosian narrative is taken to its most immanent, conspiratorial extreme. In Bailey's work, the deep irony of supposed apocalyptic "otherworldliness," when deployed in the context of a historical declension narrative such as that provided by Rose, is made apparent: With only a handful of concretizations of narrative ambiguity, ethereal enemies quickly become immanent, politicized, and worthy of counterconspiratorial resistance.

In order to be attentive to the relative power dynamics of a given platform within which the Rose narrative is received and recapitulated, I must note that, outside of the US context, the situation quickly escalates to a degree whose impact is still yet to be determined. Because Rose's writings, particularly *Orthodoxy and the Religion of the Future*, have been widely distributed in Russia (including as samizdat, or contraband material, during the Soviet era), devotion to his sanctity and writings is high at both popular and official levels there. In 2020, *Interfax News* in Moscow reported the following story, headlined "The Russian Orthodox Church Has Refused to Recognize the Existence of Other Civilizations Outside Earth":

"If civilizations really existed on other planets, our Holy Scripture, the Bible, would definitely say something about that. If it doesn't say anything about it, we assume that they don't exist," head of the external church relations department of the Moscow Patriarchate Metropolitan Hilarion said on the Rossiya-24 television channel.

To support his contention, he mentioned a book by Hieromonk Seraphim Rose, a prominent theologian of the Russian Church Abroad, called *Orthodoxy and the Religion of the Future*. The book contains testimonies by people who have seen aliens and UFOs, and the author compares these stories to manifestations of demons, stories that "exist in abundance in hagiographic literature."

"He proves in his book that people who have allegedly seen aliens really saw demons, whose existence many people now refuse to believe in," Metropolitan Hilarion said.

The church believes in the existence of angels and demons "not because this is stated somewhere, but because it is confirmed by the centuries-old experience of church people," he said.[19]

Hilarion's words here stand, on the one hand, as a simple endorsement of the most rudimentary elements of the Rose narrative that we have been describing here. However, as scholars such as Sarah Riccardi-Swartz have shown, in the Putin era (and in the context of ongoing investigations of conspiratorial disinformation in the hostilities between the United States and Russia), Orthodoxy (especially in its Russian and Russian Church Outside of Russia, or ROCOR, expressions) is a particularly tense field for the outworking of theological and geopolitical positioning.[20] To the extent that the Russian church is aligning itself with the aspects of Rose's legacy that are, as I have shown, perhaps uniquely vulnerable to being narratively bundled with conspiracy theory, that is a situation that bears watching, since it seems to have enough ambiguity around demonic/human agency built into it for it to be taken in conspiratorially fraught directions—which itself might have geopolitical consequences.

Theological Reflection

The substance of both Rose's arguments and those of the previously mentioned proponents are fundamentally epistemological—their urging is for believers to acquire and sustain an "Orthodox mind" or worldview (phronema) in order to both discern and, presumably, withstand the signs of the times (political, social, and cultural) indicated by the demonic UFO deception and its accompanying human actors.[21] If we name Rose's achievement—for better or for worse—as capturing the ambient apocalyptic anxieties of his context and reinscribing it in terms of a "patristic" worldview, then how are we to assess the theological impact of this move?

The particular confluence of conspiracy paranoia, antimodernism, cataloging of the demonic, and eschatological imagination that we see in the Rosian lineage draws upon a host of well-established (and, from an Orthodox perspective, quite defensible) theological themes. Eastern Orthodox theology does have an inescapably eschatological structure that looks to the triumph of God's love and justice over evil in the world, and spiritual discernment as to how to align one's life and vocation with this proleptic triumph (inaugurated in the life, death, and resurrection of Jesus Christ) is indeed a powerful leitmotif in both patristic and contemporary Orthodox thought. Moreover, the uneven headway made by Enlightenment epistemologies in Eastern churches (even in Western contexts) has allowed many Orthodox theologians to have more immediate recourse to the theological imagery and conceptuality of the demonic than many of their Western counterparts; in other words, the reticence to ascribe historical events to demonic activity in many post-Enlightenment Western settings has not been as much a feature in Eastern theology and rhetoric. Finally, theological critique of the more supposed deleterious aspects of modernity upon the psychic, spiritual, and political well-being of humanity is as much in keeping with the subtle critiques of academic Orthodox theologians as Bulgakov, Florovsky, Behr, Hart, etc. as it is with the more conservative, often autodidactic, thinkers favored by Rose and his progeny; in other words, critiques of modernity can and do happen on multiple fronts. Thus, there might be genuinely theological reasons why Rose's vision is captivating, including because it seems to create a sort of critical distance between Orthodoxy and deleterious aspects of modernity. This distance, in Rose's hands, does draw on elements that have been and might yet be powerfully deployed for a genuinely critical and faithful Orthodox appraisal of our day. The point is not to fault Orthodox theology for the very features that make it appealing to those who, for various reasons, have concerns about Western theology's epistemic captivity to Enlightenment and post-Enlightenment frameworks; were this critical distance to be lost, something important about Orthodoxy might be as well. At the same time, these same currents are often intermingled with levels of conspiracism and demonizing of the immanent, human Other, and the narrative logic that allows this bundling to happen, with significant affective force, needs to be interrogated. In keeping with the narrative methodology, then, we might focus less on the individual theological components woven together by those operating in Rose's wake and more on the results of the narrative weaving itself. What are the impacts, and how are they to be assessed theologically?

Cultural theorists such as Susan Lepselter and D. W. Pasulka have written poignantly—based on ethnographic research ranging from middle America to Silicon Valley—on how fascination with aliens (both in extraterrestrial and paranormal imaginaries) reflects particular American anxieties and aspirations for agency in a world in which older verities—be they economic stability or institutional trustworthiness—seem to be eroding at an accelerated pace.[22] While it is impossible to ascribe the same motivation to all who buy into, promulgate, or expand upon the Eastern Orthodox narrative of the paranormal demonic/New World Order conspiracism, narrative analysis shows us that there is sufficient thematic coherence of a corrupt government colluding (wittingly or not) with demonic forces that it allows for adherents to locate their own anxieties within the narrative while having sufficient room to improvise based on ongoing current events (such is the malleability of both conspiracy narratives and their accompanying demonology). In other words, the narrative is flexible enough so that people can find themselves and their concerns within it while being "thick" enough to have recognizable authority and plausibility. This has the seemingly paradoxical (but narratively coherent) effect of utilizing an "otherworldly" (paranormal) frame to allow for a more acute and affectively powerful diagnosis of immanent threats—the governments, conspirators, and other actors working against the perceived common good. One of the theological points of studying contemporary Orthodox demonology is to demonstrate, once again, that invocations of spiritual warfare often have all-too-human targets. Simply put, if the Antichrist remains the Other, then the result might be human solidarity; if "Antichrist" becomes an ascription for human structures and the actors within them, then something has gone awry.

We can note, too, that to the extent that the narrative inaugurated (or, rather, reinscribed as "patristic" by Rose) depends upon a vision of the patristic sources as a unified epistemic source, it recapitulates another unfortunate aspect of US fundamentalism—attribution of inerrant uniformity to a body of literature that is diverse and vital in its heterogeneity.[23] Concerns about "patristic fundamentalism" are common in contemporary

Eastern Orthodox theology. The temptation to it is to disrupt the coherence of uniform epistemic perspective in the Fathers (or to admit that such discordance and diversity is an ineradicable feature of that canon), thereby undermining the broader narrative coherence that allows for the "patristic" mindset to serve as an effective counterbalance against the forces of modernity as hypostasized demonic. The epistemic cost of this disruption, theologically speaking, would be a kind of vulnerability that a mindset of perpetual spiritual warfare (with immanent enemies) may not be able to afford. If the Orthodox "phronema" is not a static given but a perpetually contested reality, then it cannot serve as a bulwark against social flux but is always already part of that flux.

As a scholar-practitioner of Orthodoxy, I suggest that there are certain strands of "the Orthodox mind" that are attracted to the antimodernity signified somewhat by Rose and more aggressively by those operating in his name who see such refusal to truck with "secular" wisdom as somehow characteristically patristic. At the same time, there are others—myself being one—that are intrigued by the prospect of acquiring a "patristic mind" precisely because these authors, in addition to being diverse in their witness, were often some of the most lucid, subtle, and intellectually curious interlocutors with the best philosophy and science of their day. If the patristic legacy is necessarily contested in our time, then the contestation must include a protest against recruiting the patristic phronema as a cipher for constricting rather than expanding the field of dialogue (however critical) with other modes of contemporary thought. One hopes that Rose's legacy is retrievable for this project; further scholarship and time will tell.

All of this theological assessment occurs against the backdrop of the fact that, empirically and theologically, there is no "pure" Orthodoxy against which the currents described in this chapter may be judged as "more" or "less" Orthodox. My argument that a prima facie odd theologoumenon is emblematic of a powerful strand within the US Orthodox experience, if at all correct, makes the enterprise of adjudicating what constitutes "real" Orthodoxy no more helpful for the theologian than for the social scientist (since "real" Orthodoxy in the end cannot be anything other than what "real" Orthodox do, and to allow that analysis to slip from descriptive to normative is to engage a slippery slope indeed). In fact, I would argue that theologians can take a real and salutary cue from the social scientist's general unwillingness to posit a pure essence over and against lived and heterogeneous realities, because in the absence of the discourse of purity the theologian is left with less conceptually tidy but more immanently pressing questions of theological quality: What fosters life? What opens the heart to vulnerable love rather than fear? What follows the patristic authors' lead in humbly locating the demonic (or at least its potential) first and foremost in one's own being rather than in the neighbor, even (especially) the enemy? Just because an ethos is ostensibly countermodern does not make it Christian.

In any case, whether one's interests are theological or political/social, the sort of theological slippage that I have been tracking is, I would argue, relevant to those seeking to understand why certain theological gestures might track with conspiratorial thinking in Eastern Orthodoxy in the United States.

Notes

The second epigraph, along with the archbishop's crediting of Rose for the most effective articulation of his point, can be found at http://orthodoxinfo.com/praxis/alien_abduct.aspx.

1. For a helpful overview of how the rhetoric of UFOs has interacted with demonology and conspiracy theory in US religion more broadly, see David G. Robertson, *UFOs, Conspiracy Theories, and the New Age* (Bloomsbury Academic, 2016).

2. For a locus classicus of the narrative method applied in cultural sociology, see Margaret R. Somers, *Genealogies of Citizenship: Markets, Statelessness, and the Right to Have Rights* (Cambridge University Press, 2008), esp. 254ff.

3. See the essays in Leslie J. Irvine, Jennifer L. Pierce, and Robert L. Zussman, eds., *Narrative Sociology* (Vanderbilt University Press, 2019). Of special interest for my point here is Francesca Polletta's work on the narrative conceptuality of "spontaneity" in her article "It Was Like a Fever . . . : Narrative and Identity in Social Protest," 301–16.

4. Liz Przybylski argues that "in hybrid fieldwork, like physical and online work from which it germinates, the researcher engages in cultural practices as a participant while simultaneously observing the field with critical ears and eyes, all while making it known to others in the scene that participant-observation is part of an overt research process." Furthermore, she contends that because in our daily lives the lines between what is "online" and what is "physical" increasingly blur, given our technology, smart phones, etc., blends of physical and online ethnography are in many ways keeping pace with the subject formation and identity construction characteristic of everyday life in the twenty-first century. Liz Przybylski, *Hybrid Ethnography: Online, Offline,*

and In Between (Sage, 2021). Similarly, in a 2016 article on Facebook methodologies, Steffen Dalsgaard writes: "Despite being new media that provide new platforms for social life, I will wager that Facebook and perhaps social media more generally do not confront ethnographers with any challenges that are totally unprecedented. Qualitative ethnographic methodology, which has developed significantly following the crisis of representation and the advent of discourses of globalization, is already in possession of the tools to deal with online platforms. These include: training in paying attention to detail through observation; immersion into a diversity of lived lives through participation; systematic modes of questioning through interviewing; and epistemologies for working with text, images, film and other media representations of self and other. What ethnographers do online in terms of pursuing research questions, and thinking critically and systematically about data and their sources, is not that different from what they are used to doing offline. Virtual or digital ethnography, which focuses on online modes of inquiry, goes back almost two decades, and is inspired by well-tested offline approaches. . . . Scholars in media studies have produced much work outlining the methodological importance of social media, but within anthropology fewer publications have tried to grapple with the topic. . . . For this reason, there is still much need for discussions of how fieldwork is facilitated both online and offline, and how field-relationships become articulated in new forms with the new affordances of digital technologies." Steffen Dalsgaard, "The Ethnographic Use of Facebook in Everyday Life," *Anthropological Forum* 26, no. 1 (2016): 96–114.

5. Narrative, in my view, then, is one way to fulfill Sewell's injunction that we continue to give heed to "a sense of the particular shapes and consistencies of worlds of meaning in different places and times and a sense that in spite of conflicts and resistance, these worlds of meaning somehow hang together," however loosely. William H. Sewell, "The Concept(s) of Culture," in *Practicing History: New Directions in Historical Writing After the Linguistic Turn*, ed. Gabrielle M. Spiegel (Routledge, 2005), 57–58.

6. Fr. Serafim Rose, *Orthodoxy and the Religion of the Future* (St. Herman of Alaska Brotherhood Press, 1975), 109.

7. As in Lecture 9 of the "Orthodox Survival Course." While these lectures have never been formally published, they are widely available in unedited form on the internet; moreover, in 2019 Samizdat Press in Monee, Illinois, published a paperback edition with some additional historical footnotes. This published edition is the version that I will be citing in this chapter.

8. Rose, *Orthodoxy and the Religion of the Future*, 108.

9. See Jeffrey J. Kripal, *Authors of the Impossible: The Paranormal and the Sacred* (University of Chicago Press, 2010).

10. Rose, *Orthodoxy and the Religion of the Future*, 114. One sees here, as elsewhere, how any non-Christian teleology for Rose (evolution, millennialism, chiliasm, etc.) is a sure sign of both human delusion and the gathering storm of the Antichrist.

11. It is relevant here that Rose is clear that only Eastern Orthodox Christian disciplines are effective here; in fact, Rose—who regularly identified ecumenism as another chiliastic trend that would facilitate the rise of the Antichrist—specifically singles out both Protestantism and Roman Catholicism as being welcoming of the UFO phenomenon and thus catastrophic for Christian resistance. This gives more evidence that he seemed unaware of how aligned his views here are with Protestant fundamentalism at the time.

12. See, inter alia, Rob Brotherton, *Suspicious Minds: Why We Believe Conspiracy Theories* (Bloomsbury, 2017); and Carl T. Bergstrom and Javin D. West, *Calling Bullshit: The Art of Skepticism in a Data-Driven World* (Random House, 2020).

13. It should be noted, too, that this narrative has gained traction outside of Eastern Orthodoxy; the controversial Catholic priest Br. Michael Dimond, for instance, offers a narrative of UFOs as demons similar to Rose's (but with fewer apocalyptic/conspiratorial overtones). Br. Michael Dimond, *UFOs: Demonic Activity and Elaborate Hoaxes Meant to Deceive Mankind* (Most Holy Family Monastery, 2008).

14. Jonathan McCormack, "The Great Reset, UFO's [sic], Transhumanism, and the Occult Engineering of the New Man," https://katehon.com/en/article/great-reset-ufos-and-occult-engineering-new-man. Typos in original throughout. McCormack's earlier crediting and endorsement of Rose on this collusion can be found in a post one year earlier, "Could UFO's [sic] Be a Demonic Deception?," posted at https://jonathanmccormack.medium.com/could-ufos-be-demonic-deception-d6c4b97223ce but subsequently deleted.

15. The audio is available at the website of St. Timothy Antiochian Church in Lompoc, California: https://www.sttimothy.net/index.php/2020/08/13/survival-course-for-orthodox-christians/.

16. Personal correspondence with author, May 22, 2021.

17. Fr. Spyridon Bailey, *Orthodoxy and the Kingdom of Satan* (FeedaRead.Com, 2017).

18. Fr. Spyridon Bailey, *The UFO Deception: An Orthodox Christian Perspective* (FeedaRead.com, 2021).

19. "Russian Orthodox Church Equates Aliens with Demons," *Interfax*, April 20, 2020, https://interfax.com/newsroom/top-stories/68479/.

20. See, inter alia, Sarah Riccardi-Swartz, "American Conversions to Russian Orthodoxy Amid the Global Culture Wars," Berkeley Center for Religion, Peace & World Affairs, Georgetown University, https://berkleycenter

.georgetown.edu/responses/american-conversions-to-russian-orthodoxy-amid-the-global-culture-wars; Sarah Riccardi-Swartz, *Between Heaven and Russia: Religious Conversion and Political Apostasy in Appalachia* (Fordham University Press, 2022).

21. A significant virtue of David G. Robertson's compelling study of the intersection of UFO discourse and conspiracy theory is that it shows how pervasively UFOs stand as a site of epistemological contestation in a variety of settings, including explicitly "New Age" and millennialist movements. David G. Robertson, *UFOs, Conspiracy Theory, and the New Age: Millennial Conspiracism* (Bloomsbury, 2016).

22. See Susan Lepselter, *The Resonance of Unseen Things: Poetics, Power, Captivity, and UFOs in the American Uncanny* (University of Michigan Press, 2016); and D. W. Pasulka, *American Cosmic: UFOs, Religion, Technology* (Oxford University Press, 2019). In their now-classic study of susceptibility to conspiracy thinking in the United States, Joseph E. Uscinski and Joseph M. Parent assert that "conspiracy theories are a manifestation of vulnerability, a symptom of heightened danger from powerful actors. Shifts in the distribution of power condition people to communicate and coordinate against common threats." Joseph E. Uscinski and Joseph M. Parent, *American Conspiracy Theories* (Oxford University Press, 2014), 17.

23. See Aristotle Papanikolaou and George E. Demacopoulos, "Being as Tradition," in *Fundamentalism or Tradition: Christianity After Secularism*, ed. Aristotle Papanikolaou and George E. Demacopoulos (Fordham University Press, 2019).

AFTERWORD

Angie Heo

What does anthropology offer for the interdisciplinary study of Orthodox Christianity? In 2005, anthropologist Chris Hann and theologian Hermann Goltz convened a group of ethnographers working mostly in the Balkans and Eastern Europe to consider this question and later contribute to the pathbreaking volume *Eastern Christians in Anthropological Perspective* (2010). With diagnostic acuity, their application of the "anthropological perspective" to Orthodox Christianity addressed gaps created by two significant trends of scholarly attention.

The first trend was the then-emerging "anthropology of Christianity" and its founding rationale in the hypothesis that (Protestant) Christianity had been largely neglected as a subject of study given its excessive proximity or repugnance to the ethnographer—at least as it was viewed from the perspective of the scholar-anthropologist steeped in the secular, modern West. Where is Orthodoxy, and the neglect of Orthodoxy, in this specific formulation of anthropology's neglect of Christianity? The second trend, more longstanding and pervasive than the first, was and remains the East-West divide, or the imaginary that set Eastern Europe (i.e., socialism, communism, authoritarianism) as the Other of Western Europe (i.e., capitalism, democracy, liberalism). By further naming their subject of study "Eastern Christians" in their volume's title, Hann and Goltz effectively both leveraged the geopolitical binary while also indulging the future dissolution of "Eastern Christian" as a category of analysis altogether.

Nearly two decades later, this present volume, *Anthropologies of Orthodox Christianity*, offers an original and forward-looking collection of essays that urge us to reckon with the consequences of the East-West binary on current developments in Orthodox Christianity. Compared to *Praying with the Senses* (2018), a recently published volume that also brought together ethnographers of Orthodoxy, this present volume does not underscore so much the aesthetic and bodily contents of Orthodox traditional practice as it does explicitly thematize the moral politics of faith and the problematic geopolitics of theological imperialism (Kormina and Naumescu 2020). As much as they are anthropologists of Orthodoxy, Candace Lukasik and Sarah Riccardi-Swartz are scholars of political conservatism and Americanists engaged with the transnational and global aspects of religion and spirituality in the United States. Their respective research projects also pose an important challenge to the category of "Eastern Christian" in ways that realize Hann and Goltz's earlier anticipation of future work in the anthropology of Orthodox and Eastern Catholic communities. What happens to the venerable East-West divide when we reconsider its social moral purchase in what Riccardi-Swartz (2022) calls "the new Russian turn in American Christianity"? What does the uneven translation of Coptic minority identities from Egypt to the United States suggest about the East-West divide as a trope that carries real material, political effects into the world of lobbying and movement organizing (Lukasik 2025)?

By coincidence or by design, several authors featured in this volume take up related questions about the Orthodox diaspora and migration to Western Europe and North America (Kellogg, Silva, Sheklian) or else the hybridization of Orthodox discourse with ideologies and theologies understood to originate in Western Europe and North America (Saler, Goodgame). All these case studies deliver valuable insights into how Orthodoxy moves between and beyond the borders of canonical territory, hinting at new configurations of "global" Orthodox belonging that do not neatly abide with the classic Orthodox model of world church unity organized as a federated communion of autonomous churches. They also push against the stereotypical characterization of Orthodoxy as backward, stagnant, or obscure, showing instead how it serves as a creative resource for the internal critique of clerical authority (Michka) and evaluations of interpatriarchate and inter-religious relations (Lassin, Dulin). So far in my experiences teaching graduate students interested in religion in the United States (the University of Chicago) and in Europe (the University Centre Saint-Ignatius Antwerp), I have noticed a growing interest in new converts to

Orthodoxy among the disillusioned younger generations on the hunt for alternatives to evangelicalism and secular atheism. For this reason alone, I foresee various essays in this collection being eagerly picked up by researchers as well as readers outside scholarly circles.

In the remainder of my reflections, I wish to linger a bit longer on the political and theological possibilities that follow from new anthropological perspectives on the East-West divide. Admittedly, much of my desire to reconsider what "East" and "West" signify stems from the current, troubling state of world politics in Europe and Africa. As I write these words in July 2022, the Orthodox Christian world grapples with the politics of church division and their thick and sticky ties to various territorial politics of secession and annexation. Continuity in "the true faith," as many anthropologists have already noted, is central to Orthodox Christianity. Schisms are revolutionary ruptures of change, but to the extent that they occur around disputes over succession and secession, they are also fundamentally claims to the "right" and "true" line of continuity. What does an Orthodox-specific politics of schism reveal about our international politics of war and independence? And what might anthropologists of Orthodoxy, newly attuned to this volume's focus on its global and transnational dimensions, reveal about Orthodox struggles for autonomy through redefined terms of belonging to the "right" and "true" body of faith?

Earlier this year, in February 2022, Russia's brutal invasion of Ukraine sent shockwaves worldwide and demonstrated with full force Vladimir Putin's antagonism toward NATO and the European Union. For the Ukrainian Orthodox in Ukraine and abroad in the diaspora, the signs of Moscow's imperial, anti-European stance had already been long apparent in patriarchate politics across the East/West divide. The Moscow-Constantinople schism of 2018 was a spectacular fracture between the two most powerful, prominent centers of Orthodox power, whose rivalry had never actually reached the point of schism even at the most strained heights of the Cold War. The Moscow patriarchate's unilateral severing of communion ties with the Ecumenical Patriarchate of Constantinople was directly connected to splits internal to the Ukrainian Orthodox over the issue of Russian authority in Ukraine.

Compared to the Russia-Ukraine war, the Ethiopian civil war has received minimal attention, despite horrific and widespread accounts of ethnic cleansing and mass displacement. In November 2020, war broke out between the Ethiopian federal militias (and the Eritrean Defense Forces) and the Tigray Defense Force (and Oromo Liberation Army). As a result, the Ethiopian Orthodox Church, the world's second-largest Orthodox church after the Russian Orthodox Church, is currently in the throes of a potential split between a new emerging "Tigray Orthodox Tewahedo Church" and the older, established Ethiopian Orthodox Tewahedo Church, whose papal see is based in the region of Amhara, the region that seeks control over Western Tigray. As in the case of the Moscow-Constantinople schism, this rupture is largely motivated by an Orthodox community's quest for "autocephaly," a term that is loosely equated to "independence." Unlike the Moscow-Constantinople split, however, the Tigray Orthodox quest for autocephaly preserves the space of communion with the other Ethiopian Orthodox Church. Autocephaly is not the same as schism. In fact, the making of autocephalous churches may be understood as the distinguishing feature of Orthodox governance: unity-in-diversity.

Fortunately, there are scholars whose writings provide the detail and nuance that an analysis of Orthodox schism and autocephaly in each of these war-torn regions deserves.[1] For now, my initial question about what the anthropological perspective may offer for the study of Orthodoxy leads me to ask: What specific features of Orthodoxy invite anthropologists to unsettle or challenge standard narratives of war and the East-West divide?

Elsewhere, in an earlier conversation with Lukasik and Riccardi-Swartz about Orthodoxy and "the idea of global Christianity," I had forwarded the bold claim that Orthodox's uniqueness lies in the "intrinsic centrality of the ethnos or nation to its self-identity."[2] This is not to suggest that Protestantism, for example, does not have a national identity or that Protestant schisms are not subject to competing faith-based nationalisms. (The Presbyterian Church of Korea, for instance, is notorious for its internal schisms, which have produced over two hundred subdenominations over the brief fifty years since the Korean War.) Rather, what I mean to point out is that the Orthodox political order is organized along national and regional lines. Orthodox ecclesiology allows for a diffuse, decentralized structure of theological authority through a circle of multiple patriarchates at the head, with each patriarchate governing a separate jurisdiction of national and ethnic churches. By revisiting my earlier claim, I must also qualify it by emphasizing that the link between the nation and Orthodoxy is an imagined and historical one; by extension, the link between the modern nation-form (e.g., state power, territorial borders, horizontal sociality) and Orthodoxy is a relatively recent development. Indeed, there is already a significant body of research on how the nation-state, nationhood, and the primacy of national belonging has fundamentally transformed modern Orthodoxy, including my own on Coptic Orthodoxy and its relationship to Egyptian national unity and Christian-Muslim sectarianism (Heo 2018).

The key remaining question, it seems to me, is what Orthodoxy can tell us about the historical specificity, even strangeness, of the nation-form and nationalism as the central organizational terms of identity and belonging in our world today. Here is also where the politics of Orthodox division in Ethiopia and Ukraine may offer some striking hints of insight. Frequently identified as "minorities" (religious or racial), the Coptic Orthodox are rarely identified as an imperial power or seat of authority. Yet the Coptic Orthodox Patriarchate of Alexandria is also the ultimate patriarchate authority overseeing the Ethiopian and Eritrean Orthodox Churches. Under what conditions would the Coptic Orthodox Patriarchate grant recognition to the "Tigray Orthodox Tewahedo Church" today? Only recently as 1950 did the Patriarchate of Alexandria grant the Ethiopian Church autocephaly, and for the Eritrean Church, much later in 1994, following Eritrea's secession from Ethiopia. I was reminded of this historical reality when I caught sight of the famous "Virgin of the Apparition" image dangling beneath the driver's mirror in a taxi heading to O'Hare airport. Heavily accustomed to seeing the image with the Egyptian national flag, I was startled by the Ethiopian colors of green, yellow, and red. Same Orthodox family, different nation-states, and different battles over nationalism. If I had followed the "Virgin of the Apparition" in Ethiopia and Eritrea, what histories of nationhood and empire might have been uncovered? Instead of beginning with the Egyptian nation-state as the natural referent of belonging, what would a study of Coptic Orthodoxy look like if the focus were on the Orthodox politics of autocephaly in historical relation to, for example, Anglo-Egyptian Sudan, or pan-Africanism, or the Arab-Israeli wars? (I'm further willing to bet that an imagined East-West divide is active within this contentious arena of African and Arab Christendom.) Pursuing these different geopolitical frames would not mean discarding the centrality of nationhood and minoritarian nationalism; on the contrary, it would help us better understand how the nation-form is deeply embedded in multiple orders of religious, racial, and regional belonging and exclusion.

The Moscow patriarchate, compared to the Alexandrian patriarchate, is more well known for its imperial outlook toward other national churches, especially those it considers under its jurisdiction in the wake of the Soviet Union's collapse. In addition to the Ukrainian case, numerous schisms have resulted from an Orthodox Church cutting spiritual ties with its patron in Moscow by strategically seeking autocephaly from another patriarchate head. These schisms can reveal something about the fractured state of nations and separatist nationalism especially in autonomous border zones. Here, I am thinking particularly of the anthropologist Dominic Martin's (2019) work on the "rebel" monastics who live in a postnuclear wasteland in Far Eastern Russia and who openly reject Moscow and seek patronage from the Old Believer metropolitan even farther west in Romania. I am also intrigued by the moral and spiritual radicalism of these revivalist "youngsters," who, like the Orthodox converts in Appalachia seeking to "reclaim America for God" (Riccardi-Swartz 2022), are disillusioned by the corrupt state of national politics. Whether an Orthodox community breaks away from or aligns with "Moscow"—whatever "Moscow" is imagined to be, a transnational attachment to "Russia" intersects with other styles of moral nationalism, such as far-right conservatism in the United States or spiritual traditionalism in Romania.

By drawing brief attention to Ethiopia and Russia, my only aim is to show how the question of Orthodox identity and transformation is a living and contentious one. This timely volume shows us that Orthodox Christians can no longer be assimilated into the category of "Eastern Christians" without taking into serious account what the East-West divide signifies in any given context of study. To my mind, in doing so, this volume also illumines the potential for anthropologists of Orthodoxy to challenge methodological nationalism in anthropology and the social sciences at large. Far from being natural and self-stable, the world order of national Orthodox churches is perpetually changing with new demands for recognition under conditions of schism, secession, and separatism.

Works Cited

Fader, Ayala, and Naumescu, Vlad. 2022. "Religious Orthodoxies: Provocations from the Jewish and Christian Margins." *Annual Review of Anthropology* 51 (October): 325–43.

Hann, Chris, and Hermann Goltz. *Eastern Christians in Anthropological Perspective.* University of California Press, 2011.

Heo, Angie. *The Political Lives of Saints: Christian-Muslim Mediation in Egypt.* University of California Press, 2018.

Kormina, Jeanne, and Vlad Naumescu. 2020. "A New 'Great Schism'? Theopolitics of Communion and Canonical Territory in the Orthodox Church." *Anthropology Today* 36, no. 1.

Luehrmann, Sonja, ed. *Praying with the Senses: Contemporary Orthodox Christian Spirituality in Practice.* Indiana University Press, 2018.

Lukasik, Candace. *Martyrs and Migrants: Coptic Christians and the Persecution Politics of US Empire.* New York University Press, 2025.

Riccardi-Swartz, Sarah. *Between Heaven and Russia: Religious Conversion and Political Apostasy in Appalachia.* Fordham University Press, 2022.

Notes

1. See "The Idea of Global Christianity," interview with Angie Heo, https://www.new-directions.sps.ed.ac.uk/the-idea-of-global-christianity-an-interview-with-angie-heo-2/.

2. As the editor of *Praying with the Senses* (2018), the late Sonja Luehrmann (1975–2019) advanced the anthropology of Orthodoxy in a variety of significant directions after Hann and Goltz's inaugural collaboration. Most obviously, her volume was the first to advance collaboration beyond Eastern Europe and the Balkans, inviting scholars working in the Middle East and South Asia including myself, Andreas Bandak, Tom Boylston, and Vlad Naumescu. Later, Luehrmann would launch an initiative to think comparatively about Orthodox Christianity and Orthodox Judaism, an initiative that was carried out to completion by Naumescu and Fader (2022).

ACKNOWLEDGMENTS

In the spring of 2020, we organized a panel discussion titled "Orthodoxy and Anthropology in Conversation," bringing together anthropologists and theologians of Orthodox Christianity in dialogue, featuring panelists who would later become contributors to this volume. Supported by the Center for Theologically Engaged Anthropology and hosted by the Orthodox Christian Studies Center at Fordham University, the panel was intended to be an entry point to larger conversations about the disciplines of theology and anthropology working together to better understand a growing interest in the idea of global Orthodoxy. COVID had different plans for that event. After being postponed, the panel was reimagined and brought online during the pandemic. The questions asked, contestations aired, and conversations had during the webinar shaped this volume in both explicit ways and those still yet unknown.

We are grateful for the generosity and support of the Orthodox Christian Studies Center at Fordham University, which has been a crucial and much-needed academic voice for the study of Orthodoxy. For as long as we have known them, Aristotle Papanikolaou and George Demacopoulos have championed anthropological and social science research on Orthodoxy. We are thankful for their support and mentorship over the years. J. Derrick Lemmons and the Center for Theologically Engaged Anthropology have helped pave the way to have the type of work and conversations that appear in this volume. Along the way, we are immensely grateful for the engagements we have had with Bethlehem Dejene, Alexandra

Antohin, Elina Vuola, and Donna Rizk Asdourian on the intersection of anthropology and theology.

Many of the chapters you find in this book were workshopped at Northeastern University, thanks to a mentoring grant through the ADVANCE office. The Ethnographers of Orthodoxy group was pivotal for the finalization of this book. We are grateful to the university for its generous support.

LIST OF CONTRIBUTORS

Sarah Bakker Kellogg is an anthropologist by training and teaches courses on religion, gender, and ethnographic research at San Francisco State University. An interdisciplinary and publicly engaged scholar, she bridges North American, European, and Middle Eastern conversations about racism, religious difference, gender, and global migration politics.

John Dulin is an associate professor of anthropology at Utah Valley University. His research focuses on interreligious worlds. He has published on the interstices of religion in multiple regions, spanning topics such as the intersection of Evangelicals and Judaism in North America, spiritual experiences of Charismatic Christians and Traditionalists in Ghana, and Orthodox-Muslim-Pentecostal relations in Ethiopia.

Clayton Goodgame is a postdoctoral research fellow at Yale University. He received his PhD in anthropology from the London School of Economics.

Angie Heo is an associate professor of the anthropology and sociology of religion at the University of Chicago Divinity School. She is the author of *The Political Lives of Saints: Christian-Muslim Mediation in Egypt* (University of California Press, 2018).

Jacob Lassin is an assistant professor of regional and cultural studies (Russia) at the Air Force Culture and Language Center, Air University. He received his PhD from Yale University in Slavic literatures and cultures in

2019. His research focuses on the intersection of religion, politics, literature, and new media in Russia and the former Soviet Union. He is currently working on a book project titled *Sacred Sites: Russian Orthodox Cultural Politics Online*, which explores how websites run by the Russian Orthodox Church and its allies reinterpret Russian culture to attract a new educated elite that supports the church and state.

Amber Lee Silva completed her doctorate in anthropology from McGill University in 2022. Since then, she has been raising her three children in Quebec, writing, and revising her ethnography on the Alaskan and Pennsylvanian Old Believers.

Candace Lukasik is an assistant professor of religion and faculty affiliate in anthropology and Middle Eastern cultures at Mississippi State University. She is the author of *Martyrs and Migrants: Coptic Christians and the Persecution Politics of US Empire* (NYU Press, 2025).

Aaron Michka is an assistant professor of anthropology at the University of Notre Dame.

Sarah Riccardi-Swartz is an assistant professor of religion and anthropology at Northeastern University. She is the author of *Between Heaven and Russia: Religious Conversion and Political Authority in Appalachia* (Fordham University Press, 2022).

Robert Saler is an associate professor of theology and culture at Christian Theological Seminary, where he also serves as associate dean for evaluation. He is the author or editor of several books, most recently *"Death to the World" and Apocalyptic Theological Aesthetics* (Bloomsbury, 2024). He is currently working on several projects related to the intersection of conspiracy theory, public epistemologies, and aesthetics.

Christopher Sheklian is an assistant professor of philosophy and religion at Mississippi State University. He received his PhD in anthropology from the University of Chicago and was previously a Manoogian postdoctoral fellow in Armenian studies at the University of Michigan and a postdoctoral researcher at Radboud University, part of the ERC-funded Rewriting Global Orthodoxy project. Currently, he is working on a monograph entitled *Liturgical Rights: Armenian Minority Presence in Turkey*.

Sonja Thomas is an associate professor of women's, gender, and sexuality studies at Colby College. Her research examines the intersections of caste, race, gender, class, and religion in postcolonial India and the South Asian diaspora. She is the author of *Privileged Minorities: Syrian Christianity, Gender, and Minority Rights in Postcolonial India*. She has also written articles on education and Christian religious minorities in India, on South Asian American Christians, and on tap dance in the United States and globally. She is currently completing a manuscript on Indian missionary priests in the United States entitled *Indians and Cowboys: Race, Caste, and Indian Missionary Priests in Rural America*.

INDEX

ORTHODOX CHRISTIANITY AND CONTEMPORARY THOUGHT

SERIES EDITORS

Aristotle Papanikolaou and Ashley M. Purpura,
Sarah Bakker Kellogg, Sonic Icons:
Relation, Recognition, and Revival in a Syriac World
A. G. Roeber, Orthodox Christianity and the
Rights Revolution in America
Bryce E. Rich, Gender Essentialism and Orthodoxy:
Beyond Male and Female

Kristina Stoeckl and Dmitry Uzlaner, *The Moralist International: Russia in the Global Culture Wars*

Sarah Riccardi-Swartz, *Between Heaven and Russia: Religious Conversion and Political Apostasy in Appalachia*

Thomas Arentzen, Ashley M. Purpura, and Aristotle Papanikolaou (eds.), *Orthodox Tradition and Human Sexuality*

Christina M. Gschwandtner, *Welcoming Finitude: Toward a Phenomenology of Orthodox Liturgy*

George E. Demacopoulos, *Colonizing Christianity: Greek and Latin Religious Identity in the Era of the Fourth Crusade.*

Pia Sophia Chaudhari, *Dynamis of Healing: Patristic Theology and the Psyche*

Brian A. Butcher, *Liturgical Theology after Schmemann: An Orthodox Reading of Paul Ricoeur.* Foreword by Andrew Louth.

Ashley M. Purpura, *God, Hierarchy, and Power: Orthodox Theologies of Authority from Byzantium.*

Aristotle Papanikolaou and George E. Demacopoulos (eds.), *Faith, Reason, and Theosis*

Aristotle Papanikolaou and George E. Demacopoulos (eds.), *Fundamentalism or Tradition: Christianity after Secularism*

George E. Demacopoulos and Aristotle Papanikolaou (eds.), *Christianity, Democracy, and the Shadow of Constantine.*

George E. Demacopoulos and Aristotle Papanikolaou (eds.), *Orthodox Constructions of the West.*

George E. Demacopoulos and Aristotle Papanikolaou (eds.), *Orthodox Readings of Augustine* [available 2020]

John Chryssavgis and Bruce V. Foltz (eds.), *Toward an Ecology of Transfiguration: Orthodox Christian Perspectives on Environment, Nature, and Creation.* Foreword by Bill McKibben. Prefatory Letter by Ecumenical Patriarch Bartholomew.

Lucian N. Leustean (ed.), *Orthodox Christianity and Nationalism in Nineteenth-Century Southeastern Europe.*

Georgia Frank, Susan R. Holman, and Andrew S. Jacobs (eds.), *The Garb of Being: Embodiment and the Pursuit of Holiness in Late Ancient Christianity*

John Chryssavgis (ed.), *Dialogue of Love: Breaking the Silence of Centuries.* Contributions by Brian E. Daley, S.J., and Georges Florovsky

A. G. Roeber, *Orthodox Christians and the Rights Revolution in America*

Ecumenical Patriarch Bartholomew, *In the World, Yet Not of the World: Social and Global Initiatives of Ecumenical Patriarch Bartholomew*. Edited by John Chryssavgis. Foreword by José Manuel Barroso

Ecumenical Patriarch Bartholomew, *Speaking the Truth in Love: Theological and Spiritual Exhortations of Ecumenical Patriarch Bartholomew*. Edited by John Chryssavgis. Foreword by Dr. Rowan Williams, Archbishop of Canterbury.

Ecumenical Patriarch Bartholomew, *On Earth as in Heaven: Ecological Vision and Initiatives of Ecumenical Patriarch Bartholomew*. Edited by John Chryssavgis. Foreword by His Royal Highness, the Duke of Edinburgh.

George E. Demacopoulos and Aristotle Papanikolaou (eds.), *Nicaea and the Future of Christianity*

Nicholas Roumas, *Redemption: A Mimetic Soteriology*

Candace Lukasik and Sarah Riccardi-Swartz (eds.), *Anthropologies of Orthodox Christianity: Theology, Politics, Ethics*